The Bricker Amendment Controversy

The Bricker Amendment Controversy

A TEST OF EISENHOWER'S POLITICAL LEADERSHIP

Duane Tananbaum

Cornell University Press

ITHACA AND LONDON

First published 1988 by Cornell University Press.

International Standard Book Number 0-8014-2037-7
Library of Congress Catalog Card Number 88-3614
Printed in the United States of America
Librarians: Library of Congress cataloging information appears on the last page of the book.

The paper in this book is acid-free and meets the guidelines for permanence and durability of the Committee on Production Guidelines for Book Longevity of the Council on Library Resources.

This book is dedicated to my son,
Robert Daniel Tananbaum.

Contents

Preface

During the years following World War II, important changes took place in the United States government. Federal authority continued to expand at the expense of the states, and the executive branch gained power within the national government. Conservatives feared that these trends would be accelerated by America's increasingly active role in world affairs, especially its participation in the United Nations, and thus they sought to limit the domestic effects of the nation's growing international involvement.

The leaders of the American Bar Association shared these concerns. They worried especially that international agreements such as the United Nations Charter, the Genocide Convention, and the Universal Declaration of Human Rights might have adverse effects within the United States. The attorneys feared that these agreements might nullify certain laws, including segregation laws in the South, and serve as a basis for extending federal control over matters previously regulated by the states. After studying the issue, the ABA leaders concluded that a constitutional amendment was needed to limit the effects of such compacts.

The agreements emanating from the United Nations also alarmed Senator John Bricker, a conservative Republican from Ohio. Bricker viewed treaties such as the UN's draft covenant on human rights as threats to the sovereignty and independence of the United States, and he agreed with the leaders of the ABA that something should be done to safeguard the rights and freedoms of American citizens, the character and structure of the American government, and domestic matters within the United States. Consequently, on September 14, 1951, Bricker introduced a constitutional amendment to protect the United States and the American people from the dangers he saw lurking in treaties and other international agreements.

The Bricker amendment quickly became one of the major political controversies of the 1950s. By 1953 the resolution had more than sixty cosponsors in the Senate, including isolationists, conservative Democrats, and almost all the Republicans, while liberal Democrats led the opposition to the measure. In early 1954 the amendment dominated the news as senators debated Bricker's proposal and various substitute resolutions.

Despite the strong backing the amendment received from Republicans in Congress, President Dwight Eisenhower and his advisers opposed the measure. Though Bricker and his supporters viewed the amendment as a means of limiting the impact of international agreements on domestic matters, Eisenhower and his aides saw it as a measure that would cripple the president's power in foreign affairs. But Eisenhower hoped to avoid an open break with Bricker and the right wing of the Republican party, which championed the amendment, so he tried various stratagems to delay consideration of the resolution. When those failed, however, the president finally waged an all-out campaign against the amendment.

Eisenhower's handling of the conflict provides an excellent case study of his methods of operation and leadership and the workings of his administration. The president played an active role in the maneuvering against the Bricker amendment, but he did so from behind the scenes until it became clear that he had to become more visibly involved if the measure were to be defeated. The picture of Eisenhower that emerges reinforces the revisionist view of him as an active, involved, and knowledgeable president, but it also illustrates some of the weaknesses and liabilities in his "hidden-hand" leadership. Because of Eisenhower's initial reluctance to oppose the amendment directly, people were unsure of his position and doubted his understanding of the issues, the measure gained momentum, and the whole affair dragged on longer than necessary.

A study of the Bricker amendment illuminates important issues in American history and politics since 1945. The controversy extended beyond the problem of the domestic effects of treaties and executive agreements and resulted in an extensive debate over the relationship between the United States and the United Nations, the jurisdiction of the states and the federal government, and the proper balance between congressional and presidential authority in foreign affairs—issues that are all still with us today.

Over the years, many people have helped me in numerous ways in my work on the Bricker amendment. The International Studies Association, the Eleanor Roosevelt Institute, the Harry S. Truman Institute, the Lyndon Baines Johnson Institute, the Department of History and the College of Humanities at Ohio State University, and the George N. Shuster Fund of Lehman College, City University of New York, all provided financial assistance at various stages of the project. Librarians and archivists at presidential libraries and other repositories facilitated my research in manuscript collections, and John Bricker, Herbert Brownell, and others were kind enough to share their recollections with me. Chris Burton, Janice Gulker, and Maria Mazon of Ohio State University typed the manuscript and taught me how to use a word processor, and Jeanette and Harry Zubkoff and Susan Armeny Langley made my traveling and research easier with their friendship and hospitality. I am also grateful to Peter Agree and Kay Scheuer of Cornell University Press and Elizabeth Shaw for their help in preparing this book for publication.

Walter LaFeber first stimulated my interest in the history of American foreign relations in general and the Bricker amendment in particular when I was an undergraduate at Cornell University. My friends and fellow graduate students at Columbia University—James Baughman, Lauren Branhower, John D'Emilio, Lois Gilman, William McLaughlin, Gary Rubin, Nancy Tucker, and Susan Stone Wong—all gave me much-needed "constructive criticism" on the first drafts of this manuscript and helped me to work out many of the conceptual problems. John Chambers of Rutgers University, John Burnham and Marvin Zahniser of Ohio State University, and Walter LaFeber found time in their busy schedules to read portions of the manuscript and offer comments and suggestions that improved it considerably.

I can never thank William E. Leuchtenburg enough for his help and guidance. This project began as a dissertation under his supervision at Columbia University; both it and I have benefited tremendously from his advice and encouragement over the years.

Finally, I thank my parents for their love and confidence expressed in so many ways, and my wife, Joan, for her help with this project and for so many other things as well.

DUANE TANANBAUM

Mt. Vernon, New York

Abbreviations

ABA	American Bar Association
ABAJ	*American Bar Association Journal*
CR	*Congressional Record*
CUOHC	Columbia University Oral History Collection
DDEL	Dwight D. Eisenhower Library
DDEP	Dwight D. Eisenhower Papers
ERP	Eleanor Roosevelt Papers
FDRL	Franklin D. Roosevelt Library
HSTL	Harry S. Truman Library
JBP	John Bricker Papers
LBJL	Lyndon Baines Johnson Library
OHS	Ohio Historical Society

The Bricker Amendment Controversy

.

CHAPTER ONE

Human Rights vs. States' Rights

In the late 1940s, conservative leaders in the United States were concerned about changes occurring in the American government, economy, and society. They had opposed Franklin Roosevelt's expansion of federal and presidential authority over economic and social matters during the 1930s and World War II, and they feared that increased American involvement in world affairs in the postwar era would result in even greater federal and presidential control. Conservatives worried particularly that American membership in the new United Nations would accelerate these trends, and they began looking for ways to limit the effects of American participation in the UN.[1]

I

At the close of World War II, the vast majority of Americans supported membership in the United Nations organization, which was formed to maintain peace and develop friendly relations among nations. But when the U.S. Senate considered the UN Charter in 1945, Senator Eugene Millikin, a conservative Republican from Colorado and close ally of Senator Robert Taft (R-Ohio), expressed concern that the new organization might undermine American sovereignty and independence by meddling in

---

[1]I am using "conservative" here in a very general way, defining as conservatives those who opposed the extension of federal and presidential authority in the 1930s and 1940s. More precise definitions of liberals and conservatives, based on ratings compiled by Americans for Democratic Action, will be used later in this study.

the nation's domestic affairs. Millikin noted that Article 55 of the charter stated that the United Nations would promote:

(a) higher standards of living, full employment, and conditions of economic and social progress and development;
(b) solutions of international economic, social, health, and related problems; and international cultural and educational cooperation; and
(c) universal respect for, and observance of, human rights and fundamental freedoms for all without distinction as to race, sex, language or religion.

Millikin pointed out that member nations also pledged in Article 56 "to take joint and separate action in cooperation with the organization for the achievement of the purposes set forth in Article 55," and he wondered how these provisions would be interpreted and carried out. He especially feared that they might be construed as giving the United Nations the right to study American wage rates, investigate charges of racial discrimination, or otherwise involve itself in domestic matters within the United States.[2]

State Department officials assured Millikin that the United Nations would not have the power to interfere in the internal affairs of the United States. They emphasized that Article 2(7) of the charter plainly stipulated:

Nothing contained in the present Charter shall authorize the United Nations to intervene in matters which are essentially within the domestic jurisdiction of any state or shall require the members to submit such matters to settlement under the present Charter.

Hence, there was no need to worry about intrusions from the UN on domestic matters. The Senate Committee on Foreign Relations stressed this point in its report on the charter, as did Senator Arthur Vandenberg (R-Mich.), the ranking Republican on the committee, during his remarks on the floor of the Senate. Reassured that the UN would not have any jurisdiction over America's internal affairs, Millikin, Taft, and others who

[2]See U.S., Congress, Senate, Committee on Foreign Relations, *The Charter of the United Nations, Hearings,* before the Committee on Foreign Relations, Senate, 79th Cong., 1st sess., 1945, pp. 307–12 (hereinafter referred to as *Charter, Hearings*). For the complete text of the charter, see U.S., Congress, Senate, *The Charter of the United Nations,* S. Doc. 70, 79th Cong., 1st sess., 1945. On American support for the United Nations, see Gallup, *The Gallup Poll,* pp. 497, 516; and Scott and Withey, *The United States and the United Nations,* pp. 9–15. On the relationship between Millikin and Taft, see Patterson, *Mr. Republican,* pp. 253 and 336; and St. Louis *Post-Dispatch,* July 10, 1945, pp. 1, 10-A. Millikin's conservatism can be seen in the low ratings he received from Americans for Democratic Action in the late 1940s. According to the ADA, Milikin's liberal rating ranged from a low of 0 in 1949 to a high of 30% in 1947. See *ADA World,* August 26, 1947; July 20, 1948; and October 28, 1949, in "Americans for Democratic Action Papers," microfilm edition, Series IX, "*ADA World.*"

had been concerned about this issue joined with the overwhelming majority of their colleagues in supporting the charter, which was approved in the Senate by a vote of 89–2.[3]

Although the United Nations could not intervene in the internal affairs of the United States, some people soon argued that the federal government could use American ratification of the UN Charter and previous Supreme Court decisions to extend federal control over social and economic matters regulated primarily by the states. In 1914, a U.S. District Court had invalidated a federal law protecting migratory birds, ruling it an unconstitutional invasion of the powers reserved to the states and to the people by the Tenth Amendment. The United States had then entered into a treaty with Great Britain to protect such birds, and a new statute had been enacted. In 1920 the Supreme Court had upheld the new law in *Missouri v. Holland,* declaring that the statute was a valid exercise of Congress's authority to pass all laws "necessary and proper" for carrying into effect any of the powers vested in the national government. Since the Constitution gave the president and the Senate the authority to make treaties, the justices had ruled, Congress then possessed the power to implement all such agreements.[4] Citing that decision, advocates of federal legislation regulating child labor had asserted in the 1920s and 1930s that such a law could be sustained as constitutional if enacted to implement a treaty. Now, in 1946, the left-wing National Lawyers Guild insisted that Congress could enact an anti-lynching bill to carry out America's obligations under Articles 55 and 56 of the United Nations Charter.[5]

The possibility of enacting federal civil rights legislation on this basis stirred up considerable controversy over the next few years as President Truman's Committee on Civil Rights, Justice Department officials, and various lawmakers included *Missouri v. Holland* and the United Nations

---

[3]See *Charter, Hearings,* pp. 307–12; U.S., Congress, Senate, Committee on Foreign Relations, *The Charter of the United Nations,* S. Exec. Report 8, 79th Cong., 1st sess., 1945, printed in *New York Times,* July 17, 1945, p. 4; and 91 *CR* 7956–57, 7971, 8156, and 8189–90 (1945). (All citations in this book to the *Congressional Record* are to the bound volumes.) William Langer (R-N.D.) and Henrik Shipstead (R-Minn.) were the only senators who voted against the charter.

[4]*Missouri v. Holland,* 252 U.S. 416 (1920). See also Lofgren, "*Missouri v. Holland* in Historical Perspective."

[5]See "Constitutional Basis for Federal Anti-Lynching Legislation," *Lawyers Guild Review,* 6 (November-December 1946), 643–47; Chamberlain, "Migratory Bird Treaty Decision and Its Relation to Labor Treaties"; Boyd, "The Expanding Treaty Power"; and Weinfeld, "Are Labor Conditions a Proper Subject of International Conventions and May the United States Government Become a Party to Such Conventions though They Regulate Matters Ordinarily Reserved to the States?" For criticism of the decision in *Missouri v. Holland,* see Thompson, "State Sovereignty and the Treaty-Making Power" and Black, "*Missouri v. Holland*—A Judicial Milepost on the Road to Absolutism."

Charter among possible constitutional bases for such laws. In none of these instances, however, was the charter cited as the sole or even the primary basis for such legislation. The President's Committee on Civil Rights listed it tenth among eleven possible bases for civil rights legislation in its 1947 report, and the following year an assistant to the attorney general cited Congress's authority to implement the UN Charter as but one of a number of bases for an anti-lynching law. And although the Senate Committee on Labor and Public Welfare did mention the charter and *Missouri v. Holland* in its report recommending enactment of a Fair Employment Practices bill in 1948, the senators emphasized that such a measure could be adopted under Congress's power to regulate interstate and foreign commerce.[6]

Nonetheless, in their minority report opposing the Fair Employment Practices bill, Senators Allen Ellender (D-La.) and Lister Hill (D-Ala.) attacked their colleagues' reference to the UN Charter and *Missouri v. Holland*. They noted that in the migratory bird case the courts had been dealing with "creatures without reason who enjoy only animal freedom," and they maintained that the ruling could not possibly be employed as a precedent "for the violation and desecration of the rights that belong to human beings." No treaty, they declared, could "destroy the reserved and retained rights of the people or the sovereign rights of the States."[7]

II

While the executive and legislative branches of the national government considered the possibility of using the UN Charter as a basis for federal civil rights legislation, the judiciary had to deal with the relationship between the charter and existing statutes and practices. According to Article VI of the U.S. Constitution, a ratified treaty becomes part of the supreme law of the land, and, as such, overrides any state laws to the contrary. The charter had been approved by the president and the Senate, so the courts now had to decide whether the pledge in Articles 55 and 56 to promote and protect "universal respect for, and observance of, human rights and fundamental freedoms for all" was self-executing and whether it automatically

[6]See President's Committee on Civil Rights, *To Secure These Rights: The Report of the President's Committee on Civil Rights* (Washington, D.C.: United States Government Printing Office, 1947), pp. 104–11; Interview with Nancy Wechsler, former counsel to the President's Committee on Civil Rights, June 30, 1976; Assistant to the Attorney General Peyton Ford to Rep. Earl Michener, February 10, 1948, copy in Charles Murphy Files, Box 21, HSTL; and U.S., Congress, Senate, Committee on Labor and Public Welfare, *Prohibiting Discrimination in Employment Because of Race, Religion, Color, National Origin, or Ancestry*, S. Report 951, 80th Cong., 2d sess., March 2, 1948.
[7]S. Report 951, 80th Cong., 2d sess., 1948, Part 2, pp. 12–13.

invalidated state laws discriminating against one group or another, or if additional legislation was required before these provisions went into effect.

The status and effect of the UN Charter became an important issue in 1948 in the case of *Oyama v. California,* a dispute concerning a California law prohibiting aliens ineligible for citizenship from acquiring land. The U.S. Supreme Court ruled that part of the statute was unconstitutional because it violated the stipulation in the Fourteenth Amendment that "no State shall . . . deny to any person within its jurisdiction the equal protection of the laws." In concurring opinions, four justices also pointed out that, in reality, the law applied only to Japanese aliens, and they argued that the entire statute should thus be invalidated as contrary to Articles 55 and 56 of the United Nations Charter. Justices Hugo Black and William O. Douglas believed it would be impossible for the United States to carry out its obligations under the charter to promote human rights "if State laws which bar land ownership and occupancy by aliens on account of race are permitted to be enforced." Similarly, Justices Frank Murphy and Wiley Rutledge denounced the Alien Land Law as "a barrier to the fulfillment of that national pledge" made in the UN Charter, and asserted that "its inconsistency with the Charter, which has been duly ratified and adopted by the United States, is but one more reason why the statute must be condemned."[8]

The Supreme Court's decision in *Oyama v. California* nullified only one section of the state's Alien Land Law; in 1950, however, in *Sei Fujii v. California,* a California District Court threw out the remainder of the statute on the grounds that it was in "direct conflict with the plain terms of the [United Nations] Charter." The court ruled that the UN, in adopting the Universal Declaration of Human Rights in 1948, had defined the rights and freedoms referred to in the charter as including the right to own property. Therefore, the judges concluded, the California law barring Japanese aliens from owning land had to "yield to the treaty as the superior force." In effect, the California Court ruled that the UN Charter was self-executing, that even without any implementing legislation by Congress its provisions overrode state laws to the contrary.[9]

Although the California Supreme Court ruled two years later that the charter was not self-executing, that the Alien Land Law was unconstitutional only because it violated the equal protection clause of the Fourteenth Amendment, the original decision in *Sei Fujii v. California* still proved controversial. Edward Corwin, McCormick professor of jurispru-

[8]*Oyama v. California,* 332 U.S. 633 (1948), esp. pp. 650, 673 for the quotations from the concurring opinions.
[9]*Sei Fujii v. State of California,* 217 Pac. (2nd) 481 (1950); *New York Times,* April 26, 1950, p. 16.

dence at Princeton University and a noted authority on constitutional law, thought that the charter "offered a very slim basis" for the ruling of the court, and Manley Hudson, professor of international law at Harvard Law School and chairman of the United Nations International Law Commission, argued that the district court had misconstrued the charter, which was never meant to be self-executing. Arthur Krock of the *New York Times* criticized the decision and noted that it "opened the way to the contention that all discriminatory laws and practices in this country were automatically made illegal when the Charter was ratified." If the ruling were upheld, he observed, legislation might not be required to put President Truman's civil rights program into effect, since all forms of segregation would contravene the law of the land. Writing in the *Wall Street Journal,* Garet Garrett dramatized the fears of many critics of the decision when he described the district court's conclusion that "the United Nations Charter has become the supreme law of the land" as "the twelve most ominous words of legal meaning uttered in our time!"[10]

Legislators, too, denounced the district court's rationale in the *Fujii* case. Senator Millikin wondered how the judges had ignored the assurance in Article 2(7) that nothing in the charter gave the United Nations the right to intervene in the internal affairs of member states, and Tom Connally (D-Tex.), chairman of the Senate Foreign Relations Committee, declared that senators never would have approved the charter if they had realized it might be invoked for such purposes. Senator Forrest Donnell (R-Mo.) condemned the decision and reminded his colleagues of an additional threat posed by such international agreements: not only were the courts ruling that such agreements were self-executing, he pointed out, but, according to the precedent of *Missouri v. Holland,* Congress could also use such agreements to pass legislation that would otherwise be an unconstitutional invasion of the reserved powers of the states.[11]

People criticized the decision in the *Fujii* case not only because it held that the United Nations Charter was self-executing, but also because it seemed to be based in part on the Declaration of Human Rights.[12] The

[10]*Sei Fujii v. State of California,* 242 Pac. (2nd) 617 (1952); Edward Corwin to Eldon Crowell, August 16, 1950, Corwin Papers, Chronological Files, Princeton University Library; Hudson, Editorial Comment: "Charter Provisions on Human Rights in American Law"; Arthur Krock in *New York Times,* May 16, 1950, p. 30, and May 23, 1950, p. 28; and Garet Garrett, "Rewriting the Constitution: It Can Be Done by United Nations Treaties If We Don't Watch Out," *Wall Street Journal,* February 5, 1951.

[11]96 *CR* 5993–6003, 7325–28 (1950).

[12]See for example Hudson, "Charter Provisions," p. 547; "The United Nations Charter and the Constitution," *ABAJ,* 36 (August 1950), 652–53; Washington *Times-Herald,* May 21, 1950, clipping in Stephen Spingarn Papers, Box 15, HSTL; and *Saturday Evening Post,* December 29, 1951, p. 8.

declaration was not a treaty; it had never been approved by the Senate and was not part of the law of the land. Hence, it should have had no bearing on the case. Moreover, as adopted by the United Nations General Assembly in December 1948, the Declaration of Human Rights went far beyond the traditional American concept of human rights. Although many of its provisions dealt with matters such as freedom of religion that were consistent with the United States Constitution and the Bill of Rights, other sections spelled out more novel social and economic rights. Article 24, for example, proclaimed that "everyone has the right to rest and leisure, including reasonable limitation of working hours and periodic holidays with pay." Similarly, Article 25 declared that "motherhood and childhood are entitled to special care and assistance. All children, whether born in or out of wedlock, shall enjoy the same social protection." These may have been desirable social goals, but most Americans certainly did not consider them to be inalienable human rights.[13]

III

The inclusion of social and economic concerns in the Declaration of Human Rights especially perturbed the leaders of the American Bar Association. As early as May 1946, William Ransom, chairman of the ABA's special committee on the United Nations, advised Eleanor Roosevelt, American representative and chairman of the UN Commission on Human Rights, that an international bill of rights should not include any provisions on social and economic conditions, that it should be limited instead to the more traditional civil liberties and political rights. Two years later, as the General Assembly began discussing the final draft of the declaration, the ABA's Committee for Peace and Law Through United Nations concluded that the document, since it dealt with economic and social matters, "still does not reflect and express the American concept as to the appropriate contents of a Declaration to vouchsafe and protect basic rights and freedoms." Consequently, the ABA's House of Delegates, its official policy-making body, passed a resolution recommending that the Declaration of Human Rights not be approved by the United Nations General Assembly, or accepted by the United States and other member nations.[14]

[13]For the complete text of the Declaration of Human Rights, see *Department of State Bulletin,* 19 (December 19, 1948), 752–54.

[14]William Ransom to Eleanor Roosevelt, May 4, 1946, ERP, Box 4587, FDRL; ABA, "Report and Recommendations to the House of Delegates by the Committee for Peace and Law Through United Nations, with the Action Voted by the House of Delegates upon the Recommendations," September 7, 1948, pp. 3, 10, copy in Manley Hudson Papers, Box 135, Harvard Law School Library.

The ABA's opposition to the declaration reflected the conservative, discriminatory nature of the organization in the late 1940s and early 1950s. At that time the ABA included very few blacks, mainly because a prospective member had to indicate his race on his application, and four negative votes on the sixteen-member board of governors would cause an applicant to be rejected. Originally, two negative votes on the board had blocked a prospective member, but the number had been raised to four in 1943 in response to protests that the old rule had effectively excluded blacks from the ABA. The ABA had refused to liberalize the rule any further, however, rejecting a proposal to admit to membership those who received a majority vote of approval. In 1949, the House of Delegates refused to remove the question concerning race from the application, and it was not until 1950 that a black was first appointed to serve on one of the association's many committees. As for the right-wing policies pursued by the ABA and its leaders, future Supreme Court Justice Robert H. Jackson had observed in the 1930s that lawyers' organizations "generally pyramid conservatism until at the top of the structures our bar association officers are as conservative as cemetery trustees." Jackson's comment accurately describes the ABA at midcentury. According to Professor Corwin, the organization was still dominated by "your *nisi prius* lawyer"—an attorney who tried civil cases in the lower courts—and even a former president of the ABA had conceded that such men knew "no more of the principles that control the affairs of state than a titmouse knows of the gestations of an elephant." As another past president of the ABA noted, its leaders had "a new baby" in their opposition to the Declaration of Human Rights, and "it fits beautifully into highly conservative thinking."[15]

Frank Holman, the president of the American Bar Association in 1948–49, typified the organization's conservative leadership. Born in Sandy City, Utah, in 1886, Holman graduated from the University of Utah, won a Rhodes Scholarship and earned a law degree at Oxford, and for a few years taught jurisprudence back in Utah. Switching to private practice, he moved to Seattle and became a senior partner in a large firm whose clients included Boeing Aircraft. Politically, Holman actively opposed the New Deal, charging that it represented the first step on the road to socialism and communism. He regarded Franklin Roosevelt as "a great faker—

[15] See *New York Times,* August 26, 1943, p. 25; September 5, 1949, p. 15; September 6, 1949, p. 16; and December 15, 1950, p. 29; ABA, *Reports,* 68 (1943), 120–28; Robert H. Jackson, "The Lawyer: Leader or Mouthpiece?" p. 72; letter from Edward Corwin, May 24, 1955, attached to letter from Abraham Streiff to John Bricker, May 28, 1955, JBP, Box 115, OHS; and Carl Rix to Manley Hudson, November 24, 1948, Hudson Papers, Box 114. See also Auerbach, *Unequal Justice: Lawyers and Social Change in Modern America.*

perhaps one of the greatest in American politics," and he particularly resented FDR's court-packing scheme and subsequent appointments to the bench. Holman was outraged that Roosevelt had campaigned for a third term in 1940 on the promise that he would keep the nation out of war; in Holman's view, Roosevelt's actions in support of Great Britain practically guaranteed that the United States would soon become involved in the conflict. Holman also denounced what he considered to be unnecessary concessions that Roosevelt had made to the Russians at Yalta. Although Holman claimed to have supported the United Nations Charter, he emphasized that he had done so only after receiving assurances that the new organization would not constitute a world government and would not be able to interfere with either the sovereignty or the internal affairs of the United States.[16]

Holman's speeches in 1948 illustrate his general political philosophy. In an address before the Iowa State Bar Association, he railed against the dangers posed by "socialistic encroachments at home and international encroachments from abroad." He warned that by "executive fiat . . . the forces of autocracy and bureaucracy were moving toward a centralized government so powerful as to destroy the rights of the individual, the rights of the states, and the right to local self-government." Speaking later to a group of southern governors, Holman called for an alliance between the South and the West to oppose the efforts of those in the East and the large industrial states in the Midwest who would expand federal authority by "a continued whittling away of our individual rights and of our State rights." Only by working together, he maintained, could the people in the South and the West "save us from becoming a completely Socialized State at home and a puppet state in a world-wide hegemony."[17]

Holman dedicated his term as president of the ABA to publicizing what he saw as a serious threat to constitutional government in the United States—the possibility that international agreements would have far-reaching effects within the United States. He feared that "ardent internationalists . . . , by a variety of devious maneuvers and clever resorts to semantics," were endeavoring to transform the United Nations into a world government infringing on the sovereignty and independence of the United States. The efforts by Eleanor Roosevelt and the Human Rights Commission to draft a bill of rights including articles on social and economic matters, he believed, were merely the opening wedge which would enable the world organization to begin interfering in the internal affairs of

[16]See Holman, *The Life and Career of a Western Lawyer, 1886–1961,* esp. pp. 313, 333–34, and 357.

[17]Ibid., pp. 365, 362.

the United States. He realized also that if the United States were to ratify it, such an agreement could serve as the basis for increasing the powers of the federal government, since Congress, according to the doctrine of *Missouri v. Holland*, could pass any legislation necessary to implement the compact, even measures it could not enact in the absence of the agreement. To prevent any of that from happening, Holman began what President Eisenhower later derided as a crusade "to save the United States from Eleanor Roosevelt."[18]

In the spring of 1948, Holman began speaking out publicly against the proposed Declaration of Human Rights. In a talk at Gonzaga Law School, he denounced the declaration as a "strange document" that would institute "a world-wide social and economic program" through which governments would assure everyone of "adequate employment, adequate wages, adequate housing and clothing, and adequate rest and leisure." A few weeks later, Holman warned the Utah Bar Association that the declaration's provisions proclaiming freedom of residence and freedom of movement "might easily be interpreted as authorizing some agency of the United Nations like the World Court to nullify our immigration laws and enable large numbers from the over-populated areas of China, India, and of Indonesia to move into the United States." And, in an address before the annual convention of the State Bar of California in September, Holman charged that the United Nations human rights proposals diverged sharply from the fundamental American concept of individual rights and freedoms and threatened the notion of private property, which he considered the basis for real freedom and liberty. The declaration, he complained, constituted "an agreement to adopt the New Deal on an international scale by committing the member nations to a paternalistic form of government which would attempt to care for all the daily needs of the citizen and minimize the incentive for individual initiative and progress." Its approval, he stressed, would "promote state socialism, if not communism, throughout the world."[19]

Holman sought, unsuccessfully, to block the Declaration of Human Rights. In November 1948, he suggested to Secretary of State George C. Marshall that the United States try to defer final action on the declaration until its ramifications could be studied more thoroughly by lawyers, lay people, and Congress. Marshall emphasized, however, that the agreement

18Ibid., pp. 357–59, 372–73. Eisenhower's comment is quoted in James Hagerty Diary, January 11, 1954, in Ferrell, ed., *The Diary of James C. Hagerty,* p. 6.

19Holman, *Western Lawyer,* pp. 361–62, 365; *New York Times,* September 18, 1948, p. 4. See also Holman, "An 'International Bill of Rights': Proposals Have Dangerous Implications for U.S."

was not a formal treaty; it was "merely declaratory in character" and placed no legal obligations whatsoever upon the United States. He also pointed out that the declaration had been the subject of consideration for almost two years and had already been examined by attorneys both in and out of government. Marshall could see no reason for delay, since in his opinion the document generally reflected "the traditions and sentiments of the American people." Consequently, when the United Nations approved the declaration in December 1948, it did so with strong support from the American delegation.[20]

Alarmed at the dangers they saw lurking in the declaration, and concerned that a legally binding covenant on human rights would contain similar provisions on social and economic matters, the leaders of the American Bar Association, in January 1949, recommended postponing any further action on a covenant for at least one year in order to give them more time to study the complex legal and constitutional questions raised by such an agreement. Holman reminded the ABA's House of Delegates that Article 2 of the United Nations Charter prohibited the world organization from interfering in the internal affairs of member states. Nevertheless, he warned, the efforts to draft a treaty on human rights were a stratagem to allow the UN to do just that; to give it, for example, an excuse to investigate allegations of racism in the United States. Similarly, William Ransom, chairman of the ABA's Committee for Peace and Law Through United Nations, asserted that if the United States were to ratify such a convention, it would "immediately become part of the supreme law of the land, coordinate with the Constitution itself." What would happen then, he wondered, to the many state and federal statutes in violation of such an agreement? Four justices of the Supreme Court had already held in *Oyama v. California* that the United Nations Charter invalidated that state's Alien Land Law. Would the courts rule that a covenant on human rights automatically nullified state laws in conflict with its provisions? Ransom also warned that such agreements could be used, as the migratory bird convention with Great Britain had been used, to remove matters from state and local control and put them under federal jurisdiction. The leaders of the ABA wanted these issues resolved and safeguards put in place before the United States approved any covenant on human rights.[21]

[20]Holman to Marshall, November 2, 1948; and Marshall to Holman, November 13, 1948; copies of both in Manley Hudson Papers, Box 127. See also Simsarian, "United Nations Action on Human Rights in 1948."

[21]ABA, "Documents for Study in the 1949 Series of Regional Group Conferences," February 1949, esp. pp. 1–10, copy in Emanuel Celler Papers, Box 14, Library of Congress; *New York Times,* February 1, 1949, p. 8; and Frank Holman to Secretary of State Dean Acheson, February 8, 1949, copy in Manley Hudson Papers, Box 127.

IV

The American Bar Association also opposed the UN Convention on the Prevention and Punishment of Genocide. The slaughtering of Jews and other minority groups by the Nazis during World War II had convinced the world community that such actions should be made a crime against international law, and in December 1946 the UN General Assembly defined genocide as "a denial of the right of existence of entire human groups, as homicide is the denial of the right to live of individual human beings." The General Assembly proclaimed that genocide was "contrary to moral law and to the spirit and aims of the United Nations," and two years later it adopted the Genocide Convention unanimously, with the understanding that the agreement would be submitted as a treaty to member nations for their ratification. Specifically, the convention enumerated the following five acts, any one of which would constitute the crime of genocide if

> committed with intent to destroy, in whole or in part, a national, ethnical, racial or religious group, as such:
> (a) Killing members of the group;
> (b) Causing serious bodily or mental harm to members of the group;
> (c) Deliberately inflicting on the group conditions of life calculated to bring about its physical destruction in whole or in part;
> (d) Imposing measures intended to prevent births within the group;
> (e) Forcibly transferring children of the group to another group.

Applying to "constitutionally responsible rulers, public officials, or private individuals," the convention stipulated that nations approving the compact should enact, "in accordance with their respective Constitutions," any legislation necessary to give effect to the agreement. Persons charged with crimes under the convention would be tried by a court of the country in which the act had taken place, or by an international tribunal if its jurisdiction was accepted by the contracting parties.[22]

Concerned because the agreement involved many of the same issues raised by the human rights proposals, the ABA's House of Delegates resolved unanimously in February 1949 that the United States should not ratify the Genocide Convention until there had been more time to study the compact. The lawyers were uncertain what the legal effects of approving the agreement would be, since, as a ratified treaty, it would become

[22]Articles II, IV, V, and VI of the Convention on the Prevention and Punishment of the Crime of Genocide. For the complete text of the agreement, see *Department of State Bulletin,* 19 (December 19, 1948), 756–57.

part of the supreme law of the land. They worried that phrases like "causing serious mental harm" were vague and could easily be abused, and they were dubious about making private individuals subject to international law, which previously had dealt only with the actions of governments. Finally, they feared that ratification of the convention would allow Congress, following the precedent of *Missouri v. Holland,* to enact an antilynching bill or some other form of civil rights legislation.[23]

During the next six months, different groups within the ABA disagreed over how the United States should proceed with regard to the Genocide Convention. The Section of International and Comparative Law, composed of almost 1000 members of the ABA who were interested in and knowledgeable about international affairs, thought the Senate should approve the agreement subject to certain reservations that would delineate more clearly its effects within the United States. The section proposed reservations making it explicit that the convention would have to be implemented by subsequent legislation before it would go into effect, that such measures would be limited to matters over which the national government already had jurisdiction, and that any person charged with genocide in the United States would be tried by the federal court of the district in which the crime had allegedly been committed. Members of the section did not necessarily believe these reservations were needed, but they hoped their addition would make the convention more acceptable to the rest of the ABA.[24]

The proposed reservations failed to mollify Frank Holman or the ABA's Committee on Peace and Law Through United Nations, however. Holman spoke before many groups, denouncing the convention as "a fradulent instrument which provided for the taking of American citizens to some foreign country for trial—Jews as well as others." He warned that if a white person driving through Harlem happened to run over a Negro child accidently, the motorist would be guilty of genocide and subject to extradition for judicial proceedings before an international tribunal or a foreign court. The Committee on Peace and Law, a small but influential group that included several past-presidents of the ABA, echoed these

[23]See *New York Times,* February 2, 1949, p. 14; Carl Rix to William Ransom, December 20, 1948, copy in Manley Hudson Papers, Box 14; Arthur Powell to Senator Richard Russell, April 4, 1949, Russell Papers, Series XV, Box 417, Richard Russell Memorial Library, University of Georgia; and ABA, "Documents for Study, 1949."

[24]See ABA, "Report and Recommendations to the Section of International and Comparative Law by the Committee on United Nations," September 5, 1949, copy in ERP, Box 3779; ABA, "Report and Recommendations of the Section of International and Comparative Law," September 8, 1949, copy in Elbert Thomas Papers, Box 263, FDRL; *New York Times,* September 7, 1949, p. 44; and C. W. Tillett to Dana Backus, March 13, 1950, copy in Adolf Berle Papers, Box 90, FDRL.

sentiments. It asserted that the agreement raised many constitutional questions which were still unanswered, including the effectiveness of attaching reservations to a multilateral treaty like the Genocide Convention, the effects of the agreement on existing state and local regulations, and the convention's use as a possible basis for expanding federal authority over matters controlled by the states. Carl Rix, who had succeeded Ransom as chairman of the committee, suggested that a constitutional amendment might even be needed to ensure that Congress could not, through the use of such treaties, "remove from the states their power of self-government." Consequently, the committee recommended that the Senate reject the Genocide Convention, a stand endorsed by the House of Delegates in September 1949.[25]

Most of the ABA's objections to the Genocide Convention had no basis whatsoever in reality. As Acting Secretary of State James E. Webb stressed in his report to the president on the agreement, there had to be "a specific intent to destroy a racial, religious, national or ethnical group as such in whole or in part" for an act to be considered genocide. Thus, murdering an individual, much less injuring or killing someone in a car accident, would not be genocide as defined by the compact. Moreover, the convention was not self-executing; it explicitly called for implementing legislation enacted according to the contracting parties' constitutional processes, and any person charged with genocide within the United States would be tried in American courts unless the Senate were to advise and consent to a subsequent agreement establishing an international tribunal.[26]

Why then were Holman and the others so resolute in their opposition to the Genocide Convention? They feared that American ratification would facilitate changes in the U.S. government, economy, and society. Specifically, they feared that it would lead to UN involvement in America's internal affairs, accelerate federal encroachments on the reserved powers of the states, and nullify existing state laws. Rix pointed out to a Senate subcommittee that the President's Committee on Civil Rights and a proposed Fair Employment Practices bill had both referred to Congress's

[25]Holman, *Western Lawyer,* pp. 400, 415–16, 537–38; Washington *Star,* February 9, 1949, clipping in Harold M. Stephens Papers, Box 19, Library of Congress; ABA, "Report of the Special Committee on Peace and Law Through United Nations," September 1, 1949, copy in Adolf Berle Papers, Box 90; and *New York Times,* September 7, 1949, p. 44, and September 9, 1949, pp. 1, 13. See also Phillips, "The Genocide Convention: Its Effect on Our Legal System." Phillips was a member of the ABA Committee on Peace and Law Through United Nations.

[26]See Acting Secretary of State James E. Webb to President Truman, n.d., included as part of U.S., Congress, Senate, *International Convention on the Prevention and Punishment of the Crime of Genocide: Message from the President of the United States,* Executive O, Senate, 81st Cong., 1st sess., June 16, 1949, pp. 2–6.

power to enact legislation to implement a treaty, and he warned that if the Senate approved the Genocide Convention, Congress would then have the authority to pass any laws "necessary and proper" to carrying out the agreement, including an anti-lynching bill or some other civil rights measure interfering in matters best left under the control of the individual states. Similarly, George Finch, a Washington attorney and member of the Committee on Peace and Law, stressed that if the Genocide Convention were ratified, civil rights activists and minority groups would be able to claim that it superseded and invalidated segregation laws and all discriminatory state legislation.[27]

The controversy over the applicability of the United Nations Charter, the Declaration of Human Rights, and the Genocide Convention to the internal affairs of the United States led some of the leaders of the American Bar Association to start thinking in terms of a constitutional amendment to limit the effects of treaties within the United States. Rather than fighting against each and every human rights agreement that might nullify segregation laws or serve as a basis for federal civil rights legislation, they realized that the best way to protect the states against further inroads by the national government would be to adopt a constitutional amendment stipulating that ratified treaties would *not* be part of the supreme law of the land and that Congress could *not* use its authority to implement such compacts to invade the reserved powers of the states. At the meeting in September 1949, when the House of Delegates recommended that the Senate reject the Genocide Convention, various leaders of the ABA suggested that a constitutional amendment might be needed to safeguard the rights of the individual states and protect existing state laws from being superseded. Subsequently, while testifying against the Genocide Convention before a Senate subcommittee in January 1950, Carl Rix advised that if the United States were going to be asked to approve these agreements on human rights, it should first adopt a constitutional amendment "to preserve the rights of the states." A few months later, the ABA's Committee on Peace and Law began considering the possibility of drafting such a measure, and in 1951 Senator John Bricker (R-Ohio) formally introduced in Congress his own constitutional amendment to limit the effects of treaties and executive agreements within the United States.[28]

---

[27]U.S., Congress, Senate, Committee on Foreign Relations, *The Genocide Convention, Hearings,* before a Subcommittee of the Committee on Foreign Relations, Senate, 81st Cong., 2d sess., 1950, pp. 208–9, 217 (hereinafter referred to as *Genocide, Hearings*).

[28]See *New York Times,* September 9, 1949, pp. 1, 13, and January 25, 1950, p. 9; St. Louis *Post-Dispatch,* September 7, 1949, p. 2-A; *Genocide, Hearings,* pp. 208–9; Carl Rix to Manley Hudson, October 4, 1949, Hudson Papers, Box 114; and S.J. Res. 102, 82d Cong., 1st sess., September 14, 1951.

CHAPTER TWO

John Bricker and the
Covenant on Human Rights

As the cold war intensified in the late 1940s and early 1950s, many
Americans became disenchanted with the United Nations. They saw it as
paralyzed much of the time by the Soviet Union's veto power, and they
feared that the organization provided a cover for Soviet spies to operate in
the United States. Alger Hiss's conviction for perjury in 1950 exacerbated
these concerns, because Hiss, while in the State Department, had helped
in planning for the United Nations. After 1950, the UN also became a
convenient scapegoat for America's failure to win a clear-cut military victory in Korea.[1]

The UN's efforts to draft a legally binding covenant on human rights
became a particular target for conservatives who wanted to express their
growing dissatisfaction with the United Nations. Conservatives such as
Senator John Bricker and columnist George Sokolsky were still fighting
against federal intervention in social and economic matters; they certainly
opposed any initiatives in these areas by an international organization,
which they saw as dominated by communist and socialist nations. Sokolsky
believed it was absolutely necessary "to expose these efforts of Europeans
and Asiatics to control our lives," and he praised Frank Holman and the
American Bar Association for their vigorous opposition to the UN's proposals on human rights. Meanwhile, Bricker took the lead in Congress in

---

[1] See Gallup Poll, September 14, 1947, in Gallup, *Gallup Poll,* p. 672; Washington *Post,* July
21, 1948, pp. 1, 3; Alexander Uhl, *The Assault on the UN* (Washington, D.C.: Public Affairs
Institute, 1953), copy enclosed with Dewey Anderson to Adolf Berle, July 17, 1953, Berle
papers, Box 97, FDRL; James Burnham, "The United Nations Lobby," clipping from
Berkshire *Evening Eagle,* August 11, 1953, Democratic National Committee Clipping Files,
HSTL; Westbrook Pegler, "Eleanor's Effrontery Queers UN in US," Indianapolis *Star,*
December 22, 1953, p. 16, copy in ERP, Box 4716, FDRL; and Caridi, *The Korean War and
American Politics,* pp. 71–73, 113–15, and 260–62.

trying to arouse public and congressional opposition to any international agreements on human rights.[2]

I

After the adoption of the Declaration of Human Rights and the Genocide Convention in 1948, Eleanor Roosevelt and others at the United Nations attempted to draft a legally binding covenant to define and protect human rights. Over the next three years, the Commission on Human Rights, the Economic and Social Council, and the General Assembly considered various drafts and proposals, but the UN failed to approve a final text for submission to member states. On a number of issues, however, the UN reached tentative decisions that seriously weakened the proposed covenant, gave credibility to its critics, and made American ratification highly unlikely.

From the beginning, American officials realized that it would be difficult if not impossible to win Senate approval for a legally binding covenant on human rights. Eleanor Roosevelt and State Department officials knew that "certain elements among the southern contingent and the reactionaries from other parts of the country" would adamantly oppose any treaty that might serve as a basis for federal civil rights legislation or establish social and economic rights to be secured and safeguarded by the federal government. Consequently, Mrs. Roosevelt and the American delegation worked in the UN for a covenant that would assuage legitimate concerns in the United States and be able to win American acceptance.[3]

State Department officials believed that including a federal-state clause would greatly enhance the covenant's chances of winning Senate approval. Such a provision would make it clear that America's obligations under the covenant would be limited to matters already under federal jurisdiction. In matters not under federal control, Washington's only responsibility would be to recommend to states and localities that they modify their laws and customs to accord with the covenant. The State Department hoped that such a proviso would calm fears that the covenant would serve as a vehicle for increasing federal authority at the expense of the states. As a department lawyer noted, a federal-state clause would

[2]See George Sokolsky column, Washington *Times-Herald,* September 10, 1951, copy in Harold M. Stephens Papers, Box 19, Library of Congress. Bricker's conservatism will be discussed in section II of this chapter.

[3]James Hendrick, memorandum of conversation about the Commission on Human Rights, July 3, 1947, ERP, Box 4587.

enable department officials "to tell the Senate that the Covenant does not disturb States' rights."[4]

But despite the Truman administration's best efforts, the United States failed to secure a federal-state clause. At meetings of the UN Commission on Human Rights in the spring of 1950, Eleanor Roosevelt made it clear to the other delegates that there had to be such a provision for the covenant to be adopted in the United States. But the commission postponed any decision on the matter, leaving it for the Economic and Social Council or the General Assembly to decide. Mrs. Roosevelt recommended to President Truman that "a little work" be done "on the higher levels," and the president promised to "see what can be done to get our point of view across." He agreed that a federal-state clause was necessary "if we want to avoid complications here at home." In December 1950, the General Assembly instructed the Commission on Human Rights to study the possibility of including a federal-state clause in the covenant, but the commission found itself too busy to deal with this issue during its spring meeting in 1951. As a result, the draft covenant under consideration at the end of 1951 still did not include a federal-state clause.[5]

The inclusion in the covenant of provisions on social and economic matters exacerbated this problem. State Department officials preferred a covenant limited to civil and political rights, since incorporating social and economic concerns in the agreement would mean covering such topics as health, housing, education, and employment. In the United States these matters were still primarily under state jurisdiction, and their inclusion would appear to some as an attack on states' rights, especially since the covenant still lacked a federal-state clause.[6]

The United Nations, however, repeatedly rejected the American position on this issue. In December 1950, the General Assembly asked the Commission on Human Rights to broaden the proposed covenant to include economic, social, and cultural rights, and the commission proceeded to draft a new agreement with articles on such concerns as the right to work, the right to adequate housing, and the right to an education.

[4]Marjorie Whiteman, Office of the Legal Adviser, Department of State, to Eleanor Roosevelt, August 26, 1949, ERP, Box 4588; and Simsarian, "Proposed Human Rights Covenant," 948–49.

[5]Eleanor Roosevelt to President Truman, May 28, 1950, and Truman to Eleanor Roosevelt, June 30, 1950, both in Truman Papers, OF 85-RR, HSTL; *Department of State Bulletin,* 24 (January 29, 1951), 177; and Simsarian, "Economic, Social, and Cultural Provisions in the Human Rights Covenant," 1008.

[6]See Secretary of State Dean Acheson to Eleanor Roosevelt, July 11, 1949; and "Suggested Statement for January 3 Press Conference on the Covenant on Human Rights," attached to letter from Gilbert Stewart, press officer, United States Mission to the United Nations, to Eleanor Roosevelt, December 29, 1949; ERP, Boxes 3779 and 4588.

When the General Assembly discussed the issue again in December 1951, Eleanor Roosevelt and the American delegation argued for two separate covenants, one on civil and political rights, the other on social and economic matters. Including all the provisions in one covenant, Mrs. Roosevelt asserted, would only delay the ratification of any agreement on human rights, whereas dividing them into two conventions would accelerate their approval. But as she later reported, a majority of delegates voted again for a single covenant so that there would be "no differentiations in importance between civil and political rights and economic, social, and cultural rights."[7]

An even more serious defect in the draft covenant was the enumeration of all sorts of limitations on and exceptions to the rights and freedoms it was setting forth. Eleanor Roosevelt warned in her newspaper column in 1950 that in "stating exceptions . . . you cease to emphasize the right," and her words proved to be prophetic.[8] In the text approved by the Commission on Human Rights that spring, for example, Article 2 stipulated that "in the case of a state of emergency officially proclaimed by the authorities or in the case of a public disaster, a State may take measures derogating, to the extent strictly limited by the exigencies of the situation, from its obligations under . . . this Covenant." The article then went on to exempt from this proviso such basic rights as the right to life, freedom from torture and slavery, and freedom of religion. But among the rights not exempted were the rights to a fair and public trial, to hold opinions without interference and express oneself freely, and to assemble peacefully. These rights and freedoms could all be suspended under the covenant. And if that loophole were not broad enough, individual articles included additional exceptions and limitations, such as those in Article 13 subjecting "freedom of thought, conscience, and religion . . . to such limitations as are pursuant to law and are reasonable and necessary to protect public safety, order, health or morals, or the fundamental rights and freedoms of others."[9]

These limitations and exceptions may have sounded reasonable enough on the surface, but they stood in sharp contrast to the guarantees embodied in the United States Constitution and the Bill of Rights that Congress

[7]See *New York Times,* December 5, 1950, p. 25; Mr. Popper to Mr. Green, "Post-Mortem on the Third Committee," December 22, 1950, copy in ERP, Box 4583; Simsarian, "Economic, Social, and Cultural Provisions in the Human Rights Covenant"; and *Department of State Bulletin,* 25 (December 31, 1951), 1082. Quotation is from "Statement by Mrs. Franklin D. Roosevelt," *Department of State Bulletin,* 25 (December 31, 1951), 1059, 1064–66.

[8]Eleanor Roosevelt, "My Day," April 1, 1950, ERP, Box 3152.

[9]For the text of the proposed covenant on human rights, see *Department of State Bulletin,* 22 (June 12, 1950), 949–54.

can pass *no* laws abridging freedom of speech, the right of people peace-fully to assemble, or the rights of the accused to public trials. Thus, even though Article 18 of the draft covenant stated explicitly that "nothing in this Covenant may be interpreted as limiting or derogating from any of the rights and freedoms which may be guaranteed under the laws of any Contracting State," some people still feared that the covenant on human rights could be employed to justify restrictions on rights and freedoms that would otherwise be unconstitutional. After all, they had seen the UN Charter and even the Declaration of Human Rights cited in various court cases despite a similar provision in the charter that was supposed to pro-tect member states against interference in their domestic affairs. Even Eleanor Roosevelt conceded that there was little likelihood of a covenant with so many loopholes and exceptions ever being approved by the Sen-ate. Instead, the covenant soon became a convenient target for attacks from conservatives such as the leaders of the American Bar Association and Senator John Bricker.[10]

II

John Bricker first came to national prominence in the late 1930s and early 1940s when he served as governor of Ohio. Later described by a colleague as one of only two legislators "who really looked like Senators," the tall, handsome, white-haired Bricker was elected governor in 1938 by a margin of 118,000 votes, and reelected easily in 1940 and again in 1942. As governor, Bricker earned a reputation as an honest, able, economy-minded public official. "Honest John" rooted out many of the irregularities and corrupt practices of his predecessors, and he reorganized the state govern-ment to make it more efficient and less expensive. Aided by the recovery in the nation's economy, he transformed an inherited budget deficit of $40 million into a surplus in the state treasury of more than $70 million when he left office in 1945. His preoccupation with maintaining a reserve in the state treasury sometimes had unfortunate effects, however, such as when he refused to call a special session of the state legislature to deal with the relief crisis in Ohio's cities in 1939. Bricker feared that once the lawmakers reassembled in Columbus they would increase state spending and dissipate his surplus.[11]

[10]See Eleanor Roosevelt to President Truman, April 24, 1951, ERP, Box 4560.
[11]On Bricker's early career, see Pauly, *Bricker of Ohio,* an uncritical campaign biography; New York *Herald Tribune,* June 29, 1944, p. 4; *U.S. News and World Report,* January 29, 1954, pp. 73–75; and Seasongood, "John W. Bricker: Personally Honest." On the relief crisis in 1939, see Maurer, "Relief Problems and Politics in Ohio," pp. 96–99; and *New York Times,* November 29, 1939–December 9, 1939, and December 17, 1939, pp. 1, 12. The quotation about Bricker looking like a senator is from Cotton, *In the Senate,* p. 173.

Bricker's reelection in 1940 and again in 1942 thrust him into the national spotlight as a candidate for the Republican presidential nomination in 1944. His opposition to the federal government's encroachment on matters previously left to the states and localities appealed especially to many of the party regulars and business leaders. They were impressed by his record in Ohio and his pledge that after "we have freed the world from autocracy then we will free the United States from needless and costly bureaucracy." Bricker also received an early endorsement from fellow Ohioan Robert Taft, who had decided to concentrate on winning reelection to the Senate in 1944 rather than seeking the presidency. Even though Taft had his doubts about Bricker's intellect and his ability to put together an organization and run a campaign, the senator much preferred Bricker's conservatism and anti-New Dealism to Wendell Willkie's internationalism or Thomas Dewey's arrogance and connections with the New York *Herald Tribune* and the eastern establishment. But Dewey won easily in several primary contests and clinched the nomination before the convention began. Bricker then withdrew and endorsed Dewey, who accepted Bricker as his running mate to balance the ticket both geographically and ideologically.[12]

John Bricker's actions and rhetoric during the 1944 campaign illustrate his excessive partisanship and what even Taft recognized as Bricker's penchant for making mistakes. At a press conference in upstate New York in July, for example, Bricker stated that he welcomed support from any and all sources. Asked if that included Gerald L. K. Smith, an anti-semitic, isolationist, right-wing extremist, Bricker replied that Smith's ballot, too, would be counted if he voted for the GOP. A few days later, however, when Smith's America First party nominated Bricker to be its vice-presidential candidate, Bricker criticized such action as cheap demagoguery, and Dewey condemned Smith as a "Hitler-like rabble rouser."[13]

Bricker tried repeatedly during the campaign to link Franklin Roosevelt and the New Deal not only with Sidney Hillman and the CIO's Political Action Committee (PAC), but also with Earl Browder and the American Communist party. In a speech in Dallas, for instance, Bricker charged that "to all intents and purposes the great Democratic party has become the Hillman-Browder Communistic party with Franklin Roosevelt as its front." Later, Bricker named seven federal employees whose connections with PAC, he claimed, "conclusively prove that Franklin Roosevelt and

12See *New York Times*, April 20, 1944, p. 36; New York *Herald Tribune*, June 29, 1944, p. 4; Roseboom, *A History of Presidential Elections*, pp. 480–82; Mayer, "The Republican Party, 1932–1952," in Arthur Schlesinger, Jr., ed., *History of United States Political Parties*, 3, 2283–84; and Patterson, *Mr. Republican*, pp. 268–72.

13*New York Times*, July 27, 1944, pp. 1, 11; and August 2, 1944, pp. 1, 10; and Patterson, *Mr. Republican*, p. 271.

the New Deal are in the hands of the radicals and the Communists."[14]

Dewey and Bricker lost to Roosevelt and Truman in the 1944 election, and John Bricker retired temporarily from public life. But in 1946 he sought and easily won a seat in the United States Senate, defeating liberal Democrat James Huffman by more than 350,000 votes. In the Senate, Bricker was one of the conservatives who predominated among the new Republican "class of 1946" (other newly elected Republican senators included Henry Dworshak of Idaho, William Jenner of Indiana, and Joseph McCarthy of Wisconsin), and he quickly aligned himself with the conservative Republicans and southern Democrats who controlled Congress. He opposed government regulation of business, advocated reductions in federal spending, and sought to curb the federal government's expanding role in the daily lives of the American people. To Bricker, issues such as public housing and education were state and local matters better dealt with at those levels of government. Americans for Democratic Action ranked him as one of the most conservative members of the Senate, giving him liberal ratings of 10 percent in 1947, 6 percent in 1948, and 0 percent in 1949.[15]

Bricker spoke out frequently against the dangers that he saw in the constant expansion of the federal government's authority. In a December 1948 speech to the Council of State Governments, he warned that the United States was on the verge of abandoning its traditional federal system. He suggested that a commission be established to study the relationship between the federal and state governments so that the people could find out whether their state governments were merely an "expensive, archaic manifestation of a bygone day and should be dissolved," though "heaven forbid such was the case!" The question that had to be faced, he stressed, was whether the United States was confronted with "an irresistible rush to centralization—then state socialism—then dictatorship." Similarly, in a 1950 Memorial Day address at Gettysburg National Cemetery, he urged Americans to guard against "bureaucratic control," contending that "whenever you enhance the power of government, just to that degree do you suppress human freedom."[16]

On foreign policy issues, Bricker's position and his record are more

---

[14]*New York Times,* October 26, 1944, p. 15; and October 31, 1944, p. 15; and Fried, *Men against McCarthy,* p. 8.

[15]*New York Times,* November 6, 1946, p. 15; *U.S. News and World Report,* January 29, 1954, pp. 73–75; and *ADA World,* August 26, 1947; July 20, 1948; and October 29, 1949, all in "ADA Papers," microfilm edition, Series IX, "*ADA World.*" For a basis of comparison, Taft's liberal ratings from ADA were 20% in 1947, 25% in 1948, and 14% in 1949. See also Bendiner, "Retrogression in Ohio."

[16]*New York Times,* December 5, 1948, p. 47; and May 31, 1950, p. 2.

difficult to characterize. Though he claimed to be a supporter of the United Nations, he fought against any proposals that he thought might involve the United States in a world council with substantive powers. While serving on the Joint Congressional Committee on Atomic Energy in 1947, for example, he opposed any suggestions that the United States turn over control of the atomic bomb to an international commission that would then be able to use the bomb against any nation that broke the peace. Bricker rejected the plan because he feared that any such agency, if it were strong enough to punish individual nations, would clearly be more powerful than any single country, including the United States. It would constitute a world government, which he adamantly opposed.[17]

Bricker was not an isolationist, however. Unlike Taft, William Langer (R-N.D.), Kenneth Wherry (R-Neb.), and a few others, Bricker voted for both the Marshall Plan and the North Atlantic Treaty. On the other hand, he did support Taft's unsuccessful efforts to cut funding for the Marshall Plan and attach a reservation to the North Atlantic Pact disavowing any American obligation to supply its treaty partners with military equipment or atomic bombs. Moreover, in later years he often tried to cut or eliminate many foreign aid programs, denouncing them as confusing and wasteful of American taxpayers' money.[18]

Not surprisingly, Bricker, like most Republican legislators of that period, disapproved of the increasing tendency of presidents to act unilaterally in foreign affairs without consulting Congress. A frequent and vocal critic of Franklin Roosevelt and the Yalta accords, Bricker endorsed a resolution in 1950 to compel President Truman to inform Congress of any commitments or agreements he had made in recent talks with British Prime Minister Clement Attlee. And when the Senate debated Truman's power to send additional troops to Western Europe in the spring of 1951, Bricker maintained that passing an advisory sense of the Senate resolution would be ineffective; he recommended instead the enactment of a joint resolution that would have the force of law.[19]

[17]See ibid., January 31, 1947, p. 12; and John Bricker to John Weed Powers, November 19, 1951, JBP, Box 90, OHS. (For many years, the John Bricker Papers were divided. The senator donated most of his papers to the Ohio Historical Society in the 1960s and early '70s, and this material is cited herein as JBP, OHS, with specific box numbers included in the citations. Bricker retained some of his papers, however, and these were still in his personal possession when I did my research. Thus, I have cited this material simply as JBP. These too have since been deposited at the Ohio Historical Society.)

[18]See 94 *CR* 2708, 2793 (1948); 95 *CR* 9915–16 (1949); 104 *CR* 14716–17 (1958); *New York Times,* July 22, 1949, pp. 1, 2; *U.S. News and World Report,* January 29, 1954, pp. 73–75; and Jewell, *Senatorial Politics and Foreign Policy,* p. 49.

[19]See 97 *CR* 8260 (1951); S. Res. 371, 81st Cong., 2d sess., December 6, 1950; and *New York Times,* March 30, 1951, p. 6; and April 4, 1951, pp. 1, 17.

Never in the forefront of the struggle for civil rights or civil liberties, Bricker strongly supported Senator Joe McCarthy and defended what he called the Wisconsin Republican's "simple and direct" methods of rooting out Communists in the United States. Reportedly, he once told McCarthy that "Joe, you're a dirty son of a bitch, but there are times when you've got to have a son of a bitch around, and this is one of them." In 1954, when the Senate considered a resolution to censure McCarthy, Bricker opposed the measure, arguing that McCarthy, "with patriotic exuberance," had merely "grabbed his shillelagh" and gone to work to expose and destroy the "unmitigated evil" of Communism. He warned, moreover, that disciplinary action against McCarthy "would operate as a club to beat down any senator inclined to lead in Congress the never-ending fight . . . against the Communist conspiracy in America."[20]

Throughout this period, numerous commentators attacked Bricker and his record. The *New Republic* described him as "a genial handshaker, gifted in the art of avoiding issues and uncanny in the knack of making friends without influencing people," and John Gunther, in his best seller *Inside U.S.A.*, wrote that "Little record exists that Bricker has ever said anything worth more than thirty seconds of serious consideration by anybody. Intellectually he is like interstellar space—a vast vacuum occasionally crossed by homeless, wandering cliches." Similarly, a poll of 211 Washington newsmen and radio reporters conducted by *Pageant* magazine in 1949 ranked Robert Taft as the best senator and rated Bricker "The Loser—'Worst Senator,'" Bricker narrowly edging out Senators William Jenner (R-Ind.) and Kenneth McKellar (D-Tenn.) for the title. Despite such criticism, however, the voters of Ohio, the people whose opinions really mattered for the continuance of Bricker's political career, repeatedly demonstrated their support for him by electing him to office by large majorities.[21]

III

John Bricker believed that Alger Hiss, Dean Acheson, John Foster Dulles, and others had led the UN astray from its original purpose of maintaining the peace, and that the organization now focused instead on "creating a universal standard of social and economic justice, so called."

[20]100 *CR* 15998–16001 (1954). Bricker's comment to McCarthy is reported in Rovere, *Senator Joe McCarthy,* p. 65.

[21]*New Republic,* June 28, 1943, pp. 860–61; Gunther, *Inside U.S.A.,* p. 460; and "Our Best and Worst Senators," *Pageant,* October, 1949, pp. 9–16. But on the *Pageant* poll see also Drury, *Three Kids in a Cart,* pp. 108–9.

Bricker saw the UN's efforts to draft a covenant on human rights as a key part of its scheme to provide everyone with a common social and economic way of life, and he began searching for ways to limit the effects of such agreements within the United States.[22]

In opposing the draft covenant on human rights, Bricker claimed that he was protecting the rights and freedoms of the American people from the dangers posed by such agreements. His arguments gained credence from the many real defects in the draft covenant then under consideration, but his sudden concern for human rights and civil liberties stands in sharp contrast to the lack of such concern throughout his public career. Moreover, his opposition over the years to the Genocide Convention, which had been drafted much more carefully and was not marred by the faults found in the draft convenant on human rights, undermined his case against the covenant, and the wild accusations that he hurled against Franklin Roosevelt, Harry Truman, and Dean Acheson revealed the partisan nature of his attacks against the covenant.[23]

Bricker opened his campaign against the draft covenant on July 17, 1951, when he introduced S. Res. 177, a measure "opposing the proposed International Covenant on Human Rights." The resolution declared that it was the sense of the Senate that the latest version of the human rights covenant "would, if ratified as a treaty, prejudice those rights of the American people which are now protected by the Bill of Rights of the Constitution of the United States." It directed the president to advise the United Nations that the draft agreement was not acceptable to the United States, and to instruct the American representatives "to withdraw from further negotiations with respect to the Covenant on Human Rights, and all other covenants, treaties, and conventions which seek to prescribe restrictions on individual liberty which, if passed by the Congress as domestic legislation, would be unconstitutional." The purpose of his resolution, Bricker emphasized, was "to bury the so-called covenant on human rights so deep that no one holding high public office will ever dare to attempt its resurrection."[24]

In his remarks accompanying the resolution, Bricker denounced the draft covenant as a "blueprint for slavery," and suggested that its real title

22See 97 *CR* 8257; and Bricker to Carl Rix, November 30, 1951, JBP. See also Bricker to Professor Kenneth Colegrove, February 13, 1953, JBP, Box 91, OHS; and interview with Senator Bricker, June 26, 1975.

23See 97 *CR* 8254–63, 11509–14. On Bricker's opposition to the Genocide Convention, see Bricker to Joseph Wilson, April 7, 1954, JBP, Box 101, OHS; and Bricker to Senator George Aiken, December 10, 1970, Aiken Papers, Crate 38, Box 3, University of Vermont Library.

24S. Res. 177, 82d Cong., 1st sess., July 17, 1951; 97 *CR* 8254, 8263; and *New York Times*, July 18, 1951, p. 5.

should be "a Covenant on Human Slavery or subservience to government." He asserted that the agreement's authors had "repudiated the underlying theory of the Bill of Rights—freedom to be let alone"—and had substituted "a host of vaguely defined duties and responsibilities enforceable by the Government." The many qualifications and limitations on rights and freedoms contained in the covenant, he warned, "would legalize the most vicious restrictions of dictators both past and present."[25]

Bricker pointed out, for example, that Article 14 of the proposed covenant was supposed to protect the right to seek and receive information. That article stipulated, however, that such freedom carried with it "special duties and responsibilities," and was, therefore, "subject to certain penalties, liabilities, and restrictions . . . as are provided by law and are necessary for the protection of national security, public order, safety, health or morals, or of the rights, freedoms or reputations of others." The inclusion of so many qualifications, Bricker charged, proved that the Commission on Human Rights had "attempted to destroy human freedom by the subterfuge of recognizing human rights and then nullifying those rights by making their exercise a matter of responsibility and accountability to the state." He argued, moreover, that the justifications set forth in the covenant for limiting freedom of information were extremely vague; permitting governments to restrict the press whenever necessary to protect public morals would allow the state to censor or prevent the publication of almost anything.[26]

Equally alarming, the senator complained, was the covenant's inclusion of articles dealing with economic and social matters. Although such concerns might reflect legitimate aspirations to which few people would take exception, Bricker maintained, they were not constitutional rights that Americans could assert against their government. Any attempt to satisfy such hopes through government action, he warned, would result in the federal government assuming "absolute control over the lives of all its citizens," disregarding the individual liberties of the American people in the process.[27]

Bricker then focused on the legal status of the covenant if it were approved by the Senate. Acknowledging that some people contended that the agreement would be of no force or effect in the United States if it detracted from the freedoms secured by the Bill of Rights, Bricker pointed out three possible bases upon which a treaty could be ruled constitutional

[25]97 *CR* 8255.
[26]Ibid., 8255–56, 8258. For the complete text of the draft covenant on human rights then under consideration, see ibid., 8263–67.
[27]Ibid., 8258.

even if it allowed "legislative destruction" of some of the rights guaranteed to the American people. In the first place, he reminded his colleagues, Article VI of the Constitution stipulated that the Constitution, federal statutes, and ratified treaties were all part of the supreme law of the land, but it did not specify that one took precedence over the others. Bricker also noted that in *Missouri v. Holland* in 1920, the Supreme Court had upheld a treaty with Great Britain concerning the shooting of migratory birds even though that subject had previously been regulated by the states under their reserved powers. Finally, he observed, someone could argue that ratification of a treaty by the president and the Senate was not, technically speaking, an act of Congress, and therefore it did not come under the restriction in the First Amendment that Congress could pass no laws abridging freedom of speech or of the press.[28]

To illustrate the dangers posed by agreements such as the covenant on human rights, Bricker discussed the California District Court's ruling in 1950 in the *Fujii* case. The California Supreme Court had not yet handed down its decision in the case, and with the help of Senators John Marshall Butler (R-Md.) and Wayne Morse (R-Ore.), Bricker related how the lower court in California had invalidated that state's Alien Land Law because it conflicted with the human rights provisions in the United Nations Charter. The court had made that ruling, Bricker emphasized, despite the stipulation in Article 2(7) of the charter that nothing in the charter should be construed so as to alter the domestic law of member nations. Given that precedent, Bricker stressed, how could the American people rely for protection on the disclaimer in the draft covenant that "nothing in this covenant may be interpreted as limiting or derogating from any of the rights and freedoms which may be guaranteed under the laws of any contracting state"?[29]

Bricker also asserted that the draft covenant, even under the most favorable interpretation, would be of little benefit to the American people because of its stipulation that "In the case of a state of emergency officially proclaimed by the authorities, . . . a state may take measures derogating, to the extent strictly limited by the exigencies of the situation, from its obligations under . . . this Covenant." He noted that Franklin Roosevelt had often called the Depression an "emergency greater than war," and that crisis had been followed by "the prewar emergency, the World War II emergency, the postwar emergency, and now the Korean emergency." If

[28]Ibid., 8261. See also the discussion of *Missouri v. Holland* in Chapter 1, above.

[29]97 CR 8261–62. See also Article 18 of the proposed covenant, ibid., 8265; and *Sei Fujii v. State of California*, 217 Pac. (2nd) 481 (1950), discussed in Chapter 1, above.

the human rights convention would apply "only during those abnormal periods which a President cannot describe as an 'emergency,'" it would seldom be in effect in the United States.[30]

Given all the difficulties and dangers inherent in the human rights agreement, why did "the State Department and its international do-gooders at the United Nations" continue pushing the pact toward ratification? They supported the covenant, Bricker charged, because it was "an ingenious mechanism designed to stifle all criticism of the so-called Fair Deal." Both President Truman and Secretary of State Acheson had declared on numerous occasions that the administration's foreign and military policies were crucial to the defense of the United States; therefore, Bricker argued, the covenant's proviso that the press could be subjected to penalties in order to safeguard national security might become a convenient weapon to deter unfavorable comments. American approval of the covenant, Bricker warned, "would draw another iron curtain around the administration in Washington for the protection of the New Deal, or the Fair Deal, or whatever one may choose to call it."[31]

Who was the main culprit behind this plot to do away with a substantial portion of the American Bill of Rights? According to Bricker, Truman's assertion earlier in the year, during the Troops-to-Europe controversy, that the president had the power to send the armed forces "anywhere in the world" proved that "he does not understand the legal principles on which this Republic was founded." Hence, it would be unfair to charge him with deliberately trying to destroy the Constitution. Similarly, Bricker was willing to give Eleanor Roosevelt the benefit of the doubt and assume that she "and her one-world colleagues are blissfully ignorant of the fact that the United States is a constitutional republic and not a democracy." Secretary of State Acheson had the reputation of being a brilliant and able constitutional lawyer, however, and Bricker condemned his as the real villain, for he should have been aware of the effects that the covenant would have on the rights of the American people. To aid the secretary in any future negotiations on the human rights convention, Bricker reminded him of Thomas Jefferson's famous warning that: "Our liberty depends on the freedom of the press, and that cannot be limited without being lost."[32]

By this time, Acheson had become accustomed to being the target of Republican attacks. Republicans had condemned him for refusing to turn

[30]*97 CR* 8261.

[31]Ibid., 8258–60. See also Article 14(3) of the proposed covenant.

[32]Ibid., 8263. For Truman's remarks concerning the power of the president to dispatch American troops, see *Public Papers of the Presidents: Harry S. Truman, 1951* (Washington, D.C.: United States Government Printing Office, 1965), p. 19.

his back on Alger Hiss, and for "inviting" the Communist attack in Korea by defining the Korean Peninsula as outside the American defense perimeter in the Pacific. In December 1950, the vast majority of Republicans in both the House and the Senate had endorsed a resolution of "no confidence" in the secretary of state and insisted that he be replaced, and four months later Senators Bricker, Wherry, and others had blamed Acheson for President Truman's decision to relieve General MacArthur of his command in Korea. By the summer of 1951, Acheson had clearly become the Republicans' favorite "whipping boy."[33]

Not surprisingly, the State Department took exception to Bricker's remarks and his resolution. In response to a letter from Senator Connally asking for the department's comments on S. Res. 177, Assistant Secretary of State Jack McFall emphasized that his agency and its representatives had no intention of recommending any treaty that might jeopardize the rights of the American people. On the contrary, he assured the senator, department officials had been and would continue to be guided by the principles of the Bill of Rights in the negotiations for a covenant on human rights. McFall stressed that the proposed agreement was still in the process of formulation; therefore, much of the criticism of the pact was premature. He readily admitted that, as presently drafted, certain sections of the covenant were unacceptable. He explained, however, that instead of pulling back from further discussions, department representatives preferred to continue seeking modifications and improvements in the text. The only way to achieve international cooperation, he observed, was for all nations to participate in such talks. McFall was tempted to point out the similarity between the course of action recommended by Bricker and the Soviet Union's practice of walking out of UN meetings when it did not get its way, but he refrained, stating merely that instead of withdrawing when others expressed contrary opinions, delegates from the United States would stay and try to win support for the American position.[34]

IV

John Bricker spoke out again against the draft covenant in September 1951, and this time he sent a copy of his remarks to each of his colleagues. Bricker reiterated his complaints and insisted that he was not acting from

[33]See *New York Times*, December 16, 1950, pp. 1, 3; Acheson, *Present at the Creation*, pp. 354–70; McLellan, *Dean Acheson*, pp. 218–38, 301; Caridi, *Korean War and American Politics*, pp. 42, 151–52; and Westerfield, *Foreign Policy and Party Politics*, pp. 327–29.

[34]See Assistant Secretary of State Jack McFall to Senator Tom Connally, August 23, 1951; and draft of letter from McFall to Connally, attached to note from Durward Sandifer to Eleanor Roosevelt, August 6, 1951; ERP, Boxes 4584 and 3935.

partisan motives or attacking the United Nations. In fact, he suggested that the worst enemies of the UN were those who sought "to expand its role in international affairs beyond that contemplated by the Congress of the United States." If the UN were to be an effective instrument for world peace, he warned, "it must not be sabotaged by those who seek to make it an intervenor in matters which are purely the domestic concern of the member nations and their citizens."[35]

A number of Bricker's Republican colleagues applauded his efforts. Styles Bridges of New Hampshire thought Bricker's views were "completely sound" and promised to help expedite consideration of S. Res. 177. Similarly, Robert Hendrickson of New Jersey assured Bricker of his support on this "highly controversial issue," and Edward Martin of Pennsylvania declared that he was "fully in agreement." Leverett Saltonstall of Massachusetts reported that he had been worried for years that questions would arise involving the United Nations Charter, and the *Fujii* decision had exacerbated his concern. Although he realized the world had grown smaller, and it was important for the United States to get closer to its allies, he was reluctant to give up "our fundamental rights that are contained in our Constitution." He hoped that Bricker would continue keeping a close eye on the whole situation.[36]

Southern Democrats, too, endorsed Bricker's position. John Sparkman of Alabama agreed that before the Senate took any action on the human rights covenant it should have a clearer understanding of all its ramifications, and he told Bricker that he would be glad to discuss S. Res. 177 with Senator Connally and other members of the Foreign Relations Committee. Willis Smith of North Carolina reported that he had first become interested in this whole problem when it had come up in the American Bar Association, and he had decided then that the United States should not ratify the Genocide Convention or any covenant on human rights. Richard Russell of Georgia thanked Bricker for performing a great service in exposing the pitfalls in the draft covenant, observing that "the euphonious and appealing title" given that agreement was just "one of the means used to drum up public sentiment in favor of proposals that are fraught with danger to the fundamental rights of our people." He pledged his full support for Bricker's efforts to make sure that the United States did not approve the covenant.[37]

[35]See 97 *CR* 11509–14; and Bricker to Senator Harley Kilgore, September 20, 1951, Kilgore Papers, Box 75, FDRL.
[36]Bridges to Bricker, September 24, 1951; Hendrickson to Bricker, September 24, 1951; Martin to Bricker, September 24, 1951; and Saltonstall to Bricker, September 26, 1951; all in JBP, Box 90, OHS.
[37]Sparkman to Bricker, September 26, 1951; Smith to Bricker, October 9, 1951; and Russell to Bricker, September 26, 1951; all in JBP, Box 90, OHS.

Bricker received one other reply that warrants attention. Senator A. Willis Robertson (D-Va.) probably expressed the true feelings of many of the southerners and conservatives who opposed the agreement when he promised to help Bricker in the fight against the covenant because he believed there was already "enough trouble with do-gooders in our own country telling us about how the Federal government should regulate in all details the problems of human rights which the Constitution clearly left to the States." In Robertson's view, the American people certainly didn't need the United Nations joining "in that same type of pressure."[38]

John Bricker had introduced S. Res. 177 for reasons very similar to those expressed by Senator Robertson. He had never been all that concerned about the rights of a free press, but he had always opposed efforts to strengthen the United Nations or give it any jurisdiction over domestic matters within the United States. As Bricker himself once explained, he sought to "prohibit world or regional government by treaty," and "prevent the UN Human Rights Commission from regulating the civil and political rights of the American people; the World Health Organization from regulating on the subject of domestic medical care; or the International Labor Organization from regulating such purely domestic matters as social security, insurance, labor-management relations, minimum wages and hours, and maternity benefits."[39]

In other words, Bricker wanted to insure that international agreements would not lead to United Nations interference or more liberal social and economic policies and legislation in the United States. He realized, however, that S. Res. 177 was "purely a stopgap device without legal force or effect"; what was really needed was a constitutional amendment to protect the people against the "dangers" inherent in international conventions such as the draft covenant on human rights.[40]

[38]Robertson to Bricker, September 22, 1951, JBP, Box 90, OHS.
[39]See Bricker to Frank Waldrop, March 6, 1953, JBP, Box 91, OHS.
[40]Bricker to Frank Holman, July 23, 1951, JBP; and interview with Senator Bricker, June 26, 1975.

CHAPTER THREE

Drafting a Constitutional Amendment

John Bricker's opposition to the draft covenant on human rights brought him into contact with the leaders of the American Bar Association, and they soon agreed that some sort of constitutional amendment was needed to protect the United States permanently from the threats posed by the covenant and other such agreements. Bricker's perception of the dangers diverged somewhat from that of the attorneys, however, and so did his solution. Both Bricker and the ABA sought to prevent the United Nations from promoting liberal social and economic programs within the United States and from converting itself by treaty into a world government, but the leaders of the ABA pressed for an amendment that would include additional safeguards to protect the reserved rights of the states from further encroachments by the federal government. Although Bricker generally opposed the expansion of federal authority at the expense of the states, he believed there were occasions when the federal government should be able to implement a treaty even if it meant invading the traditional prerogatives of the states. This difference of opinion would hamper Bricker and the ABA in their fight to win approval for a constitutional amendment limiting the effects of treaties and executive agreements.

I

The American Bar Association condemned the draft covenant on human rights in much the same manner that it had spoken out previously against the Declaration of Human Rights and the Genocide Convention. In an August 1950 speech before the Washington State Bar Association, Frank Holman warned that the proposed covenant on human rights "might transform the United States into a socialist state and substitute 'Treaty Law' for Constitutional Law," and the Committee for Peace and

32

Law Through United Nations soon concluded that the draft covenant threatened the basic rights of the American people. Consequently, in September 1950, the ABA's House of Delegates adopted a resolution formally opposing the draft covenant.[1]

In their report to the House of Delegates, members of the Committee on Peace and Law summarized the ABA's objections to the covenant. They pointed out again that a ratified treaty became part of the supreme law of the land, superseding any contrary provisions in state laws or constitutions or federal statutes, and they cited the *Fujii* case to show that the UN Charter and any covenant on human rights would probably invalidate state laws that made distinctions on the basis of "sex, race, color, language, property, birth status, [or] political or other opinion," including "laws relating to women, to miscegenation, . . . [and] possibly even state laws undertaking to outlaw the Communist party as a political party." They also noted that American immigration and naturalization restrictions might be annulled by the covenant's proclamation that "everyone has the right to seek and enjoy in other countries asylum from persecution." Finally, repeating the standard warning based on *Missouri v. Holland,* the committee asserted that American approval of the covenant would empower the federal government to pass civil rights laws and other legislation that it could not enact in the absence of treaty.[2]

Members of the Committee on Peace and Law realized, however, that rather than opposing each such covenant as it was proposed by the United Nations, a better solution might be a constitutional amendment to clarify and limit the treaty-making power. They feared that the treaty-making power was a " 'Trojan horse' " through which "the constitutional character of our government can be substantially changed and the balance between state and federal power greatly upset." Carl Rix and others had suggested previously, in response to the Genocide Convention, that a constitutional amendment might be needed, and the committee now asked the House of Delegates for permission to study the advisability of amending the Constitution "to protect, beyond question, the federal-state character of our government as now established."[3]

The House of Delegates agreed that this matter warranted further con-

[1]Holman, *Western Lawyer,* p. 505; ABA, "Report of the Committee for Peace and Law Through United Nations," September 1, 1950, copy in Arthur Sutherland Papers, Box 11, Harvard Law School Library; and ABA, "Summary of Action Taken by the House of Delegates," September 1950, copy in Harold M. Stephens Papers, Box 137. See also Rix, "Human Rights and International Law: Effect of the Covenant under Our Constitution"; and Holman, "Treaty Law-Making: A Blank Check for Writing a New Constitution."

[2]ABA, "Report of the Committee for Peace and Law Through United Nations," September 1, 1950.

[3]Ibid. See also *Genocide, Hearings, 1950,* pp. 208–9; and Carl Rix to Manley Hudson, October 4, 1949, Hudson Papers, Box 114.

sideration, and in September 1950 it authorized both the Committee on Peace and Law and the Section of International and Comparative Law to study the feasibility of a constitutional amendment removing the dangers inherent in the treaty-making power. Specifically, both groups were instructed to focus on three questions: (1) Should the Constitution be amended so that treaties would not be self-executing upon ratification but would become part of the law of the land only to the extent provided by subsequent acts of Congress? (2) Should Congress be limited in implementing treaties to passing only those measures which it could already enact under its enumerated powers? and (3) Should international agreements be prohibited from changing the basic structure of the United States government?[4]

II

When John Bricker introduced his resolution in 1951 opposing the draft covenant on human rights, the leaders of the American Bar Association welcomed him to their cause. Frank Holman saw a brief summary of Bricker's remarks and wrote to congratulate the senator on his fine speech. He told Bricker how pleased he was "that a statesman of your ability and standing has interested yourself in this matter." Similarly, Alfred Schweppe, a Seattle attorney and chairman of the Committee on Peace and Law Through United Nations, praised Bricker for his "excellent statement" and sent him copies of the committee's reports criticizing the various agreements on human rights emanating from the United Nations.[5]

In his letter to Bricker, Schweppe also raised the possibility of amending the Constitution to eliminate the problems posed by the covenant on human rights. His committee was already studying the idea of a constitutional amendment to deal with this matter, Schweppe reported, as were Congressmen Charles Bennett (D-Fla.) and Usher Burdick (R-N.D.).[6]

Bricker agreed that a constitutional amendment might be the best way to protect against the perils presented by such compacts. He admitted in a letter to Holman that his bill opposing the human rights covenant was simply a sense of the Senate resolution, without legal force or effect; it would merely inform the president that the legislators did not favor the

---

[4]ABA, "Summary of Action Taken by the House of Delegates," September 1950; Holman, *Western Lawyer*, p. 506. See also Ober, "The Treaty-Making and Amending Powers: Do They Protect Our Fundamental Rights?"
[5]Holman to Bricker, July 18, 1951; and Schweppe to Bricker, July 20, 1951; both in JBP.
[6]Schweppe to Bricker, July 20, 1951, JBP.

draft convention. Nonetheless, he hoped that his proposal, if adopted, "might slow the State Department in its mad pursuit for a World Bill of Rights." The senator concurred, however, that "a permanent solution for the dangers inherent in treaty law-making seems to require a constitutional amendment limiting the impact of treaties on domestic law."[7]

In his replies to Holman and Schweppe, Bricker also raised the question of executive agreements. Like many Republicans, Bricker believed that the Yalta, Potsdam, and Teheran agreements were "among the greatest catastrophes in modern history," and he feared that the president and the State Department would circumvent any restrictions imposed on treaties by resorting to executive agreements. Consequently, he advised that any constitutional amendment to limit the treaty-making power should also prohibit the use of executive agreements in place of treaties.[8]

It must be emphasized, however, that curbing executive agreements was never Bricker's primary objective; scholars such as Alexander DeConde, Walter LaFeber, and William Manchester have misinterpreted the thrust of the amendment when they have argued, in Manchester's words, that "Yalta was what the Bricker Amendment was all about." Bricker and the leaders of the ABA began considering a constitutional amendment, not in response to Yalta and other executive agreements, but because they were concerned about the possible effects within the United States of *treaties* such as the UN Charter, the Genocide Convention, and the proposed covenant on human rights. The Bricker amendment would include restrictions on executive agreements too, but they were designed mainly to ensure that presidents could not evade the restrictions the measure would place on treaties.[9]

Bricker appreciated and reciprocated the support he received from the leaders of the ABA. He commended Schweppe on "the wonderful work your committee has been doing in alerting the American Bar to a danger which is not widely recognized even today," and he told Holman how encouraging it was "that you and so many other able and patriotic lawyers are fighting to save the Constitution." Bricker also asked Holman if he had any specific suggestions or proposals, since he intended in the near future to introduce a constitutional amendment.[10]

[7]Bricker to Holman, July 23, 1951, JBP. See also Bricker to Schweppe, July 24, 1951, JBP.

[8]Bricker to Holman, July 23, 1951; Bricker to Schweppe, July 24, 1951; both in JBP; and 97 CR 8260 (1951). On Yalta in particular, see Theoharis, *The Yalta Myths.*

[9]Quotation is from Manchester, *The Glory and the Dream,* p. 674. See also DeConde, *A History of American Foreign Policy,* 2d ed., p. 778; and LaFeber, *America, Russia, and the Cold War, 1945–1984,* 5th ed., p. 178. On this whole issue, see Tananbaum, "The Bricker Amendment Controversy: Its Origins, and Eisenhower's Role," pp. 73–74.

[10]Bricker to Schweppe, July 24, 1951; and Bricker to Holman, July 23, 1951; both in JBP.

III

In a short speech to the Senate on September 14, 1951, John Bricker told his colleagues about a resolution that had been adopted unanimously by the Tampa Rotary Club. The Floridians urged the Senate to reject the draft covenant on human rights because they feared the covenant "would put in jeopardy, if not abrogate entirely, existing laws which are in our Bill of Rights and our Constitution."[11]

Bricker agreed that the draft covenant "might take from citizens of the United States sacred rights which they enjoy under the Bill of Rights and the Constitution." So, he announced, to safeguard the American people from that threat, he was introducing a constitutional amendment concerning treaties and executive agreements. His amendment would protect the rights and liberties of the American people from the dangers posed by international agreements such as the covenant on human rights, and it would also clarify and limit the use of executive agreements.[12]

S.J. Res. 102 (see Appendix A for the complete text), the first of many versions of the Bricker amendment, was a very complex measure. The first two sections attempted to define more precisely the legal relationship between treaties and the Constitution by requiring that such agreements, in order to become part of the supreme law of the land, be made in pursuance of the Constitution. Previously, treaties had been entered into "under the authority of the United States," and, in the *Curtiss-Wright* case in 1936, the Supreme Court had ruled that the powers of the federal government in foreign affairs "did not depend upon the affirmative grants of the Constitution." Bricker wanted his amendment to make it clear that treaty provisions had to accord with the Constitution.[13]

The senator designed the third section of his resolution to prevent the establishment of a world government, to protect the rights of the American people from being compromised by a treaty, and to ensure that agreements with other nations were confined to traditional subjects of international transactions. This part of the amendment prohibited the government from entering into any agreements concerning the rights and freedoms of American citizens, "the character and form of government prescribed by the Constitution and laws of the United States, . . . or any other matters essentially within the domestic jurisdiction of the United States."[14]

The amendment went on to deal specifically with executive agreements.

[11]97 *CR* 11361.

[12]Ibid.; S.J. Res. 102, 82d Cong., 1st sess., September 14, 1951.

[13]S.J. Res. 102, 82d Cong., 1st sess., September 14, 1951; United States Constitution, Article VI; *United States v. Curtiss-Wright Export Corp. et al.,* 299 U.S. 304 (1936).

[14]S.J. Res. 102, 82d Cong., 1st sess., September 14, 1951.

It prohibited their use as substitutes for treaties, and spelled out a complicated procedure under which they would automatically expire six months after the end of the term of the president who had entered into them, unless the president requested and Congress approved an extension. It also required that executive agreements be published, except that those which the president believed must be kept secret could be submitted to congressional committees in lieu of publication. Finally, the resolution gave Congress the power to enact any legislation needed to enforce the amendment.[15]

Bricker and his legislative assistant, Charles Webb, had drafted the amendment on their own, without any help or specific suggestions from the leaders of the ABA, and the senator realized that there were problems with his resolution. "Any proposed amendment affecting the treaty-making power," he conceded in a letter to Schweppe, was "bound to have imperfections." Nonetheless, Bricker defended his decision to introduce his amendment without waiting for the American Bar Association to complete its study on the issue. It did not matter that the amendment was not yet in finished form, he explained to Schweppe, for his primary purpose in submitting the measure was to induce the Senate Judiciary Committee to hold hearings on the question. He favored "a full dress public debate on a wide variety of proposals" so that the judiciary committee could consider different texts and alternatives and then resolve all the "legal complexities."[16]

IV

Just after Bricker introduced his amendment, members of the American Bar Association's House of Delegates, at their annual meeting in September 1951, again discussed the dangers inherent in the treaty-making powers of the federal government. Cody Fowler, the outgoing president of the organization, warned that revolutionary changes in recent years had created an "all-powerful central government" that imperiled the basic rights and freedoms of the American people. It was the responsibility of the nation's lawyers, he asserted, to prevent this government from convert-

[15]Ibid.
[16]Bricker to Schweppe, October 18, 1951; and Bricker to Eberhard Deutsch, November 5, 1951; both in JBP. Webb was also an attorney, having graduated from the University of Virginia Law School in 1941. He had served as a staff member of the Senate Judiciary Committee for a short time, and had then worked for the Senate Republican Policy Committee before joining Senator Bricker. See Webb to Mrs. Robert Murray, August 5, 1954, JBP, Box 109, OHS; and interview with Charles Webb, July 24, 1975.

ing the United States into a socialist state "through the back door" of international agreements.[17]

Harold Stassen also spoke about the problem of treaties when he addressed the members of the ABA's Section of International and Comparative Law. The former "Boy Governor" of Minnesota, now president of the University of Pennsylvania, Stassen chaired the section's Committee on the Constitutional Aspects of International Agreements. Stassen urged that the United States continue its participation in efforts to expand international law into the realm of economic and social affairs. He stressed, however, that safeguards were needed to ensure that the various United Nations covenants and conventions would not infringe on the rights of the American people. In particular, he hoped a way could be found to preserve existing state laws, which might otherwise be superseded by such treaties. Since his committee had not yet determined whether such protection could best be provided by including specific language in each covenant, attaching reservations to an agreement when it was approved by the Senate, or amending the Constitution to limit the effects of such agreements, Stassen suggested that the Section of International and Comparative Law and the Committee on Peace and Law be authorized to continue their studies.[18]

So that the matter would not be postponed indefinitely, Frank Holman proposed that the House of Delegates consider the whole subject again at its midyear meeting in February 1952. He emphasized that he had already received numerous requests from members of Congress, the American Legion, and other organizations for information about the ABA's position on this question. Accordingly, the House of Delegates resolved that the section and the committee should report again in five months.[19]

The ABA's concern about protecting the rights of the American people must be considered carefully, as much of the association's interest in this area was based on a very limited definition of rights and freedoms. Testifying in favor of the Bricker amendment in 1953, for example, Eberhard Deutsch, a Louisiana attorney and member of the Committee on Peace and Law Through United Nations, warned that "our cherished freedoms are under attack," citing as part of this assault challenges to segregation laws in the various states and the District of Columbia.[20] To the leaders of

[17]*New York Times,* September 18, 1951, pp. 1, 24.

[18]Ibid., September 19, 1951, p. 11; New York *Herald Tribune,* September 19, 1951, pp. 1, 13; Holman, *Western Lawyer,* p. 523.

[19]ABA, *Reports of the American Bar Association,* 76 (1951), 136.

[20]U.S., Congress, Senate, Committee on the Judiciary, *Treaties and Executive Agreements, Hearings,* before a subcommittee of the Committee on the Judiciary, Senate, 83d Cong., 1st sess., 1953, pp. 80–82.

the ABA, "our cherished freedoms" included the right of states to maintain segregated facilities in the South and discriminate against the Japanese in California, and the freedom of businessmen and corporations to manage their affairs without the federal government's interference. As Frank Holman later explained, he opposed treaties stipulating that everyone had the right to "food, clothing, housing, and medical care, and necessary social services, and the right to security in the event of unemployment, sickness, disability, widowhood, [or] old age" because he feared they would transform the United States "from a republic into a completely socialistic state."[21]

The members of the Committee on Peace and Law, resuming their study of the treaty-making power a few weeks later, quickly concluded that a constitutional amendment represented "the only effective answer to the extension of federal power" by means of international agreements. But they still had to work out the text of an amendment. They first considered drafting a measure that would make a sharp distinction between foreign and domestic affairs by specifying those issues that could be dealt with legitimately in treaties, but they soon discarded that approach, fearing, as one committee member said, that it "would lead to long and complicated phraseology" and make it difficult to "sell" the amendment to the American people.[22]

The attorneys decided instead to try to limit the effects international agreements would have within the United States. They would leave the federal government with the authority to enter into all sorts of treaties, but they would limit the internal effects of such agreements by stipulating that a treaty would go into force as domestic law within the United States only as so provided by an ensuing act of Congress. This would make it clear that treaties would no longer be self-executing in the United States, and it would enable Congress, including the House of Representatives, to develop implementing legislation to limit the effects within the United States of any treaty. Schweppe in particular believed that giving the House a voice in these matters would provide further protection for the rights of

---

21Ibid., pp. 136–37. See also Carl Rix to Arthur Krock, May 26, 1950, Krock Papers, Correspondence, "Genocide Treaty," Princeton University Library; and Holman, "Treaty Law-Making: A Blank Check for Writing a New Constitution," esp. 788. The ABA's limited definition of human rights and freedoms can also be seen in its continued opposition to the Genocide Convention, which had been much more carefully drafted and was free of the defects marring the draft covenant on human rights. On the ABA and the Genocide Convention, see Chapter 1.

22Quotations are from ABA, "Report of the Committee on Peace and Law Through United Nations," February 1, 1952, p. 4, copy in Louis Waldman Papers, Box 20, New York Public Library; and Vermont Hatch to Orie Phillips, November 7, 1951, copy in JBP.

the states and the liberties of the people because congressmen were "pretty directly responsive to the electorate at home."[23]

Having agreed that treaties would have to be followed by congressional legislation before they went into effect within the United States, the committee then sought to prevent Congress from using its power to pass such laws to expand the federal government's authority at the expense of the states. As committee member Carl Rix later explained, the attorneys feared that the United Nations Charter or a covenant on human rights, when coupled with the Supreme Court's decision in *Missouri v. Holland,* would leave the rights reserved to the states by the Tenth Amendment "dead as a dodo." Specifically, the attorneys were concerned that the federal government would use the charter or the covenant as a basis for civil rights legislation or other measures infringing on the rights of the states, especially in social and economic matters. Hence, they agreed that their amendment should protect states' rights by limiting Congress, in passing legislation to implement a treaty, to enacting only those measures which it could already adopt under its enumerated powers. This part of the amendment came to be known as the "which" clause because it would allow Congress to pass only those laws *which* it could already enact without the treaty. It proved to be the most controversial part of the amendment. The "which" clause would neither roll back the expansion of federal power that had transpired since the Supreme Court "revolution" of the late 1930s nor restore the rights of corporations to their former preeminent position, but the lawyers hoped that it might at least protect the states against further encroachments by the national government through the treaty-making process.[24]

The attorneys also wanted the amendment to make it clear that treaties were subordinate to the Constitution. They believed it should be stated explicitly that treaties had the same status as federal statutes—part of the law of the land, but subject to the restrictions and limitations set forth in the nation's charter. In any conflict between an article in a treaty and a provision of the Constitution, the Constitution would prevail.[25]

After further study and deliberation, the Committee on Peace and Law drafted a constitutional amendment that its members thought would pro-

---

[23]See Schweppe to Phillips, November 6, 1951; Deutsch to Bricker, October 20, 1951; Schweppe, "Memorandum to Committee on Peace and Law," October 26, 1951; and Hatch to Phillips, November 7, 1951; all in JBP.

[24]Carl Rix to Zechariah Chafee, Jr., June 2, 1952, Chafee Papers, Box 11, Harvard Law School Library. See also Deutsch to Bricker, October 20, 1951, JBP. On the Supreme Court "revolution" beginning in the late 1930s, see Leuchtenburg, "The Constitutional Revolution of 1937."

[25]Schweppe, "Memorandum to Committee on Peace and Law," October 26, 1951, JBP.

tect the American people from the dangers they saw in the treaty-making process. To ensure that the Constitution's safeguards could not be compromised by international agreements, to eliminate the problems of self-executing covenants, and to prevent the federal government, in implementing such agreements, from intruding upon the reserved powers of the states, the committee recommended that the House of Delegates approve and send to Congress for consideration the following amendment:

> A provision of a treaty which conflicts with any provision of this Constitution shall not be of any force or effect. A treaty shall become effective as internal law in the United States only through legislation by Congress which it could enact under its delegated powers in the absence of such treaty.[26]

V

During the fall of 1951, when the ABA's Committee on Peace and Law was drafting its amendment, John Bricker remained in close contact with Frank Holman, Alfred Schweppe, and Eberhard Deutsch. They all agreed that a constitutional amendment was needed to prevent treaties from nullifying the constitutional rights of the American people, but important discrepancies began to emerge between the committee's recommendations and Bricker's own ideas. Their difficulty in reconciling their positions showed the complex and even confusing nature of both the issues and the terminology involved.

The senator believed that any amendment should differentiate between internal and external matters and clearly delineate those subjects that should not be dealt with in treaties. He recognized that it would be difficult to formulate a workable definition, but nonetheless, he maintained, "a constitutional distinction must be made between foreign and domestic affairs." That was why his own amendment had included a provision prohibiting the government from entering into any agreements concerning the rights of United States citizens, the structure of the American government, or any other matters "essentially within the domestic jurisdiction of the United States."[27]

Bricker also objected to the attorneys' plan to eliminate self-executing agreements. Knowing how busy Congress was, he argued that the legislature should not be "saddled with the burden of implementing every trea-

---

26ABA, "Report of the Committee on Peace and Law Through United Nations," February 1, 1952, copy in Louis Waldman Papers.

27See Bricker to Eberhard Deutsch, October 17, 1951, and November 5, 1951, both in JBP. See also Section 3 of S.J. Res. 102, 82d Cong., 1st sess., 1951, copy in Appendix A.

41

ty." Most agreements, he asserted, were not controversial and could easily be put into effect by the courts.[28]

Finally, and somewhat surprisingly, Bricker questioned the wisdom of the "which" clause. Although he was usually a vocal critic of any attempts to expand the power of the federal government, Bricker's years in the Senate had convinced him that there were some topics that came "within the legitimate scope of treaties, notwithstanding the fact that the States may be deprived of some of their jurisdiction." In particular, he pointed out that traditional conventions of friendship, commerce, and navigation granted Americans the right to own and inherit property abroad and engage in various business and professional activities in other countries in return for foreigners being awarded the same privileges in the United States. These matters were primarily subject to state control in the United States, however, and Bricker warned that Congress might be unable to implement such agreements if the Committee on Peace and Law's amendment were adopted, leading other nations to refuse to enter into such pacts with the United States.[29]

Bricker planned to revise his own amendment and introduce it again when Congress reconvened early in 1952, but first he sought suggestions from his colleagues on how he might improve the resolution. He sent each senator a copy of S.J. Res. 102, and explained that the draft covenant on human rights and other treaties emanating from the United Nations had made it necessary to adopt a constitutional amendment protecting "the sovereignty of the United States and the freedoms of American citizens from abuses inherent in the treaty-making power." After he had modified his proposal in accordance with their recommendations, Bricker concluded, he would welcome his colleagues' support as cosponsors of the amendment.[30]

Although he did not receive many suggestions from other senators, Bricker did pick up a large number of cosponsors, and on February 7, 1952, he introduced a new version of his amendment on behalf of himself and fifty-eight of his colleagues. With the exception of Eugene Millikin of Colorado, who basically supported the measure but preferred not to be listed as a cosponsor of someone else's legislation, every Republican senator joined in sponsoring the resolution. This near unanimity of Republican backing for the measure shows that there was a strong partisan aspect to the amendment, and that it represented, at least in part, a Re-

[28]Bricker to Deutsch, November 5, 1951, JBP.
[29]Ibid.
[30]See for example Bricker to Senator Robert Taft, January 15, 1952, Taft Papers, Box 746, Library of Congress; and Bricker to Senator Harley Kilgore, January 15, 1952, Kilgore Papers, Box 75, FDRL.

publican attack against the policies of Franklin Roosevelt and Harry Truman. The Bricker amendment cannot be explained wholly as a partisan effort, however, because fourteen conservative Democrats, including nine from southern or border states, also cosponsored the resolution. Their support for the amendment reflected their dissatisfaction with the Truman administration's liberal social and economic policies and their growing distrust of the United Nations.[31]

This coalition of Republicans and conservative, mostly southern, Democrats, was not unique to the Bricker amendment; similar combinations had managed to bottle up most liberal legislation in Congress since the late 1930s. What was new in the early 1950s, however, was that this coalition was beginning to come together in foreign affairs as well, especially since the war in Korea had bogged down into a costly stalemate after Communist China had intervened. Issues like the draft covenant on human rights and its possible effects within the United States illustrated the way in which domestic and foreign affairs were now intertwined, and the conservative coalition was responding to this development. In the spring of 1951, Republicans and conservative Democrats had passed a sense of the Senate resolution trying to limit President Truman's authority to send more troops to Western Europe, and they had conducted hearings to investigate the president's firing of General MacArthur. Now, besides sponsoring the Bricker amendment, they would soon adopt a resolution in the House of Representatives that directed the president to transmit to the House "full and complete information with respect to any agreements, commitments, or understandings" he might have entered into in a recent meeting with British Prime Minister Winston Churchill.[32]

The large number of cosponsors seemed to indicate widespread support

---

[31]S.J. Res. 130, 82d Cong., 2d sess., February 7, 1952; 98 *CR* 907–9 (1952); and interview with Senator Bricker, June 30, 1975. Although newspapers reported that fifty-six senators had signed the resolution, the names of Senators Kem (R-Mo.) and McCarran (D-Nev.) had inadvertently been omitted from the bill when it had been submitted, and Senator Chavez (D-N.M.) added his name as the measure was being introduced. See *New York Times,* February 8, 1952, p. 12; and 98 *CR* 907, 1171.

Democratic cosponsors of the measure were: Senators Byrd (Va.), Chavez (N.M), Eastland (Miss.), Frear (Del.), Gillette (Iowa), Johnson (Colo.), McCarran (Nev.), McClellan (Ark.), McKellar (Tenn.), Maybank (S.C.), O'Conor (Md.), Robertson (Va.), Smith (N.C.), and Stennis (Miss.).

[32]97 *CR* 3075, 3081, and 3282; *New York Times,* April 5, 1951, pp. 1, 12, 13; Stewart Alsop in the New York *Herald Tribune,* April 6, 1951, p. 25; H. Res. 514, 82d Cong., 2d sess., January 31, 1952; 98 *CR* 739, 1205–15; and *New York Times,* February 21, 1952, pp. 1, 3. See also Senator Ralph Flanders to Professor Zechariah Chafee, Jr., February 20, 1952, Chafee Papers, Box 11; Washington *Times-Herald,* February 8, 1952; and *Christian Science Monitor,* February 8, 1952, p. 1. On the formation of the conservative coalition in Congress in the late 1930s, see Patterson, *Congressional Conservatism and the New Deal.*

in the Senate for the Bricker amendment, but some legislators quickly made it clear that they had not necessarily endorsed Bricker's actual text. Republican Senators Eugene Millikin, Robert Taft, Leverett Saltonstall, Robert Hendrickson, James Kem (Mo.), and Arthur Watkins (Utah) all declared their support for the general thrust of Bricker's amendment, but Taft specifically reserved the right to offer amendments, and Saltonstall explained that he had cosponsored the measure primarily to ensure that the whole matter would be "thoughtfully and carefully discussed at considerable length."[33]

Bricker's new amendment, S.J. Res. 130, retained many of the provisions of his previous proposal. This bill, too, tried to specify those subjects that the senator considered inappropriate for inclusion in international agreements. It prohibited the government from entering into any treaties or executive agreements "respecting the rights of citizens of the United States protected by this Constitution," or ceding to an international organization or a foreign country "any of the legislative, executive, or judicial powers vested by this Constitution in the Congress, the president, and in the courts of the United States, respectively." Also, it again set forth various regulations for the publication and expiration of executive agreements, and required that such compacts not be used as substitutes for treaties. Finally, it left intact Congress's power, in implementing a treaty, to pass legislation that might otherwise be an unconstitutional invasion of the powers reserved to the states.[34]

The only major change from Bricker's previous amendment involved the question of whether international agreements that conflicted with state laws should be self-executing. Bricker's first resolution had stipulated that treaties made in pursuance of the Constitution would be the law of the land, thereby automatically superseding contrary provisions in state laws. However, in an attempt to bring his own bill more in line with the American Bar Association's drafts, the senator had modified his proposal so that it now provided that treaties and executive agreements would not alter or abridge state laws unless Congress so decreed in subsequent legislation. Thus, although some compacts would still be self-executing, those conflicting with state laws would require additional congressional action before going into effect.[35]

---

[33]98 *CR* 907–14; Saltonstall to Professor Chafee, February 13, 1952, Chafee Papers, Box 11.

[34]S.J. Res. 130, 82d Cong., 2d sess., February 7, 1952. For the complete text of S.J. Res. 130, see Appendix C.

[35]See Appendixes A and C to compare Section 2 of S.J. Res. 102 and Section 3 of S.J. Res. 130.

VI

In addition to John Bricker and the Committee on Peace and Law, the ABA's Section of International and Comparative Law was also studying the problems posed by the treaty-making power. The section consisted mainly of lawyers from New York and the East Coast, and, as had been the case with the Genocide Convention, members of the section reached a different conclusion from that reached by the Committee on Peace and Law. Although they conceded that the United Nations human rights conventions raised some serious constitutional issues, members of the section did not believe that immediate approval of a constitutional amendment was necessary. Rather, they suggested that the problem could better be handled by confining American participation in such programs to an advisory role and refusing to ratify such covenants until these issues were resolved. The section recommended further study before the ABA went on the record in support of a constitutional amendment limiting the treaty-making power.[36]

Leaders of the section realized, however, that it would be very difficult to win support for their position in the House of Delegates and delay action on the constitutional amendment being proposed by the Committee on Peace and Law. C. W. Tillett, a North Carolina attorney and former chairman of the section, complained to a friend that the amendment's backers intended to take advantage of "the almost complete and total ignorance of the average run-of-mine members of the House of Delegates on the subject of constitutional law and international relations." The amendment's supporters, he warned, were "both demagogues and un-scrupulous," and they would "bull-doze and frighten" the assembly into approving their proposal. The only way to counter such tactics would be for the leaders of the section to "adjust ourselves to the mental level of the House of Delegates and show them in words of one syllable and by means of language and illustrations easily within their mental grasp, that the adoption of these amendments would be an unsound move." Nothing would give him more pleasure, Tillett confided, "than to be able to erect ghosts in opposition to those amendments just as horrendous as the ones which Mr. Holman and his cohorts will erect in support of the amendments."[37]

When members of the House of Delegates met in late February 1952,

[36]See ABA, Section of International and Comparative Law, *Proceedings,* 1952, pp. 9–12, 43–44; and *New York Times,* February 25, 1952, p. 7.
[37]C. W. Tillett to Zechariah Chafee, Jr., January 25, 1952, Chafee Papers, Box 11.

representatives from the Section of International and Comparative Law tried to dissuade them from recommending adoption of the constitutional amendment submitted by the Committee on Peace and Law. Lyman Tondel, Jr., the section's new chairman, maintained that the proposed amendment would hamper the federal government's ability to negotiate extradition treaties, consular conventions, and covenants facilitating business operations by Americans in foreign countries. He pointed out that United States citizens could own or inherit property abroad and form corporations overseas only because the federal government had entered into treaties granting foreigners the same rights in the United States. If Congress were restricted to passing only those laws authorized under its enumerated powers, however, it might not be able to implement these compacts, since such matters were under state jurisdiction. Under those circumstances, Tondel stressed, foreign nations might be very reluctant to enter into such treaties with the United States or to extend similar favors to Americans. Since the draft amendment also ignored the related problem of executive agreements, Tondel suggested that final action be delayed again until September.[38]

Tondel's pleas fell on deaf ears. The ABA's Board of Governors had already endorsed the amendment before the House of Delegates had begun its meetings, and now Frank Holman and Alfred Schweppe responded to Tondel's objections. They argued that an amendment was needed immediately to protect the rights of the states and the people from being compromised by the various United Nations conventions on human rights. As for the problem of executive agreements, Schweppe explained that his group was well aware of that issue, but they had decided to deal with it separately. Since the present threat had originated in the treaties emanating from the United Nations, the committee thought it more important to act first to meet that danger. When the debate finally drew to a close, the House of Delegates voted overwhelmingly to approve the committee's amendment and forward it to Congress with a recommendation for favorable action.[39]

Critics of the proposed amendment complained bitterly about its endorsement by the ABA. Professor Zechariah Chafee, Jr., of Harvard Uni-

---

[38]See ABA, Section of International and Comparative Law, *Proceedings,* 1952, pp. 43–44; and ABA, *Reports of the American Bar Association,* 77 (1952), 447–48. See also Lyman Tondel, Jr., letter to the editor, *New York Times,* February 24, 1952, IV, 8.

[39]*New York Times,* February 27, 1952, p. 8; ABA, *Reports of the American Bar Association,* 77 (1952), 447–48; Holman, *Western Lawyer,* pp. 523–24; and Schweppe to Bricker, March 5, 1952, JBP. In September 1952, the House of Delegates approved the text of a separate constitutional amendment to limit the use of executive agreements. See *New York Times,* September 19, 1952, p. 6.

versity, a well-known and respected authority on human rights and civil liberties, charged that the ABA's approval of the amendment represented "the worst event which has happened in the law" in the last forty years. He believed that in response to the hypothetical possibility that the president and two-thirds of the Senate might someday approve a treaty nullifying part of the Bill of Rights, the ABA had recommended a constitutional amendment that would deprive Americans of the privileges of doing business or practicing a profession abroad, or suing in a foreign court. Moreover, Chafee feared that the ABA's amendment would strip the federal government of its supremacy in foreign affairs, thereby "undoing one of the most important achievements of the Philadelphia Convention of 1787."[40]

Thus, by the end of February 1952, both John Bricker and the American Bar Association had drafted constitutional amendments to deal with the dangers posed by international agreements, but fundamental differences remained between the two proposals. The ABA's amendment was a short, simple, two-sentence statement; Bricker's resolution consisted of six separate articles. The senator's proposal also applied to executive agreements, which the ABA's did not. Finally, and most significantly, the ABA's amendment included the "which" clause. Bricker's amendment, however, would have affirmed the precedent set in *Missouri v. Holland,* allowing Congress to pass laws giving effect to international agreements even if such measures involved matters otherwise under the jurisdiction of the states.[41]

Writing in the early 1960s, Frank Holman lamented that Bricker had introduced S.J. Res. 130 three weeks before the ABA's House of Delegates had officially approved its own version of the amendment. He regretted that the senator had not waited until he had received "the benefit of the American Bar's idea of a proper text," and he pointed out how confusing it had been to have had two different proposals under consideration. It should be noted, however, that Bricker had been in close contact with Holman, Schweppe, and the other members of the Committee on Peace and Law, and the senator was aware of the drafts the committee had discussed. The inconsistencies between the two resolutions were not there simply because Bricker had acted precipitously; rather, they were the result of the senator and the attorneys having slightly divergent goals. In particular, the principal concern of the leaders of the ABA was to prevent further

---

[40]Chafee to Willard Cowles, March 3, 1952; and Chafee to Erwin Canham, March 3, 1952; both in Chafee Papers, Box 11. See also Chafee, "Amending the Constitution to Cripple Treaties."

[41]To compare the two texts, see Appendixes B and C.

expansion of federal power at the expense of the states. They sought, therefore, to repeal the doctrine established in the migratory bird case: that Congress, in legislating to bring a treaty into force, could pass laws not otherwise sanctioned under its delegated powers. But that was not Bricker's main objective. As the senator explained in 1954, he believed that the "major problem is not how to protect States' Rights as such, but how to protect all purely domestic matters, Federal and State, from the consuming ambition of the United Nations and its specialized agencies to regulate those matters by treaty."[42]

Bricker's service in the Senate had convinced him that in some instances Congress should have the right in implementing treaties to deal with subjects normally under state control. Frank Holman's later statements to the contrary notwithstanding, it was this basic difference of opinion, not any jumping of the gun by Senator Bricker, that produced the discrepancies between the two amendments.

[42]Holman, *Western Lawyer,* p. 524; John Bricker, "The Fight for a Treaty-Control Amendment: Round One," address by Senator Bricker before the regional conference of the ABA, March 4, 1954, JBP, Box 110, OHS. See also Bricker to Senator H. Alexander Smith, February 18, 1953, Smith Papers, Box 123, Princeton University Library.

CHAPTER FOUR

Preliminary Skirmishing

By early 1952, the Bricker amendment was emerging as a major political controversy. Isolationists and conservatives rallied to support the amendment, which reflected their frustration over America's more active role in world affairs, particularly in the United Nations, and their fear that the federal government would use the treaty-making power to encroach on the reserved rights of the states. Moreover, the continuing war in Korea and President Truman's seizure of the steel mills in the spring of 1952 raised serious questions about the extent of presidential power, leading some people to support the Bricker amendment as a way of limiting executive autonomy in foreign affairs. As Richard Strout noted in the *Christian Science Monitor,* there was "political dynamite" in the Bricker amendment.[1]

I

On April 8, 1952, President Harry Truman put the nation's steel mills under government control to avert a strike that threatened to interrupt the production of arms and ammunition for the war effort in Korea. He was taking this action, the president explained, under the authority vested in him by "the Constitution and the laws of the United States, and as President of the United States and Commander in Chief of the armed forces."[2]

[1]Richard Strout, "Bricker, Taft Lead 56 Senators Seeking Curb Upon Treaties," *Christian Science Monitor,* February 8, 1952, p. 1. See also William Moore, "Senators Rip Globalism in Rough Session," Washington *Times-Herald,* February 8, 1952.

[2]Executive Order 10340, reprinted in *New York Times,* April 9, 1952, p. 16; and "Radio and Television Address to the American People on the Need for Government Operation of the Steel Mills," April 8, 1952, in *Public Papers: Truman, 1952–53,* pp. 246–50. On the administra-

Already concerned about the issue of presidential power because of Franklin Roosevelt's expansion of executive authority and Truman's unilateral decisions in 1950 and 1951 to send American troops to Korea and Western Europe, many legislators condemned the seizure of the steel mills. Senator Bricker charged that Truman's justification for the takeover sounded like "totalitarian philosophy and a dictatorship idea," and Senator Bourke Hickenlooper (R-Iowa) complained that the president's action constituted an unwarranted confiscation of private property. Similarly, Democratic Senator Richard Russell of Georgia warned that such conduct "sets a pattern that a potential dictator later on could follow and use as a precedent."[3]

At a press conference a few days later, Truman aroused further concern over his views on presidential power. Since the president obviously believed that he could seize the steel mills under his inherent authority, a reporter asked, did he also think he could take over the nation's newspapers and the radio stations if he deemed it necessary? Under the same circumstances, Truman replied, "the President of the United States has to act for whatever is for the best of the country." People did not find Truman's answer reassuring.[4]

When the steel companies challenged the legality of Truman's seizure of their mills, the Supreme Court ruled that the president's action represented an unconstitutional usurpation of authority. In the official opinion for the court, Justice Black emphasized that presidential power "must stem either from an act of Congress or from the Constitution itself." In this case, he stressed, it was the legislature, not the executive, that had the right to order such a seizure of private property, for the Constitution gave Congress the "exclusive constitutional authority to make laws necessary and proper to carry out the powers vested by the Constitution in the Government of the United States." In concurring opinions, Justice Douglas noted that even in an emergency the president's powers were limited to those granted him by the Constitution, and Justices Frankfurter, Jackson,

---

tion's decision to base the seizure on the president's inherent powers rather than on any specific statutory authority, see Milton Kayle to David Stowe, memorandum, "Meeting with Justice Department Staff on 'Section 18 Seizure Authority,'" April 1, 1952; and Kayle to Stowe, memorandum, "Meetings with Officials of Defense Department and Atomic Energy Commission regarding Section 18—Seizure Authority," April 3, 1952, both in Stowe Papers, Box 4, HSTL. The best account of the steel seizure incident is Marcus, *Truman and the Steel Seizure Case.*

[3]98 *CR* 3797 (Bricker), 3794 (Hickenlooper) (1952); and *New York Times,* April 14, 1952, p. 8 (Russell).

[4]*Public Papers: Truman, 1952–53,* pp. 272–73; and *New York Times,* April 18, 1952, p. 1.

Burton, and Clark, even though they believed the division between executive and legislative prerogatives was not so clear-cut, found that in this instance the president had exceeded his authority.[5]

Chief Justice Vinson and Justices Reed and Minton dissented from the court's decision, asserting that the president had to be allowed to act in "extraordinary times." They argued that in various statutes and treaties, including the United Nations Charter, the United States had taken steps to build up its defense forces and had promised to work with other nations to preserve the peace and respond to acts of aggression, such as the communist attack in Korea, that threatened international peace and security. Since these treaties and statutes had been approved by Congress, the president had the responsibility under the Constitution to carry out the programs and policies they had established, many of which depended upon continued supplies of steel. Vinson, Reed, and Minton concluded, therefore, that the president did have the authority in this case to seize the steel mills.[6]

Both legislators and the press cheered the court's ruling in the steel seizure case. Upon learning of the verdict, Senator Charles Tobey (R-N.H.) shouted "Hurrah! Thank God for the Supreme Court," and Senator Harry Cain (R-Wash.) rejoiced that the Constitution had been saved. Similarly, the editors of the *New York Times* praised the justices for preserving the balance of power between Congress and the president, and the New York *Herald Tribune* predicted that "in an epoch when executive prerogative is everywhere being enlarged, this decision will stand as an historic affirmation of the powers, the authority, the dignity of the legislative branch." Even the liberal Washington *Post* commended the court for rejecting the Truman administration's "formula for executive dictatorship."[7]

Instead of being reassured by the Supreme Court's ruling, however, Frank Holman and other supporters of the Bricker amendment denounced the reference in the dissenting opinion to the United Nations Charter. Holman seized on Vinson's comments about the charter, took them out of context, and charged that the Chief Justice had "advanced the

[5]*Youngstown Sheet & Tube Co. v. Sawyer,* 343 U.S. 579–667 (1952), esp. pp. 585 and 588–89 for the quotations from Justice Black's opinion.

[6]*Youngstown Sheet & Tube Co. v. Sawyer,* 343 U.S. 667–710, esp. p. 668.

[7]98 CR 6278, 6289; *New York Times,* June 3, 1952, p. 28; New York *Herald Tribune,* June 3, 1952, p. 22; and Washington *Post,* June 3, 1952, p. 14. See also memorandum for Mr. Steelman, "Excerpts from Editorials on Supreme Court Decision," June 3, 1952, copy in Harold Enarson Papers, Box 4, HSTL.

shocking doctrine that the United Nations Charter and other international commitments give the President of the United States authority—nowhere granted to him either by the Constitution or by the laws of the country—to seize private property." Likewise, the editors of the Washington *News* claimed that "three justices of the Supreme Court . . . held that President Truman had the power to seize the steel mills as a wartime act solely because we had ratified the United Nations treaty," and Senator Bricker maintained that the dissenting justices had delcared that the charter had given the president authority he did not otherwise possess under the Constitution and laws of the United States. Bricker warned that "if two additional justices of the Supreme Court had agreed with those three, our Republic would have been ended, and we would have been under some kind of oligarchy." The whole incident, he asserted, demonstrated the need for a constitutional amendment to ensure that a different court would not someday rule that the UN Charter or some other international covenant had endowed the president with new, extralegal powers.[8]

Concern aroused by the steel seizure controversy soon developed into support for the Bricker amendment. For example, a Vermont attorney who emphasized how happy he was "over the restoration of the American Constitutional Government by the Supreme Court decision in the Steel Case," urged Senator George Aiken (R-Vt.) to help provide additional protection for the rights of the American people by voting for the Bricker resolution. Similarly, Texas oilman H. R. Cullen explained to a friend that "It is very necessary to pass this [Bricker] amendment for we came so nearly [sic] losing our form of government when three members of the Supreme Court held that President Harry Truman had the right to take over the steel industry. If a majority of the Supreme Court had upheld Harry Truman in that case, then he could have taken over the entire nation and could have used the army to back him up."[9]

---

[8]Frank Holman, "Dangers of Treaty Law," November, 1953, copy attached to letter from Mary Boning to Senator Herbert Lehman, February 17, 1954, Lehman Papers, Legislative Files, "Bricker Amendment—Pro," Columbia University; Washington *News* quoted by Senator Carl Hayden, 100 *CR* 1217 (1954); and John Bricker in 100 *CR* 942. See also editorial, Chicago *Tribune,* January 26, 1953, p. 24; and U.S., Congress, Senate, Committee on the Judiciary, *Constitutional Amendment Relative to Treaties and Executive Agreements,* Senate Report 412, 83d Cong., 1st sess., 1953, p. 5.

[9]Osmer Fitts to Aiken, June 23, 1952, Aiken Papers, Crate 31, Box 2; H. R. Cullen to T. S. Petersen, January 11, 1954, copy in DDEP, OF 116-H-4, DDEL. See also Earl Phillips to Professor Chafee, November 24, 1952, Chafee Papers, Box 11; and Fred Moore to John W. Davis, January 22, 1954, copy in Will Clayton Papers, 1954–1960, "Committee for Defense of the Constitution by Preserving the Treaty Power," HSTL. On H. R. Cullen, see also Washington *Post,* February 19, 1954, pp. 1, 15.

II

In May 1952, while the courts were deciding the steel seizure case, a Senate judiciary subcommittee held the first formal hearings on the Bricker amendment. It was unlikely that an amendment would get through both the Senate and the House before Congress adjourned for the year, but Bricker and his supporters hoped that the hearings would make it possible to draft a better amendment in 1953. Senator Pat McCarran (D-Nev.), chairman of the full committee and a cosponsor of Bricker's resolution, named himself head of the panel that would consider the measure, and he appointed Senators Herbert O'Conor (D-Md.), Willis Smith (D-N.C.), Homer Ferguson (R-Mich.), and Robert Hendrickson (R-N.J.) as the other members of the subcommittee. All four were also among the resolution's proponents, so Bricker and his supporters were assured a friendly reception by the subcommittee.[10]

John Bricker and members of the American Bar Association's Committee on Peace and Law testified first when the hearings opened on May 21, 1952. For the most part, they repeated the arguments from their earlier statements and reports. Bricker placed the latest version of the draft covenant on human rights in the record to show why a constitutional amendment was needed to prohibit the use of treaties as instruments of domestic legislation or as vehicles for surrendering national sovereignty. He charged again that the proposed compact was "a blueprint for tyranny," which would subordinate the liberties of individuals "to the powers of the state under some form of socialism, communism, fascism, or feudalism." The senator maintained that his resolution was not an anti-United Nations measure, but rather an attempt to ensure that the world organization complied with the stipulation in its own charter forbidding it from interfering in the internal affairs of member states.[11]

Bricker then explained why his amendment dealt also with the problem of executive agreements. He contended that "the most glaring weakness in the conduct of American foreign policy has been the assumption of international obligations by the President which the Congress has not approved and which it is reluctant to implement." He warned, moreover, that restricting treaties but not executive agreements would give presi-

[10]See Bricker to Senator Francis Case (R-S.D.), May 7, 1952, Case Papers, Legislative Files, 82d Cong., on microfilm at HSTL; U.S., Congress, Senate, Committee on the Judiciary, *Treaties and Executive Agreements, Hearings*, before a Subcommittee of the Committee on the Judiciary, Senate, 82d Cong., 2d sess., 1952 (hereinafter cited as *Hearings, 1952*); and *New York Times*, May 24, 1952, p. 26.

[11]*Hearings, 1952*, pp. 1–22, esp. pp. 21–22.

dents "an additional incentive to evade constitutional provisions relative to the making of treaties." Since the executive branch might dispute Congress's authority to regulate presidential compacts by statute, he had thought it advisable to include such controls as part of his constitutional amendment.[12]

Frank Holman and members of the ABA's Committee on Peace and Law described their efforts to alert the American people to the dangers posed by international conventions. Holman condemned the State Department for its "attitude of appeasement and compromise," and asserted that a constitutional amendment was needed to "eliminate the risk that through 'treaty law' our basic American rights may be bargained away in attempts to show our good neighborliness and in attempts to indicate to the rest of the world our spirit of brotherhood." As to the actual wording of the proposal, he preferred the text recommended by the ABA, but he agreed with Senator Bricker that the resolution should also stipulate that presidential compacts should not be made in lieu of treaties and that Congress had the power to regulate the scope and use of executive agreements. An amendment along these lines, Holman concluded, was "absolutely necessary to protect American rights and to preserve the American form of government."[13]

Once again, the statements made by members of the Committee on Peace and Law showed that when they talked about safeguarding the rights of the American people, they had in mind the rights of states to continue to segregate and discriminate against blacks and other minority groups. Eberhard Deutsch warned that, without the Bricker amendment, the lower court's decision in the *Fujii* case that international agreements were self-executing might lead to a ruling "that the entire civil rights program has already effectively been imposed on the United States through the United Nations Charter itself, without the need for any congressional action whatever." Similarly, Carl Rix pointed out that the President's Committee on Civil Rights had previously suggested that a treaty dealing with human rights might open the way for federal civil rights legislation under the doctrine expounded by the courts in *Missouri v. Holland*. Consequently, he counseled that a constitutional amendment was needed to protect the system of checks and balances and to preserve the autonomy of the states.[14]

W. L. McGrath, president of the Williamson Heater Company of Cincinnati, also testified in favor of the Bricker resolution. A representative of

[12]Ibid., pp. 28–29.
[13]Ibid., pp. 144–71, esp. pp. 164, 167, and 169.
[14]Ibid., pp. 53, 46–50.

the United States Chamber of Commerce on the American delegation to the International Labor Organization (ILO), McGrath reported that the ILO was "seeking to set itself up as a sort of international legislature to formulate uniform domestic socialistic laws which it hopes, by the vehicle of treaty ratification, can eventually be imposed upon most of the countries of the world." ILO agreements, he explained, dealt with such issues as maximum hours, employment agencies, and methods of collective bargaining, and the organization's agenda for future meetings included compacts calling for holidays with pay, job and insurance protection for pregnant women, and social security. McGrath believed, however, that such matters were domestic concerns best regulated by the states, not by the federal government, and certainly not by some international association. Accordingly, he advocated passage of the Bricker amendment to preclude the adoption of new controls over labor-management relations through international agreements.[15]

Representatives from right-wing and isolationist groups supported Bricker's proposal at the hearings, primarily because of their opposition to the United Nations. A spokeswoman for the Daughters of the American Revolution emphasized her organization's opposition to world government and its fear that international covenants might "nullify the Constitution of the United States." Similarly, Henry McFarland, Jr., of the American Flag Committee stated that his group had wanted to limit the treaty-making power ever since the decision in the *Fujii* case. He endorsed the Bricker amendment and even recommended making it retroactive to January 1945, so that its restrictions would definitely apply to the United Nations Charter as well as to any future agreements.[16]

III

The hearings on the Bricker amendment provided the opposition with its first real opportunity to present the case against the resolution. The Truman administration, members of the ABA's Section of International and Comparative Law, and the Association of the Bar of the City of New York led the opposition to the proposal, and representatives of liberal, internationalist organizations, including the American Jewish Congress,

[15]Ibid., pp. 239–49, esp. p. 243.

[16]Ibid., pp. 69–73, esp. p. 69, and pp. 106–9. On the growing opposition to many of the UN's activities, see also the comments by Senators H. Alexander Smith (R-N.J.), Walter George (D-Ga.), and Tom Connally (D-Tex.) in U.S., Congress, Senate, Committee on Foreign Relations, *Executive Sessions of the Senate Foreign Relations Committee* (Historical Series), Vol. IV: 82d Cong., 2d sess., 1952 (made public in 1976), pp. 459–62.

Americans for Democratic Action, and the American Association for the United Nations, also voiced their objections to the amendment.

President Truman adamantly opposed the Bricker resolution, and he sought to ensure that administration officials had the chance to testify against the measure before the subcommittee adjourned. On May 23, 1952, the president ordered the heads of all executive departments and agencies to prepare official statements describing effects the Bricker amendment would have on matters under their jurisdiction. Representatives of the executive branch had not been invited to address the subcommittee considering the resolution, but Truman suggested that department officials ask to appear at the hearings. To ensure that no one misunderstood this "suggestion," the president warned that any agency believing it was not involved directly enough to warrant testifying would have to explain its reasons to him at the earliest possible date. Truman stressed that the gravity of the questions raised by this amendment could not be overstated. Therefore, he would see to it that the executive branch did not "default on its responsibilities" to make sure that its views were known on this issue of "fundamental importance."[17]

Besides opposing the amendment on its merits, Truman also resented that its chief sponsor was John Bricker. The animosity between the president and the senator from Ohio dated back to Bricker's failure to send Truman a telegram congratulating him in 1944 after Roosevelt and Truman had defeated Dewey and Bricker, and the controversy over treaties and executive agreements exacerbated the hostility. Years later, while touring the Truman Library and Museum with an associate, the former president summarized his feelings toward Bricker. As they passed the many gifts he had received from various world leaders, Truman stopped in front of a beautiful jeweled sword, which had been given to him by the king of Saudi Arabia. That was the only present he had ever wanted to keep, Truman confessed. He had promised the sword to his wife "if she'd kick Bricker in the ass, but she wouldn't do it."[18]

Undersecretary of State David Bruce opened the administration's case against the Bricker amendment at the hearings. He told the subcommittee that the requirement that treaties be approved by a two-thirds vote in the Senate protected the rights of the American people from being abridged by international covenants. He warned, however, that in trying to guard against a nonexistent threat, Bricker's resolution would alter the basic structure of the United States government by contravening the principles

---

[17]"Memorandum on Proposed Bills Dealing with Treaties and Executive Agreements," *Public Papers: Truman, 1952–53*, pp. 367–68; *New York Times*, May 24, 1952, p. 26.

[18]Miller, *Plain Speaking*, p. 407. For similar stories, see also Margaret Truman, *Harry Truman*, pp. 192, 327–28; and Abell, ed., *Drew Pearson Diaries, 1949–1959*, p. 501.

of separation of powers among the president, Congress, and the courts. The measure would so gravely interfere with the "historic and fundamental functions of the Executive and the Senate in the field of foreign affairs," he asserted, that it would "jeopardize the influence of the United States in the world today."[19]

Bruce pointed out that if the Bricker amendment were adopted, the federal government might not be able to negotiate important international agreements. Section 1 of the proposal, he explained, prohibited agreements concerning the rights of United States citizens. But since traditional treaties of friendship, commerce, and navigation frequently granted Americans overseas the right to own, inherit, and dispose of property, he questioned whether such treaties would still be legal if the amendment were approved. Moreover, he predicted that if Congress were not allowed to implement such conventions because they dealt with matters usually regulated by the states, then other nations would refuse to enter into such treaties with the United States. Bruce also warned that the resolution's provisions forbidding covenants delegating power to international organizations would block America's own Baruch plan to control atomic energy, since that program called for an international authority to manage all nuclear facilities.[20]

Another drawback of the resolution, the undersecretary contended, was the possibility that it might nullify federal narcotics laws, which had been upheld previously as necessary and proper to carrying out international agreements controlling such drugs. When asked by Senator Willis Smith whether such legislation could not be enacted under either the general welfare clause or the power of Congress to regulate interstate commerce, both Bruce and State Department Legal Adviser Adrian Fisher declined to speculate on whether the courts, in the absence of any treaties on the subject, would allow Congress to pass such laws under its delegated powers. Fisher noted that the extent of the inherent authority of the different branches of the federal government was presently in dispute in the steel seizure case.[21]

Bruce also informed the legislators that the decision in the *Fujii* case, which had stirred up so much controversy, should no longer be an issue. He reported on the Supreme Court of California ruling a month earlier that the United Nations Charter did not invalidate California's Alien Land Law. The court had found that the charter provisions in which members had pledged to promote human rights had been merely promises of future

[19]*Hearings, 1952*, p. 174; *New York Times*, May 28, 1952, p. 9.
[20]*Hearings, 1952*, pp. 179–83.
[21]Ibid., pp. 187–91. See also *Stutz v. Bureau of Narcotics*, 56 F. Supp. 810 (N.D. Calif., 1944).

action, not intended to supersede existing domestic legislation. Although the court had again determined that the statute was unconstitutional, it had based its conclusion solely on the equal protection clause of the Fourteenth Amendment.[22]

Representatives of other government agencies also submitted briefs or statements criticizing both Bricker's amendment and the text recommended by the American Bar Association. The Commissioner of Narcotics, the head of the Internal Revenue Service, and officials of the departments of Agriculture, Defense, Commerce, and Labor all echoed Solicitor General Philip Perlman, who charged that the "premature and vague" concerns advanced by supporters of the amendment certainly did not justify "the serious restrictions and impediments to the effective conduct of foreign relations which would result from the present proposals." Considering the tone of the memorandum President Truman had circulated, it is hardly surprising that even the Post Office and the Securities and Exchange Commission offered arguments against the resolution.[23]

As important as the administration's opposition to the bill was, the testimony of the leaders of the Association of the Bar of the City of New York and the ABA's Section of International Law proved to be even more significant. The executive branch's comments were to be expected, since the measure sought to impose limitations on the president's authority. But the attorneys' remarks showed that not all of the nation's lawyers agreed with the ABA's House of Delegates that a constitutional amendment was needed to protect the American people from the "dangerous loophole" in the treaty-making power.

Unlike the ABA, the Association of the Bar of the City of New York was a progressive, internationally minded body. Many of its members represented clients who had business dealings overseas and depended on the rights and privileges granted to Americans in treaties of friendship and commerce. In part, at least, the New York attorneys opposed both the Bricker resolution and the amendment suggested by the ABA because they feared that such measures would make it more difficult for their clients to operate abroad.[24]

After a thorough study, the New York City Bar Association's Federal

[22]*Hearings, 1952*, pp. 192–93. See also *Sei Fujii v. State of California,* 242 Pac. (2d) 617 (1952); and Fairman, Editorial Comment: "Finis to Fujii."

[23]*Hearings, 1952*, pp. 370–73, 373–75, 355–58, 360–67, 377–89, 391–96, 396–421, 345–48, and 348–49, esp. p. 421 for the quotations from Perlman's statement.

[24]Interview with Carlyle Maw, former member of the executive committee of the Association of the Bar of the City of New York, January 26, 1977; and interview with Bethuel Webster, former president of the Association of the Bar of the City of New York, May 18, 1976.

Legislation and International Law Committees recommended that the association actively oppose the Bricker resolution. The committees warned in their report to the association that the amendment would drastically alter the treaty-making process, prohibit certain kinds of treaties altogether, and limit the president's power to enter into executive agreements with other nations. The actual wording of the proposal, they cautioned, was "so broad and indefinite" that it would handicap the president in his handling of foreign affairs. They concluded that the prospect of the Senate ever approving any agreement abridging the rights of the American people or surrendering the sovereignty of the United States was "sufficiently remote to make it unwise to tinker with the existing safeguards lest the cure should prove worse than the disease."[25]

The Association of the Bar of the City of New York approved its committees' report opposing the Bricker amendment, and Dana Backus and Theodore Pearson, chairmen of the two committees, went to Washington to testify before the Senate subcommittee conducting the hearings on the resolution. Despite undergoing a hostile cross-examination by Senators Ferguson and O'Conor, the New York attorneys maintained that the proposed amendment was both unnecessary and dangerous. Surely one-third plus one of the Senate could be depended upon to reject any covenants that really threatened the rights of the American people. However, they asserted, if the Bricker amendment were adopted, the United States would no longer be able to enter into all sorts of important and favorable compacts, such as the wartime agreements that had provided for the postwar occupation of Japan but had never been submitted to the Senate for approval.[26]

In reiterating many of the New York attorneys' complaints against the Bricker resolution, C. W. Tillett stressed that there was considerable opposition even within the American Bar Association to a constitutional amendment limiting the treaty-making power. The former chairman of the Section of International Law, Tillett explained to the senators that his group, made up of lawyers having a "special interest in and knowledge of matters of international concern," had refused to endorse the text submitted to Congress by the House of Delegates. He emphasized that one could

[25]Association of the Bar of the City of New York, Committee on Federal Legislation and Committee on International Law, "Report on 'Joint Resolution Proposing an Amendment to the Constitution of the United States Relative to the Making of Treaties and Executive Agreements' (S.J. Res. 130)," April 28, 1952, copy in Association of the Bar of the City of New York, *Reports, 1952,* Association of the Bar of the City of New York Library.

[26]"Minutes of the meeting of May 13, 1952," pp. 4–6, in Association of the Bar of the City of New York, *Reports, 1952;* interview with Dana Backus, May 19, 1976; *Hearings, 1952,* pp. 72–87.

not, through a constitutional "gadget," protect the United States against bad treaties. The best safeguard, he advised, was "to elect into the treaty-making body competent people."[27]

Realizing that the resolution reflected in part the depth and vigor of isolationist sentiment in the United States and growing hostility toward the United Nations, a few of the witnesses against the amendment focused on this issue during their testimony. Clark Eichelberger of the American Association for the United Nations charged that some of the measure's proponents were not really concerned with the rights of the American people, but were using the amendment as a vehicle for attacking the UN. Passage of the resolution, he warned, would make it impossible for the United States to play an active role in international organizations. Similarly, Will Maslow of the American Jewish Congress declared that it would be a catastrophe if the proposal were adopted because it would be seen in the UN and all over the world as "a reversion to prewar isolationism."[28]

The 82d Congress adjourned shortly after the subcommittee completed its hearings on the Bricker amendment. But even though the Senate took no further action on the resolution in 1952, the hearings had served their purpose. They had provided the amendment's supporters with a wider forum for their argument that a constitutional amendment was needed. At the same time, however, the sessions had also given the Truman administration, the Association of the Bar of the City of New York, the ABA's Section of International Law, and others the opportunity to present their case against the resolution. The disagreements emerging at the hearings made it clear that this was merely the first skirmish in what promised to be a long and bitter battle.

IV

John Bricker knew that the results of the 1952 presidential election would go a long way toward determining the fate of his amendment; removing the president from the ranks of the opposition would almost guarantee approval. Consequently, Bricker sought to get an endorsement for his resolution included in the Republican party platform. Since the planks dealing with international relations would be drafted by John Fos-

[27]*Hearings, 1952*, pp. 249–64, esp. pp. 250 and 257. See also the testimony by Edgar Turlington, another member of the Section of International Law, ibid., pp. 197–203.
[28]Ibid., pp. 203–15, 264–80, esp. p. 279. See also Zechariah Chafee, Jr., to Lyman Tondel, Jr., May 28, 1952, Chafee Papers, Box 11.

ter Dulles, the GOP's leading spokesman on foreign affairs, Dulles now became a key figure in the fight.[29]

Both by background and by experience, Dulles considered himself uniquely qualified to serve as secretary of state. The son of a Presbyterian minister, he combined the moralism of a Christian missionary with the idealism of a Wilsonian and the practicality of the successful Wall Street lawyer he had become. His grandfather, John W. Foster, had been secretary of state under Benjamin Harrison, and his uncle, Robert Lansing, had served in the same post under Woodrow Wilson. Dulles himself had attended the Hague Peace Conference in 1907, and he had been the chief American counsel on reparations at Versailles in 1919. One of the leading Republican architects of the bipartisan foreign policies of the 1940s, Dulles had been a member of the American delegation at San Francisco when the UN Charter had been approved in 1945. He had served as an adviser to the Truman administration on international affairs, and he had negotiated the Japanese Peace Treaty. Generally thought to have been Dewey's choice to head the State Department if the New York governor had been elected president in 1944 or 1948, Dulles knew that 1952 represented his last chance to realize that lifelong ambition, since he was now sixty-four years old. Therefore, his main goal in 1952 was to ensure the election of the Republican candidate. To achieve that end he sought to develop attractive policy alternatives for the Republicans, such as liberating Eastern Europe rather than merely containing communism.[30]

Over the years, Dulles had vacillated when discussing the efficacy of American participation in the United Nations human rights efforts. While working in the State Department in the late 1940s, he told Eleanor Roosevelt that it would be "illusory to expect any universal covenant [on human rights] which will really be both adequate and effective." The fundamental philosophical and religious differences between nations were so great, he stressed, that any compact widely accepted would probably "depend on a use of words which had a double meaning." In 1950 in his book *War or Peace,* however, Dulles asserted that international law should be concerned with the rights and duties of individuals, and he lamented America's reluctance to enter into treaties defining people's rights and liberties. In particular, he criticized the failure of the United States to ratify the Genocide Convention even though the agreement specifically stipulated that subse-

[29]Interview with Senator Bricker, June 26, 1975. See also the handwritten note on Deutsch to Bricker, November 9, 1951; and Charles Webb, Legislative Assistant to Senator Bricker, to Deutsch, November 14, 1951; both in JBP.

[30]The literature on Dulles is vast. On his background and career before he became secretary of state, see especially Pruessen, *John Foster Dulles.*

quent legislation would be required before it went into effect in each nation. Dulles pointed out that Soviet officials had denounced such agreements as the Declaration of Human Rights, calling them a violation of national sovereignty; the communists, he noted, argued that there were no human rights except those that governments chose to grant their citizens. He urged the United States to challenge that totalitarian philosophy, support human rights, and "stand in the world as the recognized champion of human liberty as against governmental despotism."[31]

In April 1952, Dulles reversed himself again in a political speech before a regional meeting of the American Bar Association in Louisville. He condemned recent Democratic presidents for their misuse of the treaty-making power, claiming that Roosevelt and Truman had intruded on congressional prerogatives and had not afforded the Senate a chance to offer its advice until after treaties had already been negotiated. Consequently, the Senate had been forced either to approve "Constitution-stretching treaties it does not like, or imperil our international position by rejecting what has already been agreed upon with foreign governments."[32]

In remarks he knew would be well received by the members of the ABA in the audience, Dulles then proceeded to discuss the dangers posed by treaties such as the proposed agreements on human rights. The treaty-making power, he warned, was "an extraordinary power, liable to abuse." Unlike congressional statutes, treaties could "over-ride the Constitution." They could "take powers away from the Congress and give them to the President," transfer authority from the individual states to the federal government or some international body, and even abridge "the rights given the people by their Constitutional Bill of Rights."[33]

Dulles praised Senator Bricker for taking the lead on this matter and submitting "important proposals for a constitutional amendment which would prevent treaties from impinging on present constitutional rights of the Congress, the States, and the people," but he never specifically endorsed the senator's amendment. He later explained privately that his remarks had been "in part paying off Bricker for his aid to the [Japanese Peace] treaty," but nonetheless, Dulles had qualified his comments by

---

[31]Dulles, draft of March 15, 1948, copy in ERP, Box 4588; Dulles, *War or Peace,* pp. 200–204, esp. 203–204.

[32]"Treaty-Making and National Unity," address by John Foster Dulles at the regional meeting of the American Bar Association, Louisville, Kentucky, April 11, 1952, copy in the Herman Phleger Collection of Materials Relating to the Bricker Amendment and the Treaty-Making Power of the United States, Volume 12, Princeton University Library (hereinafter referred to as Phleger Collection).

[33]Ibid.

noting that there was room for "honest difference of opinion as to whether our Constitution needs to be amended as proposed or whether the President and the Senate should retain their present powers, for possible emergency use, at the same time ensuring more vigilance to the end that Treaties will not undesirably and unnecessarily encroach on Constitutional distributions of power." Whatever one's view on the advisability of a constitutional amendment, Dulles stressed, it was certainly "in the public interest that this whole problem should be thoroughly explored."[34]

In drafting the section of the 1952 Republican party platform dealing with the treaty-making power, Dulles sought to compose a policy statement that would be acceptable to both wings of the party and preserve his freedom of action if he became secretary of state. He did not want to alienate the nationalist elements that supported Taft and the Bricker amendment; yet at the same time he wanted a platform on which Eisenhower could run without jeopardizing his backing from the internationally minded businessmen and voters whose money and support were essential for a GOP victory in November. Professor Zechariah Chafee, Jr., for one, was already warning that if the platform endorsed a constitutional amendment limiting the treaty-making power, he and many others who wanted to vote for Eisenhower would find it much more difficult to do so. Accordingly, the final platform reflected the same ambiguity as Dulles's speech in Louisville. It pledged that the Republicans would see to it that "no treaty or agreement with other countries deprives our citizens of the rights guaranteed them by the Federal Constitution," but it did not specify whether this would be done by amending the Constitution or through some less drastic method.[35]

The controversy over the Bricker amendment and the treaty-making power was not a major issue during the 1952 presidential campaign. On foreign policy, Eisenhower confined himself for the most part to broad, general statements. In those few instances when he did get more specific, he criticized the Yalta agreements, discussed his program to liberate the

---

[34]Ibid.; and memorandum of telephone conversation between Dulles and Attorney General Herbert Brownell, June 17, 1953, quoted in U.S., Department of State, *Foreign Relations of the United States, 1952–54,* Vol. I: *General: Economic and Political Matters* (Washington, D.C.: United States Government Printing Office, 1983), pp. 1818–19. On the ambiguity of Dulles's warning about the dangers in the treaty-making power and in his comments on the Bricker amendment, see John Sherman Cooper Oral History Transcript, pp. 11–12, and Thruston Morton Oral History Transcript, p. 19; both part of John Foster Dulles Oral History Project, Princeton University Library.

[35]See Dulles to Eisenhower, May 20, 1952, DDEP, 1916–52, Box 33, DDEL; Chafee to Dulles, June 19, 1952, Chafee Papers, Box 11; and *New York Times,* July 11, 1952, p. 8. See also Divine, *Foreign Policy and U.S. Presidential Elections, 1952–1960,* pp. 23–27, 31–32, and 34–36; and Porter and Johnson, comps., *National Party Platforms, 1840–1968,* p. 499.

captive peoples of Eastern Europe, and, most dramatically, promised to go to Korea. Not once did he mention the problem of international covenants undermining the liberties of the American people. On the Democratic side, one Truman administration aide commented privately that the Republican plank on treaties was "double talk in support of the Bricker resolution, which, under the guise of 'protecting' rights, attacks the efforts of the United Nations, through its Declaration of Human Rights and Genocide Convention, to apply the great American ideas of 1776 to the entire world." But Democratic nominee Adlai Stevenson and his supporters concentrated in public primarily on trumpeting the twenty years of progress in domestic affairs that had been achieved under the New Deal and the Fair Deal.[36]

The Bricker amendment did emerge as a matter of contention, however, in the 1952 senatorial contest in Ohio, where Michael DiSalle, the former mayor of Toledo and head of Truman's Office of Price Stabilization, ran against John Bricker. When asked his opinion of the senator's proposed amendment, DiSalle denounced the measure, charging that it represented "an unwarranted interference with the provisions of the Constitution." Bricker, on the other hand, defended his resolution, pointing out that fifty-eight of his colleagues, Democrats as well as Republicans, had co-sponsored the bill. Its purpose, he stressed, was not to limit the authority of the president, but rather to safeguard the rights of the American people.[37]

Dwight Eisenhower, John Bricker, and the Republican party all won tremendous victories in the 1952 elections. Resentment over inflation, high taxes, the stalemate in Korea, and corruption in Washington joined with concern over possible communist influence in the Truman administration and Eisenhower's personal popularity to produce a Republican triumph. Eisenhower easily defeated Stevenson for the presidency, and Bricker beat DiSalle in Ohio by more than 300,000 votes. Moreover, the Republicans captured a majority of seats in both the Senate and the House of Representatives for the first time since 1946.[38]

[36]See Bert Gross to David Stowe, July 14, 1952, Stowe Papers, HSTL; and Research Division, Republican National Committee, "Aims of the Eisenhower Administration: A Compilation of the 1952 Republican Platform Pledges and Campaign Statements of Dwight D. Eisenhower," May 1953, copy in Leonard Hall Papers, Box 100, DDEL. See also Divine, *Foreign Policy and U.S. Presidential Elections, 1952–1960,* pp. 42–85.

[37]Radio script of August 18, 1952, broadcast by Senator Bricker over Station WVKO, Columbus; and DiSalle's remarks quoted in Charles Webb to Mrs. James Lucas, September 26, 1952; both in JBP, Box 90, OHS.

[38]*New York Times,* November 5, 1952, p. 1, and November 6, 1952, pp. 1, 26. For an analysis of the important issues in the 1952 campaigns, see Reichard, *The Reaffirmation of Republicanism,* pp. 5–27.

For John Bricker and his amendment, the events of 1952 augured well. Fifty-eight of his colleagues had joined in cosponsoring the measure in February, and Truman's seizure of the steel mills and the chief justice's dissenting opinion in that case had resulted in additional support for the amendment from people concerned about untrammeled executive power. Although the hearings on the resolution had given its opponents a chance to present their arguments against the proposal, they had also provided Bricker and the leaders of the American Bar Association with the opportunity to explain the need for such an amendment. Finally, and in Bricker's opinion most importantly, the Republicans had gained control of Congress and the White House, and Eisenhower had been elected on a platform which promised that international agreements would not be allowed to jeopardize the rights of the American people. Neither Dulles nor Eisenhower had actually endorsed his resolution, but Bricker was confident that with a few minor revisions it would win the new administration's blessing. He based that expectation on the platform plank, Dulles's warning at Louisville about the dangers in the treaty-making power, and a note he received from Dulles in late November in which the secretary of state-designate assured Bricker that he needed and looked forward to having the benefit of the senator's "counsel, advice, and support" over the next four years.[39]

[39]Interview with Senator Bricker, June 26, 1975; Dulles to Bricker, November 24, 1952, Dulles Papers, Box 58, Princeton University Library.

CHAPTER FIVE

"As Analyzed for Me by the Secretary of State"

During his first two years in office, President Eisenhower found himself at odds with Republican legislators on a number of issues, including tariffs and trade agreements, mutual security assistance to America's allies, a resolution repudiating the Yalta agreements, the nomination of Charles Bohlen to be ambassador to the Soviet Union, and McCarthyism and the question of subversives within the United States government. With the possible exception of Senator McCarthy, however, none of these problems proved to be as intractable as the controversy over the Bricker amendment. The conflict between Bricker and the Eisenhower administration over the senator's amendment began before the president had even been inaugurated, and it intensified as Eisenhower tried to deal with the matter in a way that would avoid a head-on collision with Republicans in Congress.[1]

I

Almost everyone agreed that the Eisenhower administration's position would be crucial in the fight over the Bricker amendment, but opinion varied as to what that position was likely to be. John Bricker confidently expected the new president's backing, which would practically guarantee the amendment's adoption. Frank Holman was not so sure, however. He thought that Eisenhower's point of view would be determined by his secretary of state, and Holman feared that the choice of either John Foster Dulles or Thomas Dewey would result in continued opposition from the

---

[1] See Reichard, *The Reaffirmation of Republicanism;* Theoharis, *The Yalta Myths,* pp. 154–75; and Eisenhower, *The White House Years,* Vol. I, pp. 192–222, 277–331.

Department of State and the White House. When Eisenhower did in fact pick Dulles, Holman warned that the new secretary's association over the years with the Truman administration and Secretary of State Dean Acheson made it unlikely that he would make significant changes in State Department personnel or policies.[2]

The amendment's opponents, meanwhile, hoped that the reassuring presence of Eisenhower in the White House might "dampen the ardor" of the resolution's supporters. As Professor Chafee explained to a friend, "a proposal to tie the hands of Eisenhower and Dulles may not be so popular with the American Bar Association as the proposal to tie the hands of Truman and Acheson." Conservatives might no longer feel the need for such a measure since Eisenhower, in contrast to his predecessor, was not likely to push for such liberal causes as federal civil rights legislation or national health insurance. Moreover, Republicans might not be so eager to restrict the president's powers now that they had elected a Republican president for the first time in twenty years.[3]

Even before they took office, members of the Eisenhower administration worried that the Bricker amendment would hamper the president in his conduct of foreign affairs. On January 2, 1953, in a memorandum to soon-to-be White House chief of staff Sherman Adams, Secretary of State-designate Dulles conceded that, perhaps, a case could be made "for some amendment to meet the theoretical possibility that the Executive might negotiate, the Senate might ratify, and the Supreme Court might sustain a treaty to deprive the American citizens of their Constitutional rights." He believed that Bricker's resolution went too far, however, and "might seriously impair the treaty making power and the ability of the President to deal with current matters, notably U.S. troops abroad, etc., through administrative agreements." But instead of opposing the amendment directly, which would have antagonized Bricker and his supporters, Dulles advised that the administration should try to delay any action on the measure.[4]

During the preinaugural period, administration officials tried to persuade Bricker to wait a short while rather than reintroducing his amendment as soon as the new Congress convened. Sherman Adams instructed Wilton (Jerry) Persons, the president-elect's special assistant for congressional affairs, to convey to Bricker "the personal wish of General Eisen-

[2]Frank Holman to Senator Bricker, November 6, 1952, JBP; and Holman to Bricker, December 17, 1952, JBP, Box 91, OHS.

[3]Houston Kenyon to Professor Chafee, November 5, 1952; and Chafee to Professor Quincy Wright, December 1, 1952; both in Chafee Papers, Box 11, Harvard Law School Library.

[4]Memorandum, Dulles to Sherman Adams, re: Bricker Amendment, January 2, 1953, DDEP, OF 116-H-4, DDEL.

hower to consult with him on his proposal to amend the treaty-making power of the President before he submits his resolution to the Senate." Persons relayed the message to Bricker, who promptly telephoned and assured Dulles that he wanted "to work out this problem in close cooperation with the new Administration so that there is no danger of hamstringing the President in the conduct of the Nation's foreign policy."[5]

Despite his promise to work with the administration, however, Bricker introduced a revised version of his amendment the very next day. He had told Frank Holman he intended to move promptly on the matter, and so he did, announcing on January 7, 1953, that on behalf of himself and sixty-one of his colleagues, he was submitting a constitutional amendment "to prevent international treaties or executive agreements from narrowing or destroying rights enumerated in the Constitution."[6]

By introducing the amendment without waiting for any meetings with Eisenhower or his aides, Bricker hoped to force the new administration's hand. He believed it would be very difficult for the president or the secretary of state to oppose the measure in view of Dulles's warning at Louisville about the dangers of treaty law and the pledge in the party platform that the Republicans would see to it that international agreements did not threaten the rights and freedoms of the American people. Moreover, Bricker thought that the administration would have no choice but to endorse the amendment in the interest of party unity, since 44 of the 48 Republicans in the Senate were already supporting the resolution.[7]

Bricker's new proposal, entitled S.J. Res. 1 because it was the first joint resolution introduced in the Senate in the 83d Congress, represented the senator's latest attempt to improve the text of his amendment. He had rephrased Section 1 to make it more like the American Bar Association's draft. It now declared that "a provision of a treaty which denies or abridges any right enumerated in this Constitution shall not be of any force or effect." The second part of the resolution had been modified slightly too, but it still prohibited any foreign power or international agency from exercising authority over matters "essentially within the domestic jurisdiction of the United States." Section 3 of the bill, designed to ensure that treaties would not be self-executing, stipulated that covenants would "become effective as internal law in the United States only through the enactment of appropriate legislation by the Congress." Finally, Section 4

[5]Adams to Persons, January 5, 1953, DDEP, OF 116-H-4; Dulles to Herbert Brownell and Herman Phleger, January 5, 1953, Phleger Collection, Vol. 13; and Bricker to Dulles, January 7, 1953, JBP, Box 91, OHS.

[6]Bricker to Holman, December 9, 1952, JBP; press release for January 8, 1953, JBP, Box 91, OHS; and 99 *CR* 160 (1953).

[7]Interview with Senator Bricker, June 26, 1975. See also Bricker to Attorney General Herbert Brownell, April 2, 1953, JBP, Box 91, OHS.

affirmed the authority of Congress to regulate executive agreements, and subjected all such agreements to the same restrictions being imposed on treaties. Again, however, unlike the amendment recommended by the ABA, Bricker's proposal did not include the "which" clause. Rather than trying to protect states' rights by limiting Congress's authority in implementing treaties, Bricker's amendment would allow the doctrine of *Missouri v. Holland* to stand, enabling Congress to pass any legislation "necessary and proper" to implementing a duly ratified treaty.[8]

Within a few weeks of its introduction, two more senators joined as cosponsors of the Bricker amendment. All of the Senate's Republicans except Eugene Millikin, John Sherman Cooper (Ky.), Joseph McCarthy (Wisc.), and Alexander Wiley (Wisc.) had endorsed S.J. Res. 1 when it had first been submitted, and Senator Bricker reported a few days later that Senator McCarthy also supported the amendment. On the other side of the aisle, 18 Democrats, mostly conservatives and southerners, had been among the measure's original cosponsors, and they were joined on February 4 by Senator George Smathers of Florida. Counting McCarthy and Smathers, the amendment now had 64 cosponsors, exactly the two-thirds majority it would need for approval if everyone were present and voting.[9]

Why did so many senators support the Bricker amendment? Some, including Irving Ives (R-N.Y.) and Leverett Saltonstall (R-Mass.), cosponsored the resolution because they hoped it would make it clear that international agreements were subordinate to the Constitution. Ives believed it was necessary to spell out and limit the internal effects of treaties and executive agreements, and he wanted the Constitution to state explicitly that such covenants would be null and void if they conflicted with the Constitution. Similarly, Saltonstall explained that he favored S.J. Res. 1 because it would put "forever beyond doubt the possibility that exercise of the treaty power could diminish individual rights safeguarded by the Constitution."[10]

---

[8]S.J. Res. 1, 83d Cong., 1st sess., January 7, 1953. For the complete text of S.J. Res. 1 as introduced by Senator Bricker, see Appendix D.

[9]See 99 *CR* 160, 397; and press release for February 5, 1953, JBP, Box 91, OHS. The 18 Democrats who were among the amendment's original cosponsors were: Senators Byrd (Va.), Chavez (N.M.), Daniel (Tex.), Eastland (Miss.), Ellender (La.), Frear (Del.), Gillette (Iowa), Hoey (N.C.), Johnson (Colo.), Johnston (S.C.), Kerr (Okla.), McCarran (Nev.), McClellan (Ark.), Magnuson (Wash.), Maybank (S.C.), Robertson (Va.), Smith (N.C.), and Stennis (Miss.).

[10]Quotation is from Senator Saltonstall to Mrs. Robert Murray, January 9, 1954, JBP, Box 100, OHS. See also Saltonstall to Professor Chafee, February 13, 1952, Chafee Papers, Box 11; and Senator Ives to Roderick Stephens, January 21, 1954, Irving Ives Papers, Box 48, Cornell University Library. For other senators expressing similar reasons for supporting the Bricker amendment, see Prescott Bush (R-Conn.) to Mrs. Murray, January 8, 1954; Dennis Chavez (D-N.M.) to Mrs. Murray, January, 1954; and William Purtell (R-Conn.) to Frank Gannett, March 2, 1954; all in JBP, Box 100, OHS.

Many Republicans also viewed the amendment as a vehicle for express-ing their displeasure with the foreign policies of the Roosevelt and Truman administrations, particularly the growing use of executive agree-ments such as those reached at Yalta and Potsdam. George Aiken of Vermont supported Bricker's resolution because he believed it would pre-vent future presidents "from endangering the safety of our country through any secret executive agreements which might plunge the United States into needless and ominous commitments abroad." Likewise, H. Alexander Smith of New Jersey asserted that the "outrageous" Yalta ac-cords, "entered into by President Roosevelt individually with Stalin and Churchill without even the knowledge of Secretary of State Stet-tinius, . . . and certainly without conferring with our ally Chiang Kai-shek," had clearly demonstrated the need to amend the Constitution to restrict the uses and effects of such agreements.[11]

Ralph Flanders (R-Vt.) and William Jenner (R-Ind.) agreed that the amendment represented a rebuke to the Roosevelt and Truman admin-istrations, and they both singled out former Secretary of State Dean Acheson for special criticism. Flanders commented privately that the "de-ceit and contempt" displayed by Acheson during his appearances before Senate committees had helped convince him of the need to impose some restraints on the executive branch, and Jenner argued that Congress had to adopt the Bricker amendment because "we do not know when another Acheson will occupy the office of Secretary of State."[12]

Some senators supported S.J. Res. 1 because of their growing dissatis-faction with the activities of the United Nations. Like Senator Bricker, H. Alexander Smith of New Jersey believed the amendment was necessary to keep the UN from overstepping its authority, especially in the area of human rights. Senator Price Daniel (D-Tex.) concurred, declaring that the Bricker amendment was essential because the United Nations was adopting covenants and conventions that would "impose domestic laws which are binding upon the people of the United States."[13]

Conservatives in both parties endorsed the Bricker amendment to pre-vent the federal government from using the treaty-making power to en-croach on matters they believed should remain under state jurisdiction.

[11]See Senator Aiken to Helen Baker, July 3, 1952; and Aiken to Mr. and Mrs. John Gleason, May 28, 1953; Aiken Papers, Crate 31, Box 2 and Box 1, University of Vermont Library; and Senator Smith to Robert Clothier, January 21, 1954, Smith Papers, Box 123, Princeton University Library.

[12]Senator Flanders to Clark Eichelberger, January 19, 1954, Flanders Papers, Box 100, Syracuse University Library; and Jenner in 100 *CR* 2121 (1954).

[13]See the comments by Senator Smith in U.S., Congress, Senate, Committee on For-eign Relations, *Executive Sessions of the Senate Foreign Relations Committee* (Historical Series), Vol. IV: 82d Cong., 2d sess., 1952 (made public in 1976), pp. 459–62; and Senator Daniel's remarks in 100 *CR* 2350–52, esp. 2350.

Senators McCarran and Jenner both maintained that without the Bricker amendment, Congress could, in implementing the articles of the United Nations Charter dealing with economic and social conditions and human rights, enact federal legislation regulating and controlling education, civil rights, public health, and even intrastate commerce. In their view, adoption of the Bricker amendment was absolutely essential to preserve the nation's federal system.[14]

Southern Democrats found the Bricker amendment particularly appealing because of their fear that the United Nations Charter, the Genocide Convention, or a covenant on human rights could be used to invalidate segregation laws in the various states or enact federal civil rights legislation. Senator A. Willis Robertson noted that there had been "considerable agitation" for the courts to declare the provisions in the United Nations Charter dealing with human rights to be self-executing, and that various legislators had asserted that since the UN Charter had been ratified as a treaty, Congress could enact civil rights legislation under its authority to implement the charter. Accordingly, Robertson favored the Bricker amendment because he believed it would prevent the courts from ruling that the charter automatically superseded segregation laws in the southern states, and keep Congress from passing civil rights legislation under its power to give effect to such agreements.[15]

II

President Eisenhower appreciated the concerns that had given rise to the Bricker amendment, but he feared the measure would strip the president and the executive branch of the power and flexibility they needed in foreign policy, and signal a retreat from the nation's responsibilities in international affairs. A self-styled conservative, Eisenhower agreed with the amendment's proponents that international agreements should not be used to bring about fundamental changes in American society or alter the relationship between the federal government and the states. He worried, however, that the amendment, particularly its restrictions on executive agreements, would impede cooperation among nations, which he considered essential to the defense of the United States, Western Europe, and the free world. As he once explained to a friend, he believed that:

> the transfer, by force or by subversion, to Communistic control of the great industrial complex of Western Europe, including its tremendous numbers in

[14]100 *CR* 934–37 (McCarran), and 2121–26 (Jenner).
[15]See Senator Robertson to Virginius Dabney, July 31, 1953, Dabney Papers, Box 1, University of Virginia Library; and Newsletter, "Washington as Viewed by Your Senator, A. Willis Robertson," January 31, 1954, copy in DDEP, OF 116-H-4.

skilled labor, would be for us a major catastrophe. If the Eurasian Continent were one solid mass of Communist-dominated people and industry, there would be no possible military dispositions on our part that could protect the Continent of Africa except possibly its southern areas. Among other areas, the Belgian Congo, the Mid-East, and the Suez Canal would be gone!

Eisenhower pointed out also that the loss of Western Europe would deprive American industry of needed raw materials and markets, thereby creating serious economic problems for the United States. This realization of Europe's importance, which had led Eisenhower to accept the appointment in 1951 as military commander of NATO, had been a key factor in his 1952 decision to seek the Republican presidential nomination. He feared that the election of Robert A. Taft might result in the United States abandoning its commitment to rebuild and protect Western Europe.[16]

In a "personal and confidential" letter to his brother Edgar, an attorney in Washington State who favored the Bricker amendment, Eisenhower set forth his reasons for opposing the resolution. He asserted that the amendment's adoption would "cripple the executive power to the point that we become helpless in world affairs." The president, he explained, had to make numerous arrangements with other governments that could not possibly be classified as treaties or successfully concluded if they had to be submitted to the Senate. Agreements to hire workers for an American air base in North Africa, set up a NATO command post in France, or exchange vital information with allies would be impossible to negotiate if they had to be approved by Congress. He believed that "the wisdom of our founding fathers in establishing the balance between the Executive and Legislative Departments had been proven time and time again," and he saw no reason to tinker with that relationship.[17]

The president and his advisers realized, however, that they faced serious problems if they were going to oppose the Bricker amendment. Secretary of States Dulles had himself warned of dangers inherent in the treaty-making power in his speech at Louisville, and the party platform had pledged that the Republicans would protect the American people against threats posed by international agreements. Although neither Dulles nor the platform had specifically endorsed the Bricker amendment, both of

[16]See Eisenhower to Edward Bermingham, February 28, 1951, DDEP, 1916–1952, Box 9, DDEL; Eisenhower's comments in minutes of cabinet meeting of February 20, 1953, reprinted in U.S., Department of State, *Foreign Relations of the United States, 1952–1954,* Vol. I: *General: Economic and Political Matters* (Washington, D.C.: United States Government Printing Office, 1983), pp. 1781–82 (hereinafter cited as *Foreign Relations,* with the year and volume); and Eisenhower, *Mandate for Change,* pp. 12–14, 16–23.
[17]President Eisenhower to Edgar Eisenhower, March 27, 1953, DDEP, Diary Series, DDEL.

these statements were sure to prove embarrassing if the administration opposed the amendment. Moreover, administration officials realized that more than sixty senators, including all but three of the Republicans, were cosponsoring S.J. Res. 1. Determined to avoid the mistakes of their predecessors, Eisenhower and Dulles put a high premium on establishing and maintaining good relations with Congress, and they were reluctant to come right out and oppose a measure that enjoyed such widespread support among Republican senators.[18]

Administration officials sought, therefore, to delay any action on the Bricker amendment in order to buy time during which they could develop a strategy for dealing with the resolution. On February 11, Attorney General Herbert Brownell met with Bricker and tried to persuade the senator not to press for quick action on S.J. Res. 1. Brownell explained that the proposed amendment affected not only the president and Congress, but most of the federal agencies as well. He emphasized that the State, Defense, Treasury, Commerce, Labor, Agriculture, and Post Office departments; the Mutual Security Agency; and the Atomic Energy and Securities and Exchange commissions all had to be given a chance to analyze the measure before either the legislature or the executive branch reached any decisions.[19]

Bricker refused to be put off by the attorney general's arguments. He pointed out that he had introduced the first version of his amendment almost eighteen months ago, giving the various agencies plenty of time to make their views known. Although he wanted to cooperate with the administration, Bricker made it clear that he would push for prompt action.[20]

Brownell reported to the president on his conversation with Bricker and suggested that Eisenhower survey the federal agencies for their comments on S.J. Res. 1. The attorney general warned that the proposed amendment "may represent a serious curtailment of executive and legislative power and facility of operation in foreign affairs." Since Bricker would not agree to postpone consideration of the measure, Brownell advised that the administration should begin moving against the amendment by obtaining statements from the various departments detailing how the resolution would affect matters under their jurisdiction.[21]

[18]See Dulles to Brownell and Phleger, January 5, 1953; and Dulles to Phelger, January 7, 1953; both in Phleger Collection, Vol. 13. See also Homer Ferguson Oral History Transcript, p. 27, John Foster Dulles Oral History Project, Princeton University Library.

[19]See Dulles to Bricker, January 12, 1953; Brownell to Bricker, January 24, 1953; and Brownell to Bricker, February 13, 1953; all in JBP, Box 91, OHS; and Brownell to the president, February 13, 1953, DDEP, OF 116-H-4.

[20]See Brownell to the president, February 13, 1953, DDEP, OF 116-H-4.

[21]Ibid.

By this time State Department officials had concluded that Bricker's proposal would sharply reduce the president's authority, and they seconded the idea of requesting the agencies' views. Herman Phleger, the department's legal adviser, stressed in a memorandum for Dulles that the amendment's restrictions on executive agreements would limit the president's negotiating power, making it much more difficult for him to deal with other nations. Dulles agreed that the measure "would radically alter the President's constitutional authority in dealing with foreign affairs," and he recommended that Eisenhower instruct the different departments to ask to testify at the Senate Judiciary Committee's hearings on the resolution.[22]

At the cabinet meeting on February 20, the president and his advisers considered the Bricker amendment. Secretary of State Dulles warned that S.J. Res. 1, by giving Congress the power to regulate executive agreements, would seriously impair the president's authority in foreign affairs. Brownell and Secretary of Defense Charles E. Wilson echoed Dulles's concern, and the secretary of state agreed to prepare a formal memorandum analyzing the amendment and all its implications. Vice-President Richard Nixon explained that Bricker and his supporters had introduced the measure not to hamstring the president, but because of their fear that international agreements such as the Genocide Convention imperiled the sovereignty of the United States and the rights of the American people. Dulles revealed, however, that the State Department did not intend to ask for ratification of the Genocide Convention and planned to end American involvement in the effort to draft a covenant on human rights. He hoped this change in policy would dampen some of the enthusiasm behind the Bricker amendment.[23]

At this point, the president joined in the discussion. He did not comment on Bricker's proposal directly, but he indicated some sympathy with the professed goals of its supporters, making it clear that he opposed any attempts to change the Constitution through international agreements. Any altering of the nation's charter, he declared, should be accomplished through the regular amending process.[24]

Five days later, the president circulated the message, which Brownell and Dulles had recommended, to the executive departments. Dulles had drafted the note, and it repeated almost verbatim Truman's letter of the previous year. Eisenhower stressed the importance of the matter, maintaining that Bricker's resolution "would not only impose restraints upon the President or agencies of the executive branch, but would affect the powers of the

---

[22]Phleger to Dulles, February 16, 1953, Phleger Collection, Vol. 9; and Dulles, memorandum for Mr. Adams, February 19, 1953, DDEP, OF 116-H-4.

[23]Minutes of cabinet meeting of February 20, 1953, in *Foreign Relations, 1952–1954*, I, 1781–82.

[24]Ibid., p. 1782.

federal government as a whole and those of the states." Accordingly, he wanted each department to study the proposal and be ready to express its views to the Senate Judiciary Committee.[25]

The same day he sent the memorandum, Eisenhower met with Frank Holman and Alfred Schweppe of the ABA. The attorneys informed the president that although they did not support Senator Bricker's text, they did favor a constitutional amendment clarifying and limiting the effects of international agreements. Eisenhower replied that he appreciated their concern, and that he, too, objected to any attempts to use such compacts to expand the powers of the federal government at the expense of the states. The president explained, however, that rereading the *Federalist Papers* had convinced him that the nation's founding fathers had adequately safeguarded the rights of the American people by requiring that treaties be approved by a two-thirds vote in the Senate.[26]

Eisenhower did not consider it significant that so many of the nation's lawyers had endorsed some sort of constitutional amendment. Legal counselors, he noted a few weeks later, were trained to take either side of a case and then make an "impassioned defense of their adopted viewpoint." Moreover, attorneys he respected, men with practical experience in government such as Dulles, Brownell, and John W. Davis, had advised him that the Bricker amendment would damage America's efforts to lead the defense of the free world. Consequently, the ABA's position did not carry as much weight with the president as might have been expected.[27]

The various departments and agencies informed the president and his staff of their misgivings about the Bricker amendment and asked for more time to examine the proposal and its ramifications. Department of Defense officials, for example, warned that the measure's restrictions on executive agreements would make it difficult for the president to act quickly and in concert with other nations during crises. If intelligence agencies were to learn that an attack on the United States or its possessions was imminent, the president might need to make arrangements with an ally involving deployment of American forces or aircraft in its territory, or joint action to combat the threat. But if the Bricker amendment were in effect, the president would first have to seek legislative approval, wasting time that

[25]Memorandum by the president to the heads of executive departments and agencies, February 25, 1953, in *Foreign Relations, 1952–1954*, I, 1782–83. See also draft for memorandum by the president, attached to Dulles to Sherman Adams, February 19, 1953, DDEP, OF 116-H-4.

[26]Bernard Shanley Diary, February 25, 1953, Seton Hall University Library and DDEL; and Holman, *Western Lawyer*, pp. 528–29. Shanley was special counsel to the president at this time.

[27]Eisenhower, memorandum for the record, April 1, 1953, in Ferrell, ed., *The Eisenhower Diaries*, p. 233.

could be critical to the nation's survival. Additional objections to S.J. Res. 1 were raised by the departments of State, Commerce, and the Post Office; the Central Intelligence and Mutual Security agencies; the Atomic Energy Commission; and others.[28]

The president and his advisers met with Bricker and his staff during the next few weeks in an apparent attempt to work out a compromise, but administration officials really had no intention of agreeing to anything. At the cabinet meeting on March 13, Dulles talked about the desirability of finding an alternative to Bricker's amendment, but then he concluded that the measure was "impossible" even if revised. The following week he explained to members of the cabinet that even a seemingly harmless amendment might be dangerous, since one could never be sure how it would be interpreted by the courts. A few days later, White House chief of staff Sherman Adams suggested that the executive branch should draft a proposal that "theoretically we could use for a compromise." Since it was unlikely that administration officials would like the new text any better than the original, they could then tell Bricker that they had tried to write a satisfactory resolution but had failed. They could then propose setting up a commission, to be headed by Senator Bricker, to consider the whole matter for six months or so. Of course, Adams noted, the president would not be bound to implement the study group's recommendations.[29]

This idea of a study commission stemmed from the administration's desire to avoid directly opposing a measure favored by so many Republican senators, and from a misreading of Bricker's willingness to compromise on specific language. Because the senator told Eisenhower, Dulles, and Secretary of the Treasury George Humphrey that he would not insist on the exact text he had introduced, administration officials assumed that Bricker was interested only in having enacted something that would bear his name. If that were the case, the attorney general counseled, then appointing Bricker to chair a special "Bricker Commission" to study the problem might be enough to satisfy him.[30]

[28]See Roger Kent, general counsel of the Department of Defense, to Bernard Shanley, March 10, 1953, and attached draft statement, DDEP, OF 116-H-4; Dulles to the president, March 2, 1953; and "Views of U.S. Departments and Agencies on S.J. Res. 1 and S.J. Res. 2," n.d.; both in *Foreign Relations, 1952–54*, I, 1785–89; Secretary of Commerce Sinclair Weeks to the president, March 3, 1953; and Postmaster General Arthur Summerfield to the president, n.d.; both in DDEP, OF 116-H-4.

[29]Minutes of cabinet meeting of March 13, 1953, in *Foreign Relations, 1952–54*, I, 1794–95; minutes of cabinet meeting of March 20, 1953, DDEL; and Shanley Diary, March 23 and 27, 1953.

[30]Minutes of cabinet meetings of March 20 and 27, 1953, DDEL; Shanley Diary, March 19, 20, and 27, 1953; and minutes of telephone calls, Secretary Humphrey to Dulles, March 13 and 26, 1953, in "Minutes of Telephone Conversations of John Foster Dulles and of Christian Herter, 1953–1961," microfilm edition (Washington, D.C.: University Publications of America, 1980) (hereinafter cited as "Telephone Conversations, Dulles").

Although Bricker was not wedded to the specific language of S.J. Res. 1, he was not willing to accept any amendment just because it would bear his name. He had already changed the wording of the measure twice, and he expected the judiciary committee to modify it again. The senator knew that a different text might still accomplish his objectives; thus, he had offered to alter his proposal to win the administration's support. He would not endorse any resolution, however, unless he believed it protected the rights of the American people and the sovereignty of the United States, and limited the use and effects of executive agreements.[31]

Bricker realized that the administration was just trying to put off any action on his amendment, and he rejected the suggestion that he head a commission to study the treaty-making power. He appreciated the courtesy and consideration that Brownell and George Humphrey had shown him, but he bitterly resented Dulles's failure to offer any concrete ideas as to how the measure could be changed to meet the administration's objections. After all, the secretary of state himself had pointed out the dangers of "treaty law" in his remarks a year ago at Louisville. Bricker emphasized to Brownell that there was too much support for his amendment to put it off. Moreover, he warned, a year's delay would make the resolution look like an attack on President Eisenhower.[32]

III

When reporters raised the issue of the Bricker amendment at one of the president's press conferences in mid-March, Eisenhower, typically, refused either to endorse or reject the proposal. He often evaded questions or answered ambiguously when sensitive matters came up at his news conferences. When all else failed, he would use his wandering syntax intentionally to confuse the issue. When asked if he favored the Bricker amendment, the president masterfully avoided answering the question. The whole issue, he declared, "was one of the most argumentative" that he had ever heard discussed. Recalling the old adage that a man had two ears and one tongue, he stated that he was trying "to keep twice as still as I would in other places." The president, he observed, had no formal role in the amending process, so he did not have to take a position on the resolution. Eisenhower

---

[31]See Bricker to Frank Holman, January 15, 1953; Bricker to Herbert Brownell, April 2, 1953; and Bricker to Senator Arthur Watkins, April 15, 1953; all in JBP, Box 91, OHS; Bricker to Senator Ives, February 18, 1953, Ives Papers, Box 48; Bricker to Senator Smith (N.J.), May 12, 1953, Smith Papers, Box 123; and Bricker to Vice-President Richard Nixon, May 26, 1953, Nixon Papers, Vice-Presidential Series, "Bricker Amendment," Federal Archives and Records Center, Los Angeles.

[32]Bricker to Brownell, April 2, 1953, JBP, Box 91, OHS.

did comment, however, that it seemed to him that most of the amendment's proponents did not really want to change the Constitution; rather, they were merely seeking to ensure that the nation's charter could not be altered by international agreements. But it struck the president as a bit irregular to amend the Constitution "in order to show that it is going to remain the same."[33]

When a reporter raised the issue again the following week, the president came out against the Bricker resolution, but in a somewhat circumspect manner. "As analyzed for me by the Secretary of State," Eisenhower explained, the amendment would "restrict the authority that the President must have, if he is to conduct the foreign affairs of this Nation effectively." He was certain that was not the intent of its framers, who believed it would help protect the United States and the rights of American citizens. Nonetheless, he emphasized, the resolution "would work to the disadvantage of our country, particularly in making it impossible for the President to work with the flexibility that he needs in this highly complicated and difficult situation."[34]

Eisenhower's early handling of the Bricker amendment controversy, as typified by his remarks at the press conference, illustrates both the strengths and weaknesses of his "hidden-hand leadership." As Fred Greenstein and others have noted, Eisenhower often played an active role behind the scenes in the administration's decision making, but downplayed his involvement in public, leaving Dulles or Sherman Adams to take any criticism or blame that the administration's policies might engender. Dulles and the State Department were willing, in Dulles's words, to be the "whipping boy" on the Bricker amendment, and Eisenhower used them in exactly that way. When the president first announced his opposition to the proposal, he based it on the secretary of state's analysis of the resolution and its probable effects, thereby deflecting public and congressional criticism away from himself and onto Dulles and the State Department. Arthur Krock, for example, writing in the *New York Times,* concluded that Dulles was "largely responsible" for the president's opposition, and Senator Bricker blamed the secretary of state, not Eisenhower, for the administration's opposition. By avoiding the hostility that Bricker and his supporters soon came to feel

---

[33]President's news conference, March 19, 1953, in *Public Papers: Eisenhower, 1953,* pp. 109–10. Eisenhower's confidence in his ability to duck tough questions at his press conferences was evident in March 1955, when Press Secretary James Hagerty urged him not to answer any questions concerning the possible use of atomic bombs in a war resulting from the Communist Chinese shelling of Quemoy and Matsu. The president reassured Hagerty that "if that question comes up, I'll just confuse them." See Eisenhower, *Mandate for Change,* 477–78. On Eisenhower's evasiveness and ambiguity at press conferences in general, see Greenstein, *The Hidden-Hand Presidency,* pp. 67–70.

[34]President's news conference, March 26, 1953, in *Public Papers: Eisenhower, 1953,* p. 132.

toward Dulles, the president was able to work with them on other issues.[35]

But Eisenhower's willingness to use Dulles and the State Department as the "whipping boy" had its drawbacks too. The president's failure to take a more direct stand against the amendment led Bricker, Frank Holman, and others to question both his understanding of the issue and the firmness of his opposition. As a result, they persisted in their efforts to win approval of an amendment, and the fight dragged on for years. Dulles and Brownell both believed that support for the amendment would have collapsed if only Eisenhower had taken a strong stand against it at the start.[36]

The president moved cautiously in opposing the Bricker amendment because he wanted to avoid a confrontation with Senate Republicans, and because he was reluctant to commit himself to battle unless he was confident of the outcome. He had concluded that the amendment was too restrictive, but he knew it had been endorsed by sixty-four senators, including almost all of the Republicans. Even administration loyalists such as Senator H. Alexander Smith of New Jersey were urging the president and his advisers to reach some sort of compromise with Bricker to avoid splitting the Republican party. Accordingly, Eisenhower was reluctant to come out publicly against the amendment. Only when the administration had failed in all its efforts to persuade Bricker to delay consideration of his proposal did the president speak out against the amendment, and even then he did not do so in a straightforward and forthright manner. Although this spared him from the wrath of the amendment's supporters and even preserved for him the option of accepting a revised amendment if necessary, it also gave the resolution's proponents hope that they might eventually win the president's backing. Thus the stage was set for a protracted struggle over the Bricker amendment.[37]

[35]See minutes of telephone call, Dulles to Phleger, March 30, 1953, in "Telephone Conversations, Dulles"; Shanley Diary, March 27, 1953; Arthur Krock in *New York Times,* March 27, 1953, p. 22; Bricker to Brownell, April 2, 1953, JBP, Box 91, OHS; and interview with Senator Bricker, June 26, 1975. On Eisenhower's "hidden-hand leadership," see Greenstein, *The Hidden-Hand Presidency;* Kempton, "The Underestimation of Dwight D. Eisenhower"; and Cook, *The Declassified Eisenhower.*

[36]See memorandum of telephone conversation between the secretary of state and the attorney general, June 4, 1953, in *Foreign Relations, 1952–1954,* I, 1812–13; Cater, "Congress and the President"; Holman to Bricker, May 21, 1953, JBP, Box 92, OHS; and editorial, "Two Pledges Written Off," Washington *Times-Herald,* February 17, 1954, clipping in DDEP, GF 3-A-5.

[37]See Eisenhower, memorandum for the record, April 1, 1953, in Ferrell, ed., *The Eisenhower Diaries,* p. 233; Senator Smith to Dulles, March 28, 1953; and Smith to Herman Phleger, May 18 and May 25, 1953; all in Smith Papers, Box 123. Smith voted against the Eisenhower administration only 7 times during the 83d Congress (1953 and 1954), a record of support for the administration surpassed only by Senators James Duff (Pa.) and Ralph Flanders. See *Congressional Quarterly Almanac, 1953,* p. 82, and *Congressional Quarterly Almanac, 1954,* p. 62.

CHAPTER SIX

Battle Lines Are Drawn

The Senate Judiciary Committee scheduled hearings on the Bricker amendment to begin in mid-February 1953. The hearings posed problems, however, for both the resolution's proponents and the Eisenhower administration. John Bricker and the leaders of the American Bar Association were still haggling over the wording of the amendment, while administration officials were trying to delay action on the matter. The president and his advisers worried that opposing the amendment would be embarrassing in light of Dulles's previous remarks, the party platform plank on treaties, and the widespread support the measure enjoyed among Republican senators. Nevertheless, administration officials would have to go public at the hearings with their opposition to the amendment.

I

Although Bricker had received strong support from his colleagues for S.J. Res. 1, he had never resolved his differences with the leaders of the American Bar Association over the wording of the measure. Frank Holman complained that Bricker's new proposal was still inadequate because it invalidated only treaty provisions denying or abridging rights "enumerated" in the Constitution. He feared that such wording left at risk liberties and freedoms not specifically listed in the Constitution, especially rights reserved to the states and to the people by the Tenth Amendment. Holman pointed out also that Bricker had not included the "which" clause in his amendment, thereby leaving in effect the Supreme Court's decision in the migratory bird case, which "was and is largely the basis for the need of a Constitutional Amendment." In Holman's opinion, the federal government had to be stopped from using its authority to implement treaties as a means of encroaching further on the jurisdiction of the states. Finally, Holman believed that Bricker's proposal was "too long to be readily grasped and understood, particularly by state legislatures."[1]

Unhappy with Bricker's resolution, Holman and members of the ABA's Committee on Peace and Law Through United Nations drafted their own amendment. At a meeting in New Orleans in late January 1953, the attorneys refined the text they had recommended to Congress in 1952. They tightened the language and added a section on executive agreements, so that the measure now read:

> Section 1. A provision of a treaty which conflicts with any provision of this Constitution shall not be of any force or effect. A treaty shall become effective as internal law in the United States only through legislation which would be valid in the absence of treaty.
> Section 2. Executive agreements shall be subject to regulation by the Congress and to the limitations imposed on treaties by this article.

At the request of Holman and the leaders of the ABA, Senator Arthur Watkins (R-Utah) introduced their proposal in the Senate so that it, too, would be considered by the judiciary committee.[2]

In relaying the new text to Bricker, Holman and the attorneys tried to persuade him to drop his own resolution and endorse theirs. Alfred Schweppe, chairman of the Committee on Peace and Law, maintained that the revised proposal would stand up better against the opposition's attacks because it embodied all the essential principles and stated them "most precisely and succinctly." Holman emphasized that the "simplicity and directness" of the ABA's measure would give it greater appeal. Moreover, he warned, unless the senator substituted the new resolution for his own bill, those favoring an amendment might dissipate their energy defending a text that still had serious weaknesses.[3]

Bricker still objected, however, to the "which" clause. He feared that limiting Congress's authority in implementing a treaty to passing only those laws it could already enact without the treaty might actually accelerate the growth of federal power by forcing the Supreme Court to stretch the commerce or general welfare clauses of the Constitution in order to uphold a statute passed to effectuate an advantageous agreement.[4]

[1]Holman to Bricker, January 12, 1953, JBP, Box 91, OHS. See also Eberhard Deutsch to Bricker, January 9, 1953; and Alfred Schweppe to Bricker, January 16, 1953; both in JBP, Box 91, OHS. For the text of S.J. Res. 1, see Appendix D.

[2]See Holman to Bricker, February 2, 1953; Schweppe to Bricker, February 3, 1953; and Deutsch to Bricker, February 13, 1953; all in JBP, Box 91, OHS.

[3]Schweppe to Bricker, February 3, 1953; Holman to Bricker, February 2, 1953; JBP, Box 91, OHS.

[4]See Bricker to Holman, January 15, 1953, JBP, Box 91, OHS.

The senator detailed his objections to the ABA's proposal in a letter to all the cosponsors of S.J. Res. 1. He explained that the ABA's amendment (S.J. Res. 43) would make it difficult if not impossible to negotiate reciprocal agreements securing for Americans the right to own property or engage in business in other countries in exchange for foreign nationals being granted similar privileges in the United States. Since these matters were regulated by the individual states, Congress would be unable to implement such compacts if it were stripped of its authority to adopt any legislation necessary and proper to carrying out such a treaty. State action would be required, and Bricker questioned the wisdom of an amendment that gave the states "what amounts to a veto power over foreign policy." He was no defender of growing federal authority, but even Bricker realized that the ABA's amendment, especially the "which" clause, went too far in trying to prevent federal encroachments.[5]

Nonetheless, Bricker still hoped that some sort of agreement could be worked out between himself and the leaders of the ABA. He stressed to his colleagues that he was still in close contact with the attorneys, but even if they failed to reconcile their differences, he was confident that the judiciary committee would be able to draft an amendment they could all support.[6]

II

Both S.J. Res. 1 and S.J. Res. 43 were referred to the Committee on the Judiciary, and on February 18, 1953, that group's Subcommittee on Constitutional Amendments began its hearings on the measures. Senators William Langer (R-N.D.), Everett Dirksen (R-Ill.), John Marshall Butler (R-Md.), Harley Kilgore (D-W.Va.), and Estes Kefauver (D-Tenn.) made up the preliminary panel, and, in contrast to the situation the previous year, only the three Republicans were among the cosponsors of Bricker's proposal. Even so, the sessions were hardly conducted in an evenhanded manner, as Langer, chairman of the committee, granted Holman and representatives of the ABA the extraordinary privileges of questioning the other witnesses and testifying again after all the opponents had been heard. Also, other members of the judiciary committee, including Willis Smith and Pat McCarran, sat in on the hearings occasionally to voice their strong support for the Bricker amendment.[7]

---

[5]See for example Bricker to Senator Ives, February 18, 1953, Ives Papers, Box 48; and Bricker to Senator Smith (N.J.), February 18, 1953, Smith Papers, Box 123.

[6]Ibid. See also Bricker to Frank Waldrop, March 6, 1953, JBP, Box 91, OHS.

[7]U.S., Congress, Senate, Committee on the Judiciary, *Treaties and Executive Agreements, Hearings,* before a Subcommittee of the Committee on the Judiciary, Senate, 83d Cong., 1st

Senator Bricker spoke first at the hearings, and for the most part he merely reiterated the arguments he had offered previously. This time, however, he emphasized that Secretary of State Dulles had himself warned in his remarks at Louisville of the dangers lurking in the treaty-making power. Bricker also explained that he was not necessarily wedded to the text of S.J. Res. 1 as introduced. The amendment's objectives, he declared, were "too important . . . for any words to stand in the way of ratification."[8]

Hostility toward the United Nations became much more blatant during these hearings than had been the case in 1952. Witness after witness condemned the world organization. Frank Holman denounced the UN for "meddling in the affairs of the member states" when it should have been working for world peace, and Senator Langer charged that American boys were still dying in Korea because the UN had prevented the United States from winning a decisive military victory. Complaints about the UN were so common during the hearings that Senator Kefauver concluded, not incorrectly, that the Bricker Amendment represented a belated attack against the UN Charter and was designed to keep the United States from joining such organizations in the future.[9]

Many of the resolution's proponents also condemned the executive agreements entered into by Presidents Roosevelt and Truman and urged the amendment's adoption to prevent future presidents from entering into important agreements without the consent of Congress. Senators Dirksen and McCarran blamed the Yalta accords for most of America's problems in the world, including the war in Korea. Senator Willis Smith concurred. For him, the real question was "whether or not we shall allow executive agreements to go to the point of giving us in effect a totalitarian government, or if we shall continue our protection of the citizens by constitutional process, which means enactment of laws by the people's elected representatives." Senator Langer even asked one witness if he thought "the American people, after Abraham Lincoln freed the slaves, would have ratified the Potsdam agreement selling five or six million people into slavery, white people?"[10]

Speaking for the American Bar Association, Frank Holman and Alfred Schweppe explained and defended the merits of their proposal as compared to Senator Bricker's resolution. Without the restrictions embodied

---

sess., 1953 (hereinafter referred to as *Hearings, 1953*). On Holman and representatives of the ABA interrogating other witnesses, see *Hearings, 1953*, pp. 13, 19, 211–13, 401. For Holman's and Schweppe's rebuttal testimony, see ibid., pp. 1193–94, 1216–28, 1228–67.

[8]Ibid., pp. 2–16, esp. 16.

[9]Ibid., pp. 133 (Holman), 355–56 (Langer), and 397–98 (Kefauver).

[10]Ibid., pp. 225–27 (Dirksen), 380 (McCarran), 1095 (Smith), and 229 (Langer). See also Alfred Schweppe's comments, ibid., pp. 64–68.

in their amendment, Holman cautioned, Congress could, under the doctrine of *Missouri v. Holland,* "take over vast areas heretofore reserved respectively to the States and to the people." Schweppe dismissed as groundless the fear that the ABA's amendment would make it impossible for Congress to implement traditional treaties of friendship and commerce allowing foreigners to own businesses or inherit property in the United States. Congress could still bring such agreements into force, he maintained, under its constitutional authority to regulate commerce with foreign nations.[11]

Even though talk of rights and freedoms dominated much of the hearings, Holman and representatives of the business community showed that for many of the amendment's supporters, economic interests and concerns were really uppermost in their minds. Holman stressed that the United Nations human rights program endangered the "life, liberty and *property*" (emphasis added) of American citizens. Charles Rhyne, an attorney from Washington D.C. appearing on behalf of the United States Chamber of Commerce, argued that the social and economic rights set forth in the proposed covenant on human rights "would, if made effective in our Nation, destroy in many respects vital parts of our free enterprise system." A spokesman for the National Association of Manufacturers noted that the decision in the migratory bird case had set a precedent that could be used to extend federal control over labor and management. He warned that unless the Bricker amendment were adopted, ratification of international compacts on such subjects as private employment agencies, vocational guidance and training, annual holidays with pay, and pension insurance would allow the national government to supersede the states in regulating these matters.[12]

W. L. McGrath of Cincinnati, testifying for the U.S. Chamber of Commerce, again discussed his experiences as a member of the United States employer delegation to the annual conferences of the International Labor Organization. McGrath used the ILO to illustrate how treaties could transfer authority over domestic affairs to an international agency. In its early years, McGrath explained, the ILO had concentrated on matters directly related to labor. As "state socialism" had become more prevalent in Europe and the concept of a planned economy had gained acceptance, however, the organization had begun to focus more of its attention on government itself. McGrath believed the agency was now "almost completely in the hands of a socialistic government-labor coalition, which apparently has as its objective the enactment of socialistic legislation, stan-

[11]Ibid., pp. 156 (Holman), and 60–61 (Schweppe).
[12]Ibid., pp. 134–37, esp. 134 (Holman); 583–90, esp. 584 (Rhyne); and 599–600 (National Association of Manufacturers).

dardized along ILO lines, in the largest possible number of countries in the world."[13]

To show how far the ILO had gone, McGrath detailed for the senators the provisions of a convention on maternity benefits that the organization had approved the previous summer. He pointed out that the covenant made no distinction between legitimate children and those born "without benefit of marriage," and that it accorded employed women at least twelve weeks off to have their babies, as well as free medical care and hospitalization if needed. During that period, the women would receive in cash from the government an amount equal to two-thirds of their pay, and, after they returned to their jobs, interruptions from work for nursing their babies would be counted as working hours and paid for by the employer. When the issue of nursing mothers had first come up, McGrath recalled, "labor and employer delegates, from nations all over the world, debated the question as to whether a woman nursing her baby, on time paid for by the employer, should do so in a single period of one hour per day, or two periods of one-half hour each. . . . On this great international point the representatives of the United States Government appeared neutral."[14]

An even more "crucial" problem that had been considered, McGrath continued, concerned nursing mothers unable to provide their own milk. It was decided that in such cases the government should buy milk for them. But that seemed unfair to those who could supply their own milk, so it was agreed that "a mother who could furnish her own milk should likewise be paid by the Government for doing so, and while dispensing it she would also be paid an hourly rate by her employer." Though there had been some "facetious discussion about time and a half" for overtime, McGrath reported, no action had been taken on that question.[15]

Times had changed since 1787, McGrath emphasized. Had the founding fathers of the United States been thinking of compacts regarding layettes and mothers' milk when they had written that treaties would be part of the supreme law of the land? McGrath was sure that in those days "nobody could have dreamed that proposed international treaties could ever be devised which would include subject matter such as is now included in ILO conventions." He believed the nation needed a constitutional amendment to deal with this new situation.[16]

[13]Ibid., pp. 530–36, esp. 536. See also McGrath to Senator Herbert Lehman, October 15, 1952, and enclosed report by McGrath, "The 35th International Labor Conference of the International Labor Organization," Geneva, Switzerland, June, 1952, in Herbert H. Lehman Papers, Departmental Files, 1951–52, Columbia University.
[14]*Hearings, 1953*, pp. 539–41.
[15]Ibid., p. 542.
[16]Ibid.

In response to McGrath's comments, George Delaney of the American Federation of Labor defended the ILO. He complained that McGrath and others had misrepresented and distorted the organization's record because, "to some persons, any proposition which looks in the direction of the social or economic improvement of the conditions of life and labor is socialistic." Most of the matters under ILO consideration, Delaney reported, such as social security, had already been enacted into law in the United States. Moreover, he informed the committee, the ILO exercised no legislative authority whatsoever; its influence was limited to friendly persuasion and the "inherent virtues of proposed standards" included in its recommendations. Its charter also stated specifically that in a nation with a federal system of government, it would be up to that nation to decide for itself if a particular ILO convention could be implemented by the central government, or if state and local action would be required.[17]

Delaney assured the senators that the AFL did not regard an ILO agreement as an easy way of enacting into law programs that could not be adopted in the usual manner. Agreements such as the covenant on maternity benefits, which McGrath had discussed at such length, would have to be approved by a two-thirds vote in the Senate and then implemented by legislation approved by both the House and the Senate before they would go into effect in the United States. Clearly, this method was much more cumbersome and difficult than the regular legislative process.[18]

Other witnesses also tried to convince the senators that there was no need for a constitutional amendment. Dana Backus and Theodore Pearson of the Association of the Bar of the City of New York detailed their group's opposition to the resolution again, and Bernard Bernstein of B'nai B'rith and Irving Ferman of the American Civil Liberties Union both stressed that the draft covenant on human rights stated explicitly that none of its provisions would derogate in any way from freedoms that people already enjoyed. Similarly, Will Maslow of the American Jewish Congress observed that if the Senate worried that a particular compact endangered the liberties of the American people, the proper course of action would be simply to reject it. Surely that remedy was preferable to adopting a vague constitutional amendment "which will tie our hands for years to come and which would be a source not only of domestic ill health but which would hurt our foreign relations as well." Covey Oliver, professor of international law at the University of California, summed up the arguments of most of the measure's opponents. Noting the resolution's apparent wide-

---

[17]Ibid., pp. 1082–96, esp. 1086 and 1083 for the quotations. See also the statement by Rudolph Faupl of the International Association of Machinists, ibid., 779–89.

[18]Ibid., pp. 1085–88.

spread support, he declared: "Seldom in human history would so much be risked by so many for so little cause!"[19]

III

Senator Langer hoped to conduct the hearings on S.J. Res. 1 as quickly as possible, but the Eisenhower administration sought to prolong the sessions so that it would have more time to formulate its response. On February 25, as the subcommittee concluded its first week of hearings, Langer announced that the hearings would conclude on March 4 whether or not representatives of the executive branch were ready to testify by that date. Subsequently, however, Vice-President Nixon prevailed upon Langer to give administration officials until April 6 to prepare their testimony.[20]

On April 3, President Eisenhower and his advisers made final plans for presenting the administration's testimony. They decided that cabinet members would be free to express their own opinions, but anyone considering endorsing S.J. Res. 1 was urged to meet first with officials from the State Department. In case anyone had missed the hint, Eisenhower reminded everyone that he had recently stated at a press conference that the amendment was unnecessary and dangerous because it would prevent presidents from entering into necessary agreements with other nations.[21]

Although the president did not testify at the hearings, he played an important role in shaping the administration's case. When Dulles sent him a draft of the statement he planned to make to the subcommittee, Eisenhower returned it and suggested a number of changes. He questioned "the usefulness or appropriateness" of arguing before a legislative body that the measure "would make the President the 'servant' of the Congress"; too many legislators supported the amendment for that very reason. The president recommended that the secretary save that argument for public audiences, stressing instead to the committee that the resolution would "impede and stifle necessary action in the international field."[22]

Eisenhower's other comments on the draft showed similar insight. He noted that Dulles's description of the proposal as something that "might

[19]Ibid., pp. 191–208 (Backus and Pearson), 253–57 (Bernstein), 281 (Ferman), 359 (Maslow), and 683 (Oliver). See also the remarks by Senator Kefauver, ibid., p. 395.

[20]See ibid., pp. 15, 24–25, 32, 376, and 378; and Bernard Shanley Diary, March 6, 9, and 12, 1953.

[21]Minutes of cabinet meeting of April 3, 1953, in *Foreign Relations, 1952–54*, I, 1806–7.

[22]Memorandum by the secretary of state to the president, March 31, 1953, and enclosed draft statement, "The Pending Resolutions," March 30, 1953; and memorandum by the president to the secretary of state, April 1, 1953; all in *Foreign Relations, 1952–54*, I, 1796–1806.

under other circumstances be a desirable Constitutional amendment"
seemed to imply that "with a different kind of administration, it might be a
good thing to adopt such a Resolution." If that were so, the president
declared, *"then I am for the Resolution."* If the American people did need
protection against "the treaty-making powers of a stupid President and a
partisan Senate," Eisenhower pointed out, then the fact that there was no
danger during the next four years was not a very good argument against the
amendment. The basis for their position, Eisenhower emphasized, had to
be the soundness of the Constitution, not the "personal ability and
wisdom" of the present administrators of the government.[23]

Dulles, Brownell, and other administration spokesmen followed the
president's advice at the hearings, testifying that the Bricker amendment
would cause more problems than it would solve. The secretary of state
warned that the amendment "would deprive the nation of treaty-making
powers in large areas" and impede the conduct of foreign affairs, and a
representative from the Department of Defense counseled that approval of
the measure "would seriously interfere with essential military operations
both in peace and in war," since international agreements played a key role
in developing "an integrated defense system for the free nations of the
world." Restricting the president's authority to enter into such compacts,
Defense Department officials asserted, would limit America's ability to
acquire and utilize overseas bases, making it difficult for the president "to
act in moments of serious emergency where speed and decisions are
essential for the safety of this country."[24]

Still seeking to avoid a confrontation with Senate Republicans, administration officials praised Bricker and the leaders of the American Bar
Association for alerting the nation to the dangers posed by international
agreements, and confined their objections to the specific texts under
consideration. Brownell endorsed the "very laudable" goals of the amendments' proponents, and even promised to support any resolution that
would accomplish their objectives without impairing the president's
powers under the Constitution. He opposed the measures presently before
the committee, however, because he believed they had "grave implications
for the principle of separation of powers on which our Constitution is
based." Dulles, too, professed great sympathy for the proposals' objectives.

[23]Memorandum by the president to the secretary of state, April 1, 1953, in *Foreign Relations,
1952–54,* I, 1805–6.

[24]*Hearings, 1953,* pp. 823–900, esp. 823–24 (Dulles); 901–47 (Brownell), and 951–84, esp.
951, 960, 969, and 975 (Department of Defense officials). Administration witnesses testifying
against the amendments included: Dulles, Brownell, Assistant Secretary of Defense Frank
Nash, General Counsel of the Treasury Department Elbert Tuttle, General Counsel of the
Commerce Department Stephen Dunn, and Mutual Security Director Harold Stassen.

But careful analysis had convinced him that the amendments under consideration would curtail "necessary power in the area of foreign relations at a very critical time." The fact that Senator Bricker and the ABA had each submitted their own resolutions showed how difficult it was to draft a suitable amendment. Accordingly, despite Bricker's previous rejection of the idea, the secretary again suggested that a "Bricker Committee" be established to study the problem of treaties and executive agreements.[25]

Administration officials never defended the United Nations human rights proposals that had evoked the Bricker amendment. On the contrary, in an attempt to undercut support for the resolution, or at least remove some of the urgency from the movement for its adoption, Dulles announced at the hearings that the administration would neither sign nor seek Senate approval for the covenant on human rights or any other agreements involving the nation's internal affairs. The secretary reported that President Eisenhower was "committed to the exercise of the treaty-making power only within traditional limits"; he would not allow agreements with other nations to be used "to circumvent the constitutional procedures established in relation to what are essentially matters of domestic concern." The United States would continue "to encourage the promotion everywhere of human rights and individual freedoms," Dulles declared, but it would do so by "persuasion, education, and example rather than formal undertakings." Consequently, members of the Senate could take their time and consider the whole problem carefully without worrying that a treaty would alter conditions within the United States while they were still debating the issue.[26]

Dulles also made it clear that the administration considered the ABA's resolution with its "which" clause even more objectionable than Bricker's amendment. In terms reminiscent of Bricker's letter to the cosponsors of S.J. Res. I, the Secretary explained that the nation's founders had drafted

[25]*Hearings, 1953,* pp. 939 and 934 (Brownell), and 895 and 898–99 (Dulles). See also Brownell to Bricker, April 6, 1953, JBP, Box 91, OHS; and Cater, "Congress and the President."

[26]*Hearings, 1953,* p. 825. See also memorandum by the legal adviser and the assistant secretary of state for United Nations affairs to the secretary of state, February 18, 1953, and attached memorandum, "United States Policy Regarding International Covenants on Human Rights," February 17, 1953; the secretary of state to the U.S. representative on the Commission on Human Rights, April 3, 1953; the secretary of state to the consulate general at Geneva, for Mrs. Lord, April 6, 1953; memorandum by the secretary of state to the president, April 7, 1953, and attached proposed statement by the president, April 7, 1953; statement made by the U.S. representative before the Commission on Human Rights, Geneva, April 8, 1953; the consul general at Geneva, from Mrs. Lord, to the Department of State, April 8, 1953; and the acting secretary of state to the consulate general at Geneva, for Mrs. Lord, April 10, 1953; all in *Foreign Relations, 1952–54,* III: *United Nations Affairs,* pp. 1549–54 and 1564–75; and *New York Times,* April 7, 1953, pp. 1, 14, and April 8, 1953, p. 7.

the treaty-making provisions of the Constitution to ensure that the country spoke with one voice in foreign affairs and that the individual states complied with agreements entered into by the national government. He warned, however, that the ABA's proposal, in its attempt to overturn the doctrine of *Missouri v. Holland,* would create a "no-man's-land" by requiring that each of the forty-eight states approve such conventions as treaties of friendship and commerce before they could go into effect. If the states could accept or reject such agreements, Dulles maintained, one of the primary accomplishments of the framers of the Constitution would have been undone.[27]

Following the secretary's formal statement, Senator Alexander Wiley (R-Wisc.) asked him to elaborate on his comments at Louisville the previous year. Dulles had prepared carefully for such a question, and he explained that he had never said, and certainly not in his speech at Louisville, that a constitutional amendment was the proper remedy for the threat posed by treaties. Rather, he had called for further study of the matter. Now that he had examined the problem thoroughly, he believed that a constitutional amendment would not be in the nation's best interests. The best way to protect the rights of the American people, he had concluded, was through "constant vigilance," not a constitutional amendment that would itself endanger the nation's security and well-being.[28]

After all the testimony against the amendment had been heard, Frank Holman lashed back bitterly in his rebuttal statement. He noted that the Association of the Bar of the City of New York was the only bar association objecting to the proposal, and he charged that its report reflected the biases of its authors, Dana Backus and Theodore Pearson. Holman pointed out that Backus had worked for Secretary of State Stettinius during the San Francisco Conference on the UN Charter in 1945, and he claimed, erroneously, that Pearson had been with the State Department for a number of years and thus had acquired "the State Department slant on these matters." Why was it, Holman wondered, that attorneys from all over the country, men "with no ax to grind, with no selfish interest to pursue, with no motive involving their own power," supported the resolution, but those connected with the State Department and the executive branch, whether under Truman or now under Eisenhower, opposed it? Was there, perhaps, "a conflict of ideology between the men in power who wanted more power, who did not want to be annoyed or fettered by a constitutional restraint,"

[27]*Hearings, 1953,* pp. 824, 829. On the problems between the national government and the states over treaties before the Constitution, see Frederick W. Marks III, *Independence on Trial: Foreign Affairs and the Making of the Constitution.*
[28]*Hearings, 1953,* pp. 861–64, 880. On Dulles's preparation for such a question, see Department of State, "Questions and Answers Prepared for 1953 Hearings," Phleger Collection, Vol. 12.

and those motivated only by the desire to protect the American people? Unless this amendment were adopted, Holman warned, the treaty-making power would continue to be "a method by which you can put a dictatorship in this country just as easily . . . as the Reichstag turned Germany over to Hitler!"[29]

IV

After the subcommittee completed its hearings, John Bricker and the leaders of the ABA resumed their efforts to draft a constitutional amendment that they would all support. Senator Langer advised that it would greatly facilitate the judiciary committee's task if Bricker, Holman, and the members of the ABA's Committee on Peace and Law could resolve their differences over the wording and endorse the same proposal. Consequently, Bricker and the others met a number of times in April and May. After considering many different texts, they recommended that the senators approve the following amendment:

Section 1. A provision of a treaty which conflicts with this Constitution shall not be of any force or effect.
Section 2. A treaty shall become effective as internal law in the United States only through legislation which would be valid in the absence of treaty.
Section 3. Congress shall have the power to regulate all executive and other agreements with any foreign power or international organization. All such agreements shall be subject to the limitations imposed on treaties by this article.[30]

In both style and substance, the revised resolution resembled the ABA's proposal more than Bricker's own amendment. It was short and to the point, and, most importantly, it included the "which" clause reversing the doctrine of *Missouri v. Holland* and restricting Congress, in implementing treaties, to passing only those laws *which* it could already enact under its delegated powers.[31]

Given his previous opposition to the "which" clause, why did Bricker give in at this point? In part, he finally conceded because Holman and the

[29]*Hearings, 1953*, pp. 1216–28, esp. 1217–19. See also letter from Theodore Pearson to author, September 12, 1979.

[30]See Frank Holman to Charles Webb, March 23, 1953; Bricker to Senator Watkins, April 15, 1953; Senator Smith (N.C.) to Bricker, April 15, 1953; Langer to Bricker, April 21, 1953; all in JBP, Boxes 91 and 92, OHS; Bricker to Vice-President Nixon, May 26, 1953, Nixon Papers, Vice-Presidential Series, "Bricker Amendment"; and Bricker to Senator Ives, June 2, 1953, Ives Papers, Box 48.

[31]To compare the various texts, see Appendixes A–F. See also Frank Holman's letter of June 5, 1953, to "Key Individuals and Heads of Organizations," copy attached to Holman to Bricker, June 8, 1953, JBP, Box 92, OHS.

others assured him that Congress would still be able to implement treaties of friendship and commerce under its authority to regulate interstate and foreign commerce. They also convinced him that a provision safeguarding the powers reserved to the states would help the amendment win ratification in the required three-fourths of the states. Most important, however, was that Holman and the leaders of the ABA remained adamant about including the "which" clause in the resolution, and as Bricker recalled years later, he "had to keep the American Bar's support." He realized that the legitimacy and stature the measure gained from endorsement by the ABA were crucial to its chances of winning Senate approval, especially now that the administration had made clear its opposition to any meaningful amendment.[32]

On June 4, 1953, the Senate Judiciary Committee voted 8-4 to approve the revised version of the Bricker amendment that had been agreed upon by Bricker and the leaders of the ABA. Despite the Eisenhower administration's opposition to the measure, five of the committee's eight Republicans—Senators Butler (Md.), Hendrickson (N.J.), Jenner (Ind.), Watkins (Utah), and Welker (Id.)—endorsed the resolution, and they were joined by three southern Democrats—Senators Eastland (Miss.), Smith (N.C.), and Johnston (S.C.). Only Senators Kefauver (D-Tenn.), Kilgore (D-W.Va.), Langer (R-N.D.), and Wiley (R-Wisc.) voted against the amendment, and Langer's opposition stemmed not from objections to the measure but from his hope that Bricker and the administration might work out a compromise if they had more time. In order to give other members of the committee a chance to record their positions, the senators decided to wait ten days before forwarding their recommendation to the full Senate. During that interval Senator McCarran (D-Nev.) voted for the resolution and Senator Hennings (D-Mo.) voted against it, making the final count 9-5 in favor of the amendment, with Senator Dirksen (R-Ill.), who had supported the proposal in the subcommittee, unrecorded. There was some indication, however, that the amendment's backing might not be as solid as it seemed. Under pressure from administration officials, Senator Hendrickson qualified his vote for the resolution by reserving the right to oppose it after further study.[33]

[32]See Bricker to Senator Taft, June 29, 1953, and enclosed memorandum on the "Effect of the 'which' clause of S.J. Res. 1"; Bricker to Senator Magnuson, July 21, 1953; and Holman to Bricker, June 26, 1953; all in JBP, Boxes 92 and 95, OHS. Quotation is from interview with Senator Bricker, June 30, 1975.
[33]See New York *Herald Tribune,* June 5, 1953, pp. 1, 24; Washington *Post,* June 5, 1953, p. 2; *New York Times,* June 5, 1953, pp. 1, 9, and June 16, 1953, pp. 1, 13; Bernard Shanley Diary, June 3, 1953; and Hendrickson to Shanley, June 5, 1953; Shanley to Hendrickson, June 11, 1953; and Hendrickson to Shanley, June 16, 1953; all three in DDEP, OF 116-H-4. On Dirksen's support for the amendment in the subcommittee, see summary of telephone conversation, Senator Langer to Secretary Dulles, May 1, 1953, in "Telephone Conversations, Dulles."

The amendment's supporters on the committee explained in their majority report why they favored the resolution. They asserted that evidence presented at the hearings "certainly establishes that there exists no express limitation on the treatymaking power," and that the rights of the states were "in jeopardy of destruction by abuse of the treatymaking power and liberal application of the decision in the case of *Missouri v. Holland*." In addition, they contended that the many "improper and unwise" executive agreements entered into in recent years had clearly shown that Congress should have the authority to supervise and regulate such agreements as well. Moreover, they stressed, "it would be absurd . . . to limit the treatymaking power without attaching comparable limitations to the executive agreement-making power," because presidents with any common sense would simply circumvent the restrictions imposed on treaties by using executive agreements instead. In order to close all these "loopholes" in the Constitution, the senators recommended that S.J. Res. 1 "be favorably considered by the Senate of the United States."[34]

In a minority report, Senators Kefauver, Kilgore, Hennings, and Wiley set forth their reasons for voting against the proposal. They maintained that the hearings had "convincingly demonstrated the complete lack of need for any constitutional amendment" limiting the treaty-making power. If an international agreement threatened the rights of the American people, they emphasized, the proper course of action would be to reject that particular covenant. They believed that the judiciary committee's deliberations had revealed that all of the measures that had been considered, including the text recommended by their colleagues, contained "serious pitfalls." Approval of such an amendment, they warned, would "leave the United States as a nation stripped of a part of the normal attributes and necessary powers of sovereign nations," and "reduce the President to a mere figurehead in foreign affairs, unable to deal effectively or with dispatch in matters which may be of the utmost urgency."[35]

Senator Langer refused to join in either the majority or minority reports on S.J. Res. 1. He had voted against the measure at the request of Senator Taft, the Republican majority leader, in an attempt to give Bricker and administration officials a chance to reach a compromise on the wording of the amendment. As he explained in a separate statement attached to the committee report, he recognized the concerns that had alarmed the resolution's proponents. Since the amendment "so vitally affects the operation of the office of the President and the whole executive branch," however, he thought every effort should be made to draft a measure that the administra-

[34]U.S., Congress, Senate, Committee on the Judiciary, *Constitutional Amendment Relative to Treaties and Executive Agreements*, S. Report 412, 83d Cong., 1st sess., June 15, 1953, pp. 1–34, esp. pp. 25, 30, and 33–34.
[35]Ibid., pp. 35–54, esp. pp. 35, 45, 48, and 53–54.

tion, too, would support. He believed it was premature to send the amendment to the floor when the two sides might yet work out their differences.[36]

By the time the judiciary committee completed its consideration of S.J. Res. 1, the battle lines had been clearly drawn. On one side were John Bricker and many of his Senate colleagues, Frank Holman and the leaders of the ABA, and representatives of various business organizations, patriotic societies, and isolationist and right-wing groups. As Holman had testified before the subcommittee, they believed that a constitutional amendment was needed to protect the rights of the American people and prevent Congress from enacting legislation, under the guise of implementing agreements such as the UN Charter, on "all manners of social, economic, and property matters which in the absence of a treaty the Congress would have no right under the Constitution to deal with."[37]

On the other side, the Eisenhower administration now led the opposition to the amendment. Spokesmen for the New York City Bar Association, organized labor, and other groups had attacked the resolution too, but the administration's opposition was the key. Dulles, Brownell, and the others had praised Bricker and the ABA for alerting the country to the problems that might arise if treaties were not carefully scrutinized, but, they had stressed, by taking from the president the powers he needed to conduct the nation's foreign affairs safely and effectively, the amendment would create new dangers even more hazardous than those it sought to eliminate. Therefore, they had urged senators to reject the measure.

Based on the results in the judiciary committee, however, the administration's efforts against S.J. Res. 1 had failed completely. The committee had not only approved Senator Bricker's proposal, but it had made the measure even more objectionable by recommending a text that included the "which" clause. Despite the administration's opposition to the amendment, only two of the committee's eight Republicans had voted against reporting it favorably to the floor, and Senator Langer had voted against it only because he wanted to give the president and his advisers more time to work out a compromise with the resolution's proponents. The committee's actions indicated that the administration needed a new strategy if it hoped to keep the Bricker amendment from becoming part of the supreme law of the land.

---

[36]Ibid., p. 55; and Langer to Vice-President Nixon, February 18, 1954, Nixon Papers, Vice-Presidential Series, "Bricker Amendment."

[37]*Hearings, 1953*, p. 1225.

CHAPTER SEVEN

Compromise?

In June of 1953, as the Senate Judiciary Committee was approving S.J. Res. 1, members of the Eisenhower administration and John Bricker resumed their negotiations. Both sides were willing to make some concessions, but the "which" clause still loomed as the major stumbling block to reaching an agreement. Many of Bricker's supporters saw that provision as the heart and soul of the amendment, but the president and his advisers detested it. A summary of a telephone conversation between the president and the attorney general reflected the administration's hostility when it referred to the provision as the *"witch"* clause—a Freudian slip no doubt. This disagreement would have to be settled somehow if a compromise were to be effected.[1]

I

Both John Bricker and Frank Holman worried that the administration's opposition to S.J. Res. 1 might cause various senators who had endorsed the amendment to change their minds. Holman reported that he had heard that Senators Potter (R-Mich.), Beall (R-Md.), Smith (R-N.J.), and Smathers (D-Fla.) were wavering, and he pointed out there was no guarantee that all sixty-four senators who had cosponsored the proposal would vote for it when it reached the floor. Holman believed the matter had moved beyond the legal issues to the point where officials at the State Department and others within the executive branch now felt their "pride and prestige" were involved as well. He feared that administration officials

[1]Summary of telephone conversation between the president and the attorney general, December 18, 1953, DDEP, Diary Series.

would do everything they could to persuade senators to vote against the Bricker amendment.[2]

Despite the administration's clear and emphatic opposition to S.J. Res. 1 at the hearings, Holman still hoped that the president himself might be persuaded to support the measure, or at least remain neutral in the battle. The manner in which Eisenhower had opposed the amendment at his press conferences, basing his objections on the secretary of state's analysis of the resolution and its probable effects, had left some doubt as to the president's own position. In a letter to Bricker in mid-May, Holman recalled that when he and Al Schweppe had talked with the president in February, Eisenhower had agreed that treaties should not be used to override constitutional rights. Holman believed, therefore, that the fact that Dulles was opposed to S.J. Res. 1 did not necessarily mean that Eisenhower was opposed to it. He suggested that Bricker meet with the president and urge him to make a public statement clarifying his position. If nothing else, perhaps such a meeting would keep the president from "falling into the 'trap' of being importuned by Mr. Dulles or others to come out with a damaging statement at the time the matter reaches the floor of the Senate for a vote."[3]

Bricker advised against any efforts to solicit a public statement from the president. He realized the administration's active opposition jeopardized the amendment, and he was still hoping to win its support. As he explained to Holman, however, this was "a difficult and delicate undertaking which could easily be upset by the intervention of those who do not have all the facts or full knowledge of the political factors involved." In Bricker's judgment, bringing pressure on the president at this time would force him to "back up Secretary Dulles by reaffirming his opposition to the amendment."[4]

Rather than publicly challenging the administration, Bricker preferred to try working quietly behind the scenes to soften the opposition. He reminded Vice-President Nixon that S.J. Res. 1 had the support of almost every Republican senator. Ever since he had introduced the amendment in January, Bricker emphasized, he had repeatedly asked administration officials to give it serious consideration and suggest modifications or improvements, but the president's advisers had not offered any constructive ideas. Nevertheless, the senator told Nixon, he still hoped the administration would "show some willingness to arrive at a compromise of this vital

[2]See Holman to Bricker, April 13, 1953; Holman to Charles Webb, May 20, 1953; Holman to Clarence Manion, May 20, 1953; and Bricker to Holman, May 27, 1953; all in JBP, Boxes 91 and 92, OHS.

[3]Holman to Bricker, May 21, 1953, JBP, Box 92, OHS.

[4]Bricker to Holman, May 27, 1953, JBP, Box 92, OHS.

problem" and align itself with "the overwhelming majority of Republicans."[5]

When the Senate Judiciary Committee approved the revised text of S.J. Res. 1, Bricker claimed that the new amendment met "all valid criticisms" that had been advanced against the previous proposals and conformed completely with the administration's treaty-making policy as explained by Dulles at the hearings. The senator argued that the most controversial part of his original amendment—the section prohibiting international organizations from exercising authority over the rights of American citizens or matters within the domestic jurisdiction of the United States—had been dropped from the measure. According to Bricker, the amendment as now worded merely limited the internal effects of treaties; it would have no effect on treaties dealing only with foreign affairs, and thus would not hinder the president "in the performance of his vital foreign affairs responsibilities." Adopting this amendment, Bricker maintained, would ensure that the present administration's policy of opposing treaties involving the nation's internal affairs would be "preserved in perpetuity."[6]

The senator's description of his amendment highlighted those aspects of the resolution that were in accord with administration policy. Other provisions remained, however, to which the administration objected. The president's advisers had made clear in the hearings their opposition to the "which" clause. In addition, the provision in the amendment giving Congress the right to regulate executive agreements was seen as a violation of the doctrine of separation of powers that would, in Dulles's words, tie the president's hands in wartime and leave the nation "incapable of taking care of itself in the world today."[7]

II

In early June, members of the administration discussed how to proceed on the Bricker amendment. Secretary of State Dulles and Attorney General Brownell both thought the measure could be defeated if Eisenhower stood firm. But the Republican Senate leaders, particularly William Knowland of California and Eugene Millikin of Colorado, warned the

[5]Bricker to Nixon, May 26, 1953, Nixon Papers, Vice-Presidential Series, "Bricker Amendment." See also Bricker to Senator Smith (N.J.), May 12, 1953, and May 29, 1953, Smith Papers, Box 123.

[6]*New York Times,* June 5, 1953, pp. 1, 9; and Bricker to Henry Luce, July 10, 1953, JBP, Box 95, OHS. To compare S.J. Res. 1 as introduced by Bricker with the text approved by the judiciary committee, see Appendixes D and F.

[7]Minutes of cabinet meeting of June 5, 1953; and memorandum by the secretary of state to the president, June 14, 1953; both in *Foreign Relations, 1952–54,* I, 1813–14, and 1816–17.

president and his advisers not to underestimate the resolution's support in the Senate, and they urged administration officials to work out a reasonable compromise with Bricker. Dulles believed, however, that constitutional principles were involved that could not be compromised, and he did not see any way in which the amendment could be modified to render it harmless. The president agreed that a compromise would be ill-advised, but he was concerned about the proposal's strong backing in the Senate. The cabinet decided, therefore, that Brownell and State Department Legal Adviser Herman Phleger should try to work out an "alternative solution" that would not be a compromise, but would enable interested senators to save face by adopting some sort of resolution.[8]

The president and his aides determined that this alternative solution should be an amendment stating explicitly that treaties and executive agreements could not violate the Constitution. They believed that such an amendment merely reiterated the existing situation, but they were willing to accept it in order to settle the whole matter. This was as far as they would go, however. They would not support any resolution that included the "which" clause or gave Congress the power to regulate executive agreements.[9]

Attorney General Brownell conveyed the administration's proposal to Bricker, but the senator was noncommittal. Brownell tried to reassure him that even if he lost the support of the ABA, the administration would "get behind the compromise to get it ratified." Bricker wanted more time, though, to study the administration's proposal.[10]

The president met with Bricker on June 16 to discuss S.J. Res. 1. Eisenhower explained that although he still believed that no amendment was needed, he would accept one making it clear that international agreements could not override the Constitution. Such a measure would not cause any real harm and would calm people's fears about the treaty-making power. The president told Bricker that he was delegating the attorney general to work with the senator on the actual wording of the resolution, and he hoped a reasonable compromise would be reached in the near future.[11]

---

[8]Memorandum by the assistant to the president to the director of the Bureau of the Budget, June 4, 1953; memorandum of telephone conversation between the secretary of state and the attorney general, June 4, 1953; and minutes of cabinet meeting of June 5, 1953; all in *Foreign Relations, 1952–54,* I, 1811–14. See also Dulles to Phleger, June 11, 1953, Phleger Collection, Vol. 9.

[9]See Bernard Shanley Diary, June 12, 1953.

[10]See memorandum of telephone conversation between the secretary of state and the attorney general, June 16, 1953, quoted in *Foreign Relations, 1952–54,* I, 1818.

[11]Bernard Shanley Diary, June 12 and 16, 1953; and Eisenhower, memorandum for the record, July 24, 1953, in Ferrell, ed., *The Eisenhower Diaries,* p. 248.

Bricker left the meeting with the president hopeful that the dispute over his amendment would soon be ended, with Eisenhower endorsing the measure after some minor revisions. As presidential counsel Bernard Shanley noted in his diary, the senator "was walking on air as he thought the President was going to capitulate or, in any event, go along with what he demanded as the minimum language in the Bricker resolution." But Shanley thought Bricker was being "over-bullish," for he doubted that the president would concede anywhere near as much as Bricker seemed to be anticipating.[12]

After further negotiations with Bricker, administration officials, too, believed that a settlement was near—but on their terms. Bricker and Brownell met on June 17, and the attorney general later reported to Dulles that Bricker was "about beaten." According to Brownell, Bricker had accepted a compromise amendment that basically reiterated the Constitution's supremacy over international agreements, and he had also agreed that a study group would be set up to consider the whole problem. Bricker had asked Brownell to draft the actual proposal and then clear it with George Finch, a Washington attorney and member of the ABA's Committee on Peace and Law Through United Nations.[13]

Despite the optimism on both sides, it soon became apparent that they were still far from an agreement. Brownell thought that Bricker had abandoned the "which" clause, and thus he drafted a resolution without such a provision. Brownell's amendment would have nullified international agreements that conflicted with the Constitution, authorized the courts to determine when such a conflict existed, and required roll-call votes in the Senate on all treaties. In addition, the proposal stipulated that the Senate could require subsequent congressional legislation before a particular treaty went into effect within the United States.[14]

Much to the administration's dismay, however, Bricker refused to yield on the "which" clause. He offered to eliminate the section of the amendment giving Congress the right to regulate executive agreements, but he would not drop the "which" clause. Although he himself had previously voiced many of the same objections that administration officials were now raising, Bricker feared that eliminating the "which" clause would cost him

[12]Shanley Diary, June 16, 1953.
[13]Memorandum of telephone conversation between the secretary of state and the attorney general, June 17, 1953, in "Telephone Conversations, Dulles."
[14]Ibid.; memorandum of telephone conversation between the secretary of state and the attorney general, June 24, 1953, in *Foreign Relations, 1952–54*, I, 1819; and Herbert Brownell to Vice-President Nixon, July 2, 1953; Brownell to Mr. Rankin, July 2, 1953; and "Revision of Bricker Amendment," July 2, 1953; all three in Nixon Papers, Vice-Presidential Series, "Bricker Amendment." See Appendix G for complete text of the resolution proposed by the administration.

the support of the ABA and those senators who regarded the clause as "the heart of the amendment." Moreover, he worried that the states would have little incentive to approve the amendment if it "enabled Congress to destroy the Federal-State relationship by legislating in pursuance of a treaty." He was willing to add a proviso to the resolution giving Congress the right to implement agreements relating to the rights and privileges of foreigners in the United States, but other than that, he insisted that the "which" clause remain intact.[15]

Bricker had good reason to be concerned that his followers might desert the cause if he abandoned the "which" clause. Frank Holman advised him that "it would be 'less than half a loaf'" if the Senate were to adopt an amendment without the "which" clause. Without such a restriction safeguarding the American people, Holman asserted, Congress could, in implementing a treaty, "avoid all constitutional restraints, . . . destroy all states' rights," and transform the United States into "a government of legislative absolutism." The "internationalists" would be able "to put us into a world government merely through a treaty and the implementation thereof by Congress." Similarly, W. L. McGrath warned that the elimination of the "which" clause "would be a serious threat to the sovereignty of the individual states, and an invitation to socialistically minded 'economic planners' to continue to try to achieve, by convention ratification, legislation which would not be obtained in the usual way. In short, the same old loophole would still be there."[16]

Administration officials remained adamant in their opposition to the "which" clause. The president's advisers contended that such a provision, even if amended to permit Congress to implement traditional treaties of friendship, navigation, and commerce, would still cause "irreparable damage" to the nation by making it impossible for the United States to enter into agreements to control narcotics or atomic weapons, settle the claims of American citizens against foreign governments, or protect the rights of American soldiers overseas. Dulles in particular argued that the "which" clause "cuts the treaty power back to what it was under the Articles of Confederation," leaving the federal government without the authority to enter into various compacts with other nations "except by the agreement of

[15]See Charles Webb, legislative assistant to Senator Bricker, to Frank Holman, June 17, 1953, JBP, Box 92, OHS; transcript of telephone conversation between the attorney general and the president, June 23, 1953, DDEP, Diary Series; memorandum of telephone conversation between the secretary of state and the attorney general, June 24, 1953, in *Foreign Relations, 1952–54*, I, 1819; Bricker to Senator Taft, June 29, 1953, and Bricker to Holman, July 22, 1953, both in JBP, Boxes 92 and 95, OHS; and Brownell to Senator Knowland, July 14, 1953, Phleger Collection, Vol. 9.

[16]Holman to Bricker, June 26, 1953; and McGrath to Senator Taft, July 6, 1953; both in JBP, Boxes 92 and 95, OHS.

the forty-eight states." Neither the administration nor Bricker would give in, and negotiations between them reached an impasse.[17]

Actually, President Eisenhower misunderstood the implications of the "which" clause, believing it "would completely wreck the traditional and prescribed balance between the executive and the legislative branch in the making of treaties." In fact, the "which" clause would not have affected the balance of power between the president and Congress. Rather, it was aimed at preventing the federal government as a whole from infringing on the reserved powers of the states. Eisenhower's misinterpretation probably stemmed from the fact that while Bricker and his supporters sought through S.J. Res. 1 mainly to limit the impact of international agreements on domestic matters, the president and his advisers saw the amendment primarily as an attempt to limit the executive's power in foreign affairs. Parts of the amendment, particularly the restrictions on executive agreements, certainly would have had that effect, and, as can be seen in many of their later accounts of the struggle over the amendment, that aspect of the resolution dominated the thinking of members of the administration.[18]

The president eventually realized that the "which" clause threatened the powers of the federal government as a whole rather than just the executive branch, and he then opposed it on the grounds that it would make it impossible for the United States to encourage and protect American businesses operating overseas. As he explained to his brother Edgar, "one of the most desperate needs of the free world today is *more international trade*." The United States, he pointed out, needed other nations to absorb its industrial and agricultural surpluses and provide raw materials. American business firms were "ready and anxious to invest abroad," but they demanded first that the government enter into treaties protecting them against expropriation. Such treaties were traditionally made on a reciprocal basis, with the United States granting to foreign nationals the same privileges it was seeking for American citizens. The president feared, however, that if the Bricker amendment and the "which" clause were adopted, then the federal government would be unable to protect for-

[17]Brownell to Senator Knowland, July 14, 1953, in Phleger Collection, Vol. 9; memorandum by the secretary of state to the president, June 14, 1953, and memorandum of telephone conversation between the secretary of state and the attorney general, June 24, 1953, both in *Foreign Relations, 1952–54*, I, 1816–17 and 1819; and transcript of Secretary Dulles's press conference, June 30, 1953, Carl McCardle Papers, Box 6, DDEL. See also comments by Senator Bricker in 99 *CR* 10824 (1953).

[18]Eisenhower, memorandum for the record, July 24, 1953, in Ferrell, ed., *The Eisenhower Diaries*, p. 248. For the view by administration officials that the Bricker amendment was aimed primarily at limiting the president's powers in foreign affairs, see Hughes, *The Ordeal of Power*, p. 143; Adams, *Firsthand Report*, pp. 104–9; and Eisenhower, *Mandate for Change*, p. 284.

eigners' property against expropriation or eminent domain proceedings by state and local authorities. Consequently, few nations would enter into such agreements with the United States, and American businesses would have to curtail their overseas operations.[19]

As Bricker kept insisting that the resolution had to include the "which" clause, administration officials became more and more incensed at his intransigence and his refusal to endorse any proposal not acceptable to Holman and the leaders of the ABA. Dulles charged, with some justification, that Bricker "was a prisoner of the little Bar Association group" that had originally drafted the provision, and, as a result, had thrown away his chance to work with the administration on this matter. Similarly, the president thought that Bricker had introduced the amendment "as his one hope of achieving at least a faint immortality in American history," but was now demanding that the "which" clause be retained because of the influence of "a certain fearful section of the American Bar Association."[20]

Nonetheless, administration officials realized they could not ignore the strong support in the Senate for the Bricker amendment, especially since public opinion seemed to favor the resolution as well. Knowland and the legislative leaders advised that most of the Republicans in Congress backed the proposal, and Secretary of Agriculture Ezra Taft Benson and others reported that the amendment enjoyed broad support at the grass roots level. As the president told his cabinet, he was "quite concerned about the complete readiness of the Republican Party to tear us apart" on this matter, and therefore he sought some way to reassure both the legislators and the public that the treaty-making power would not be abused. At the same time, however, he did not want to hamstring the federal government and the executive branch in their conduct of foreign affairs.[21]

At this point, Brownell suggested and the president agreed that the best way to proceed would be to get one of the Republican Senate leaders to sponsor a harmless substitute amendment that Eisenhower would then

[19]Dwight Eisenhower to Edgar Eisenhower, January 12, 1954, DDEP, Diary Series. On Eisenhower's belief in the importance of raw materials and foreign markets, see also Griffith, "Dwight D. Eisenhower and the Corporate Commonwealth," p. 94.

[20]Memorandum of telephone conversation between the secretary of state and the attorney general, June 24, 1953, in *Foreign Relations, 1952–54,* I, 1819; and Eisenhower, memorandum for the record, July 24, 1953, in Ferrell, ed., *The Eisenhower Diaries,* p. 248. See also interview with Herbert Brownell, June 23, 1975.

[21]See minutes of cabinet meeting of June 5, 1953, in *Foreign Relations, 1952–54,* I, 1813–14; Benson to the president, June 30, 1953, DDEP, Diary Series; Malcolm Champlin to Maxwell Rabb, June 11, 1953, DDEP, GF 3-A-5; and transcript of telephone call from the attorney general to the president, June 23, 1953, DDEP, Diary Series. For more on public opinion, see Chapter 8, below.

endorse. The attorney general began discussing the possibility with the congressional leaders, and at a press conference on July 1, President Eisenhower announced that he had modified his position with respect to the Bricker amendment. Although he still did not believe that treaties could circumvent or override the Constitution, the president declared that he would support an amendment specifically incorporating that principle into the Constitution. He was taking this action, Eisenhower explained, to "quiet fears anywhere in this whole country" that treaties could threaten the rights of the American people. The president emphasized, however, that he would "never agree to anything that interferes with the constitutional and traditional separation of powers."[22]

III

During this period, the controversy over the NATO Status of Forces Agreement further complicated the struggle over the Bricker amendment. This multilateral treaty was designed to supersede a number of executive agreements that had defined the legal status of troops of one signatory when they were stationed in another. Specifically, it gave American military officials primary jurisdiction over American soldiers in Europe who violated local ordinances in the line of duty. American servicemen who committed crimes under any other circumstances, however, would be subject to the legal system of the host nation, with the proviso that local authorities give "sympathetic consideration" to requests that they waive their rights and allow the American military justice system to handle such incidents. In other words, an American G.I. in France who was charged with robbery or driving while intoxicated would have to face judicial proceedings in a French court unless his actions had occurred in the line of duty or the French waived their rights and turned him over to American military authorities.[23]

President Eisenhower strongly supported the Status of Forces Agreement. He had been the military commander of NATO when the pact had been signed in 1951, and he considered it essential to America's defense

[22]Transcript of telephone call from the attorney general to the president, June 23, 1953, DDEP, Diary Series; memoranda of telephone conversations between the secretary of state and the attorney general, June 24 and 30, 1953, in *Foreign Relations, 1952–54,* I, 1819 and 1822; president's news conference, July 1, 1953, in *Public Papers: Eisenhower, 1953,* pp. 469–70; Arthur Krock in *New York Times,* July 2, 1953, p. 22; and Brownell to Vice-President Nixon, July 2, 1953, Nixon Papers, Vice-Presidential Series, "Bricker Amendment."
[23]For the text of the NATO Status of Forces Agreement, see 99 *CR* 8724–28.

program. When he transmitted the treaty to the Senate in February, 1953, he emphasized its importance in providing "a workable, equitable, and desirable framework for NATO activities."[24]

Critics of the agreement charged, however, that the State Department had bartered away the constitutional rights of American servicemen. Alfred Schweppe of the ABA and Senators Bricker, Knowland, and Langer argued that international law provided that soldiers stationed in a foreign country with the host nation's consent were immune from local laws and could be disciplined only by their own authorities. They maintained, therefore, that the Status of Forces Agreement, by subjecting American troops to foreign courts in some instances, had deprived the soldiers of their rights to a jury trial, the presumption of innocence until proven guilty, and protection against cruel and unusual punishments. Schweppe also warned that this treaty set a dangerous precedent. He noted that in some Moslem countries a person's hand might be cut off for certain crimes, and he questioned the legality of exposing draftees to such tortures if similar covenants were negotiated with those nations.[25]

Administration officials, on the other hand, held that the treaty safeguarded the rights of American servicemen stationed in Europe. The attorney general showed that there really was no generally accepted rule of international law on this issue. Previous agreements varied considerably, he explained, including a recent treaty among Great Britain, France, Belgium, the Netherlands, and Luxembourg that completely rejected the idea of exempting foreign troops from local prosecution. Since the Status of Forces Agreement gave American military officials dominion over offenses committed in the line of duty and required the European nations to consider sympathetically requests that they waive their jurisdiction, Brownell concluded that the convention afforded the soldiers more protection than they would have in its absence.[26]

In an attempt to ensure that the Status of Forces Agreement was consistent with his proposed constitutional amendment and would not abrogate any of the rights of American servicemen, Senator Bricker suggested a reservation to the treaty. Unlike some of his colleagues, who wanted the United States to have jurisdiction over both foreign soldiers in the United

[24]See president's message to the senate, February 27, 1953, in 99 *CR* 1487. See also minutes of cabinet meeting of March 20, 1953, DDEL; Eisenhower to Senator Knowland, July 14, 1953, DDEP, Administrative Files, Box 30, "NATO"; and Shanley Diary, March 20 and 23, 1953.

[25]See Schweppe to Bricker, May 4, 1953, JBP, Box 92, OHS; *New York Times,* April 8, 1953, p. 14; and 99 *CR* 4659–74.

[26]Brownell, "International Law and the Status of Forces Agreement," May 27, 1953, DDEP, OF 116-H-3(1). See also "Criminal Jurisdiction over American Armed Forces Abroad"; and Re, "The NATO Status of Forces Agreement and International Law."

States and American forces stationed overseas, Bricker was willing to extend to others the same rights in the United States that he sought for American troops in NATO countries. Thus he proposed a reservation to the agreement that would give American military authorities exclusive jurisdiction over American forces in Europe, and, in return, give the NATO allies authority over any of their troops who might commit criminal offenses in the United States.[27]

Administration officials realized immediately that Bricker had ensnared himself in a difficult position demonstrating the incompatibility of the Status of Forces Agreement and the Bricker amendment. State Department Legal Adviser Herman Phleger noted that in trying to reconcile the treaty with S.J. Res. 1, Bricker had made the agreement exactly like those that would be blocked by his amendment, since his reservation would deprive the states and localities of "their normal jurisdiction over crimes committed in their territories." Moreover, Phleger pointed out, Bricker's reservation would leave the United States without the authority to bring to justice a foreign soldier who assassinated the president or committed some other grievous offense. Administration officials feared, however, that senators, seeing the conflict between the treaty and the Bricker amendment, might reject the former because of their support for the latter.[28]

The president and his advisers waged an all-out fight to win approval of the Status of Forces Agreement without any reservations. Eisenhower described the pact to the Senate as a "necessary part of the new machinery we need to carry forward the vital program for the integrated defense forces of the North Atlantic Treaty Organization." Chairman of the Joint Chiefs of Staff Omar Bradley, Secretary of Defense Charles E. Wilson, and Undersecretary of State Bedell Smith all emphasized that same point when they testified in favor of the treaty before the Senate Committee on Foreign Relations. Just before the Senate was to vote on Bricker's reservation, Eisenhower sent a public letter to Senator Knowland, which the senator read to his colleagues. The president urged senators to approve the agreement without any amendments or qualifications, declaring that such

[27] 99 CR 4320; Washington *Times-Herald*, May 5, 1953; and Bricker to Senator Saltonstall, May 15, 1953, copy in Gerald Morgan Records, A67-19, Box 8, DDEL. See also the comments by Senator Willis Smith in *Hearings, 1953*, pp. 961–63.

[28] Herman Phleger to Bernard Shanley, May 6, 1953, and enclosed memorandum re: Proposed Bricker Reservation to NATO Status of Forces Treaty, DDEP, OF 116-H-3(1); Phleger to Dulles, April 8, 1953, Phelger Collection, Vol. 9; Bricker to Schweppe, May 20, 1953, JBP, Box 92, OHS; and Shanley Diary, June 29, 1953. According to Bernard Shanley, Bricker once admitted to Herman Phleger at a cocktail party "that he didn't care about the Status of Forces Treaty and that all he was interested in was the Bricker Amendment." See Shanley Diary, May 8, 1953.

action would be "a great forward step toward cementing the mutual security effort among the nations of the free world." On the other hand, he warned, rejecting the treaty or attaching reservations "could result in undermining the entire United States military position in Europe."[29]

On July 14, 1953, the Senate defeated Bricker's reservation to the Status of Forces Agreement by a vote of 53-27. This test of strength indicated that the treaty enjoyed considerable support, but administration officials still worried that it might fall one or two votes short of the two-thirds required for approval. On the final vote the following day, however, thirteen senators (seven Republicans and six Democrats) who had favored Bricker's reservation now sided with the administration, and the treaty was approved 72-15. Senator Hendrickson spoke for many of the thirteen when he explained that it was only because of his "unfailing faith in the President" that he would, "with reluctance," support the Status of Forces Agreement. The only votes against the treaty came from isolationist Republicans such as William Jenner, and a few southern Democrats.[30]

Proponents of the Bricker amendment asserted that the ratification of the Status of Forces Agreement provided further proof that a constitutional amendment was needed to protect the rights of the American people. Bricker argued that the treaty's approval showed that the nation could not rely upon the president and the Senate to reject an agreement that deprived American citizens of their constitutional rights. One group supporting the amendment even circulated a pamphlet with a picture of the severed hand of a man allegedly tried and convicted in a foreign court for stealing firewood. The leaflet warned that "THIS COULD HAPPEN TO YOUR SON, BROTHER OR HUSBAND" unless the Bricker amendment were adopted to prohibit treaties and executive agreements allowing American soldiers to be tried in foreign courts! Similarly, Hearst's New York *Daily*

---

[29]President's message to the Senate, February 27, 1953, in 99 *CR* 1487; U.S., Congress, Senate, Committee on Foreign Relations, *Agreements Relating to the Status of the North Atlantic Treaty Organization, Armed Forces, and Military Headquarters, Hearings,* before the Committee on Foreign Relations, Senate, 83d Cong., 1st sess., 1953; and President Eisenhower to Senator Knowland, July 14, 1953, in 99 *CR* 8779. See also minutes of cabinet meetings of March 20 and May 29, 1953, both in DDEL.

[30]99 *CR* 8782, 8837–38; and *New York Times,* July 16, 1953, pp. 1, 3. The thirteen senators who had supported Bricker's reservation but voted for the agreement in the end were: Senators Bennett (R-Utah), Bridges (R-N.H.), Cordon (R-Ore.), Eastland (D-Miss.), Hendrickson (R-N.J.), Hunt (D-Wyo.), Johnson (D-Colo.), Langer (R-N.D.), Magnuson (D-Wash.), McClellan (D-Ark.), Symington (D-Mo.), Watkins (R-Utah), and Young (R-N.D.). Those who voted against the treaty were: Senators Bricker (R-Ohio), Dirksen (R-Ill.), Dworshak (R-Id.), Frear (D-Del.), Jenner (R-Ind.), Johnston (D-S.C.), Long (D-La.), Malone (R-Nev.), McCarran (D-Nev.), McCarthy (R-Wisc.), Russell (D-Ga.), Schoeppel (R-Kan.), Smathers (D-Fla.), Welker (R-Id.), and Williams (R-Del.).

Mirror seized upon the case of Private Richard Keefe to mobilize support for the Bricker amendment. The editors claimed that Keefe, an American soldier, had been sentenced by a French court to five years in prison for stealing a taxicab, and charged that Keefe's harsh punishment represented "another instance of legislating away the rights of American citizens by treaty." The only way to prevent such occurrences in the future, they advised, was to "pass the Bricker amendment!" What the editors had omitted from the story, however, was that, according to a spokesman for the Army, Keefe had received the harsh sentence because he and another soldier had "very nearly strangled the driver to death" while stealing the taxi.[31]

The Senate's approval of the Status of Forces Agreement had important implications for the fight over the Bricker amendment. As the *New York Times* observed, the treaty's ratification marked "a significant foreign policy victory" for the president; he had committed his influence and prestige to the battle, and he had triumphed with votes to spare. Moreover, the debate over the treaty had illustrated some of the debilitating effects the Bricker amendment would have, such as preventing the United States from entering into the Status of Forces Agreement. The question now was whether the administration would follow up its victory with an all-out campaign against the amendment or continue its efforts to draft some sort of harmless substitute measure.[32]

IV

At the cabinet meeting on July 17, the president and his advisers considered their next move on the Bricker amendment. Dulles argued that the time had come to make up their minds "and stop being fuzzy on this"; they should arrange either to have the Senate delay action on S.J. Res. 1 until the following year, or they should make the president's position known "unequivocally" to all senators. Eisenhower denied that he had been fuzzy on this matter. He maintained that he had told Bricker that

[31]99 *CR* 8835; Phleger to Shanley, June 1, 1955, and enclosed pamphlet from the Texas Women for Constitutional Government, DDEP, GF 3-A-5; "The Tragedy of Pvt. Keefe," editorial, New York *Daily Mirror*, January 7, 1954, copy in Herbert Lehman Papers, Senate Legislative Files, "Bricker Amendment-Pro"; and Lt. Colonel Tench Tilghman to Senator Lehman, January 26, 1954, copy attached to memorandum from Julius Edelstein to Coleman Rosenberger, February 10, 1954, Harley Kilgore Papers, Box 25, FDRL. See also excerpts from Paul Harvey news broadcasts, July 18 and August 1, 1954, included as extension of remarks of Senator Bricker, August 6, 1954, 100 *CR* A5833 (1954).
[32]*New York Times*, July 16, 1953, pp. 1, 13; and Shanley Diary, July 15, 1953.

"we'd go just so far and no further." Dulles complained, however, that the president may have told that to Bricker, but he had not told it to anybody else.[33]

Dulles and Mutual Security Director Harold Stassen both urged that the administration try to defeat the Bricker amendment once and for all. They had beaten Bricker decisively on the Status of Forces Agreement, and they were confident they could do it again on S.J. Res. 1 if they mobilized all their resources. Eisenhower noted, however, that public opinion had been aroused on this issue, and he worried that simply defeating the Bricker amendment might not be enough to quiet the agitation for it. Attorney General Brownell and Vice-President Nixon warned that a full-fledged battle over the measure would split the Republican party. They thought that Bricker, in view of the Senate's rejection of his position on the treaty, might now be willing to accept the administration's substitute proposal. The cabinet agreed, therefore, that Brownell should continue his talks with Bricker and the Senate leaders to see if they could agree upon a satisfactory text.[34]

In an effort to work out a compromise, Brownell, Dulles, and Bricker all attended the Senate Majority Policy Committee meeting on July 21. The attorney general and the secretary of state informed the senators that the administration would support the following amendment as a substitute for the resolution recommended by the judiciary committee:

> Section 1. A provision of a treaty or other international agreement which conflicts with the Constitution shall not be of any force or effect. The judicial power of the United States shall extend to all cases, in law or equity, in which it is claimed that the conflict described in this amendment is present.
> Section 2. When the Senate consents to the ratification of a treaty the vote shall be determined by yeas and nays, and the names of the persons voting for and against shall be entered on the Journal of the Senate.
> Section 3. When the Senate so provides in its consent to ratification, a treaty shall become effective as internal law in the United States only through the enactment of appropriate legislation by the Congress.

This was the same text that Bricker had turned down a few weeks earlier because it did not include the "which" clause.[35]

[33]Hughes, *The Ordeal of Power*, p. 144; and minutes of cabinet meeting of July 17, 1953, in *Foreign Relations, 1952–54,* I, 1823–24.

[34]Minutes of cabinet meeting of July 17, 1953, in *Foreign Relations, 1952–54,* I, 1823–24. See also memorandum of telephone conversation between the secretary of state and the attorney general, July 17, 1953, ibid., pp. 1824–25.

[35]See "Resume of Meeting of the Senate Majority Policy Committee," July 21, 1953, copy in JBP. See also Brownell to Nixon, July 2, 1953, Nixon Papers, Vice-Presidential Series, "Bricker Amendment."

Bricker had not changed his position because of the defeat of his reservation to the Status of Forces Agreement, and he again rejected the administration's proposal. He reiterated what he had told Brownell previously—he would not accept any amendment that left the reserved powers of the states subject to further encroachments by the federal government under the guise of implementing compacts with other nations. He would support this resolution only if the following language was inserted instead of section 3:

> A treaty or other international agreement shall become effective as internal law in the United States only through legislation which would be valid in the absence of a treaty, except that Congress shall have power to make effective as internal law provisions of a treaty relating to the rights and privileges of aliens in the United States.

Such a provision was unacceptable to the administration, however, so the talks remained deadlocked over the "which" clause.[36]

At this point, the president and his advisers decided to proceed on their own without Senator Bricker. As Brownell had suggested a few weeks earlier, administration officials asked Senator Knowland, acting majority leader, to introduce their proposal as a substitute for the judiciary committee's text. Knowland agreed to do so, and on July 22, 1953, he formally introduced the resolution that Brownell and Dulles had offered at the policy committee meeting the previous day.[37]

In a public statement released that same afternoon, President Eisenhower announced his "unqualified support" for Knowland's substitute resolution. Eisenhower declared that he was still "unalterably opposed to any amendment which would change our traditional treaty-making power or which would hamper the President in his constitutional authority to conduct foreign affairs." He maintained, however, that the Knowland substitute would reassure the American people that treaties could not override the Constitution, and it would do so without interfering with the president's ability to carry out his responsibilities. Accordingly, Knowland's resolution enjoyed his full and complete support.[38]

The administration's role in sponsoring the substitute amendment infu-

---

[36]"Resume of Meeting of the Senate Majority Policy Committee," July 21, 1953, JBP. See also Bricker to Frank Holman, July 22, 1953, JBP, Box 95, OHS.

[37]Memorandum of telephone conversation between the secretary of state and the attorney general, June 24, 1953, in *Foreign Relations, 1952–54*, I, 1819; 99 CR 9757–58; Shanley Diary, July 22, 1953; and President Eisenhower, memorandum for the record, July 24, 1953, in Ferrell, ed., *The Eisenhower Diaries*, p. 248.

[38]"Statement by the President on a Proposed Amendment to the Constitution Relating to Treaties," July 22, 1953, *Public Papers: Eisenhower, 1953*, pp. 509–11.

riated Bricker and Holman. Bricker complained that White House officials and the majority leader had never told him that they were considering introducing the measure unilaterally. He denounced the resolution as "woefully inadequate and an obvious political trick to defeat the amendment that would really do the job." Holman condemned the proposal too and advised Bricker that "the time has come to take off the gloves and slug it out with the administration."[39]

Bricker detailed his objections to the Knowland substitute in a short speech to the Senate on August 1. He began very politely, stating that he was "deeply gratified that the President and administration leaders have concluded that some additional constitutional protection against treaties and executive agreements is desirable." He charged, however, that the substitute proposal had serious defects: it did not reaffirm Congress's right to regulate executive agreements; it would still allow most treaties to be self-executing and go into effect without subsequent legislation by Congress; and, most importantly, it would not prevent Congress from infringing on the reserved powers of the states when implementing treaties. Consequently, Bricker dismissed the substitute resolution as "unimportant, meaningless, and possibly very dangerous."[40]

Reluctant to attack Eisenhower directly, Bricker blamed the president's opposition to S.J. Res. 1 on bad advice that he must be receiving from "administration leaders." Bricker pointed out that Eisenhower was not a lawyer and was probably relying on the expertise of others who were, presumably, more knowledgeable about the legal and constitutional issues involved. The senator thought the president had been poorly served by his advisers, however. Even before the inauguration, Bricker recalled, he had asked members of the new administration to work with him and representatives of the American Bar Association to draft an acceptable amendment. But for months White House officials had contented themselves with criticizing proposals submitted by others and refused to offer any constructive ideas of their own. Only after the judiciary committee had recommended the resolution's adoption had the administration shown any inclination whatsoever to cooperate, and that had been in response to the force of public opinion in favor of the measure. And now, Bricker lamented, the administration had come forward with this "absurd" substitute proposal designed to delay action and confuse the whole issue. Nonetheless, Bricker professed great respect for the president and ex-

[39]See Bricker to Kenneth Ingwalson, July 27, 1953; Bricker to Dr. L. A. Alesen, July 27, 1953; Charles Webb to W. L. McGrath, July 27, 1953; Bricker to Senator John Marshall Butler, July 29, 1953; and Frank Holman to Bricker, July 28, 1953, all in JBP, Box 95, OHS.
[40]99 *CR* 10822–23.

pressed confidence that Eisenhower eventually would repudiate the Knowland resolution.[41]

Bricker never specified which "administration leaders" were supposedly leading the president astray. Years later, however, he blamed Dulles especially for Eisenhower's opposition, charging that the secretary of state had represented the bankers and lawyers in New York who "wanted to run the government through treaties . . . to protect themselves and the international trade." According to Bricker, the president's advisers had found picayune flaws in every proposal he had submitted, and Dulles had been "the head nit-picker in the whole bunch." Bricker believed that Dulles had "dominated the administration's position and finally converted them" against the amendment.[42]

Although it was true that the business and legal communities in New York played an important role in organizing the opposition to the Bricker amendment, it would be inaccurate to conclude that Dulles, as their representative, determined the administration's position. Brownell, Stassen, Secretary of Defense Wilson, and others within the administration also considered the amendment a threat to the president's authority to conduct the nation's foreign affairs and urged Eisenhower to oppose it. Moreover, the president himself, especially after the debate over the Status of Forces Agreement, believed the amendment would critically impede America's economic and military cooperation with its allies, and thus he did not need much convincing from his advisers to oppose it. Behind the scenes, Eisenhower played a much more active part in opposing the amendment than Bricker ever realized.[43]

Introduction of the Knowland substitute guaranteed that the Senate would not formally consider the Bricker amendment before recessing for the year. Debate over the various proposals promised to be a long and bitter affair, and the Senate adjourned in early August with the Bricker amendment among its unfinished business. Both sides hoped to use the

[41]Ibid., 10824–26. On the confusion generated by the introduction of the Knowland substitute, see for example Frances Barrett Lucas, executive secretary, Daughters of the American Revolution, to Senator Bricker, August 6, 1953, JBP, Box 95, OHS.

[42]Interview with Senator Bricker, June 26 and 30, 1975. See also Bricker to Brownell, April 2, 1953, JBP, Box 91, OHS; and memorandum of telephone conversation between the secretary of state and the attorney general, June 11, 1953, in *Foreign Relations, 1952–54,* I, 1815–16.

[43]See minutes of cabinet meeting of February 20, 1953; memorandum by the president to the secretary of state, April 1, 1953; minutes of cabinet meeting of April 3, 1953; and minutes of cabinet meeting of July 17, 1953; all in *Foreign Relations, 1952–54,* I, 1781–82, 1805–7, and 1823–24; President Eisenhower to Edgar Eisenhower, March 27, 1953, DDEP, Diary Series; and Dwight Eisenhower, memoranda for the record, April 1 and July 24, 1953, in Ferrell, ed., *The Eisenhower Diaries,* pp. 233–34, and 248.

time before Congress reconvened in January to mobilize public support for their respective positions.[44]

[44]See Bricker to Holman, July 22, 1953; Bricker to Dr. L. A. Alesen, July 27, 1953; and Charles Webb to W. L. McGrath, July 27, 1953; all in JBP, Box 95, OHS. See also Holman to Judge Harold Stephens, July 29, 1953, Stephens Papers, Box 19, Library of Congress.

CHAPTER EIGHT

Mobilizing for the Final Battle

After Congress adjourned in August 1953 without taking further action on the Bricker amendment, each side tried to take its case to the American people. John Bricker and the leaders of the American Bar Association continued their campaign to win support for S.J. Res. 1, while the Eisenhower administration and members of the Association of the Bar of the City of New York kept up their efforts to defeat the proposal. Others soon joined the fray, establishing organizations and committees to arouse support for, or opposition to, the Bricker amendment.

I

Although the proponents of S.J. Res. 1 had originally pushed for quick action, they now planned to use the time before Congress reconvened to their advantage. John Bricker believed that they could "take this fight to the people with a view toward impressing on all members of Congress by the first of next year the overwhelming grass-roots support for the Amendment," and he hoped that a demonstration of the strength behind the proposal might even lead the Eisenhower administration to drop its active opposition rather than risk a significant defeat. Similarly, Cincinnati businessman W. L. McGrath recommended that the amendment's supporters use the next several months to make clear to the American people that they needed the Bricker amendment to ensure that they were not "sold down the river by the internationalist group."[1]

Clarence Manion, former dean of the University of Notre Dame Law School and an ardent advocate of states' rights, first proposed in April 1953

[1]John Bricker to Frank Holman, July 22, 1953; and W. L. McGrath to Charles Webb, July 30, 1953; both in JBP, Box 95, OHS. See also Clarence Manion to Bricker, July 6, 1953; and Holman to Bricker, July 28, 1953; both in JBP, Box 95, OHS.

that a national committee be formed to aid in the fight for the Bricker amendment. Although registered as a Democrat, Manion had originally supported Robert Taft for the presidency in 1952, but he had endorsed Eisenhower after the Republican convention. Subsequently, he had delivered a nationwide radio broadcast urging people to vote for Eisenhower and the Republicans to prevent Stevenson, Acheson, and the Democrats from using treaties to extend the powers of the president and the federal government. As Manion later explained to Republican National Chairman Leonard Hall, he had worried about "the doctrine of treaty supremacy ever since it was gratuitously announced by Justice Holmes in *Missouri v. Holland,*" and he believed that "with the present propagation of UN treaties dealing with every intimate phase of American life, personal rights and States' rights may be riddled any moment." Manion became concerned when the Eisenhower administration opposed S.J. Res. 1 at the judiciary committee's hearings, and he suggested to Senator Bricker at that time that they set up some sort of committee to mobilize support for the amendment. They discussed how such a committee could be helpful in distributing "accurate and easily understood material" clarifying the legal and constitutional issues and coordinating the activities of organizations supporting the resolution, but neither of them took any specific actions to create such a committee.[2]

After the introduction of the Knowland substitute in July, however, Manion, Bricker, and McGrath began working in earnest to establish a national committee to promote the Bricker amendment. The senator forwarded to Manion a list of persons he thought might be willing to invest time and/or money in the effort to secure approval of S.J. Res. 1, and McGrath also began compiling lists of businessmen and others who might want to get involved. Manion thought that the committee, once it was formed, should use the next few months to "flood the country with truth about the Bricker amendment and the fault by omission and otherwise of the Knowland substitute."[3]

Manion knew that it would be expensive to establish a national committee in support of the Bricker amendment, so he sought to persuade various midwestern businessmen to help underwrite the costs. He prevailed upon Robert E. Wilson, chairman of the Standard Oil Company of Indiana, and A. W. Peake, president of the company, to invite prominent Chicago area industrialists and corporate leaders to a series of meetings to discuss

[2]See Manion to Leonard Hall, July 10, 1953; John Bricker to Manion, April 16, 1953; and Manion to Bricker, April 20, 1953; JBP, Boxes 95 and 91, OHS; Clarence Manion Oral History Transcript, pp. 40–41, 47–51, and 58–64, DDEL; and Manion, *The Conservative American,* pp. 71–125.
[3]Bricker to Manion, July 23, 1953; McGrath to Manion, August 10, 1953; and Manion to McGrath, August 28, 1953; all in JBP, Box 95, OHS.

setting up such an organization. At these meetings, Robert E. Wood, chairman of Sears, Roebuck and Company, Fred Gurley, president of the Santa Fe Railroad, and others heard Manion and Frank Holman describe the treaty-making power as a serious threat to the United States and American capitalism. Holman explained to the businessmen that international agreements on wages and labor conditions would become the law of the land if approved by the Senate, enabling Congress, under the doctrine of *Missouri v. Holland,* to enact additional regulations in implementing these agreements. Holman emphasized, however, that adoption of the Bricker amendment would nullify these threats.[4]

Impressed by Holman's and Manion's presentations, the businessmen agreed to help set up an organization to work for the adoption of the Bricker amendment. The Foundation for Study of Treaty Law that they established, however, proved to be fatally flawed from the start. Because they insisted on organizing it as an educational project so that all contributions would be tax deductible, the foundation had to present both sides of the issue in any literature it distributed or at any meetings it sponsored. This alienated many of the amendment's more zealous supporters, who refused to work with an organization that would allow speakers to criticize the resolution, no matter how controlled the setting. Having dedicated themselves to seeing the measure enacted, they would not get involved with or participate in any such nonpartisan endeavors, even though the foundation's publications and activities were all heavily weighted in favor of the amendment. Consequently, though the foundation did publish some pamphlets on the subject of treaty law, it never enjoyed much influence, even among the amendment's supporters.[5]

Although the Foundation for Study of Treaty Law foundered, Manion traveled across the country giving speeches in favor of the Bricker amendment, warning that treaties could take powers from the individual states and transfer them to the federal government or international organizations. He contended that such changes, by concentrating authority in the national government, "would grease the track for the success of the Communist conspiracy to take America from the inside."[6]

Despite Manion's outspoken advocacy of the Bricker amendment, Presi-

---

[4]See Manion to McGrath, August 28, 1953; and McGrath, memo, September 14, 1953; copies of both in JBP, Box 95, OHS; and Holman, *The Life and Career of a Western Lawyer,* pp. 561–63.

[5]See Vigilant Women for the Bricker Amendment to William Simon, November 28, 1953; and Frank Holman to W. L. McGrath, December 16, 1953; both in JBP, Box 96, OHS; Holman, *Western Lawyer,* p. 563; and Foundation for Study of Treaty Law, "Treaty Law Manual," esp. pp. 3–7, 59, copy in Lyndon Johnson Papers, Senate Papers, Work Papers of Gerald Siegel, 83d Cong., "Bricker Amendment," LBJL.

[6]See Clarence Manion, "The Cancer of Despotism: An Antidote—The Bricker Amendment," text of radio broadcast as substitute on Paul Harvey's ABC program, August 1953,

dent Eisenhower, in September 1953, appointed him chairman of a special Commission on Intergovernmental Relations. Manion had already testified in support of S. J. Res. 1 at the judiciary committee's hearings and had endorsed the measure in letters and telegrams to various officials; nonetheless, Eisenhower named him to head the new commission as a concession to the Taft wing of the party and a favor to House Majority Leader Charles Halleck of Indiana. The president and his advisers regretted this decision almost immediately, however, as Manion continued to devote most of his time to making speeches for the Bricker amendment. When a few commission members complained that Manion had failed to provide the leadership that the group needed, administration officials saw a way out of this embarrassing situation, and in mid-February 1954, White House chief of staff Sherman Adams, citing the commission's lack of progress, demanded Manion's resignation. Manion agreed and resigned officially at the commission's next meeting.[7]

The president's aides were concerned about Manion and his activities not only because of the embarrassment but because they feared his background, especially his long association with Notre Dame, and his anticommunist rhetoric would persuade large numbers of Catholics to support S.J. Res. 1. The president was already worried about possible problems with Catholic voters, who were seen as some of Senator McCarthy's staunchest supporters, and he did not want to alienate them on the Bricker amendment. Hence, administration officials were relieved to learn from Monsignor Howard Carroll, general secretary of the National Catholic Welfare Conference, that Manion's views on the Bricker resolution were "diametrically opposed to the nearest thing there is to an official Catholic position" on the

---

Economic Council Papers, Vol. 8, No. 8, November 15, 1953, copy attached to memorandum from Bernard Shanley to General Carroll, December 3, 1953, DDEP, OF 116-H-4. See also Herman Phleger to Shanley, October 30, 1953; and memorandum from Shanley to Sherman Adams, November 3, 1953; both in DDEP, OF 116-H-4; and Mrs. Franklin Moore to President Eisenhower, November 6, 1953, DDEP, GF 190-A.

[7]On Manion's early support for the Bricker amendment, see Manion to the president, March 2, 1953, DDEP, GF 3-A-5; and *Hearings, 1953,* pp. 809–23. On Manion's appointment to head the Commission on Intergovernmental Relations, see Charles Halleck to Sherman Adams, July 14, 1953; and Manion to Adams, August 10, 1953, and attachments; DDEP, GF 190-A and OF 239; and Manion Oral History Transcript, pp. 42–46, and 50–56, DDEL. On the administration's displeasure with Manion and his eventual firing, see Shanley to Adams, November 3, 1953; and Shanley to General Carroll, December 3, 1953, and attachments; both in DDEP, OF 116-H-4; Gabriel Hauge to Adams, October 27, 1953; and John E. Burton to Dean Manion, October 24, 1953; both in DDEP, OF 239; Shanley Diary, December 18, 1953; Manion to Adams, February 8, 1954; and Manion to President Eisenhower, February 17, 1954; both in DDEP, OF 239; President Eisenhower's news conference, March 10, 1954, *Public Papers: Eisenhower, 1954,* p. 302; *Time* Magazine, February 8, 1954, p. 16; and Manion Oral History Transcript, pp. 69–73.

measure. Carroll reported that the Catholic Association for International Peace, whose honorary chairman was Archbishop O'Boyle of Washington, D.C., had, through one of its subcommittees, issued a public statement arguing that the Bricker amendment was both unnecessary and ill-advised, and that the president and the Senate could be relied upon to reject any treaties or covenants that jeopardized the rights of the American people. In terms of Catholic opinion, the administration could also take solace in the fact that the editors of *America,* the national Catholic weekly, were waging a vigorous campaign in the magazine against S.J. Res. 1 on similar grounds.[8]

In addition to Manion and the Foundation for Study of Treaty Law, newspaper publisher Frank Gannett and his Committee for Constitutional Government worked to build support for the Bricker amendment. Originally founded in 1937 as the National Committee to Uphold Constitutional Government, the organization had been established by Gannett and others to oppose Franklin Roosevelt's court-packing plan. Subsequently, it had fought against FDR's attempt to reorganize the executive branch of the federal government, national legislation regulating wages and hours, and the Roosevelt policy of aiding Britain and France before Pearl Harbor. Now, in 1953 and 1954, the committee sent out millions of letters and telegrams to legislators, businessmen, and others on its "screened list of opinion molders across the nation," bought full-page advertisements in the *Wall Street Journal,* and sponsored radio broadcasts urging people to support the Bricker amendment. Committee spokesmen called S.J. Res. 1 the "gravest constitutional issue of our time," and asked for financial contributions to help in the committee's "nationwide mobilization like that which helped save [the] independence of [the] Supreme Court."[9]

[8]See Sherman Adams to Bernard Shanley, September 28, 1953; Shanley to Monsignor Carroll, October 15, 1953; Carroll to Shanley, October 22, 1953, and enclosed statement of the subcommittee on juridical institutions, Catholic Association for International Peace, "The Bricker Resolution: Restricting Conduct of U.S. Foreign Relations," April 5, 1953; Shanley to John Foster Dulles, October 28, 1953; and Shanley to Herbert Brownell, October 30, 1953; all in DDEP, OF 116-H-4. On the opposition of the editors of *America* to the Bricker amendment, see "Associated Press Pushes Bricker Bill," *America,* January 17, 1953, 88: 413–14; "The Bricker Amendment," *America,* March 7, 1953, 88: 615; "Bricker Opponents Unite," *America,* January 9, 1954, 90: 374; "How Much to Give Bricker?" *America,* January 30, 1954, 90: 429; and "Warning: The Treaty Boobytrap Ahead," *America,* February 6, 1954, 90: 465. See also the articles by *America* associate editor Fr. Edward A. Conway, S. J., "Straight-Jacketing the Treaty Power," *America,* March 14, 1953, 88: 647–49; and "'Darling Daughter' Amendment," *America,* January 23, 1954, 90: 415–17.
[9]See Committee for Constitutional Government to Wilmer Thomson, May 5, 1953, copy in Edward Corwin Papers, Chronological Files, Princeton University Library. See also Frank Gannett to Senator Wiley, June 5, 1953, copy in JBP, Box 92, OHS; Committee for Constitutional Government to Senator Harley Kilgore, February 1954, and enclosed copy of full-page advertisement from the *Wall Street Journal,* February 15, 1954, p. 13, Kilgore Papers, Box 24,

In their appeals on behalf of S.J. Res. 1, leaders of the Committee for Constitutional Government urged people to enlist in "the battle to safeguard our Constitution" against "the dangers and menace of treaty law." Sumner Gerard, treasurer and trustee of the committee, warned that "the socialists abroad, and some from this country, are planning to use treaty law to undermine our Constitution and Bill of Rights, taking us step by step into international socialism." Specifically, he charged that organized labor, "with its hundreds of millions of dollars of annual income, knows that its pet project, socialized medicine, can be brought to the USA, without action by Congress, by the backdoor method of treaty law." The committee also mailed out reprints of an article by Senator Bricker entitled "United Nations Treaties: A Threat to the Freedom of the American People," and an essay by Frank Holman detailing the reasons "Why *You* Should Support the Bricker Amendment." In a letter accompanying Holman's piece, Gerard compared it to the *Federalist Papers*. As the writings of Hamilton, Madison, and Jay had persuaded the nation in 1787 to ratify the Constitution, Gerard hoped that Holman's tract would persuade people to protect that Constitution now by adopting the Bricker amendment.[10]

The fear that socialized medicine might come to the United States through an international agreement also led many physicians and their professional organizations to lobby for the amendment. As an article in the *Columbus [Ohio] Academy of Medicine Bulletin* explained, doctors worried that "under the present law it would be entirely possible for socialized medicine, as well as many other equally undesirable things, to be foisted upon the American people through ratification by the Senate of treaty commitments made in the United Nations organizations, including the International Labor Organization." Consequently, the American Medical Association and other physicians' groups passed resolutions opposing ILO covenants calling for minimum standards of health care and sickness

FDRL; Samuel Pettengill, "Why the Bricker Amendment Should Be Adopted," radio address sponsored by the Committee for Constitutional Government and broadcast by the Mutual Broadcasting System, February 14, 1954, copy in JBP, Box 100, OHS; and Committee for Constitutional Government to Doctor and/or Fellow Citizen, attached to Dr. Peter Kornfeld to Senator Herbert Lehman, March 7, 1956, Lehman Papers, Legislative Files, "Bricker Amendment," Columbia University.

[10]Sumner Gerard to Friend and Fellow American, January 1954, and attached article, Frank Holman, "Why *You* Should Support the Bricker Amendment," "Spotlights," C-249–252, Zechariah Chafee, Jr. Papers, Box 11, Harvard Law School Library; and John Bricker, "United Nations Treaties: A Threat to the Freedom of the American People," "Spotlight," No. 89, copy in Sterling Cole Papers, Box 42, Cornell University Library.

benefits, and pressed for the enactment of S.J. Res. 1. Dr. Edward McCormick, president of the AMA, assured Senator Bricker that "doctors at the grass roots in every state in the Union are supporting . . . your bill to prevent the United States from getting into trouble by treaties which transgress the fundamentals of our Constitution."[11]

Many conservative business, patriotic, and religious organizations endorsed the Bricker amendment too, hoping it would ensure that international agreements could not affect domestic matters within the United States. Representatives of both the United States Chamber of Commerce and the National Association of Manufacturers asserted that compacts and covenants emanating from the UN and the ILO threatened the free enterprise system, and that S.J. Res. 1 had to be adopted to preserve it. A spokesman for the American Legion declared that his group was proud to be part of "the tremendous movement in the United States to limit the treaty power by clearly written law," and the leaders of the Daughters of the American Revolution could not understand "why any United States Senator would hesitate to vote for a resolution which will protect American rights under the Constitution." The Christian Parents for Better Education were confident that the Bricker amendment would pass "to safeguard our Republic" because they knew that "God is directing our efforts."[12]

One organization requiring special mention is the Vigilant Women for the Bricker Amendment. In August 1953, eight women from Wisconsin and Illinois met in Milwaukee to discuss what they could do on behalf of S.J. Res. 1. Mostly housewives and clubwomen active in such groups as the Daughters of the American Revolution and the Minute Women, they were concerned that the UN and the ILO were trying to impose international controls over the American people and the American economy, and they believed that the Bricker amendment was essential to protect individual liberties, states' rights, and national sovereignty against this threat.

[11]*Columbus [Ohio] Academy of Medicine Bulletin,* 19 (March 1953), p. 41, attached to letter from Dr. Claude Perry to Senator Bricker, n.d.; and Dr. Edward McCormick to Bricker, July 25, 1953; JBP, Boxes 91 and 95, OHS. See also the resolutions on international treaties and covenants acted upon by the House of Delegates, American Medical Association, December 1952, enclosed with letter from Lee Garling, business manager, Washington office, AMA, to President Eisenhower, February 27, 1953, DDEP, GF 3-A-5.

[12]See *Hearings, 1953,* pp. 530–65, 571–91, and 596–600; Ray Murphy, "Which Constitution Do We Want?" *American Legion Magazine,* February 1954; and Daughters of the American Revolution to Senator Kilgore, July 30, 1953; both in Kilgore Papers, Box 25, FDRL; and Christian Parents for Better Education to Senator Lehman, June 16, 1953, Lehman Papers, Departmental Files, 1952–53, "Bricker Amendment." See also the "List of Legislatures, Bar Associations and Important Lay Organizations that have taken Official Action in Support of a Constitutional Amendment on Treaties and Executive Agreements," JBP, Box 110, OHS.

In order to rouse public support for the resolution among the women of the nation, they formed the Vigilant Women for the Bricker Amendment.[13]

The organization's members worked vigorously on behalf of the proposal. They wrote to senators to determine how the legislators intended to vote on S.J. Res. 1; at meetings of the Daughters of the American Revolution and other such groups they circulated petitions calling on the president and Congress to support the measure; and in January 1954, more than 600 representatives of the organization came to Washington to lobby for the amendment. They conferred with senators who were wavering or doubtful and tried to persuade them to back the resolution, and a few of them even met briefly with President Eisenhower, trying to convince him that the amendment was needed to eliminate the danger lurking in the treaty-making power. The highlight of their efforts in Washington came when they presented Senator Bricker with their petitions, tied in bundles with red, white, and blue ribbons, and bearing more than 300,000 signatures.[14]

Some notable individuals also spoke out in favor of the Bricker amendment. Phyllis Schlafly, then just beginning her career as a political activist and champion of conservative causes, contended in 1953 that a constitutional amendment invalidating "the pernicious doctrine of *Missouri v. Holland* . . . is the most important and necessary legislation that the present Congress can pass." Columnist Raymond Moley, a former adviser to Franklin Roosevelt, asserted that S.J. Res. 1 was needed to counter "the fallibility of an unrestrained executive and bureaucracy" and to prevent treaties from radically altering the American economy and society. Former governor and future senator Strom Thurmond of South Carolina thought that the measure should be adopted to protect states' rights. Right-wing Texas oil millionaire H. L. Hunt argued that the amendment would safeguard the people "against capricious laws which the members of Congress

[13]On the background and formation of the Vigilant Women for the Bricker Amendment, see U.S., Congress, Senate, Committee on the Judiciary, *Treaties and Executive Agreements, Hearings,* before a Subcommittee of the Committee on the Judiciary, Senate, 84th Cong., 1st sess., 1955 (hereinafter referred to as *Hearings, 1955*), pp. 422–24; and Milwaukee *Journal,* January 29, 1954, p. 2. On the group's concerns and beliefs, see Vigilant Women to Senator Lehman, January 6, 1954, Lehman Papers, Legislative Files, "Bricker Amendment"; and pamphlet, "Facts about the Vigilant Women for the Bricker Amendment," n.d., Thomas Hennings Papers, Folder 7485, University of Missouri Library.

[14]Vigilant Women for the Bricker Amendment to Senator _____, January 6, 1954, JBP, Box 100, OHS; Ruth Murray to Tom Stevens [sic], January 21, 1954, DDEP, OF 116-H-4; *New York Times,* January 26, 1954, p. 14; Washington *Post,* January 26, 1954, p. 23; and Milwaukee *Journal,* January 29, 1954, p. 2.

would not enact," but which might come into effect through treaties and presidential agreements.[15]

As in the congressional hearings of 1953, many of those who urged lawmakers in Washington to support the Bricker amendment also denounced the United Nations, an indication of the proposal's appeal to isolationists. One woman condemned the UN as a "diabolic plot of international conspirators to destroy the national sovereignty of the United States of America," while another claimed that it had been the UN that had kept the United States from winning a military victory in Korea. A California man emphasized that the Bricker amendment had to be adopted to "protect us from the many, many treaties prepared . . . by that hydra-headed monster the United Nations and all of its many specialized agencies," and he recommended that the American people "get the U.S. out of the UN and the UN out of the U.S." Similarly, another woman advocated "an immediate withdrawal from this anti-Christ dominated United Nations," charging that "when the Congress of the United States accepted the one-CommUNist world inspired and Alger Hiss written Charter of the United Nations Organization, they betrayed their God and their Country and violated their OATH of OFFICE, as Senators and Congressmen, to UPHOLD the CONSTITUTION."[16]

II

Dana Backus of the Association of the Bar of the City of New York believed that the opponents of S.J. Res. 1 needed some sort of national committee to show that there was considerable opposition to the Bricker amendment and to help lead the fight against the measure. He had discussed the possibility of forming such an organization with Professor Zechariah Chafee, Jr., of Harvard University in May 1952, but neither of them had followed up on the idea. After the Senate Judiciary Committee approved S.J. Res. 1 in June 1953, however, Backus sent out an "Alert and

[15]Phyllis Schlafly to Senator Kilgore, February 24, 1953, Kilgore Papers, Box 25, FDRL; Raymond Moley, "The Bricker Amendment," address before the Cleveland Bar Association, February 10, 1954, copy enclosed with letter from Senator Bricker to Senator George Aiken, February 15, 1954, Aiken Papers, Crate 31, Box 1, University of Vermont Library; Strom Thurmond to Bricker, February 26, 1953, JBP, Box 91, OHS; and H. L. Hunt, letter to the editor, *New York Times,* March 11, 1954, p. 30.

[16]Nancy Applewhite to Senator McCarthy, n.d., copy in Kilgore Papers, Box 24, FDRL; Edith Miller to President Eisenhower, February 4, 1954, DDEP, GF 3-A-5; Carroll Hampton to Senator Kilgore, May 28, 1953; and Mrs. L. S. Malcolm to Kilgore, January 5, 1954; both in Kilgore Papers, Box 24, FDRL.

Call to Action" to friends he knew from his days as a student at Harvard and attorneys he had met over the years. Backus warned that Bricker's proposal represented "an isolationist assault upon the power of the United States to conduct its foreign policy" that would "cripple the treaty-making power" and "hamper our leadership in the United Nations, in NATO, and in the world." He urged people to write their senators and congressmen to make known their opposition to the amendment.[17]

Shortly thereafter, Backus, Carlyle Maw, Lyman Tondel, Jr., and other leaders of the New York City bar began working to establish a formal committee to direct the campaign against the Bricker resolution. Encouraged by Herman Phleger of the State Department to create a central organization to coordinate opposition to the amendment, the New York group sought to enlist nationally prominent people whose prestige would increase the influence of the new association. Their first choice to head the committee was John W. Davis, who had just capped a distinguished legal career by successfully representing the steel companies in their suit contesting President Truman's seizure of the steel mills. The Democratic presidential nominee in 1924, Davis enjoyed a well-earned reputation as a brilliant corporate attorney and a committed constitutional conservative. He had been a leading critic of Franklin Roosevelt and the New Deal in the 1930s, and had even bolted the party in 1936 because of FDR's expansive view of the powers of the federal government and the presidency. Davis's involvement with the committee would mean that it could not be dismissed as a group of liberals who believed in unchecked federal and executive authority.[18]

Davis's interest in the treaty-making power actually dated back to his years as solicitor general during the Wilson administration in the 1910s. At that time, he had had to decide whether to appeal to the Supreme Court a lower court's ruling that a federal law regulating the hunting of migratory birds was unconstitutional. Davis had concluded that the federal government had no chance of winning the case, so he had suggested instead that

[17]Professor Chafee to Lyman Tondel, Jr., May 28, 1952, Chafee Papers, Box 11, Harvard Law School Library; Dana Backus, "An Alert and Call to Action," July 4, 1953, and attached statement by Backus, "Defend the Constitution: Beat the Bricker Amendment," copies in Will Clayton Papers, 1950–53, "Committee for Defense of the Constitution," HSTL; and in Dana Backus and Theodore Pearson, comps., "Collection of Reports and Documents on the Bricker Amendment" (hereinafter referred to as Backus Collection), Vol. 3, Association of the Bar of the City of New York Library; and interview with Dana Backus, May 19, 1976.

[18]Interview with Carlyle Maw, January 26, 1977; interview with Dana Backus, May 19, 1976; Herman Phleger to Lyman Tondel, Jr., September 3, 1953, Phleger Collection, Vol. 9. On John W. Davis's career, and particularly his opposition to the New Deal, see Harbaugh, *Lawyer's Lawyer*; and Schlesinger, *The Age of Roosevelt*, Vol. III: *The Politics of Upheaval*, pp. 311, 517–19.

the State Department negotiate a treaty with Canada to protect such birds, and that Congress then enact a new statute under its authority to pass all laws "necessary and proper" to carrying out the treaty. The administration had followed his recommendation, and in 1920 the Supreme Court had upheld the new law in its decision in *Missouri v. Holland.* As Bricker noted on an Edward R. Murrow "See It Now" broadcast in January 1954, Davis had helped bring about the court's decision in the migratory bird case, and the former solicitor general did not want to see that ruling reversed by a constitutional amendment. Davis was eager to help in the fight against S.J. Res. 1, but he did not feel that he could devote the time and energy necessary to serve as chairman, so while he agreed to join the committee, he recommended that Backus and the others find someone else to head the effort.[19]

The attorneys next approached Lucius Clay, former commander of American forces in Germany after World War II and one of the heroes of the airlift that had broken the Berlin blockade in 1948. Clay was now retired from the army and had become chairman of the board and chief executive officer of the Continental Can Company, and the lawyers thought his presence on the committee would demonstrate support from the business community. Moreover, because of Clay's close friendship with President Eisenhower, the attorneys knew that his participation would signify that the committee had the president's blessing. Clay was impressed with the caliber of the people involved in the project, and, after making sure that administration officials had no objections, he agreed to serve as a sponsor, although not as chairman, of the committee.[20]

That still left the committee without a chairman, and members of the Eisenhower administration became concerned over the delay in getting the committee organized. Administration officials preferred not to involve themselves directly in the committee's efforts, but the president and his advisers were anxious that the committee commence its work against the Bricker amendment as soon as possible. Consequently, Secretary of State Dulles began working behind the scenes to find a chairman for the committee, and on November 25, 1953, he asked Robert Lovett, a Wall Street banker who had been secretary of defense and undersecretary of state

---

[19]See transcript of "See It Now" broadcast, January 12, 1954, p. 10, JBP, Box 110, OHS. On Davis's early interest in the treaty-making power, see John W. Davis to John J. Davis, December 13, 1914, John W. Davis Papers, Yale University Library. On his role in *Missouri v. Holland,* 252 U.S. 416 (1920), see New York State Bar Association, *Proceedings of the 76th Annual Meeting, January 1953* (Albany: Fort Orange Press, 1953), pp. 99–100.

[20]Interview with Carlyle Maw, January 26, 1977; summary of telephone call, Secretary Dulles to the president, November 10, 1953, in "Telephone Conversations, Dulles"; and letter from General Clay to this author, December 21, 1976.

during the Truman administration. Lovett declined, however, and at the end of November the committee still had no chairman.[21]

The New York group then turned to Professor Edward Corwin of Princeton University, a noted legal scholar and one of the country's foremost authorities on the Constitution and the powers of the presidency. Corwin had denounced FDR's decision in 1940 to proceed without congressional consent in transferring American destroyers to Britain in exchange for bases on British territory in the Western Hemisphere, and he still believed that legislation should be enacted to prevent presidents from entering into such agreements without congressional approval. In his opinion, however, the Bricker amendment went too far; adopting the Bricker amendment to solve the problem of executive agreements, he declared, would be like "burn[ing] down the house to get roast pig." Corwin objected particularly to the "which" clause, which he feared "would gravely disable the treaty-making power as we have known it and lived under it for 164 years." Hence, when Carlyle Maw asked him to chair the committee against the Bricker amendment, Corwin accepted immediately. The leadership was now set, and the Commitee for Defense of the Constitution by Preserving the Treaty Power was formally established in December 1953, with Corwin as its national chairman, and Davis and Clay as cochairmen of a distinguished group of sponsors.[22]

The leaders of the committee sought to involve well-known and influential people from all over the country in the new organization to demonstrate that opposition to the Bricker amendment was nationwide and not confined to New York and Washington. Accordingly, they wrote to prominent attorneys, educators, and other "outstanding citizens" to ask them to participate in the fight against S.J. Res. 1. Among those who agreed to serve as sponsors of the committee were: James Brand, former chief justice of the Oregon Supreme Court; Harry Bullis, chairman of the board of General Mills in Minneapolis; Will Clayton, former undersecretary of state for economic affairs and a cotton merchant in Houston; Erwin Griswold, dean of Harvard University Law School; Palmer Hoyt, editor and publisher of the Denver *Post;* Jacob Lashly, a past president of the American Bar Association and a resident of St. Louis; Joseph O'Meara, Clarence Manion's successor as dean of the University of Notre Dame Law School; and Owen Roberts, former associate justice of the

[21]See summary of telephone conversation, Secretary Dulles to the president, November 10, 1953; summary of telephone conversation, Dulles to Dean Rusk, November 24, 1953; and summary of telephone conversation, Dulles to Robert Lovett, November 25, 1953; all in "Telephone Conversations, Dulles."

[22]Interview with Carlyle Maw, January 26, 1977; Edward Corwin, letter to the editor, *New York Times,* October 13, 1940, IV, 6–7; Corwin, *The President: Office and Powers,* pp. 288–89; and Corwin, "The President's Treaty Making Power," reprint from July 1953 issue of *Think,* p. 6, copy in Corwin Papers, "Bricker Amendment," Princeton University Library.

United States Supreme Court. The presence of such distinguished individuals and others like them on the committee's list of sponsors showed that many noted individuals whose opinions carried considerable weight were opposed to the Bricker amendment, making it easier for the Eisenhower administration and various legislators to justify and explain their own opposition.[23]

The committee concentrated its efforts on trying to persuade the president, administration officials, and individual senators to reject not only the Bricker amendment, but also any substitute measures that might be proposed. Clay, Corwin, and Davis all advised Eisenhower not to accept any "hasty political compromise," and distributed a circular imploring committee members to urge their congressmen to vote against the Bricker amendment and any other resolutions that might impair the nation's ability to conduct its foreign relations. Griswold and Roberts appeared with Bricker on "See It Now" to refute his arguments on the need for his amendment, and Clay warned in a letter to Senator Kefauver that the measure would have delayed, probably fatally, the agreements with Britain and France for the Berlin airlift. When negotiations were proceeding between administration officials and various senators in January 1954, Davis and Clay met with Brownell and Justice Department officials and counseled against accepting even a watered-down version of the Bricker amendment. The committee's leaders emphasized that the Constitution had served the nation well, and they saw no need to tamper with it in any way.[24]

[23]See Jefferson Fordham, dean of the University of Pennsylvania Law School, to Julius Edelstein, executive assistant to Senator Lehman, September 29, 1953, Lehman Papers, Special Files, "Fordham"; Frederick McKee to Mrs. Garwood, November 27, 1953; Will Clayton to McKee, December 10, 1953; McKee to Clayton, December 15, 1953; Carlyle Maw to Clayton, December 16, 1953, and enclosed "Plan of Organization for the Committee for Defense of the Constitution by Preserving the Treaty Power"; and Robert Eichholz to Clayton, December 23, 1953; all in Will Clayton Papers, 1950–53, "Committee for Defense of the Constitution"; Committee for Defense of the Constitution, press release for December 28, 1953, copy in Backus Collection, Vol. 3; and *New York Times,* December 28, 1953, p. 3. On the prestige and impact of the committee, see Arthur Krock in *New York Times,* December 29, 1953, p. 22; editorial, "Don't Shackle the President," San Francisco *Chronicle,* January 3, 1954, p. 16; editorial, "Bricker Opponents Unite," *America,* January 9, 1954, 90: 374; *New York Times,* January 18, 1954, p. 10; and Eisenhower, *Mandate for Change,* pp. 283–84.

[24]See Clay, Corwin, and Davis to President Eisenhower, February 3, 1954, DDEP, Diary Series; Committee for Defense of the Constitution to committee members, January 11, 1954, Backus Collection, Vol. 3; transcript of "See It Now" broadcast, January 12, 1954, copy in JBP, Box 110, OHS; Lucius Clay to Senator Kefauver, January 12, 1954, in 100 CR A344–45 (1954); John W. Davis to President Eisenhower, January 12, 1954; Eisenhower to Davis, January 18, 1954; Erwin Griswold to Eisenhower, January 9, 1954; and Eisenhower to Lucius Clay, February 9, 1954; all in DDEP, Diary Series; and summaries of telephone calls, Eisenhower to Brownell, January 9, 1954, and Bedell Smith to the president, January 28, 1954, both in DDEP, Diary Series.

Besides the Committee for Defense of the Constitution, other groups, including labor unions, church and civic organizations, and even a few bar associations, spoke out against the Bricker amendment. Representatives of the American Federation of Labor condemned S.J. Res. 1 as an attempt to "curb the treaty-making power of the government, cripple United States participation in the United Nations, and put a brake on U.S. action on Jim Crow laws." A spokesman for the CIO charged that the measure represented "an effort to turn the clock back to a period when the United States was a far less significant force in the world." The American Civil Liberties Union, the national board of the YWCA, the American Association for the United Nations, the American Jewish Congress, the League of Women Voters, and Americans for Democratic Action also opposed the amendment. And by January 1954, attorneys in Philadelphia, St. Louis, and Boston had joined the New York City bar in formally recommending the defeat of the Bricker amendment.[25]

Events at the ABA's convention in Boston in August 1953 also demonstrated that the nation's attorneys were far from unanimous in their support for the Bricker amendment. By a vote of 65 to 14, the Section of International and Comparative Law proposed that the ABA rescind its earlier endorsement of S.J. Res. 1 and urge instead that the measure be rejected. However, the House of Delegates defeated the section's motion 117–33, thereby reaffirming the organization's official support for the Bricker amendment. At that point, two young Boston lawyers, Stuart DeBard and future governor of Massachusetts Endicott Peabody, entered the fray. Later dismissed by Frank Holman as the "Harvard Rabble," DeBard and Peabody tried to carry the fight to the association's assembly. That body, comprised of all paid-up members of the ABA who were

[25]See AF of L *News-Reporter,* January 30, 1953, clipping in Hennings Papers, Folder 4787; Jacob Potofsky and Nathan Cowan to Senator Langer, March 6, 1953, copy in Kilgore Papers, Box 25, FDRL; American Civil Liberties Union, "Statement on the Constitutional Amendment to Limit Treaties—(S.J. Res. 1)," attached to letter from Ernest Angell, chairman of the board of directors, ACLU, to Senator Bricker, July 9, 1953, JBP, Box 95, OHS; Mrs. Edward Macy, president of the national board of the YWCA, to President Eisenhower, December 18, 1953, DDEP, OF 116-H-4; American Association for the United Nations, "Statement of Policy for 1952," April 27, 1952, copy in Dorothy Norman Papers, Box 83, Columbia University Library; Commission on Law and Social Action of the American Jewish Congress, "Memorandum on the Revised Bricker Resolution," July 2, 1953, copy in Senator Kilgore Papers, Box 25, FDRL; Mrs. John Lee, president of the League of Women Voters of the United States, to President Eisenhower, January 13, 1954, copy in Lehman Papers, Legislative Files; Americans for Democratic Action, "Legislative Newsletter," March 1, 1954, copy in Hennings Papers, Folder 4772B; Jefferson Fordham to Herman Phleger, December 10, 1953; Lon Hocker, president of the Bar Association of St. Louis, to Phleger, January 4, 1954; and Robert Haydock, Jr., to Phleger, January 26, 1954; all in Phleger Collection, Vols. 9 and 10; and editorial, "Against the Bricker Plan," St. Louis *Post-Dispatch,* December 21, 1953, p. 2-B.

registered for the convention, had the power to call for a referendum of
the entire membership of the organization if it differed from the House of
Delegates on an issue. After a long debate, the assembly refused to order a
polling of the members, but, as Peabody reported to Professor Chafee, the
clash had "shown up a real split in the Bar Association which will prevent
adherents of S.J. Res. 1 from saying that the ABA is completely for it."[26]

Although most of the business community supported the Bricker
amendment, leaders of corporations heavily involved in foreign trade vehemently opposed the resolution. State Department Legal Adviser Herman Phleger emphasized to the chairman of the board of the General
Electric Company and other business executives that the adoption of the
Bricker amendment would have a "disastrous effect" on companies en-
gaged in overseas commerce because it would make it impossible for the
United States to negotiate the traditional treaties of friendship and commerce that facilitated and protected such trade. It was not surprising,
therefore, that such men as Harry Bullis of General Mills and Will Clayton
joined the Committee for Defense of the Constitution, or that Sam Baggett, a vice-president of the United Fruit Company, expressed his concern
about the possible impact of S.J. Res. 1. The United States Council of the
International Chamber of Commerce warned specifically that the "which"
clause would "prevent the inclusion in treaties and agreements of many
provisions heretofore included for the protection and benefit of American
business interests," a view with which delegates to the National Foreign
Trade Convention concurred wholeheartedly.[27]

Many prominent individuals also denounced the Bricker amendment.
Eleanor Roosevelt rejected the notion that the draft covenant on human
rights and similar treaties posed a real threat to the United States, and
warned that the Bricker amendment, in response to this nonexistent
threat, would wreck the "carefully thought-out balance of powers" de-

[26]See ABA, Section of International and Comparative Law, Committee on Constitu-
tional Aspects of International Agreements, "Report on S.J. Res. 1 and the Knowland
Substitute Amendment," August 24, 1953, copy in Hennings Papers, Folder 4771; Endicott
Peabody to Professor Chafee, September 3, 1953, Chafee Papers, Box 11; Peabody to Senator
Kilgore, September 10, 1953, Kilgore Papers, Box 24, FDRL; interview with Endicott Pea-
body, November 10, 1976; and Holman, *Western Lawyer,* p. 530.

[27]Phleger to Philip Reed, chairman of the board, General Electric Company, September 8,
1953; Phleger to T. Brooke Price, November 10, 1953; and Sam Baggett to Phleger, May 4,
1953; all in Phleger Collection, Vol. 9; United States Council of the International Chamber of
Commerce, Inc., "The Effects of the Bricker Amendment on Commercial Treaties and
Agreements Benefiting American Business," January, 1954, copy in DDEP, GF 3-A-5; and
"Final Declaration of the 40th National Foreign Trade Convention," attached to letter from
Austin Foster, general counsel, Socony-Vacuum Oil Company, to Bernard Shanley, De-
cember 16, 1953, DDEP, OF 116-H-4. See also J. F. Drake, chairman of the board, Gulf Oil
Company, to Sherman Adams, January 25, 1954, DDEP, GF 3-A-5.

signed by the founding fathers in the Constitution. Adlai Stevenson called the measure "a dangerous, radical and unnecessary proposal" that reflected "a lack of confidence in the Senate itself, which must approve treaties by a two-thirds vote." Harry Truman labeled it a "vicious" bill that would "absolutely ruin any attempt of the President to carry out a foreign policy for the United States." Supreme Court Justice Felix Frankfurter encouraged a friend to "give most of your time on non-lucrative matters to the Bricker amendment until that most mischievous proposal is out of the way," and former assistant secretary of state Dean Rusk implored Senator Lehman to "use every Parliamentary and other means available to defeat said amendment." Socialist Norman Thomas charged that many of the amendment's proponents were motivated by their fear that a treaty might somehow undermine "the sacred doctrine of white supremacy," and Reverend Harry Emerson Fosdick of the Riverside Church condemned the resolution as "the most dangerous assault on the integrity of our Federal system that has been made in my lifetime." Finally, United States Circuit Court Judge John J. Parker of North Carolina stood one of the measure's supporters' favorite comparisons on its head when he warned that the Bricker amendment was "fraught with more danger to the institutions of our country than anything that has been brought forward since the court packing plan."28

III

Despite the efforts of the ABA, the AMA, the Foundation for Study of Treaty Law, the Committee for Constitutional Government, the Committee for Defense of the Constitution by Preserving the Treaty Power, and the Vigilant Women for the Bricker Amendment, Senator Bricker's resolution never became a burning issue to most Americans. According to a Gallup Poll released in October 1953, when people were asked if they had "heard or read anything about Senator Bricker's proposal of an amendment to the Constitution to limit the President's treaty-making power," 81 percent of the respondents replied that they had not. Those few who were

28Eleanor Roosevelt, "My Day," May 26, 1952, ERP, Box 3154, FDRL; Adlai Stevenson, "Statement on the Bricker Amendment," reprinted in Johnson, ed., *The Papers of Adlai Stevenson,* Vol. IV, pp. 317–19; *New York Times,* January 31, 1954, p. 26; Harry Truman to John W. Davis, December 30, 1953, copy in Corwin Papers, Chronological Files; Felix Frankfurter to George Roberts, January 25, 1954, Frankfurter Papers, Box 96, Library of Congress; Dean Rusk to Senator Lehman, January 9, 1954, Lehman Papers, Special Files, "Rusk"; Norman Thomas to Professor Corwin, February 9, 1954, Corwin Papers, "Bricker Amendment"; Reverend Fosdick to Senator Lehman, January 22, 1954, Lehman Papers, Special Files, "Fosdick"; and Judge Parker to Bernard Shanley, May 25, 1953, DDEP, OF 116-H-4.

familiar with the measure were divided, with almost as many against it as in favor.[29]

There were some indications that the Bricker amendment enjoyed widespread public backing, but closer examination reveals that the evidence is less than convincing. The Associated Press, for example, reported on December 27, 1952, that most incoming congressmen supported Senator Bricker's attempt "to prohibit the U.S. from entering into binding international agreements in such fields as human freedoms and social and economic rights." But, as the editors of *America* pointed out, the AP had actually asked the legislators if they believed "that the Constitution should be amended along the lines of the Bricker resolution to specify that treaties may never take precedence over rights and guarantees in the Constitution." The editors complained that such a question was "a gross oversimplification" of the issues involved, asserting that a differently phrased question, asking if people feared that President Eisenhower and the Senate would conspire to use the treaty-making power to weaken the rights and liberties of the American people, would have produced a very different result.[30]

Similarly, although the Vigilant Women for the Bricker Amendment gathered more than 300,000 signatures on their petitions in support of S.J. Res. 1, the petitions were so worded that even those who had never heard of the measure were likely to sign their names. The petitions warned that "proponents of world government" were trying "to destroy our national sovereignty, states' rights, and individual rights," and asked President Eisenhower and the Congress to "work for early adoption of the Bricker-American Bar Association Amendment . . . which has as its purpose the preservation of our basic freedoms." That may have been how the women involved viewed the amendment, but others certainly saw it very differently. Yet most people reading the petitions would have gladly endorsed the measure to protect their basic rights and freedoms.[31]

A review of incoming mail at the State Department, the White House, and the Senate Judiciary Committee reinforces the conclusion that the American people did not rise up in arms to demand the adoption of the

[29]See Washington *Post,* October 7, 1953, p. 13.

[30]"Associated Press Pushes Bricker Bill," *America,* January 17, 1953, 88: 413–14.

[31]See *New York Times,* January 26, 1954, p. 14. The figure of 300,000 signatures is from *Hearings, 1955,* p. 424. Similar examples of heavily pro-Bricker amendment responses generated by one-sided phrasings of the issues can be found in constituent polls conducted by Representatives George Bender (R-Ohio), Paul Schenck (R-Ohio), and Timothy Sheehan (R-Ill.). See "Bender Poll of Ohio Republican Workers Finds Bricker Amendment in Top Rating," press release from the office of Representative Bender, August 12, 1953, copy in Hennings Papers, Folder 4771; Thomas Calhoun to Bricker, December 21, 1953, Bricker Papers; and 100 *CR* A468.

Bricker amendment. Although the number of correspondents who favored the proposal far exceeded the number who opposed it, the volume of letters and cards received was relatively small in each case. When the judiciary committee held its hearings on S.J. Res. 1 in the spring of 1953, more than 500 people wrote to urge the legislators to approve the measure, while only 30 people recommended its rejection. In the ten days following Secretary Dulles's testimony against the amendment, the State Department received only 143 pieces of mail on the issue (121 in favor of the resolution, 22 against it). And in the weeks following President Eisenhower's announcement on July 1, 1953, that he was opposed to the Bricker amendment but would support a substitute resolution reaffirming the Constitution's supremacy over treaty provisions, 108 people wrote to the president to defend Bricker's proposal, while only four wrote in to express their opposition to the amendment. These lopsided tallies in favor of the resolution seem impressive, but it should be noted for the sake of comparison that senators reported receiving hundreds of letters each day during the court-packing fight in 1937, and almost 5,000 people wrote to President Truman in one week in 1949 to protest his program for "socialized medicine." Moreover, Eisenhower and his advisers received more than 50,000 letters, cards, and telegrams in one week in December 1953, in the midst of a dispute with Senator McCarthy over American aid to nations that traded with Communist China.[32]

Nonetheless, the communications received by the State Department and the judiciary committee revealed some interesting geographic patterns. Department of State officials noted that almost half the mail endorsing the Bricker amendment came from California, with most of the remainder coming from the Midwest, particularly Ohio and Illinois. They observed, however, that the arguments advanced for the resolution by those in the Far West differed significantly from those coming from the Midwest. Californians focused their comments on the dangers emanating from the United Nations and the need to limit the UN's activities; midwesterners, though, seemed to be more concerned with the general problems of "closing loopholes in the Constitution and ensuring a government of laws rather than men." As for the opponents of the Bricker amendment,

---

[32]See *Hearings, 1953*, pp. 1204–14; Howard Cook to Herman Phleger, "Public Comment on the Bricker Resolution," April 17, 1953, Phleger Collection, Vol. 9; and White House Mail—Weekly Reports, weeks ending July 10 and 17, 1953, DDEP, OF 72-A-12. On senators' mail during the court-packing fight, see Leuchtenburg, "Franklin D. Roosevelt's Supreme Court 'Packing' Plan," p. 77. On protests against Truman's national health insurance plan, see Cornwell, *Presidential Leadership of Public Opinion*, p. 246. On letters to Eisenhower during the controversy with McCarthy, see Donovan, *Eisenhower: The Inside Story*, p. 250; and *New York Times*, December 4, 1953, pp. 1, 2; December 7, 1953, p. 1; and December 10, 1953, p. 29.

half of those who wrote to the judiciary committee to criticize the measure lived in the New York City area. That fact, coupled with the Association of the Bar of the City of New York's key role in organizing the amendment's foes, led Senator Bricker to complain bitterly years later that New Yorkers had defeated his amendment—"New York and nobody else. . . . The bankers down there were opposed to it and the lawyers went along with them."[33]

A study of Senator Lyndon Johnson's (D-Tex.) mail on this issue also provides some important insights. Again, the cards, letters, and petitions were overwhelmingly in support of the measure, but George Reedy, Jr., one of the senator's chief aides, advised Johnson that almost all the communications in favor of the proposal were "pressure" mail "inspired by single sources." In particular, he reported, many doctors had written in after a bulletin distributed by the Association of Physicians and Surgeons had recommended that doctors urge their congressmen to vote for the resolution, and most of them had not even bothered to change the wording suggested by the organization. He further informed the senator that a number of the postcards had been addressed on the same typewriter, indicating that they had all been passed out at some sort of meeting. Reedy concluded that "the pro-Bricker amendment people are probably small in numbers," but they included some "extremely prominent personalities and important organizations, such as the medical societies." He believed, however, that "if a few people could be neutralized, the amendment would have no political importance whatsoever."[34]

As the controversy over the Bricker amendment neared its climax early in 1954, people became more aware of the resolution and more of them began to express their views on the proposal. A Gallup Poll in January 1954 showed that 28 percent of those surveyed had heard or read about the measure, 9 percent more than in October. This poll also indicated that 7 percent of the people now opposed the amendment and only 4 percent supported it, but the validity of these results is questionable because only people who were able to summarize the amendment correctly in the interviewer's judgment were asked to state their position on the resolution.[35]

More people were also writing to the president about the Bricker amendment in early 1954, and more and more of them were urging him to oppose the measure. More than 1,400 cards and letters on this issue were

[33]See Cook to Phleger, "Public Comment on the Bricker Resolution," April 17 and May 7, 1953, Phleger Collection, Vol. 9; *Hearings, 1953,* p. 1214; and interview with Senator Bricker, June 26 and 30, 1975.

[34]See memorandum, George Reedy, Jr., to Senator Lyndon Johnson, January 21, 1954, Johnson Papers, Senate Papers, "Bricker Amendment," LBJL.

[35]Gallup Poll reported in Washington *Post,* January 27, 1954, p. 11.

received at the White House during the week ending January 29, 1954. In contrast to the people who had written in 1953, most of whom had endorsed S.J. Res. 1, 886 people now argued against the amendment, and only 526 supported it. The following week, too, more people wrote opposing the measure than in its favor. Apparently, the Committee for Defense of the Constitution and others opposed to the Bricker amendment had succeeded in mobilizing more people against it than the Foundation for the Study of Treaty Law, the Committee for Constitutional Government, and other such groups had stirred in its favor.[36]

For the most part, however, the controversy over the Bricker amendment remained a dispute among politically active elites, dominated by lawyers, doctors, businessmen, and such organizations as the Daughters of the American Revolution and the American Association for the United Nations. Evidence indicates that despite all the activities of the Foundation for Study of Treaty Law, the Vigilant Women for the Bricker Amendment, the Committee for Defense of the Constitution by Preserving the Treaty Power, and all the rest, almost three-quarters of the American people had not heard and did not care very much about the Bricker amendment. Of those who were expressing their opinions, however, more and more were urging the resolution's rejection as the controversy wore on.[37]

[36]White House Mail—Weekly Reports, weeks ending January 29 and February 5, 1954, DDEP, OF 72-A-12.
[37]Gallup Poll reported in Washington *Post*, January 27, 1954, p. 11.

CHAPTER NINE

"The Mud and Dirt of France ...
and the Name of Senator Bricker"

I

While both supporters and opponents of S.J. Res. 1 mobilized for the upcoming Senate debate on the measure, members of the Eisenhower administration and Senator Bricker tried once again to reach a compromise. The president and his advisers were willing to consider a compromise to avoid a split within the Republican party, but they would not accept the "which" clause or restrictions on presidential prerogatives in foreign affairs. Bricker realized the difficulty of winning approval for any resolution in the face of an "all-out attack by the President," so he, too, sought to work out some sort of settlement. He met with Attorney General Brownell on October 5, 1953, and although they failed to resolve the substantive issues dividing them on the amendment, they "agreed on the necessity of agreeing."[1]

At a White House conference between administration officials and Republican congressional leaders and committee chairmen in mid-December 1953, Bricker again discussed S.J. Res. 1 with the president and his advisers. The senator reiterated that he had no desire to limit the president's authority to carry out the nation's foreign affairs, but was simply trying to protect the rights of the American people against the dangers posed by treaties and executive agreements. Everyone agreed that a compromise was needed to preserve party unity, and Senators Ferguson and Wiley were asked to meet with Bricker, Brownell, and Dulles to try to work out a satisfactory solution.[2]

[1]See Bricker to Representative Lawrence Smith, January 18, 1954; Charles Webb, legislative assistant to Senator Bricker, to Robert Minor, first assistant to the deputy attorney general, October 7, 1953; and Webb to Attorney General Brownell, October 7, 1953; all in JBP, Box 100 and Box 95, OHS.

[2]See notes on the Legislative Leadership Conference, December 17–19, 1953, p. 11, copy in Jack Martin Records, DDEL; Bernard Shanley Diary, December 18, 1953; and "Memoran-

At first, it looked as if Bricker and administration officials might be able to reconcile their differences. Recognizing that the "which" clause had been the major obstacle blocking agreement in previous negotiations, Charles Webb, Bricker's legislative assistant, informed presidential assistant Jack Martin that Bricker might be willing to eliminate that provision if a suitable legislative history could be developed during the debate over the amendment. Specifically, Webb suggested that a resolution stipulating that "a provision of a treaty or other international agreement which conflicts with this Constitution shall not be of any force or effect" might be acceptable to the senator if they could develop a legislative history ensuring that the amendment would be so construed as to prevent such agreements as the draft covenant on human rights from going into effect as internal law. Although Bricker would want to consult with the leaders of the American Bar Association, "both as a matter of courtesy and for the sake of insuring success of the amendment," the senator would drop the "which" clause if administration officials would agree that the remaining sections of the resolution would prohibit the use of international agreements to change social and economic conditions within the United States or surrender American sovereignty to an international organization.[3]

Now that the "which" clause apparently no longer constituted a major problem, executive agreements emerged as the primary point of contention. Bricker feared that any reference to "treaties or other international agreements" would give the impression that these were "interchangeable instruments of foreign policy." Moreover, although he was willing to see certain treaties go into effect immediately upon ratification, Bricker insisted that implementing legislation be required before executive agreements became the law of the land. Otherwise, he asserted, the president would be able to make internal law without Congress having any opportunity to accept or reject a particular agreement. Realizing that the restrictions on executive agreements accounted for much of the support for his amendment (and especially after compromising on the "which" clause) Bricker was reluctant to give in on executive agreements as well.[4]

Bricker continued to confer with administration officials into January 1954, as both sides still sought to reach a compromise. The senator and his

---

dum of Meeting with Congressional Leaders on the Bricker Amendment, December 19, 1953," *Foreign Relations, 1952–54,* I, 1826.
[3]Charles Webb to Jack Martin, "Possible Basis for Compromise on S.J. Res. 1," December 16, 1953, p. 1, copy in Gerald Morgan Records, A67-19, Box 2, DDEL.
[4]See memorandum, December 19, 1953, DDEP, OF 116-H-4; "Draft of December 28, 1953," copy in JBP; and Bricker to Jack Martin, January 7, 1954, JBP, Box 100, OHS.

legislative assistant discussed the matter with Attorney General Brownell and Senator Ferguson on December 28, and they met at the White House on January 7 with the president, Brownell, Dulles, Senators Ferguson, Knowland, and Wiley, and various staff aides. Dulles, Wiley, and State Department Legal Adviser Herman Phleger argued against any amendment, but Ferguson and Knowland pressed for an accommodation for the sake of party unity. Most of the conferees were willing to accept an amendment which stated explicitly the Constitution's supremacy over treaties and executive agreements and required implementing legislation before most agreements went into effect as internal law. They still disagreed, however, as to whether the states or Congress should have the power to implement such agreements, and whether the resolution should be phrased in such a way as to avoid implying that presidents could use executive agreements instead of treaties. When they failed to resolve these disputes, it was decided that Bricker, Brownell, and Ferguson would meet again the following day.[5]

At the meeting on January 8, Bricker, Brownell, and Ferguson finally arrived at a compromise solution. They agreed on an amendment stipulating that provisions of treaties or other international agreements that conflicted with the Constitution would not be of any force or effect, and that treaties should not be used to regulate matters normally under state or local jurisdiction unless they were related to the nation's foreign affairs. In addition, they agreed to drop the "which" clause from the measure and require only that treaties and executive agreements be implemented by congressional legislation before going into effect within the United States. According to the terms of the compromise resolution, the individual states would be involved in putting a treaty into force only when a particular treaty dealing with the rights of aliens so provided.[6]

This compromise amendment would have satisfied most of Bricker's original objectives. The new text would have confined treaties to foreign affairs issues, ensured that international agreements were not self-execut-

[5]See Charles Webb to Senator Ferguson, December 29, 1953, JBP, Box 96, OHS; draft urged by Bricker at White House meeting, January 5, 1954; draft prepared at White House, January 5, 1953 [sic, 1954]; draft dictated by Mr. Rankin, January 6, 1954; and memorandum from Charles Webb to Senator Bricker, January 7, 1954; all in JBP; Bricker to Jack Martin, January 7, 1954, and Bricker to Senator Knowland, January 7, 1954, both in JBP, Box 100, OHS; memorandum of conversation, by Jeffrey C. Kitchen of the executive secretariat, Department of State, January 8, 1954; and Senator Wiley to the president, January 8, 1954; both in *Foreign Relations, 1952–54*, I, 1827–29; and Frank Holman to Clarence Manion, January 9, 1954, copy in JBP, Box 96, OHS.

[6]See Holman to Manion, January 9, 1954, copy in JBP, Box 100, OHS; and supplementary notes on the Legislative Leadership Conference, January 11, 1954, by the assistant White House staff secretary, *Foreign Relations, 1952–54*, I, 1829–31. See Appendix H for the complete text of this resolution.

ing in terms of domestic law, and protected the constitutional rights and liberties of the American people by making it clear that treaties and executive agreements could not supersede or abrogate provisions of the Constitution. All in all, the compromise text would have achieved most of what Bricker had set out to accomplish, and it would have done so without hamstringing the president and the executive branch in their conduct of foreign affairs.

After returning to Ohio and conferring with Frank Holman, however, Bricker repudiated the compromise the very next day. The senator had been under considerable pressure from Holman and others all along not to give up the "which" clause, and as Holman explained to Clarence Manion, the only reason Bricker had accepted the new proposal was that Brownell and Ferguson had presented him with a virtual ultimatum and spent two hours "working on him, trying to argue him into submission," and "brain washing" him. In a phone call to the attorney general on January 9, Bricker told Brownell that the philosophical differences between his position and that of the administration were too basic to compromise; he would fight for S.J. Res. 1 as approved by the judiciary committee—i.e., with the "which" clause intact—to safeguard the rights of the states against further encroachments. According to Brownell, Bricker went on to say that he would not be very upset if the "which" clause were defeated, but he felt he had to make the effort on behalf of his supporters. As in June 1953, Bricker had once again pulled back from a compromise at the last minute at the behest of Holman and the leaders of the ABA.[7]

The news that Bricker was again demanding the inclusion of the "which" clause infuriated President Eisenhower. At the legislative leaders' meeting on January 11, when Senators Knowland, Millikin, and Saltonstall recommended that administration officials try once more to reach some sort of settlement with Bricker, the president maintained that certain important principles could not be compromised. Although he was still willing to see if an agreement could be worked out with Bricker, Eisenhower emphasized that he would never accept the "which" clause. If need be, he stressed, he was prepared to fight against it in every state in the Union, for in foreign affairs there could be only one United States, not the national government and the forty-eight states that would be involved under the "which" clause. "No President or Secretary of State," he declared, "sitting down with Malenkov or Molotov, can operate for forty-

---

[7]Bricker's claim that he had been "brain washed" into accepting the compromise proposal is reported in Holman to Manion, January 9, 1954, copy in JBP, Box 100, OHS. On Bricker's phone call to Brownell, see supplementary notes on the Legislative Leadership Conference, January 11, 1954, *Foreign Relations, 1952–54*, I, 1829–31; Shanley Diary, January 11, 1954; and interview with Herbert Brownell, June 23, 1975.

nine governments." In foreign affairs the United States had to speak with one voice—that of the federal government.[8]

The president reiterated his opposition to the "which" clause at his press conference on January 13. When a reporter asked him if he would support an amendment "which would make it impossible to use the treaty-making power to impose conditions on the individual states which cannot be imposed by regular legislation," Eisenhower replied by characterizing himself as a "States' Righter." He pointed out, however, that the failure of the states to comply with treaties entered into by the national government under the Articles of Confederation had been one of the major factors leading to the drafting and adoption of the federal Constitution, and the Founding Fathers had made sure in the Constitution that ratified treaties would supersede state laws and regulations. That made it possible, the president asserted, for American officials to meet with foreign dignitaries as representatives of one sovereign nation rather than separate principalities, and he would never accept any proposal that would take the country "right back to the general system that prevailed before our Constitution was adopted."[9]

Some of Eisenhower's concerns were well founded, since the Bricker amendment, particularly the "which" clause, would have altered the constitutional design of 1787, but the president and his advisers greatly exaggerated in predicting such dire consequences to the nation if the measure were adopted. Even if the amendment were in effect, the individual states would become involved only in those aspects of foreign policy that dealt with matters normally under their jurisdiction. In areas such as national defense, military alliances, and control of nuclear weapons, the federal government would retain exclusive authority.

Angered by what he felt was the president's misrepresentation of his amendment, Bricker retaliated by criticizing Eisenhower himself publicly for the first time. In a press release the same day, the senator denied that his resolution would take the nation back to the 1780s or require that treaties be approved by state legislatures, and he challenged the administration to let the matter come to a vote and then "accept in good grace the Senate's decision." He charged that Eisenhower's continued opposi-

---

[8]Supplementary notes on the Legislative Leadership Conference, January 11, 1954, and memorandum by the assistant White House staff secretary, "The Bricker Amendment," January 11, 1954, both in *Foreign Relations, 1952–54,* I, 1829–32; James Hagerty Diary, January 11, 1954, in Ferrell, ed., *The Diary of James Hagerty,* p. 6; and Shanley Diary, January 11, 1954.

[9]President's news conference, January 13, 1954, in *Public Papers: Eisenhower, 1954,* pp. 51–53. See also Eisenhower to Earl Schaefer, January 22, 1954, DDEP, Diary Series; and *New York Times,* January 14, 1954, pp. 1, 12, 13. On the problems under the Articles of Confederation, see Marks, *Independence on Trial: Foreign Affairs and the Making of the Constitution.*

tion to the "which" clause showed that the president "believes that the federal government, merely by making a promise to another country, should be able to clothe itself with authority inconsistent with the Constitution of the United States." Bricker agreed that the Constitutional Convention had been "a great gathering of patriots, . . . possibly the greatest assembly in the world's history outside the Disciples of Christ," but that did not mean that the Constitution could not be changed. After all, he noted, it had been amended during George Washington's presidency with the addition of the Bill of Rights. "The blessings of the American people stem from the Bill of Rights," Bricker concluded, and those liberties and freedoms could "only be preserved by adopting S.J. Res. 1 in principle into our basic law."[10]

Once Bricker publicly attacked him, Eisenhower resolved to wage an all-out campaign to defeat the amendment. Many of his advisers and other people whose opinions he valued, including Senator Wiley, Secretary Dulles, Thomas Dewey, John J. McCloy, Professor Corwin, John W. Davis, and Dean Erwin Griswold of Harvard Law School, were urging him to reject S.J. Res. 1 and all the proposed substitutes as unnecessary and potentially dangerous. The president himself was reluctant to see the Constitution rewritten, and he resented Bricker's remarks against him. After conferring with various aides, Eisenhower instructed them to draft a speech he could deliver over radio and television making it clear that he was opposed to any measure that would take the country back to the days "when American Ambassadors were subject to ridicule abroad because [they] represented thirteen states, not one central government." Administration officials were to rally newspaper columnists and editorial writers behind the president's efforts, stressing that the United States had to speak as one government in foreign affairs—not forty-nine. Eisenhower vowed that he would "fight up and down [the] country," and "call names"; he would denounce the amendment as a "stupid, blind violation of the Constitution by stupid, blind isolationists." The president also authorized Jerry Persons, his special assistant for congressional relations, to tell House Majority Leader Charles Halleck that he could promise congressmen "anything within reason" if they would vote against the Bricker amendment.[11]

---

[10]Press release from the office of Senator Bricker, January 13, 1954, JBP, Box 117, OHS; *New York Times,* January 14, 1954, p. 14; and Chicago *Tribune,* January 14, 1954, pp. 1, 12.

[11]Hagerty Diary, January 14, 1954, DDEL.; Senator Wiley to the president, January 8, 1954, in *Foreign Relations, 1952–54,* I, 1828–29; Pat Holt Oral History Transcript, pp. 102–4, Senate Historical Office; summaries of telephone calls, Dulles to Hagerty, January 8, 1954; Dulles to the president, January 9, 1954; Dulles to Thomas Dewey, January 9, 1954; Dulles to Brownell, January 13, 1954; Dulles to Hagerty, January 14, 1954; and Dulles to Sherman

The administration enjoyed considerable success in getting its point of view across in the press. Press Secretary James Hagerty spoke with James Reston of the *New York Times,* and the *Times* emphasized Eisenhower's opposition to the Bricker amendment in its front-page story on the president's news conference. The editors of the *Times* also published an editorial on January 17 in which they warned that the Bricker amendment would take the country back to the days before the Constitution and "paralyze foreign policy." Similarly, syndicated columnists Walter Lippmann, Marquis Childs, Roscoe Drummond, and Anne O'Hare McCormick all criticized the Bricker amendment as a measure that would restore to the states the power over treaties that they had exercised under the Articles of Confederation, making it impossible for the president, in McCormick's words, "to conduct a consistent and rational foreign policy."[12]

A few days later, in a letter to his colleagues and a Senate speech, Bricker attempted to answer what he described as Eisenhower's "erroneous charges" and "absurd" objections to his amendment. Bricker himself had argued in 1953 that the "which" clause would give the states "what amounts to a veto power over foreign policy." Now, however, he maintained that the provision would have little effect on agreements confined to international affairs; compacts such as the North Atlantic Treaty or agreements dealing with foreign commerce and other matters "within the constitutional domain" of the federal government would simply have to be implemented by acts of Congress. Even in the case of a treaty establishing rules for granting divorces, Bricker explained, his resolution would not prevent the national government from entering into such an agreement.

Adams, January 14, 1954; all in "Telephone Conversations, Dulles"; summary of telephone call from the president to Brownell, January 9, 1954, DDEP, Diary Series; John J. McCloy to the president, January 8, 1954; Eisenhower to McCloy, January 13, 1954; and McCloy to Eisenhower, January 18, 1954; all in DDEP, Diary Series; Professor Corwin to President Eisenhower, January 11, 1954, Corwin Papers, Chronological Files; and John W. Davis to the president, January 12, 1954, and Dean Griswold to the president, January 9, 1954, both in DDEP, Diary Series. The excerpt from Hagerty's diary reprinted by Ferrell leaves out the specific steps Hagerty recorded the president as outlining for the fight against the Bricker amendment. See Ferrell, ed., *Hagerty Diary,* p. 7. John Bricker later attributed Eisenhower's opposition to his amendment to letters the president received from John McCloy arguing against any change in the Constitution. The senator overstated the impact of McCloy's letters, however. They may have helped stiffen the president's resolve, but Eisenhower had already been opposing the amendment for months, and he was receiving the same advice from other sources as well. See interview with John Bricker, June 26, 1975.

[12]See James Hagerty Diary, January 13 and 19, 1954, DDEL; *New York Times,* January 14, 1954, p. 1, and editorial, "Back to 1787?" January 17, 1954, IV, 8; Walter Lippmann column, Washington *Post,* January 19, 1954, p. 15; Marquis Childs column, Washington *Post,* January 16, 1954, p. 9; Roscoe Drummond column, St. Louis *Post-Dispatch,* January 18, 1954, p. 1-B; and Anne O'Hare McCormick column, *New York Times,* January 18, 1954, p. 22.

But, since divorce was a matter reserved to state control by the Tenth Amendment, any such treaty would have to include a stipulation that state legislation would be required before it would go into effect in the United States. Bricker noted that many treaties already included such provisions, including an 1853 agreement with France, recent treaties of friendship and commerce with China (1946) and Greece (1953), and all the conventions sponsored by the International Labor Organization. Therefore, he insisted, his amendment would neither give the states "a veto power over foreign affairs" nor "turn back the clock to the old Articles of Confederation."[13]

In his remarks to the Senate, Bricker also complained that it was "highly improper" for Eisenhower to be injecting himself into the debate over S.J. Res. 1. He emphasized that under the Constitution the president had no formal role in the amending process, and he hoped that Eisenhower would not "try to transform a great constitutional issue into a personal issue." When challenged by Senator Knowland, Bricker conceded that the president had every right to express his views on the proposal, but he still argued that it would go against the spirit of the Constitution for Eisenhower to wage a vigorous campaign and use "extra-legal pressures in an effort to defeat the amendment."[14]

The president had no intention of removing himself from the debate. Although he never delivered his broadcast address on the measure because of the possibility that some sort of compromise might be worked out, he did restate his views on S.J. Res. 1 in another letter to Senator Knowland. Eisenhower reaffirmed that he would accept a simple amendment making it clear that international agreements could not override the Constitution, but he warned that the resolution insisted on by Senator Bricker "would so restrict the conduct of foreign affairs that our country could not negotiate the agreements necessary for the handling of our business with the rest of the world." Adoption of the Bricker amendment, he asserted, "would make it impossible for us to deal effectively with friendly nations for our mutual defense and common interests, . . . would be notice to our friends as well as our enemies abroad that our country intends to withdraw from its leadership in world affairs, . . . [and] would impair our hopes and plans for peace." Consequently, the president declared, he was still "un-

---

[13]Senator Bricker to Senator Richard Russell, January 20, 1954, Russell Papers, Series IX, Box 20, "Bricker Amendment," Richard Russell Memorial Library, University of Georgia; Bricker to Senator H. Alexander Smith, January 20, 1954, Smith Papers, Box 123, Princeton University Library; 100 *CR* 633–40 (1954); and *New York Times,* January 23, 1954, pp. 1, 2. On Bricker's earlier criticism of the "which" clause, see Bricker to Senator Irving Ives, February 18, 1953, Ives Papers, Box 48, Cornell University Library.

[14] 100 *CR* 633–40; and *New York Times,* January 23, 1954, pp. 1, 2.

alterably opposed to the Bricker amendment as reported by the Senate Judiciary Committee."[15]

II

The president's opposition led a number of his followers in the Senate to waver in their support for S.J. Res. 1. Senator Irving Ives (R-N.Y.) stated that he still favored the general idea of a constitutional amendment ensuring that international agreements conformed to the Constitution, but he now claimed that he had been listed as a cosponsor of Bricker's resolution "by accident." Senator Leverett Saltonstall (R-Mass.) explained to one of the leaders of the Vigilant Women for the Bricker Amendment that he had helped introduce the measure in order "to put forever beyond doubt the possibility that exercise of the treaty power could diminish individual rights safeguarded by the Constitution." He now believed, however, that certain aspects of the amendment—especially its effects on "the inherent powers of the President in the field of foreign affairs"—had to be clarified, and he was waiting to see the actual text submitted to the Senate for final consideration before deciding whether to vote for the resolution. Similarly, Senator George Aiken (R-Vt.) informed a constituent that he would support Bricker's proposal if language could be found that could not be "misinterpreted." He reported, however, that the amendment would be defeated if "the uncertain 'which' clause remains in it."[16]

Senator H. Alexander Smith of New Jersey typified the "Eisenhower Republicans" and their discomfort over the Bricker amendment. Smith thought that Bricker had raised an important issue, and he had agreed to cosponsor S.J. Res. 1 because he felt something like it was necessary to

[15]President Eisenhower to Senator Knowland, January 25, 1954, in *New York Times*, January 26, 1954, pp. 1, 4, 13; and Eisenhower to Brownell, January 22, 1954, DDEP, Diary Series.

[16]See Senator Ives to Roderick Stephens, January 21, 1954, Ives Papers, Box 48; Senator Saltonstall to Mrs. Robert Murray, January 9, 1954, copy in JBP, Box 100, OHS; and Senator Aiken to Francis Billado, January 25, 1954, Aiken Papers, Crate 31, Box 1. Ives and Saltonstall were two of the president's strongest supporters in the Senate, voting against his position only two and three times respectively in 1953. *Congressional Quarterly* rated them both as Eisenhower supporters 94% of the time in 1953 based on their "pro Eisenhower" votes on those issues that were defined as "testing support for the President's program and leadership." Senator Aiken was rated as supporting President Eisenhower 74% of the time based on the same criteria, but on foreign policy issues he supported President Eisenhower 83% of the time in the 83d Congress. See *Congressional Quarterly Almanac, 1953* (Washington, D.C.: Congressional Quarterly News Features, 1953), p. 82; and Reichard, *The Reaffirmation of Republicanism*, p. 272.

prevent future Yaltas. Smith was one of Eisenhower's most loyal supporters in the Senate, however, and he was willing to defer to "the President and the Secretary of State in their conception of the functions of the Executive and Legislative Departments." He tried numerous times to bring Bricker and administration officials together to work out a compromise, but when all such efforts failed, he had to side with either Bricker or the president. He finally chose the latter, as Dulles, Brownell, and Professor Corwin convinced him that the Bricker amendment imperiled the nation's security. By January 1954, Smith had concluded that S.J. Res. 1 "would complicate our whole situation terrifically and would handicap the President and Dulles at a time when we have to put our full confidence behind them." As he wrote in his diary, he now thought that "the strongest position may be against any change in the Constitution."[17]

Of the various legislators who were wobbling on the Bricker amendment, Senator Prescott Bush (R-Conn.) became the first to retract publicly his endorsement of the measure. Bush had supported President Eisenhower consistently in 1953, voting for the president's position 42 out of 43 times, and he would support the administration again on the Bricker amendment. In early January 1954, he told one of the resolution's proponents that he had cosponsored Bricker's original proposal because he believed it would protect the United States. He explained, however, that the administration's insistence that the measure would interfere with the nation's foreign affairs was causing him to reexamine his position, and he now preferred to wait until after the Senate's debate on the amendment before making a final decision on the bill. Subsequently, in a speech on January 21, Bush declared that the resolution as presently drafted, with the "which" clause having been added by the judiciary committee, was "much too drastic" a remedy for the abuses committed by previous presidents. Adopting the amendment in its present form, he warned, would "hamstring this great nation in a time of world crisis when we must be able to

[17]See Senator Smith to Carl Rix, July 21, 1953; and Smith to Robert Clothier, January 21, 1954; both in Smith Papers, Box 123; and H. Alexander Smith Diary, January 21, 1953, Princeton University Library. According to *Congressional Quarterly,* Smith voted against President Eisenhower only four times in 1953 and three times in 1954. His record of opposing the administration only 6% of the time during the 83d Congress was the third best of all senators. See *Congressional Quarterly Almanac, 1954,* p. 62. On Smith's efforts to bring Bricker and the administration together, see Smith to Bricker, May 18 and May 25, 1953; and Smith to Phleger, May 18 and May 25, 1953; all in Smith Papers, Box 123. On the influence of Dulles, Brownell, and Corwin, see Smith to Dulles, March 28, 1953; Corwin to Smith, May 6, May 15, June 6, June 14, June 22, July 28, and October 26, 1953; Smith to Corwin, May 25, June 17, and June 30, 1953; and Corwin to Smith, January 9, 1954; all in Smith Papers, Box 123. See also "Senator Smith Supports President Eisenhower's Position on Bricker Amendment," remarks of Senator Smith on the floor of the Senate, January 27, 1954, Smith Papers, Box 123; and 100 *CR* 857–59.

move swiftly and resolutely," and shake the confidence of those allies whose help was essential "in the worldwide struggle against Communism." Therefore, Bush announced, although he would support a simple amendment providing that international agreements that conflicted with the Constitution were null and void, he would vote against S.J. Res. 1 as presently worded.[18]

Other senators too, out of loyalty to the administration, prepared to disavow their sponsorship of the Bricker amendment. The *New York Times* reported that a number of Eisenhower Republicans who had been listed among the resolution's backers had decided to oppose the measure. A few days later, *Newsweek* named Senators Bush, Ives, Smith (N.J.), Duff (R-Pa.), Flanders (R-Vt.), and Hendrickson (R-N.J.) as legislators who would be voting against the amendment in its present form despite their previous endorsements of the resolution. According to *Newsweek*, they had changed their minds because of the insertion of the "which" clause that had not been part of the original bill they had cosponsored. As the magazine also pointed out, the senators believed that President Eisenhower's prestige was at stake, and they did not want to vote for an amendment that might weaken his power and his influence either at home or abroad.[19]

With all these defections from the ranks of the Bricker amendment's supporters, administration officials knew they had succeeded in warding off the threat posed by the "which" clause. But the president feared that failure to enact any resolution would lead to an even more dangerous proposal being introduced in the next Congress. Thus he returned to the idea of a simple amendment that would make it clear that international agreements could not override the Constitution—something similar to the Knowland substitute that he had endorsed the previous summer. He wanted to be certain, however, not to give the impression that he was capitulating to the Brickerites and the isolationists and reactionaries in the Republican party and the nation at large.[20]

[18]See Bush to Mrs. Murray, January 8, 1954; and Bush to Senator Bricker, January 19, 1954; both in JBP, Box 100, OHS; press release from the office of Senator Bush, January 21, 1954, copy in JBP; and *New York Times,* January 22, 1954, p. 10. On Bush's support for the Eisenhower administration, see *Congressional Quarterly Almanac, 1953,* p. 82.

[19]*New York Times,* January 21, 1954, pp. 1, 16, and January 22, 1954, p. 10; and *Newsweek,* February 1, 1954, p. 17. See also Senator Flanders to Paul Hoffman, January 27, 1954, Flanders Papers, Box 105, Syracuse University Library. Duff and Flanders had two of the best records of supporting the Eisenhower administration, 100% and 96% respectively in 1953. In the 83d Congress as a whole, Duff and Flanders ranked first and second in opposing the administration's programs the fewest times. Hendrickson supported the administration 84% of the time in both 1953 and 1954. See *Congressional Quarterly Almanac, 1953,* p. 82; and ibid., *1954,* p. 62.

[20]See Dulles, memorandum of breakfast conference with the president, January 20, 1954, *Foreign Relations, 1952–54,* I, 1834; Homer Gruenther to Persons, Morgan, and Martin, Janu-

The president determined that the best strategy would be to line up bipartisan support for a less stringent amendment that would be approved instead of Bricker's resolution. Even though a two-thirds majority was required to approve a constitutional amendment, only a simple majority would be needed to substitute a new text for the measure approved by the judiciary committee, meaning that forty-nine votes would be sufficient to replace the Bricker amendment with a compromise proposal. The administration would need help from the Democrats to effect such a change, however, because many of the more conservative Republicans were sure to oppose any softening of the amendment. Therefore, on January 20, President Eisenhower suggested to Dulles that the secretary meet with Senator Walter George, the senior Democrat on the foreign relations committee and a man with whom Dulles had developed a close relationship over the years, to try to draft a bipartisan, compromise resolution. Such an amendment would reassure the American people that they were protected against any dangers posed by treaties, and it would avoid knuckling under to Bricker. Accordingly, Dulles met with George on January 20, and the president conferred with the Georgia Democrat at the White House five days later in an effort to persuade him to endorse an amendment along the lines of the Knowland proposal.[21]

At this point, Senator George became an important figure in the fight over the Bricker amendment. A senator since 1922, George was regarded as a hero by many conservatives for his opposition to much of the New Deal and his survival of Franklin Roosevelt's attempt to purge him in 1938. Moreover, he had earned a reputation as one of the best constitutional lawyers in Congress, and Democrats and Republicans alike respected him and recognized his influence. Senator Willis Smith, a North Carolina Democrat, had recommended to Bricker and Holman that George be included on any strategy committee established to work for the adoption of S.J. Res. 1, and Senator Knowland advised the president that in win-

---

ary 23, 1954, Morgan Records, A67-19, Box 2, DDEL; Hagerty Diary, January 22 and 25, 1954, DDEL; Eisenhower to John W. Davis, January 18, 1954; and Eisenhower to John McCloy, January 19, 1954; both in DDEP, Diary Series; and minutes of cabinet meeting of January 29, 1954, in *Foreign Relations, 1952–54,* I, 1842–43.

[21]Summary of telephone call, Eisenhower to Dulles, January 20, 1954, "Telephone Conversations, Dulles"; memorandum by the secretary of state to the president, January 20, 1954, in *Foreign Relations, 1952–54,* I, 1834–35; Hagerty Diary, January 22, 1954, in Ferrell, ed., *Hagerty Diary,* p. 9; Gruenther to Persons, Morgan, and Martin, January 23, 1954, Morgan Records, A67-19, Box 2; and summaries of telephone calls, Senator Knowland to the president, Eisenhower to Senator George, Knowland to the president, and Eisenhower to Knowland, all on January 25, 1954, all in DDEP, Diary Series.

ning support for a bipartisan amendment, George would be the "key man, particularly with southerners."[22]

As White House officials conferred with Senator George, the Senate Democrats now entered the fray in earnest. Most of the Democrats had been content to sit on the sidelines while the Republicans wrangled over the Bricker amendment. By January 1954, however, Senate Minority Leader Lyndon Johnson of Texas saw a chance for his party to capture the initiative. He realized that if a Democrat were to sponsor a less restrictive amendment that would serve as the basis for a suitable compromise, the Democrats could take credit for saving Eisenhower and the nation from the isolationist Republicans who wanted to hamstring the president and limit the country's role in world affairs. Consequently, Johnson and the Democratic Policy Committee began working with Senator George to draft a substitute resolution of their own.[23]

Johnson had an additional reason for wanting the Democrats to introduce a less stringent amendment: he saw such a measure as a way out of a serious political dilemma of his own. A supporter of Eisenhower's foreign policy whenever possible, Johnson considered the Bricker amendment a mischievous bill that would cripple the president's authority. He had advised Secretary Dulles in June 1953 that the administration could defeat the measure if the president held firm against it. When commenting publicly on the resolution, however, Johnson waffled, saying that he hoped the administration and the amendment's proponents would resolve their differences over "technicalities" and agree on a compromise text. The senator explained that he favored an amendment that would "assure the American people that their constitutional rights cannot be lost through any treaty," but only if the measure did not deprive the president of "the proper authority he needs for the conduct of foreign affairs." Johnson realized that the Bricker amendment enjoyed great popularity among influential groups back in Texas, particularly the medical societies, and "Landslide Lyndon," who had won the Democratic primary in 1948 by 87 votes, was up for reelection in 1954. Fearful of the political consequences of opposing

[22]See Senator Willis Smith to Frank Holman, April 15, 1953, copy in JBP, Box 91, OHS; and summary of telephone call, Knowland to Eisenhower, January 25, 1954, DDEP, Diary Series. On George's influence in the Senate, see also Matt Connally, memorandum for the president, May 29, 1952, Harry Truman Papers, PSF 98, HSTL; Senator Alton Lennon (D-N.C.) to Professor Chafee, February 3, 1954, Chafee Papers, Box 12; Jay Hayden in the Detroit *News,* March 4, 1955, copy in Phleger Collection, Vol. 8, Princeton University Library; White, "Senator George—Monumental, Determined"; Roberts, "Strong Man from the South"; and *New York Times,* May 10, 1956, p. 1.

[23]See George Reedy Oral History Transcript, pp. 15–17, LBJL; and interview with Gerald W. Siegel, formerly chief counsel to the Democratic Policy Committee, December 23, 1980.

the resolution directly, Johnson preferred to have the Democrats come up with a harmless substitute, which he and others facing similar difficulties could support for political reasons without jeopardizing the nation's well-being.[24]

On January 27, after having worked with Johnson and the Democratic Policy Committee for a few days, Senator George introduced a new proposal as a substitute for S.J. Res. 1. The Georgia Democrat favored the objectives of the Bricker amendment, but his talks with the president and the secretary of state had convinced him that the judiciary committee's text went too far. Consequently, he submitted the following resolution to the Senate for consideration:

> Section 1. A provision of a treaty or other international agreement which conflicts with this Constitution shall not be of any force or effect.
> Section 2. An international agreement other than a treaty shall become effective as internal law in the United States only by an act of the Congress.[25]

The George substitute offered a reasonable basis for compromise. Senator George believed that requiring treaties to be approved by a two-thirds vote in the Senate already afforded adequate protection against ill-advised agreements that might trample the rights of the states; hence, his proposal did not contain a "which" clause or require that treaties be implemented by subsequent legislation. The only restriction it would impose on treaties was to ensure that their provisions did not violate the Constitution. As for executive agreements, George did not think that the president, on his own, should be able to make agreements that would override state laws and constitutions, so he included in his amendment a provision requiring congressional action before presidential agreements became effective as domestic law within the United States.[26]

[24]See memorandum by the secretary of state to the president, June 27, 1953, in *Foreign Relations, 1952–54*, I, 1819–20; text of radio broadcast by Senator Lyndon B. Johnson, September 13, 1953; and press release from the office of Senator Johnson, September 14, 1953; both in Johnson Papers, Senate Papers, "Bricker Amendment," LBJL; *New York Times*, September 14, 1953, pp. 1, 18; memorandum from George Reedy to Johnson, January 21, 1954; and memoranda from Gerald Siegel to Johnson, January 23 and 26, 1954; all in Johnson Papers, Senate Papers, "Bricker Amendment"; George Reedy Oral History Transcript, pp. 15–17; and interview with Gerald Siegel, December 23, 1980.

[25]For George's views on the Bricker amendment, see George to Mrs. Murray, January 8, 1954; and George to Walter Wuerdeman, February 16, 1954; copies in JBP, Boxes 100 and 101, OHS. On George's own substitute amendment, see 100 *CR* 853; and *New York Times*, January 28, 1954, pp. 1, 10. Senator George proposed his substitute resolution on January 27, but he did not formally offer it in the Senate until February 2. He waited the extra days while talks continued with administration officials. See 100 *CR* 853, 1103; and *New York Times*, January 28, 1954, pp. 1, 10, and February 3, 1954, pp. 1, 10.

[26]See Senator George's remarks, 100 *CR* 1401–2, 1416. See also memorandum from G.

Initially, President Eisenhower responded enthusiastically to Senator George's proposal. When asked by a reporter if his substitute had the president's backing, George replied that he had discussed the measure with the president and his advisers, but they had not specifically endorsed it. Eisenhower told Undersecretary of State Bedell Smith, however, that he had no objection to George's resolution. In fact, he said, he thought the new text might work to the administration's advantage by serving as the basis for a bipartisan amendment that would safeguard the rights of the American people without interfering with the executive branch's authority to conduct the nation's foreign affairs.[27]

State and Justice Department officials urged the president not to commit himself on the new proposal until they had more time to study it. Undersecretary Smith asserted that the substitute was even worse than the original resolution because it would require congressional legislation to implement executive agreements. Similarly, despite the fact that Brownell himself had used the phrase "internal law" in some of his own previous proposals, he now advised the president that the meaning of the phrase was unclear, and he did not know how the courts would interpret it. The attorney general promised that his staff would study the new language carefully, and that he would report back as quickly as possible.[28]

Eisenhower questioned the need for such caution. He maintained that executive agreements with other nations dealt with foreign affairs and thus would be unaffected by the new proposal's restrictions. Could the State Department show him one international agreement that the courts had ruled was part of the internal law of the United States? He wanted proof, he told Brownell, before he would accept the argument that the George substitute would be injurious to the nation's best interest. The president did agree, though, not to endorse the amendment publicly until his aides had more time to review it.[29]

Brownell conferred in New York with John W. Davis, and they concluded that the George resolution would severely limit the president's authority. Along with State Department Legal Adviser Herman Phleger,

W. Siegel to Senator Johnson on Senator George's proposed substitute for S. J. Res. 1, January 28, 1954, Johnson Papers, Senate Papers, "Bricker Amendment."

[27]*New York Times,* January 28, 1954, pp. 1, 10; summary of telephone call, Eisenhower to Bedell Smith, January 27, 1954, DDEP, Diary Series; and Hagerty Diary, January 27, 1954, excerpt in *Foreign Relations, 1952–54,* I, 1837.

[28]Summaries of telephone calls, Bedell Smith to the president, and Eisenhower to Brownell, both on January 27, 1954, DDEP, Diary Series. On Brownell's own use of the phrase "internal law," see memorandum, December 19, 1953, Eisenhower Papers, OF 116-H-4.

[29]Summaries of telephone calls, Smith to the president, and Eisenhower to Brownell, both on January 27, 1954, DDEP, Diary Series.

they warned the president that the George amendment would require an act of Congress to implement every executive agreement, thereby interfering with the president's power to receive ambassadors and enter into agreements for the nation's defense, and possibly preventing future presidents from negotiating agreements like the Korean armistice or the Destroyers-Bases deal of 1940. Davis, Brownell, and Phleger argued that the strength of the American system of government lay in the conflict among the executive, legislative, and judicial branches; that friction, they asserted, ensured that no one branch of government accumulated too much power. But they advised that the George amendment would wreck the essential balance of power between the executive and the legislature by transferring authority from the president to Congress.[30]

Secure in the knowledge that they had defeated the Bricker amendment and the "which" clause, the president's aides now saw no need to compromise, and thus they exaggerated the possible negative effects of the George amendment. The resolution was actually less restrictive than the text Brownell had agreed to in his talks with Bricker a few weeks earlier. That measure would have required congressional legislation before treaties and executive agreements could have gone into effect within the United States, but the George resolution imposed such a restriction only on executive agreements—not on treaties. Moreover, despite the statements of administration officials to the contrary, the George amendment would not have required implementing legislation for all executive agreements, but only for those agreements affecting domestic matters. But the president's advisers now preferred that no substantive measure be enacted, and they argued against the George substitute just as strenuously as they had objected to Bricker's amendment.[31]

The president and State Department officials also sought the opinion of Secretary Dulles, who was in Berlin attending a Big Four Foreign Ministers' meeting. At first, Dulles cabled that he "like[d] George's substitute very well." But Phleger reported to the secretary that Davis, Justice Department officials, and others were against the resolution, and the legal adviser emphasized his own concern that the proposal would limit the president's authority to recognize foreign governments, "cut down Presidential power to conduct foreign affairs, and . . . preclude agreements made by [the] President as Commander in Chief." According to Under-

---

[30]See summaries of telephone calls, Bedell Smith to the president, and Eisenhower to Smith, both on January 28, 1954, and Eisenhower to Brownell, January 29, 1954, all in DDEP, Diary Series; and "Memorandum on Legal Effect of Section 2 in Constitutional Amendment Proposed by Senator George," January 28, 1954; and "The proposed amendment . . . submitted by Senator George . . . ," n.d.; both in Phleger Collection, Vol. 10.

[31]To compare Senator George's proposal to the measure on which Brownell and Bricker had tentatively agreed earlier in January, see Appendixes H and I.

secretary Smith, however, Eisenhower wanted Dulles to bear in mind the "grave political damages resulting from hysterical build-up of pressure" if the administration rejected any and all measures. Because of practical considerations, the secretary was to advise whether they could "live with this amendment without serious impairment of our ability to conduct foreign relations."[32]

The secretary of state immediately cabled back his analysis of the George resolution. Dulles conceded that the new proposal "might diminish somewhat the authority of the President." As he understood the measure, however, he did not think it would affect the powers expressly granted to the president by the Constitution, especially his prerogatives as commander in chief and his authority to receive ambassadors. It would simply "prevent international agreements from serving as a means of enlarging the President's authority beyond what it would be otherwise under express grants of power to the President." Thus, although he still preferred that no amendment be enacted, Dulles believed that Senator George's amendment, if properly interpreted, would not seriously diminish "the capacity of the United States to preserve its vital international interests."[33]

Administration officials on the scene in Washington, however, feared that the George resolution could be construed more broadly and restrict the president's power. They noted that Bricker seemed willing to accept the new text if the administration did, and that the senator had even said on "Meet the Press" that it met "the cardinal principles" of his amendment. Bricker obviously interpreted the measure differently than the secretary of state, and the president's advisers worried that the courts might go along with Bricker's view. To ensure that the judiciary construed the resolution as narrowly as possible, Brownell and Phleger proposed adding a proviso stating explicitly that the amendment would not affect the president's authority as commander in chief or in the field of foreign affairs. But Senator George thought such language would "largely nullify" his resolution, and he refused to accept it, and negotiations between the senator and administration officials soon collapsed.[34]

[32]The secretary of state to the Department of State, January 28, 1954; and the acting secretary of state to the secretary of state, at Berlin, January 28, 1954; both in *Foreign Relations, 1952–54*, I, 1838–41.
[33]The secretary of state to the Department of State, "Message for President, Information Smith and Phleger, from Secretary," January 29, 1954, *Foreign Relations, 1952–54*, I, 1841–42.
[34]See transcript of "Meet the Press" broadcast, January 31, 1954, p. 2, copy in JBP, Box 110, OHS; Atlanta *Constitution*, February 1, 1954, pp. 1, 5; summaries of telephone calls, Eisenhower to Brownell, January 29 and February 3, 1954; and draft of January 30, 1954; all in DDEP, Diary Series; the acting secretary of state to the secretary of state, at Berlin, February 1, 1954; and the legal adviser to the secretary of state, February 2, 1954; both in *Foreign Relations, 1952–54*, I, 1845, 1846–47; and *New York Times*, February 3, 1954, pp. 1, 10.

III

The Republican congressional leaders objected to the George substitute too, but for reasons very different from those of the administration. In contrast to the president and his advisers, Senators Knowland, Ferguson, and Millikin had no real complaints about the text of Senator George's resolution and its possible effects on presidential authority. They were reluctant, however, to let the Democrats claim that they had saved President Eisenhower and the nation from extremists in the Republican party. The Republican leaders decided that the best way out of this situation would be to draft and submit a compromise amendment of their own that everyone, including the president, Senator George, and Senator Bricker, would support.[35]

Knowland and the others began with the proposal the majority leader had introduced the previous summer. The measure had provided that international agreements contravening the Constitution would be null and void, the courts would have the power to determine if a particular covenant violated the Constitution, and roll call votes would be required in the Senate in approving treaties. The Republican leaders decided to drop the section concerning the judiciary, concluding that it was superfluous. But, to emphasize that international agreements were subservient to the Constitution, they added a new section proclaiming that no treaty entered into after the Constitution had gone into force would be part of the supreme law of the land unless it had been made "in pursuance of" the Constitution. Finally, to win the support of Senator George and Senator Bricker, and because it followed their own predilections, they included a stipulation that congressional legislation would be required to bring executive agreements into effect as internal law within the United States.[36]

Administration officials found the Republican leaders' resolution just as objectionable as the George substitute since it contained essentially the same restrictions on executive agreements. As the president now realized and explained to Senator Knowland, many executive agreements affected matters within the United States. In recognizing new governments, for example, the president granted foreign diplomats immunity from local

[35]See Hagerty Diary, January 28, 1954, excerpt in *Foreign Relations, 1952–54,* I, 1838; summaries of telephone calls, Bedell Smith to the president, and Eisenhower to Knowland, both on January 28, 1954; and Eisenhower to Knowland, January 29, 1954; all in DDEP, Diary Series; and Hagerty Diary, January 29, 1954, DDEL.

[36]See summaries of telephone calls, Eisenhower to Knowland, January 28 and 29, 1954, DDEP, Diary Series; the acting secretary of state to the secretary of state, January 28, 1954; excerpt from Hagerty Diary, February 1, 1954; and the legal adviser to the secretary of state, February 2, 1954; all in *Foreign Relations, 1952–54,* I, 1839–41, 1843–45, and 1846–47; and *New York Times,* January 31, 1954, pp. 1, 27.

laws in return for American representatives abroad being given the same privilege. Moreover, Eisenhower pointed out, in an emergency the president might have to enter into an agreement with a neighboring country allowing its troops into the United States but exempting them from local ordinances. In such a crisis, time would be of the essence, and a president would not be able to wait for an act of Congress to put the agreement into effect. Consequently, Eisenhower refused to support the new proposal unless the section dealing with executive agreements was amended so that its restrictions would not apply during wartime or affect either the president's authority as commander in chief or his power to receive ambassadors and recognize foreign governments.[37]

By this time, Eisenhower was completely fed up with John Bricker, the Republican congressional leaders, and the whole Bricker amendment controversy. Given his own indecision in the matter—originally basing his opposition to the amendment on the secretary of state's analysis, his willingness to consider various compromise proposals, and his own initial favorable reaction to the George substitute—the president's criticism of the congressional leaders seems unduly harsh. Nonetheless, along with many of his advisers, he was annoyed at what he considered the ineptitude of the Republican leaders on Capitol Hill. If only they had stood their ground rather than trying to mollify Bricker and the reactionaries and the isolationists in the party, the president complained, then the whole problem would have been resolved by now. The president directed most of his wrath at Bricker, however. He was "getting so tired of the name—the time it's consumed." In a conversation with Press Secretary James Hagerty, Eisenhower lamented that "if it's true that when you die the things that bothered you most are engraved on your skull, I am sure I'll have there the mud and dirt of France during [the] invasion and the name of Senator Bricker."[38]

In deference to the president's objections, the Republican leaders finally dropped from their amendment the provision requiring congressional implementation of executive agreements. Knowland warned that even though the administration's supporters could defeat the original resolution with the "which" clause, they probably would not prevail in the fight against restrictions on executive agreements. George and Bricker were insisting upon some sort of legislative control over executive agreements that became internal law, Knowland reported, and many senators con-

[37]See summaries of telephone calls, Eisenhower to Knowland, January 28, 1954; Bedell Smith to the president, January 28, 1954; Eisenhower to Brownell, January 29, 1954; and Knowland to Eisenhower, February 1 and 2, 1954, all in DDEP, Diary Series.

[38]Hagerty Diary, February 1 and 2, 1954, excerpts in *Foreign Relations, 1952–54,* I, 1843–44, 1845–46.

curred with them on that issue. When Eisenhower and Brownell refused to accept any such curbs on the president's powers, however, Knowland, Ferguson, and the others reluctantly agreed to eliminate that section from their proposal and seek Senate approval for the rest of their resolution. On February 2, 1954, Ferguson introduced for himself and Senators Knowland, Millikin, and Saltonstall the following amendment:

> Section 1. A provision of a treaty or other international agreement which conflicts with this Constitution shall not be of any force or effect.
> Section 2. Clause 2 of Article VI of the Constitution of the United States is hereby amended by adding at the end thereof the following: "Notwithstanding the foregoing provisions of this clause, no treaty made after the establishment of this Constitution shall be the supreme law of the land unless made in pursuance of this Constitution."
> Section 3. When the Senate consents to the ratification of a treaty the vote shall be determined by yeas and nays, and the names of the persons voting for and against shall be entered on the Journal of the Senate.

To ensure that this proposal would be voted on before Senator George's substitute resolution, Ferguson submitted it as a series of perfecting amendments to the judiciary committee's text of S.J. Res. 1.[39]

At his press conference on February 3, President Eisenhower reiterated his position on the Bricker amendment. He refused to discuss specific texts, but he said again that in order to reassure the American people that treaties could not supersede the Constitution, he would accept an amendment stipulating that international agreements had to conform to the Constitution. The president emphasized, however, that "when it comes to the point of using any amendment to change or alter the traditional and constitutional balances of power among the three departments of Government, . . . I won't compromise one single word."[40]

The day after the president's news conference, John Bricker announced his own substitute text for S.J. Res. 1. The senator had expressed a willingness to endorse the Republican leaders' original proposal with its restrictions on executive agreements, but he had hardened his position after the president had rejected that version. Bricker now stated that the Ferguson amendments were fine as far as they went, but he insisted that the

[39]Summary of telephone call, Knowland to the president, February 1, 1954, DDEP, Diary Series; Hagerty Diary, February 1 and 2, 1954, excerpts in *Foreign Relations, 1952–54,* I, 1843–44, 1845–46; *New York Times,* February 3, 1954, pp. 1, 10; Washington *Post,* February 3, 1954, pp. 1, 6; and 100 *CR* 1119–20. For the printing of the leaders' amendments in the form presented above, see 100 *CR* 1239–40.
[40]President's news conference, February 3, 1954, in *Public Papers: Eisenhower, 1954,* pp. 225–28; *New York Times,* February 4, 1954, pp. 1, 14; and Hagerty Diary, February 3, 1954, DDEL.

following provision be inserted to provide meaningful protection for the rights and liberties of the American people:

> Section 3. A treaty or other international agreement shall become effective as internal law in the United States only through legislation by the Congress unless in advising and consenting to a treaty the Senate, by a vote of two-thirds of the Senators present and voting, shall provide that such treaty may become effective as internal law without legislation by the Congress.

Under this new section, congressional legislation would be required to implement an international agreement, even a treaty, if it involved the nation's internal affairs, except that senators could stipulate by a two-thirds vote that a specific treaty would go into force immediately upon ratification. With this new proviso added, Bricker declared, the amendment would accomplish almost all the original objectives of his resolution and "completely vindicate the efforts of those patriotic organizations and individuals who have alerted the American people to the dangers of treaty law."[41]

Bricker's new proposal represented a significant retreat from the text that had been approved by the Senate Judiciary Committee. The senator had dropped the provision giving Congress the right to regulate executive agreements, and he had also eliminated the infamous "which" clause. Although this resolution would require that international agreements affecting domestic matters be implemented by legislation, Congress would retain the authority to pass all such laws whether it could do so in the absence of treaty or not.[42]

Why had Bricker finally abandoned the "which" clause? He had never been very enthusiastic about the provision, arguing against it himself for almost two years in discussions with Frank Holman and the leaders of the ABA and tentatively agreeing to drop it at various times during negotiations with administration officials. The senator had retained the "which" clause as long as he had only because of constant pressure from Holman and other supporters who saw it as the heart of the amendment and the key to winning the approval of state legislatures. By February 1954, however, Bricker could see that the "which" clause was hurting the cause more

[41]Press release from the office of Senator Bricker, February 4, 1954, JBP, Box 110, OHS; *New York Times,* February 1, 1954, pp. 1, 12, and February 5, 1954, pp. 1, 13; summary of telephone call, Eisenhower to Knowland, January 29, 1954, DDEP, Diary Series; the legal adviser to the secretary of state, February 2, 1954; and the acting secretary of state to the secretary of state, February 4, 1954; both in *Foreign Relations, 1952–54,* I, 1846–47, 1848; and 100 *CR* 1307, 1916–17.

[42]To compare the two texts, see Appendixes F and K. See also *New York Times,* February 5, 1954, pp. 1, 13.

than helping; Senator George, Senator Aiken, and others had made it clear that they would oppose any measure containing that provision. Therefore, much to the displeasure of some of his more ardent backers, Bricker chose to delete the "which" clause in the hope that its elimination would enable him to regain support from moderate Republicans and from Democrats who were following Senator George's lead. He realized that he needed votes from both groups if his amendment were to secure the two-thirds majority required for adoption.[43]

Thus, as the Senate was about to begin its formal debate on S.J. Res. 1, it had before it the substitute and perfecting amendments introduced by Bricker, George, and the Republican leaders (Knowland-Ferguson). As can be seen from Table 1 (below), all three proposals contained the same first section stipulating that international agreements could not override the Constitution. After that, however, the texts diverged. Bricker and the Republican leaders had inserted another provision reiterating that treaties had to conform to the Constitution, but George believed that such an article was superfluous. He felt that adequate safeguards already existed against possible abuses in treaties, especially if section one of the amendment were approved. George did think though that closer supervision was needed for executive agreements, so he had added an article requiring congressional legislation before such agreements went into effect as law within the United States. Ferguson and Knowland had omitted such a restriction from their amendment because of the president's objections; Bricker's resolution included similar limitations on both treaties and executive agreements. Since no consensus had been reached, the question now was which of the proposals if any would be able to command the two-thirds majority required in the Senate.

However the issue was resolved, the conflict had already had a significant impact on the Eisenhower administration. Many observers noted that the controversy seemed to have transformed President Eisenhower into a much more active and involved chief executive.[44] Although he had still relied heavily on advice from Brownell, Dulles, John W. Davis, and others,

[43]See Senator Bricker's remarks, 100 *CR* 1890; Bricker to Loren Berry, February 9, 1954; Charles Webb to Mrs. Francis Lucas, February 9, 1954; Bricker to Homer Hockett, February 17, 1954; and Bricker to Henry Brandt, February 24, 1954; all in JBP, Box 100, OHS; and Aiken to Francis Billado, January 25, 1954, Aiken Papers, Crate 31, Box 1. On the unhappiness of some of Senator Bricker's supporters over his abandonment of the "which" clause, see Edward Rumely, executive secretary, Committee for Constitutional Government, to Bricker, February 15, 1954; W. Henry MacFarland, Jr., executive chairman, American Flag Commitee, to Bricker, February 23, 1954; and Madalen Leetch, secretary, American Coalition of Patriotic Societies, to Alfred Schweppe, February 12, 1954; all in JBP, Box 100, OHS.
[44]See for example Arthur Krock, "Eisenhower Changing Concept of His Job. . . ; Bricker Amendment Is Test," *New York Times,* January 17, 1954, IV, 3; Marquis Childs, "Eisenhower's

TABLE I. *Texts of various amendments*

Knowland-Ferguson	George	Bricker
1. A provision of a treaty or other international agreement which conflicts with this Constitution shall not be of any force or effect.	1. (Same as Knowland-Ferguson.)	2. (Same as Knowland-Ferguson.)
2. Clause 2 of Article VI of the Constitution of the United States is hereby amended by adding at the end thereof the following: "Notwithstanding the foregoing provisions of this clause, no treaty made after the establishment of this Constitution shall be the supreme law of the land unless made in pursuance of this Constitution."		1. (Same as Knowland-Ferguson.)
3. On the question of advising and consenting to the ratification of a treaty the vote shall be determined by yeas and nays, and the names of the persons voting for and against shall be entered on the Journal of the Senate.		4. (Same as Knowland-Ferguson.)
	2. An international agreement other than a treaty shall become effective as internal law in the United States only by an act of the Congress.	3. A treaty or other international agreement shall become effective as internal law in the United States only through legislation by the Congress unless in advising and consenting to a treaty the Senate, by a vote of two-thirds of the senators present and voting, shall provide that such treaty may become effective as internal law without legislation by the Congress.

The table comparing the three texts was compiled from a document prepared by the Committee for Defense of the Constitution by Preserving the Treaty Power which was inserted by Senator Kilgore in 100 *CR* 2042.

the president had played an active role in the deliberations within the administration and the efforts to work out a compromise with Senator George and the Democrats and the Republican leaders. Moreover, he had finally spoken out publicly and forcefully against the more restrictive versions of the amendment, and he was now using the full resources of his office to block the Bricker amendment.

The president's more active role carried risks, however. The fight over the Bricker amendment was now seen by many as a test of Eisenhower's political leadership.[45] He had beaten back the despised "which" clause, but Senator George's resolution and Bricker's new proposal still loomed as measures that enjoyed considerable support in the Senate. Eisenhower had reluctantly endorsed the Knowland-Ferguson amendment to try to ward off the more stringent measures, but he was by no means assured of success as the Senate moved to consider the various proposals. A defeat on such an important issue despite his all-out efforts would seriously weaken his power and influence as president.

States Rights View," St. Louis *Post-Dispatch,* January 20, 1954, p. 3-B; Drew Pearson, "Ike Putting Spurs to Congress," Washington *Post,* January 31, 1954, p. 5-B; and editorial, "The 'Different' Eisenhower," St. Louis *Post-Dispatch,* February 7, 1954, p. 2-C.

[45]See "President to Fight Treaty Curb Plan in Leadership Test," *New York Times,* January 14, 1954, p. 1; Richard Strout, "President Faces Showdown," *Christian Science Monitor,* January 15, 1954, p. 6; Drew Pearson, "Ike Putting Spurs to Congress," Washington *Post,* January 31, 1954, p. 5-B; and editorial, "The President Stands Fast," St. Louis *Post-Dispatch,* February 4, 1954, p. 2-B.

CHAPTER TEN

Showdown in the Senate

In late January and early February 1954, the focus of the Bricker amendment controversy shifted to the Senate, where the outcome remained very much in doubt. With all the different proposals before the Senate, neither the Eisenhower administration nor the senators themselves knew which measure, if any, would be approved and sent on to the House of Representatives. Nonetheless, both supporters and opponents of the various resolutions welcomed the final confrontation. For John Bricker, it marked the culmination of a crusade he had begun more than two and one-half years earlier to close "a loophole in our Constitution" through which the American people could be subjected to "a tyrannical world government and a Marxist covenant on human rights." On the other hand, critics of the measure such as Senator Hubert Humphrey (D-Minn.) looked to the debate and votes in the Senate to provide "a timely funeral service to this carcass which needs to be buried, . . . the Bricker amendment."[1]

I

As the Senate considered S.J. Res. 1 and the various substitute proposals, it became clear from the speeches and the votes that senators divided into four major factions on this issue (see Table 2). The first group, led by John Bricker, consisted of approximately 40 senators who wanted to enact a strong amendment that would limit the internal effects of both treaties and executive agreements. This bloc included the Senate's most conservative Republicans, such as Senators Hickenlooper (Iowa), McCarthy (Wisc.), and Welker (Id.); conservative Democrats such as Senators Byrd (Va.), Daniel (Tex.), and Ellender (La.); isolationists or

---

[1]100 *CR* 938 (Bricker), and 1229 (Humphrey) (1954).

TABLE 2.

Senate voting blocs

Bricker's supporters—senators favoring a strong amendment

Republicans		*Democrats*
Barrett (Wyo.)	Kuchel (Cal.)	Byrd (Va.)
Bennett (Utah)	Langer (N.D.)	Chavez (N.M.)
Bricker (Ohio)	Malone (Nev.)	Daniel (Tex.)
Butler (Md.)	Martin (Pa.)	Eastland (Miss.)
Butler (Neb.)	McCarthy (Wisc.)	Ellender (La.)
Capehart (Ind.)	Mundt (S.D.)	Hunt (Wyo.)
Case (S.D.)	Payne (Me.)	Johnson (Colo.)
Cordon (Ore.)	Potter (Mich.)	Johnston (S.C.)
Dirksen (Ill.)	Schoeppel (Kan.)	Long (La.)
Dworshak (Id.)	Smith (Me.)	Maybank (S.C.)
Goldwater (Ariz.)	Watkins (Utah)	McCarran (Nev.)
Griswold (Neb.)	Welker (Id.)	Russell (Ga.)
Hickenlooper (Ind.)	Williams (Del.)	Smathers (Fla.)
Jenner (Ind.)	Young (N.D.)	Stennis (Miss.)

Remaining Eisenhower Republicans
(with % support for Eisenhower on foreign policy issues)*

Aiken (Vt.)	83%	Knowland (Cal.)	83%
Bush (Conn.)	85%	Millikin (Colo.)	87%
Carlson (Kan.)	83%	Purtell (Conn.)	78%
Cooper (Ky.)	87%	Saltonstall (Mass.)	83%
Duff (Pa.)	94%	Smith (N.J.)	83%
Ferguson (Mich.)	78%	Thye (Minn.)	83%
Flanders (Vt.)	85%	Upton (N.H.)	88%
Hendrickson (N.J.)	78%	Wiley (Wisc.)	91%
Ives (N.Y.)	94%		

*Support for Eisenhower on foreign policy issues is from Reichard, *Reaffirmation of Republicanism*, pp. 272–73.

George's supporters—Democrats favoring restrictions on executive agreements

Anderson (N.M.)	Holland (Fla.)
Burke (Ohio)	Johnson (Tex.)
Clements (Ky.)	Kerr (Okla.)
Frear (Del.)	Lennon (N.C.)
George (Ga.)	Mansfield (Mont.)
Gillette (Iowa)	McClellan (Ark.)
Gore (Tenn.)	Robertson (Va.)
Hoey (N.C.)	Sparkman (Ala.)

TABLE 2. *(Continued)*

Senators opposed to any amendment
(with their liberal ratings from Americans for Democratic Action) †

Democrats				Independent	
Fulbright (Ark.)	92%	Kennedy (Mass.)	77%	Morse (Ore.)	87%
Green (R.I.)	93%	Kilgore (W.Va.)	100%		
Hayden (Ariz.)	57%	Lehman (N.Y.)	100%		
Hennings (Mo.)	77%	Monroney (Okla.)	73%		
Hill (Ala.)	85%	Murray (Mont.)	100%		
Humphrey (Minn.)	100%	Neely (W.Va.)	100%		
Jackson (Wash.)	100%	Pastore (R.I.)	85%		
Kefauver (Tenn.)	83%				

†ADA ratings are from ADA, press release, September 24, 1953, in "ADA Papers." Senator Hayden's liberal rating in 1953 was unusually low for him. In 1954, he voted liberal 92.3% of the time. See ADA, press release, October 1, 1954, "ADA Papers."

strong nationalists such as Senators Jenner (R-Ind.), Johnson (D-Colo.), Langer (R-N.D.), and Malone (R-Nev.); and four "Eisenhower Republicans"—Senators Cordon (Ore.), Griswold (Neb.), Kuchel (Cal.), and Payne (Me.)—who usually followed President Eisenhower's lead on foreign policy issues, but did not do so in this instance.[2] The rest of the Eisenhower Republicans comprised the next set of legislators. Most of these 17 senators personally favored a curb on treaties and executive agreements, as shown by the fact that they had cosponsored S.J. Res. 1, but

[2]See St. Louis *Post-Dispatch*, February 4, 1954, pp. 1, 17; and editorial, Fort Worth *Star-Telegram*, February 19, 1954, clipping in Thomas Hennings Papers, Folder 4787, University of Missouri Library. Designation of senators as liberals or conservatives is based on their percentage of "liberal" votes cast on key issues in 1953 or 1954 as judged by Americans for Democratic Action. According to ADA, Hickenlooper, McCarthy, and Welker never voted "liberal" in 1953, while Byrd, Daniel, and Ellender had the lowest liberal ratings of any Democratic senators, 10%, 20%, and 20% respectively. See Americans for Democratic Action, press release, September 24, 1953, in "Americans for Democratic Action Papers," microfilm edition, Series 7, Public Relations Files, "Press Releases." Justus Doenecke included both Langer and Johnson among the more prominent "old isolationists" still active in the 1950s, and Gary Reichard rated Jenner, Langer, and Malone among the strongest nationalists of the Republican senators returning in the 83d Congress. See Doenecke, *Not to the Swift*, and Reichard, *The Reaffirmation of Republicanism*, p. 250. Reichard also broke down into separate issue areas the *Congressional Quarterly*'s lists of roll calls testing Eisenhower's support in the 83d Congress. Using Reichard's results in the area of foreign policy, there were 22 Republican senators who supported the president more than 75% of the time and thus could be considered "Eisenhower Republicans" on foreign policy issues. Senators Cordon (80%), Griswold (82%, but based on a small number of votes because of his death in 1954), Kuchel (85%), and Payne (91%) were normally Eisenhower Republicans on foreign policy matters, but on the Bricker amendment all four disregarded the president's position and voted con-

now, out of deference to the president, they were trying to accommodate their own views with Eisenhower's opposition to the more stringent versions of the amendment. The third group of senators was headed by Walter George and was composed of 16 Democrats who sought to adopt some sort of restrictions on executive agreements, but preferred not to tamper with the treaty-making power. The final bloc consisted of those senators who were opposed to all the various amendments, and it included 15 liberal Democrats and Independent Wayne Morse (Ore.).

These divisions in the Senate meant that no one could be certain of victory as the final debate began. Bricker's supporters fell considerably short of the two-thirds majority needed to approve a constitutional amendment, but those opposed to all the resolutions were not strong enough to ensure that all the measures would be rejected. The key would be whether the proponents of the various resolutions would coalesce behind a particular amendment to secure its approval—a question which only Bricker's supporters and the Eisenhower Republicans could answer. If Bricker's own proposal were defeated, would the senator and his followers settle for "half a loaf" and support one of the less stringent resolutions that still had a chance to be passed? What would the Eisenhower Republicans do if it became impossible to reconcile their desire to side with the administration and their belief that something should be done to limit the internal effects of international agreements? How would they vote if forced to choose between the George substitute, which the president opposed, and no amendment at all? In resolving these dilemmas, Bricker's supporters and the Eisenhower Republicans would determine the outcome of the fight over the Bricker amendment.

The Republican Senate leaders tried to maneuver so that senators would not have to choose between rejecting all the various resolutions or approving a measure that the president opposed. Knowland and Ferguson introduced their proposal as separate perfecting amendments that would be debated and voted on first. They hoped that Bricker's supporters would join with the Eisenhower Republicans to substitute the Knowland-Ferguson amendment for the judiciary committee's bill. After that, they reasoned, the

---

sistently for the most stringent proposals. On this issue, therefore, I have included them among Bricker's supporters rather than with the Eisenhower Republicans. See Reichard, *Reaffirmation,* pp. viii and 272–73. Senator Styles Bridges (R-N.H.), a 79% supporter of the president on foreign policy issues, was in Europe on Senate business in early 1954 and missed most of the debate and crucial votes on the various amendments; thus he has not been included in any of the four groups. Besides Bridges, four other senators have not been included in any of the four groups: Stuart Symington (D-Mo.) was in Europe with Bridges, and J. Glenn Beall (R-Md.), Paul Douglas (D-Ill.), and Warren Magnuson (D-Wash.) have been omitted for reasons that will be discussed later in the chapter.

two groups would part company on Bricker's attempt to insert additional restrictions in the measure, the president's supporters siding with Senator George's followers and those opposed to all the amendments to defeat Bricker's new resolution. If all went according to plan, the final vote would then come on the Knowland-Ferguson amendment, which the Eisenhower Republicans would support with the president's blessing and Bricker and his cohorts would finally accept as better than nothing.[3]

The Eisenhower Republicans, Bricker's supporters, and Senator George all favored section 1 of the Knowland-Ferguson amendment, which stipulated that "a provision of a treaty or other international agreement which conflicts with this Constitution shall not be of any force or effect." Leverett Saltonstall (R-Mass.) spoke for many of his colleagues when he argued for this provision to make explicit the Constitution's supremacy over international agreements. This section, Saltonstall emphasized, would ensure that rights protected by the Constitution could not be abridged by treaties or executive agreements.[4]

Some senators opposed even this section of the resolution, however. John Pastore (D-R.I.), Wayne Morse, and others who preferred that no amendment be adopted maintained that international agreements already had to conform to the Constitution and that this provision was superfluous. These senators realized that they had a better chance of defeating a more stringent measure than of blocking a moderate proposal. Hence, in an attempt to have the final vote be on the most restrictive amendment, namely the judiciary committee's text that included the "which" clause, they opposed the effort to replace that measure with the more innocuous Knowland-Ferguson resolution.[5]

Nonetheless, on February 15, 1954, the Senate voted 62–20 to make this provision the first section of S.J. Res. 1. Those senators opposed to all the amendments voted against it, as did liberal Democrats Warren Magnuson (Wash.), John Sparkman (Ala.), and Stuart Symington (Mo.), and liberal Republicans John Sherman Cooper (Ky.) and William Langer (N.D.). But most of the Eisenhower Republicans, Bricker and his supporters, and those following Senator George joined together to approve it. Moreover, since a number of senators who missed the vote also favored the provision, the results of this first vote indicated that more than two-thirds of the senators believed some sort of amendment should be adopted to limit the

---

[3]100 *CR* 1119–20; summary of telephone call, Senator Knowland to the president, February 1, 1954, DDEP, Diary Series; and the legal adviser to the secretary of state, at Berlin, February 16, 1954, in *Foreign Relations, 1952–54,* I, 1851.

[4] 100 *CR* 1239–40. See also the comments by Senator George, ibid., 1663–64.

[5]Ibid., 1739 (Pastore and Morse); and editorial, "No Unity on Bricker," Washington *Post*, February 17, 1954, p. 8. See also the comments by Senator Fulbright, 100 *CR* 1747.

internal effects of international agreements. The question remained, however: would the coalition of senators who wanted to restrict the use of treaties and executive agreements hold together long enough to secure the enactment of a specific resolution?[6]

The Senate next postponed consideration of section 2 of the Knowland-Ferguson proposal—the most controversial provision—and moved on instead to discuss section 3, which required a roll-call vote when the Senate gave its advice and consent to a treaty. Senator Paul Douglas (D-Ill.) complained that this provision was like "using an atom bomb to kill mosquitos." The same objective, he stressed, could be achieved simply by modifying the Senate's rules. In response, Bricker conceded that this change, in and of itself, did not warrant a constitutional amendment. But, he contended, it would help prevent abuses of the treaty-making power and thus should be included in any resolution enacted. Similarly, Senator Knowland argued that the provision would lead to more careful scrutiny of treaties when they were presented to the Senate, a particularly desirable goal since treaties, unlike regular statutes, were not reviewed by the House of Representatives. Most of the legislators concurred with the majority leader's views, and senators voted 72–16 to include this article in the amendment.[7]

After the Senate had accepted these two provisions of the Knowland-Ferguson amendment, senators returned to section 2 of the resolution, the provision adding to Article VI of the Constitution the stipulation that treaties made after the adoption of the Constitution would not be the supreme law of the land unless made "in pursuance of" the Constitution. Ferguson asserted that this section was essential to avoid confusion between the present statement in Article VI that all treaties made under the authority of the United States were part of the law of the land and the proviso in the first section of the amendment declaring that international agreements in conflict with the Constitution were null and void. Moreover, he argued, this section would provide an additional safeguard against treaties that were "repugnant" to the Constitution, such as an agreement delegating executive, legislative, or judicial authority to an international organization, or a compact depriving American citizens of

[6]100 CR 1740; *New York Times,* February 16, 1954, pp. 1, 11; and editorial, "No Unity on Bricker," Washington *Post,* February 17, 1954, p. 8. In 1954, ADA gave Magnuson, Sparkman, and Symington liberal ratings of 76.9%, 88.9%, and 90.9%, respectively, and rated Langer (63.6%) and Cooper (61.5%) as the two most liberal Republicans in the Senate. See ADA, press release, October 1, 1954, "ADA Papers."
[7]100 CR 1740 (Douglas), 1759 (Bricker), 1741 (Knowland), and 1782.

their liberties and freedoms as guaranteed by the Constitution and the Bill of Rights.[8]

A number of senators raised serious objections to this provision. Edward Thye, an Eisenhower Republican from Minnesota, and Spessard Holland, a Democrat from Florida, had both voted for the first two sections of the Knowland-Ferguson amendment, but they found this provision too confusing and ambiguous to support. Wayne Morse, who was opposed to all the resolutions, charged that this clause possessed "all the clarity of the fine print in a footnote to a lease," and regretted that the judiciary committee had not been given the opportunity to study this article and all the other measures that had been hastily "drafted on the backs of envelopes." Thye, Holland, Morse, John Sherman Cooper, Thomas Hennings (D-Mo.), and others wondered how the courts would interpret the phrase "in pursuance of this Constitution," and whether the amendment would be applied retroactively to treaties previously ratified, such as the United Nations Charter. They also thought the provision was redundant since the first section of the amendment already stipulated that treaties had to conform to the Constitution. Hennings in particular feared that the article was intended, or might be construed, as "a rejuvenation of what has been described as the moribund 'which' clause." However, when Senator Bush (R-Conn.) asked Senator Ferguson if this provision was "the 'which' clause in sheep's clothing," Ferguson assured his colleagues that the provision was "naked" with "no clothing on it" at all.[9]

On February 17, senators voted 44–43 to insert the "in pursuance of" provision into the amendment, but the narrow margin by which the section was approved indicated that the Knowland-Ferguson proposal was in serious trouble. Eisenhower Republicans, Bricker's supporters, and Senator George's followers had all backed the previous sections of the resolution, but the bipartisan coalition collapsed now as the legislators divided primarily along party lines. Only six Democrats supported the article, and only four Republicans voted against it. Most of the Democrats, including the bulk of those who wanted to see some amendment adopted, agreed with Hennings and Holland that this provision was confusing, superfluous, and potentially dangerous, since no one could be certain how the courts would interpret it. Without more support from Democrats, the

[8]Ibid., 1786–91, 1891–93, and 1898–99. See also the comments by Senator Knowland, ibid., 1790, 1893–94, and 1898.
[9]Ibid., 1896 (Thye), 1914–16 (Holland), 1759–62 (Morse), 1789–91 (Cooper), 1891–1908 (Hennings and Cooper), and 1325 (Bush and Ferguson). Quotations are from pp. 1759, 1904, and 1325.

Knowland-Ferguson resolution would never secure the two-thirds majority required for final approval.[10]

II

Concerned all along that the Democrats might not support the Republican leaders' amendment, administration officials had continued to meet with Senator George in an attempt to draft a resolution they could all endorse. Eisenhower's advisers acknowledged that George had first introduced his proposal in an effort to help the president, but they feared that requiring congressional legislation for executive agreements to go into effect as internal law would curtail the president's power as commander in chief and his authority to receive ambassadors and recognize foreign governments. George stressed repeatedly that his amendment was not intended to limit the president's prerogatives in either of those areas, but he was reluctant to state that explicitly in the resolution because he worried that in enumerating those powers not affected by the amendment, Congress might inadvertently leave out other powers that also should be exempted, resulting in the latter being subjected to the restrictions in the measure.[11]

After further consideration, however, Senator George agreed to modify his amendment to meet the administration's objections. He offered to add a provision to his resolution stating that the restrictions being imposed on executive agreements "shall not be construed to affect the power of the President as Commander in Chief of the Army and Navy of the United States as provided in Article II, Section 2, of the Constitution, or the power of the President to receive ambassadors and other public ministers as provided in Article II, Section 3, of the Constitution." The measure would then go on to stipulate that "The enumeration of certain powers of the President in this section shall not be construed to deny or disparage other powers vested in him by the Constitution." This new language, George

[10]Ibid., 1916; and *New York Times,* February 18, 1954, pp. 1, 12. See also memoranda, G. W. Siegel to Senator Lyndon Johnson, on the administration's proposed substitute for the Bricker amendment, January 29 and 30, 1954, Johnson Papers, Senate Papers, "Bricker Amendment," LBJL. The four Republicans who voted against this provision were Cooper, Thye, Upton, and Duff. The six Democrats who voted for it were Burke, Byrd, Daniel, Johnson (Colo.), McClellan, and Russell.

[11]See remarks by Senator George, 100 *CR* 1404–6, 1416, 1664, and 1668; the acting secretary of state to the secretary of state, at Berlin, February 1, 1954; the legal adviser to the secretary of state, February 2, 1954; and the acting secretary of state to the secretary of state, February 4, 1954; all in *Foreign Relations, 1952–54,* I, 1845, 1846–47, and 1848; and summary of telephone call, Dulles to George, February 25, 1954, in "Telephone Conversations, Dulles."

believed, would make it clear that his amendment was not designed to interfere with the legitimate exercise of the president's authority.[12]

But administration officials objected even to George's revised proposal. Secretary Dulles advised from Berlin that the amendment was "probably innocuous as could be devised" and something the executive branch "could live with without serious embarrassment" if it had to for political reasons. He cautioned, however, that it might lead to "years of legal controversy and uncertainty," and recommended that it be avoided if possible. Justice Department officials warned that the measure would still transfer authority from the president to Congress, and they feared that it might be construed by the courts as limiting the president's powers. They suggested instead the following language, which they believed would leave the president's authority unimpaired:

Section 2. An international agreement other than a treaty shall become effective as internal law in the United States only by an act of Congress, but this section shall not apply to any agreement made under the power of the President as Commander in Chief of the Army and Navy of the United States as provided in Article II, Section 2, of the Constitution, or under his power to receive ambassadors and other public ministers as provided in Article II, Section 3, of the Constitution, or under any other power vested in him by the Constitution.

But Senator George rejected that text as virtually meaningless, since it meant the amendment would not apply to any agreements the president entered into under any of his constitutional prerogatives. Talks between the two sides soon collapsed again, and George announced on February 20 that he would work for the adoption of his original resolution.[13]

The administration's rejection of Senator George's modified proposal shows that at this point the president and his advisers were not seeking a compromise but rather an unconditional surrender from the proponents of an amendment. George had gone a long way to meet the objections to his resolution and ensure that the measure would not unduly restrict the president's ability to conduct the nation's foreign affairs, but Lucius Clay, John W. Davis, Professor Corwin, Senators Cooper, Hennings, and

[12]See the acting secretary of state to the secretary of state, February 9, 1954, *Foreign Relations, 1952–54,* I, 1849; and text of Senator George's effort to make his amendment satisfactory to the administration, n.d.; and Assistant Attorney General J. Lee Rankin to Sherman Adams, February 11, 1954, and enclosed memorandum; all in DDEP, OF 116-H-4.

[13]See the secretary of state to the Department of State, February 10, 1954; and the acting secretary of state to the secretary of state, February 13, 1954; both in *Foreign Relations, 1952–54,* I, 1849–50; J. Lee Rankin to Sherman Adams, February 11, 1954, and enclosed memorandum, DDEP, OF 116-H-4; and Washington *Post,* February 21, 1954, p. 5.

Wiley, and others were all urging Eisenhower not to accept any "hasty political compromise" that would rewrite the Constitution. Concerned that the George amendment, even in its revised form, might alter somewhat the balance of power between the president and Congress, administration officials refused to endorse the resolution. In doing so, they clearly showed their real opposition to any new limitations or restrictions, no matter how minor, on presidential power and executive agreements.[14]

III

While negotiations between Senator George and the administration were breaking down, the Senate moved on to consider the Bricker and George amendments. Both measures would require congressional legislation to make executive agreements effective as internal law in the United States, but Bricker's proposal would impose similar restrictions on treaties as well, unless two-thirds of the senators voted that a particular treaty should be self-executing. From the administration's point of view, adoption of either resolution would seriously limit the president's power to act to protect the nation's security.[15]

John Bricker maintained that both the Knowland-Ferguson amendment and the George substitute were fine as far as they went, but that neither proposal would fully safeguard the liberties and freedoms of the American people. It was not enough to check "the unlimited, dangerous, poisonous power of the President to make domestic laws by his own executive determinations," Bricker told his colleagues; Congress also had to restrict the effects of treaties if it wanted to afford real protection "to personal rights, to States' rights, and to the independence of our great nation." Of all the measures before the Senate, Bricker stressed, his resolution was the only one that would prevent abuses through executive agreements *and* treaties.

[14]Quotation is from Clay, Corwin, and Davis to the president, February 3, 1954, DDEP, Diary Series. See also Cooper to the president, January 27, 1954; and Hennings to the president, February 5, 1954; in DDEP, OF 116-H-4 and GF 3-A-5; and remarks by Senator Wiley, 100 *CR* 2056–65. On Eisenhower's concern about proposals that might alter the balance of power between the president and Congress, see informal remarks of the president to the members of the executive committee of the Young Republican National Federation, February 5, 1954, DDEP, Speeches, "Young Republican National Federation"; president's news conference, February 10, 1954, *Public Papers: Eisenhower, 1954*, p. 251; and the legal adviser to the secretary of state, February 16, 1954, *Foreign Relations, 1952–54*, I, 1851.

[15]See the memorandum on the George amendment enclosed with Rankin to Adams, February 12, 1954, DDEP, OF 116-H-4. Although this memo was directed to the George proposal, its arguments applied to Bricker's resolution as well, since the latter included all the provisions of the former and then went one step further.

Therefore, the vote on his proposal would be "justly interpreted as a vote for or against the substance of the Bricker amendment."[16]

Many senators, including Senator George, the Republican leaders, and those opposed to all the amendments, argued against Bricker's resolution. George asserted that the present requirement that treaties be approved by a two-thirds majority adequately protected the rights of the states. Since the Senate, in approving a treaty, could always attach a stipulation requiring that the agreement be implemented by congressional legislation before it could go into effect, he saw no need to amend the Constitution to prohibit self-executing treaties. Senators Knowland, Ferguson, Lehman (D-N.Y.), and Fulbright (D-Ark.) all warned that Bricker's resolution, like Senator George's amendment, would weaken the protection afforded through the two-thirds rule by establishing what Knowland described as "a method of short-circuiting the treaty-making power of the Senate." They pointed out that both proposals suggested that treaties, which had to be approved by a two-thirds vote in the Senate, were interchangeable with executive agreements, which could be put into force by simple majority votes in both the House and the Senate. As Ferguson noted, any president given the freedom to choose between those alternatives would surely choose the latter, thereby negating the safeguards provided by the two-thirds rule.[17]

If the vote on Bricker's resolution was the vote on "the substance of the Bricker amendment," then Bricker had to be sorely disappointed at the outcome. On February 25, 1954, the Senate rejected Bricker's proposal 50–42, as Senator George and his followers and the Eisenhower Republicans joined with those opposed to all the amendments to defeat the measure (see Table 3). Although 64 senators had originally cosponsored S.J. Res. 1, now, in the wake of President Eisenhower's determined opposition to the measure, only 42 of them supported Bricker's attempt to impose stringent limitations on treaties and executive agreements. Of the various amendments that came to a vote in the Senate, Bricker's was the only one that failed to win even a majority.[18]

After the senators rejected Bricker's proposal, Wayne Morse moved that the whole matter be referred back to the judiciary committee for further study. He argued that the various texts had created a great deal of confusion, and he recommended that the committee be given a chance to examine the different measures more carefully to consider their meanings and implications. But Bricker, George, and the Republican leaders all realized

[16]100 *CR* 2051, 2132–35, and 2254–55. Quotations are on pp. 2051, 2132, and 2133.

[17]Ibid., 2195–2205, and 2256–61, esp. pp. 2204, 2258, 2195–96, and 2260. Quotation is on p. 2195.

[18]Ibid., 2262; *New York Times*, February 26, 1954, pp. 1, 8.

TABLE 3.
Final vote on Senator Bricker's proposal

	Yeas: 42	
Barrett	Eastland	Maybank
Beall	Ellender	McCarthy
Bennett	Goldwater	Mundt
Bricker	Griswold	Payne
Butler (Md.)	Hickenlooper	Potter
Butler (Neb.)	Hunt	Russell
Byrd	Jenner	Schoeppel
Capehart	Johnson (Colo.)	Smathers
Case	Johnston	Smith (Me.)
Chavez	Kuchel	Stennis
Cordon	Langer	Watkins
Daniel	Long	Welker
Dirksen	Malone	Williams
Dworshak	Martin	Young

	Nays: 50	
Aiken	Hayden	Magnuson
Anderson	Hendrickson	Mansfield
Burke	Hennings	McClellan
Bush	Hill	Millikin
Carlson	Hoey	Morse
Clements	Holland	Murray
Cooper	Humphrey	Neely
Douglas	Ives	Pastore
Duff	Jackson	Purtell
Ferguson	Johnson (Tex.)	Robertson
Flanders	Kefauver	Saltonstall
Frear	Kennedy	Smith (N.J.)
Fulbright	Kerr	Sparkman
George	Kilgore	Thye
Gillette	Knowland	Upton
Gore	Lehman	Wiley
Green	Lennon	

	Not Voting: 4	
Bridges	Monroney	Symington
McCarran		

that the suggestion to recommit really represented an attempt to bury the issue in committee. Accordingly, all those who hoped to see the adoption of some sort of amendment voted against Morse's motion, which was defeated 74–18.[19]

Having disposed of both the Bricker resolution and the proposal to send the matter back to committee, senators proceeded to consider the George amendment requiring congressional legislation before an executive agreement could go into effect as internal law within the United States. Senator George explained that he had focused on the problem of presidential agreements because that was where "the wide expansion of powers in the realm of foreign affairs" had occurred. He worried that the executive branch could bypass the legislature completely by entering into conventions that were not submitted to the Senate for approval, and he emphasized that his amendment was designed to ensure that the president could not, on his own authority, "conclude an agreement which will make it unlawful for me to kill a cat in the back alley of my lot at night, . . . [or] make a treaty with India which will preclude me from butchering a cow in my own pasture."[20]

Much of George's concern about executive agreements stemmed from the Supreme Court's decision in 1942 in the *Pink* case. The justices had ruled 5–2 in *United States v. Pink* that an executive agreement between President Roosevelt and Soviet Commissar of Foreign Affairs Maxim Litvinov superseded New York State's policy for distributing the assets of a Russian insurance company that had been nationalized by the Soviet government in 1919. The New York courts had refused to recognize the Soviet Union's confiscation decree against the company's New York assets, and, in accordance with state law, New York Superintendent of Insurance Louis Pink had seized the company's funds and used them to satisfy the claims of American citizens and policyholders against the company. When there had still been a substantial sum of money left over, Pink had begun distributing it among the company's foreign creditors. In the Roosevelt-Litvinov agreement accompanying American recognition of the Soviet Union in 1933, however, the Soviets had transferred their rights to all such properties in the United States to the American government, which had then filed suit to force Pink to turn over any funds still under his jurisdiction. New York officials had challenged the federal government's authority to seize the money, asserting that both New York state

[19]100 *CR* 2264–67. The 18 senators who voted for the motion to send the matter back to committee were: Douglas, Fulbright, Gillette, Hayden, Hennings, Hill, Humphrey, Jackson, Kennedy, Kilgore, Lehman, Magnuson, Morse, Murray, Neely, Pastore, Sparkman, and Wiley.
[20]Ibid., 1401–2, 1416–17, and 1663–68. The quotations are on pp. 1417 and 1668.

law and the Fifth Amendment of the United States Constitution prohibited such taking of private property without due process and just compensation. When the case reached the Supreme Court, the justices determined that the Roosevelt-Litvinov agreement, even though never submitted to the Senate for approval, represented the national government's foreign policy, thus taking precedence over New York law. The justices also ruled that the agreement did not contravene the Fifth Amendment, since it had been the Soviet government, not the United States, that had nationalized the company.[21]

Senator George argued that the court's decision in the *Pink* case had set a dangerous precedent that could only be countered by requiring congressional action before executive agreements went into force as domestic law. He noted that commentators had criticized the decision at the time, maintaining that the justices had given the Litvinov Assignment a much broader interpretation than had ever been intended, and he emphasized to his colleagues that he had offered his resolution "solely because the Supreme Court of the United States has said that an executive agreement which was nothing but an answer to a letter written by the Russian representative in this country had the effect of overcoming the fifth amendment to the Constitution of the United States, and, also, had the effect of overriding a State law." George urged other senators to help in overturning the *Pink* decision, which he claimed had elevated executive agreements to the status of treaties, freed such compacts from the restrictions of the Fifth Amendment, and empowered presidents, on their own, to enter into agreements abrogating state laws and regulations.[22]

Thomas Hennings, a liberal Democrat from Missouri, took the lead in the Senate in opposing the George resolution. A lawyer himself, with a special interest in the Constitution, Hennings believed it was self-evident under existing law that treaties had to conform to the Constitution, and he feared that the Bricker amendment or any of the various substitute proposals would jeopardize the nation's well-being by stripping the president of the flexibility he needed to conduct foreign policy. Hennings had voted against S.J. Res. 1 in the judiciary committee, and he warned now that the George substitute was almost as bad as the original measure. In his view, the George amendment was "rather fatal medicine for a hypothetical disease."[23]

[21]See *United States v. Pink*, 315 U.S. 204 (1942). On the Roosevelt-Litvinov agreements, see Browder, *The Origins of Soviet-American Diplomacy;* and Bishop, *The Roosevelt-Litvinov Agreements: The American View.*

[22]100 CR 1401–2. See also Senator George's remarks, ibid., 1313, 1416–17, 1663–68; Senator Bricker's comments, ibid., 2047–50; Alfred Schweppe, memorandum, "The Bricker Amendment—Executive Agreements," reprinted in ibid., 1104; Borchard, "Extraterritorial Confiscations"; and Jessup, "The Litvinov Assignment and the Pink Case."

[23]Ibid., 1656. Hennings received a 100% liberal rating from Americans for Democratic

Concerned that Senator George might have persuaded senators to support his resolution with his remarks about the *Pink* case, Hennings made it a special point to answer George's charges and show that the decision in the *Pink* case was not a dangerous precedent and did not warrant a constitutional amendment. He contacted former Supreme Court Justice Owen Roberts, one of the two dissenters in the case and now one of the sponsors of the Committee for Defense of the Constitution by Preserving the Treaty Power. Hennings reported to the Senate that Roberts agreed with his own view that the ruling in the *Pink* case would have been exactly the same even if the George amendment had been in effect. The senator and the justice noted that Congress had actually implemented the Roosevelt-Litvinov agreement in 1939 when it had created a commission to examine claims and distribute any funds accruing to the federal government under the agreement. Moreover, they pointed out that the case had arisen from an agreement concluded in 1933 when President Roosevelt had formally recognized the Soviet Union, and Hennings reminded his colleagues that George had said repeatedly that his resolution was not intended to limit the president's power to receive ambassadors and recognize foreign governments. Hence, if the George amendment were construed by the courts as intended by its sponsor, it would not affect such agreements as the Litvinov Assignment. Hennings also challenged George's contention that the court had ruled the Roosevelt-Litvinov agreement did not have to comply with the Fifth Amendment, quoting from the decision to show that the justices had in fact specifically determined that the agreement did not violate anyone's rights under the Fifth Amendment. All in all, Hennings maintained, the *Pink* case was neither the "judicial monster" nor the "bogey under the bed" it had been portrayed as, but just "a very sensible case that has been misconstrued and exaggerated."[24]

Besides the *Pink* case, the Eisenhower administration's decision to ap-

---

Action in 1954. See ADA, press release, October 1, 1954, "ADA Papers." For his views on the Bricker amendment itself, see Hennings to Jacob Lashly, January 24, 1953; Hennings to H. G. Zelle, May 21, 1953; and press release from the office of Senator Hennings, June 14, 1953; all in Thomas Hennings Papers, Folders 4776, 4777, and 4765. On his key role in the fight against the Bricker amendment, see Robert Riggs, "Two Democrats Share Spotlight in Bricker Drama," clipping from Louisville *Courier-Journal,* February 15, 1954; and Doris Fleeson column, clipping from Washington *Star,* March 3, 1954; both in Hennings Papers, Folders 4780A and 8241; *New York Times,* February 27, 1954, pp. 1, 8; Herman Phleger to Hennings, February 27, 1954, Phleger Collection, Vol. 10; and interview with J. William Fulbright, November 11, 1976. See also Kemper, *Decade of Fear: Senator Hennings and Civil Liberties.*
[24]100 *CR* 1651–55, esp. 1653 and 1655, and 1729–33. See also Hennings to Owen Roberts, February 10, 1954, Hennings Papers, Folder 4780; Roberts to Hennings, February 11, 1954, reprinted in 100 *CR* 1732; and the remarks by Senators Morse and Cooper, 100 *CR* 1415–16, 1904. For Senator George's statements that his amendment was not designed to limit the president's power to receive ambassadors and recognize foreign governments, see 100 *CR* 1404–6, 1664, and 1668.

peal a lower court's ruling in *United States v. Guy W. Capps, Inc.* worried senators concerned about the use and effects of executive agreements. In April 1953, a United States Circuit Court of Appeals had held unanimously that the government could not enforce an executive agreement with Canada prohibiting the importation of Canadian potatoes except for seed purposes. The judges had ruled that the Constitution gave Congress, not the president, power to regulate foreign commerce; therefore, the agreement in question was unconstitutional because it had not been authorized by Congress and actually disregarded procedures established by the legislature to deal with such matters. The Justice Department had asked the Supreme Court to overturn the lower court's decision, arguing that the president could enter into such agreements as long as they did not directly contravene any federal laws. In this case, the attorney general had asserted, the compact had not violated any statutes and merely represented an alternative method of achieving a common goal. If Congress had objected to the arrangement, he observed, it could easily have nullified the agreement by enacting new legislation.[25]

John Bricker, Walter George, and others condemned the executive branch's decision to appeal the lower court's ruling in the *Capps* case. Like Senator McCarthy, who had moved from attacking Truman and the Democrats to criticizing the Eisenhower administration, Bricker now charged that the present administration's actions in the *Capps* case proved that Eisenhower and his aides, like Roosevelt and Truman before them, believed that the president should have the authority to repeal state laws, void federal statutes, and "amend, suspend, or revoke local legislation." Congress had an obligation, Bricker insisted, to check this "grab for power." George warned that if the Supreme Court sustained the attorney general's arguments, "then we have the possibility of a one-man rule in the United States."[26]

Senator Hennings and Senator Knowland both tried to minimize any fears engendered by the *Capps* case. Hennings saw no threat to American liberties in the administration's seeking a final review of the decision, and Knowland predicted that the Supreme Court would affirm the lower court's ruling. In the meantime, the majority leader stressed, the Circuit Court's unanimous opinion should reassure people "that the President does not have unlimited power in the field of executive agreements, but, to the contrary, is kept within due constitutional bounds when he deals in matters which are clearly within the power of the Congress."[27]

[25]See *United States v. Guy W. Capps, Inc.*, 204 F. (2d) 655 (1953), reprinted in 100 *CR* 1792–94; and memorandum on the *Capps* case, n.d., copy in DDEP, OF 116-H-4.

[26]100 *CR* 1312 and 2049 (Bricker), and 1401–2 (George). See also the comments by Senator Ferguson, ibid., 1312.

[27]Ibid., 1656 (Hennings), and 2197 (Knowland). In 1955 the Supreme Court upheld the

Once his own amendment had been defeated, John Bricker announced that he would vote for the George resolution and urged his supporters to do the same. Bricker conceded that the measure was not as stringent as he would have liked, but he hoped the House of Representatives, if given the chance, would strengthen the amendment by requiring congressional legislation to implement treaties as well as executive agreements if they involved the nation's internal affairs. But even in its present form, Bricker declared, the George amendment would prohibit American acceptance of the draft covenant on human rights or any other agreements that conflicted with the Constitution, such as a treaty to establish a world government. As he had stated previously, he believed it would also "prevent an executive agreement from overriding the Constitution, as in the *Pink* case," and curb "the power of the President to make domestic law dictatorially and single-handedly." Consequently, Bricker recommended that senators vote for the George resolution as their best chance to enact a meaningful amendment.[28]

Senator Mike Mansfield (D-Mont.) also delivered a strong speech in support of the George amendment. One of the few liberals to endorse the measure, Mansfield criticized the tendency in recent years to use executive agreements as substitutes for treaties. He did not question the president's right to make such compacts, either as commander in chief or under authority delegated to him by Congress, but he pointed out that a "provisional" agreement of friendship and commerce with Saudi Arabia entered into in 1933 remained in effect twenty years later, never supplanted by a formal treaty. Similar agreements had been made with Yemen and Nepal in 1946 and 1947, he noted, and they, too, had never been submitted to the Senate for approval. Mansfield suggested that Congress should adopt the George resolution as a warning to the executive branch to stop using executive agreements in place of treaties.[29]

Although there was considerable discussion of executive agreements during the debate on the George amendment, there was little mention of the Yalta accords. Senator Burnet Maybank (D-S.C.) was one of the few who referred to Yalta, explaining that he supported the George resolution because he believed Franklin Roosevelt had exceeded his authority at Yalta and Teheran by entering into agreements that were never approved by the legislature. But as Senator Bricker conceded during an appearance on

---

Circuit Court's decision in favor of Capps, but it did so on different grounds and did not discuss the constitutionality of the executive agreement. See *United States v. Guy W. Capps, Inc.,* 348 U.S. 296 (1955).

[28]Press release from the office of Senator Bricker, "The George Amendment," February 26, 1954, JBP; and 100 *CR* 2374 and 2049. See also Bricker to Friend, March 15, 1954, JBP.

[29]100 *CR* 2238–42. Mansfield received an 84.6% liberal rating from ADA in 1954. See ADA, press release, October 1, 1954, "ADA Papers."

"Meet the Press," the George resolution would not have prevented Yalta. Unlike the text reported by the judiciary committee, which would have given Congress the power to "regulate" all executive agreements, the George substitute required congressional implementation only of executive agreements affecting domestic matters. Thus, even if the measure had been in effect in 1945, it would not have stopped Roosevelt from making agreements concerning Eastern Europe or the Far East.[30]

In the last few days before the vote, those senators opposed to all the amendments, realizing they needed the votes of the Eisenhower Republicans if they were to defeat Senator George's proposal, sought to emphasize the administration's disapproval of the measure. On February 24, Hennings asked Senator Knowland if he had received any indications from the president or the attorney general that they had dropped their objections to the George amendment. Knowland replied that there had been no change in the administration's position: Eisenhower and his advisers still opposed the George resolution. Hennings reminded the majority leader the following day that he had agreed earlier in the debate to make available to senators a Justice Department memorandum analyzing the George substitute, and later that afternoon Knowland read into the record the statement detailing the attorney general's objections to the amendment.[31]

As the vote drew near, administration officials stepped up their lobbying efforts against the measure. Bernard Shanley, Jerry Persons, and other members of the president's staff personally contacted every Republican senator to impress upon them Eisenhower's opposition to the amendment. Most senators had already made up their minds, however. Guy Cordon of Oregon, for example, who usually supported the president on foreign policy issues, explained that he would have liked to help on this matter, but he felt he could not go back on his commitment in favor of the proposal. The only senator Shanley made any headway with at all was Frank Barrett of Wyoming, who promised to side with the administration if his vote were needed. The president's aides continued to lobby in the Senate cloakrooms right up to the final vote, but Eisenhower still worried that Republican senators, including some of his supporters, might furnish the votes to approve the amendment.[32]

[30]See 100 *CR* 2354; and transcript of "Meet the Press" broadcast, January 31, 1954, p. 9, copy in JBP, Box 110, OHS.

[31]100 *CR* 2198, 2252, 2253, and 2255–56. See also the exchange between Senator Fulbright and Senator Knowland (the presiding officer), ibid., 1788–89.

[32]See list of senators and aides assigned to contact them, n.d., DDEP, OF 116-H-4; Shanley Diary, February 17 and 26, 1954, DDEL; and Dwight Eisenhower, memorandum for the record, February 26, 1954, in Ferrell, ed., *The Eisenhower Diaries*, p. 276. On the admin-

IV

On February 26, after a month of long and sometimes bitter debate on the various proposals, the Senate voted 61–30 to substitute the George resolution for the Knowland-Ferguson text (see Table 4). Bricker's supporters and Senator George's followers, both of whom wanted a strong bill with at least some restrictions on executive agreements, voted for the George amendment, as did Eisenhower Republicans Frank Carlson (Kan.) and Ralph Flanders (Vt.), and liberal Democrats Mike Mansfield, Lister Hill (Ala.), Henry Jackson (Wash.), and Warren Magnuson (Wash.). Most of the Eisenhower Republicans joined with those opposed to all the resolutions, however, and voted against the measure, as did J. Glenn Beall (R-Md.) and Paul Douglas (D-Ill.). Significantly, even though only a simple majority was needed to make the substitution, on this preliminary test the George resolution received one vote more than the two-thirds majority that would be required to approve it on the final vote and send it on to the House of Representatives.[33]

Certain senators' votes on the motion to replace the Knowland-Ferguson proposal with the George amendment require further comment. Hill and Jackson both voted for the resolution on this occasion mainly out of respect for Senator George, not because they wanted to see the amendment adopted. Jackson had voted against all the previous measures except the provision calling for roll-call votes on treaties, and Hill had opposed even that section. In addition, they had both voted to send the whole matter back to the judiciary committee, a further indication of their opposition to all the amendments. Magnuson's position was not so clear-cut, but it seems that his vote for the resolution was also prompted by loyalty to Senator George. A cosponsor of S.J. Res. 1, he apparently believed that some sort of limitations should be imposed on international agreements. At one point he had even proposed an amendment of his own to require roll-call votes to approve executive agreements as well as treaties. He had voted against the major provisions of the Knowland-Ferguson resolution, however—even

istration's lobbying against the measure, see also John Bricker, "The Fight for a Treaty-Control Amendment—Round One," address by Senator Bricker before the regional conference of the American Bar Association, Atlanta, Georgia, March 4, 1954, pp. 2–3, copy in JBP, Box 110, OHS; Eisenhower's comments on "Eisenhower on the Presidency—Part II," CBS television program, November 23, 1961, reported in *New York Times,* November 24, 1961, pp. 1, 23; and interview with Senator Bricker, June 26, 1975.

[33]100 *CR* 2358; and summary of telephone call, Phleger to Dulles, February 26, 1954, in "Telephone Conversations, Dulles." Hill, Jackson, and Magnuson received liberal ratings of 85%, 100%, and 93% respectively from ADA in 1953, and 84.6%, 84.6%, and 76.9% respectively in 1954. See ADA, press releases of September 24, 1953, and October 1, 1954, "ADA Papers."

TABLE 4.
Vote on substituting the George amendment for S.J. Res. 1

Yeas: 61

Anderson	George	Mansfield
Barrett	Gillette	Martin
Bennett	Goldwater	Maybank
Bricker	Gore	McCarthy
Burke	Griswold	McClellan
Butler (Md.)	Hickenlooper	Mundt
Butler (Neb.)	Hill	Payne
Byrd	Hoey	Potter
Capehart	Holland	Robertson
Carlson	Hunt	Russell
Case	Jackson	Schoeppel
Chavez	Jenner	Smathers
Clements	Johnson (Colo.)	Smith (Me.)
Cordon	Johnson (Tex.)	Sparkman
Daniel	Johnston	Stennis
Dirksen	Kerr	Watkins
Dworshak	Kuchel	Welker
Eastland	Langer	Williams
Ellender	Long	Young
Flanders	Magnuson	
Frear	Malone	

Nays: 30

Aiken	Hendrickson	Monroney
Beall	Hennings	Morse
Bush	Humphrey	Neely
Cooper	Ives	Pastore
Douglas	Kefauver	Purtell
Duff	Kennedy	Saltonstall
Ferguson	Kilgore	Smith (N.J.)
Fulbright	Knowland	Thye
Green	Lehman	Upton
Hayden	Millikin	Wiley

Not Voting: 5

Bridges	McCarran	Symington
Lennon	Murray	

the article nullifying international agreements that conflicted with the Constitution—and he had supported the motion to return the amendment to committee. Moreover, even though he voted now to substitute the George resolution for the Knowland-Ferguson amendment, later that same day he would vote against final passage of the measure on the grounds that it had been changed so drastically from the proposal he had originally cosponsored.[34]

Paul Douglas decided only at the last minute to oppose the George amendment. A liberal Democrat from Illinois, Douglas, like Mike Mansfield, thought the measure might serve as a warning to State Department officials and future presidents not to abuse their power to enter into executive agreements. He had shown his willingness to support some sort of amendment when he had voted for the first section of the Knowland-Ferguson proposal, but as the vote on the George amendment drew near, Douglas became concerned that its approval would be seen as a victory for isolationists and those opposed to the United Nations. He concluded, therefore, that the resolution's adoption would not be in the nation's best interests.[35]

With the George resolution now the only measure before the Senate, the Eisenhower Republicans faced the uncomfortable dilemma they had tried to avoid. Most of the president's supporters favored enactment of some sort of constitutional amendment to limit the internal effects of treaties and executive agreements; that was why they had cosponsored Bricker's original resolution and voted for the Knowland-Ferguson proposals. They also wanted to back the president, however, and he had made it clear that he opposed the George amendment. Most of the Eisenhower Republicans had voted against replacing the Knowland-Ferguson text with the George resolution in an effort to have the final vote take place on the Knowland-Ferguson resolution, which had the president's endorsement. That strategy having failed, they now had to choose between supporting the president or voting for the only amendment that could still be

[34]See *New York Times,* February 27, 1954, pp. 1, 8; *Christian Science Monitor,* March 1, 1954, p. 1; S.J. Res. 1, 83d Cong., 1st sess., January 7, 1953; Magnuson to Bricker, July 8, 1953, JBP, Box 95, OHS; and 100 *CR* 1740, 1742, 1748–50, 1782, 1916, 2262–63, 2267, 2358, 2373, and 2374–75. Because of their consistent opposition to the various measures, Hill and Jackson have been included all along in this chapter in the group of senators opposed to all the amendments. Magnuson was not placed in any of the four groups.

[35]See Douglas to Professor Chafee, February 17, 1954, Chafee Papers, Box 12; handwritten note from T.V.R. to L.C.R., on Thomas Rankin to Leverett Saltonstall, February 17, 1954, copy in Kilgore Papers, Box 25, FDRL; 100 *CR* 1740; and Douglas, *In the Fullness of Time: The Memoirs of Paul H. Douglas,* pp. 476–78. Douglas received a 100% liberal rating from ADA in 1954. See ADA, press release for October 1, 1954, "ADA Papers."

adopted. They knew, moreover, that their votes would prove decisive in what was certain to be an extremely close contest.[36]

Just prior to the final vote on the George amendment, Senator Knowland took the floor to explain how he was going to vote. To make it clear that he was speaking only as an individual senator and not as a representative of the administration or the party, Knowland left his seat as majority leader and reported that as far as he knew the president was still opposed to the George resolution. Knowland asserted, however, that the long debate had shown the need to end the executive branch's encroachments on the powers of the legislature. He readily conceded that there were problems with the George amendment, but he was confident the House of Representatives would improve the measure and then send it back to the Senate through a conference committee, giving senators the opportunity to accept or reject a revised amendment. Knowland believed Congress had to do something to stop presidents from arrogating to themselves powers that properly belong to the legislature. Therefore, he announced, he would vote for the George resolution to give the House a chance to produce a better amendment.[37]

Knowland's argument that the Senate should approve the George resolution with the expectation that the House would modify it and the senators would consider it again in the form of a conference report was patently absurd, especially for a constitutional amendment. If senators had followed his example they would have abdicated their senatorial responsibility by approving a constitutional amendment that they regarded as seriously flawed. What if members of the House of Representatives did not change the text but merely acquiesced in the Senate's bill in order to increase the House's role in foreign affairs? Then the Senate would have no chance to reconsider the resolution or rescind its approval, and the amendment would go on to the states for ratification. The Senate's role in the amending process is that of a deliberative body, not merely a conduit to pass such measures on to the House and the state legislatures.[38]

[36]See Senator Knowland's remarks, 100 *CR* 2372; H. Alexander Smith Diary, February 26 and 27, 1954; Senator Irving Ives, Lincoln Day dinner address on "Lincoln and Eisenhower," February 11, 1954, Ives Papers, Box 48; Senator Ralph Flanders to Clark Eichelberger, January 19, 1954, Flanders Papers, Box 100; Flanders to John Bricker, January 27, 1954, and Senator William Purtell to Frank Gannett, March 2, 1954, both in JBP, Box 100, OHS; and Leverett Saltonstall Oral History Transcript, p. 150, CUOHC.

[37]100 *CR* 2371–72; Chicago *Tribune*, February 27, 1954, pp. 1, 4; and *New York Times*, February 27, 1954, pp. 1, 8. On Knowland's sometimes stormy relationship with the Eisenhower administration, see Eisenhower to William Robinson, March 12, 1954, DDEP, Diary Series; Adams, *Firsthand Report*, pp. 25–26; Reichard, *Reaffirmation of Republicanism*, pp. 194–95; and Jewell, *Senatorial Politics and Foreign Policy*, pp. 61–66.

[38]See Roscoe Drummond's criticism of Knowland's rationale in his column in the New

While Knowland's speech demonstrated that some of the Eisenhower Republicans were deserting the president on this issue, Senator Ferguson promptly showed that others were standing behind the chief executive, holding firm in their opposition to the George resolution. Ferguson agreed with Knowland that a constitutional amendment was needed to make it clear that international agreements had to conform to the Constitution, but he maintained that the George resolution would cause more problems than it would cure. Specifically, he warned that adoption of the George amendment would encourage presidents to use executive agreements more and more to circumvent the protections afforded to the states by the requirement that treaties be approved by a two-thirds majority in the Senate. Forced to decide between what he considered to be a badly flawed amendment and no amendment at all, Ferguson chose the latter, informing his colleagues he would vote against the George resolution. Senator Bush quickly concurred with Ferguson's remarks, and declared that he too would vote against the amendment.[39]

As the clerk began calling the roll that evening for the final vote on the George resolution, the outcome remained uncertain. The situation looked bleak for the administration and other opponents of the amendment when Knowland and fellow Eisenhower Republicans Frank Carlson, Robert Hendrickson, and Eugene Millikin voted with Bricker and George and their supporters in favor of the measure. The resolution's opponents began to take heart, however, when the rest of the Eisenhower Republicans—including Ralph Flanders, who had supported the amendment earlier in the day—voted against the proposal, as did Democrats Lister Hill, Henry Jackson, and Warren Magnuson, all three of whom had voted for the measure previously. Republican J. Glenn Beall also voted against the resolution, along with those senators present who had opposed all the previous measures. Nonetheless, as the vote was ending, 60 senators had voted for the amendment and only 30 had voted against it. It appeared that the George resolution would pass by exactly the two-thirds majority needed for approval.

At that point, however, Harley Kilgore, a liberal Democrat from West Virginia who had voted against all the amendments, staggered into the Senate chamber. Apparently, Kilgore had had a little too much to drink, and according to various accounts, had either been sleeping it off in his office or had to be fetched from a nearby tavern. Regardless, he had almost missed the crucial roll call when he was brought in and propped up by

---

York *Herald Tribune*, March 1, 1954, p. 3. See also the remarks by Senator Lehman, 100 *CR* 2372–73; and Rovere, *Affairs of State,* pp. 206–15.

[39]100 *CR* 2374; *New York Times,* February 27, 1954, pp. 1, 8.

various aides and colleagues. The clerk saw Kilgore and his companions enter the chamber, and asked for the senator's vote. A "nay" was heard—whether from Kilgore or one of the others is uncertain—and Kilgore was recorded as casting the decisive vote against the George resolution. Kilgore's vote made the final tally 60–31, meaning the George amendment had fallen one vote short of the two-thirds required to approve a constitutional amendment (see Table 5 for the vote). A few years later, Senator Bricker recalled bitterly how the George amendment had been defeated at the last minute by the vote of a senator who had to be brought from a tavern.[40]

With the George resolution failing by one vote, every vote against it was crucial, and none more so than that cast by Ralph Flanders of Vermont. An Eisenhower Republican who seldom voted against the president's policies (only six times during the 83d Congress, less than any other senator), Flanders had been one of the original cosponsors of the Bricker amendment. He had withdrawn his support from S.J. Res. 1 because of the insertion of the "which" clause, but, as he had explained in a speech to the Senate in early February 1954, he still believed a constitutional amendment should be adopted to counter the growing tendency of the executive branch in recent years "to depreciate the constitutional role of the Senate in the making of treaties." In particular, Flanders had charged that Secretary of State Dean Acheson had misled senators when he had assured them in 1949 that American troops would not be sent to Europe under the North Atlantic Treaty Agreement. Truman had sent four American divisions to Europe two years later, and in the senator's opinion, such actions had helped create "the climate of experience and feeling in which the seed of S.J. Res. 1 was planted." Flanders had urged his colleagues to enact the George amendment or some such limitation on executive agreements so that there would be "no question as to the authority of the Congress to deal with such agreements, nor any misunderstanding as to the status of such agreements as compared with treaties."[41]

[40]100 *CR* 2374–75; *New York Times,* February 27, 1954, pp. 1, 8; Chicago *Tribune,* February 27, 1954, pp. 1, 4; *Time* Magazine, March 8, 1954, p. 27; Shanley Diary, February 26, 1954; James Hamilton, Methodist Board of Temperance, to Senator Bricker, April 11, 1957; and Bricker to Hamilton, April 16, 1957; both in JBP, Box 129, OHS; and letter from Ben H. Brown, Jr., to author, March 21, 1977. Brown served as deputy assistant secretary of state for congressional relations from 1953 to 1955.

[41]100 *CR* 1106–7. See also Flanders to Professor Chafee, February 20, 1952, Chafee Papers, Box 11; Flanders to Clark Eichelberger, January 19, 1954, Flanders Papers, Box 100; and Flanders to Bricker, January 27, 1954, JBP, Box 100, OHS. On Flanders's support for President Eisenhower's policies, see *Congressional Quarterly Almanac, 1953,* p. 82; and ibid., *1954,* p. 62. On Acheson's assurances during the hearings on the North Atlantic Treaty in 1949 that American troops would not be sent to Europe under that agreement, see U.S., Congress, Senate, Committee on Foreign Relations, *North Atlantic Treaty, Hearings,* before the Senate Committee on Foreign Relations, 81st Cong., 1st sess., 1949, pp. 79–81.

TABLE 5.
Final vote on Senator George's substitute amendment

Yeas: 60		
Anderson	George	Mansfield
Barrett	Gillette	Martin
Bennett	Goldwater	Maybank
Bricker	Gore	McCarthy
Burke	Griswold	McClellan
Butler (Md.)	Hendrickson	Millikin
Butler (Neb.)	Hickenlooper	Mundt
Byrd	Hoey	Payne
Capehart	Holland	Potter
Carlson	Hunt	Robertson
Case	Jenner	Russell
Chavez	Johnson (Colo.)	Schoeppel
Clements	Johnson (Tex.)	Smathers
Cordon	Johnston	Smith (Me.)
Daniel	Kerr	Sparkman
Dirkson	Knowland	Stennis
Dworshak	Kuchel	Watkins
Eastland	Langer	Welker
Ellender	Long	Williams
Frear	Malone	Young

Nays: 31		
Aiken	Hennings	Morse
Beall	Hill	Neely
Bush	Humphrey	Pastore
Cooper	Ives	Purtell
Douglas	Jackson	Saltonstall
Duff	Kefauver	Smith (N.J.)
Ferguson	Kennedy	Thye
Flanders	Kilgore	Upton
Fulbright	Lehman	Wiley
Green	Magnuson	
Hayden	Monroney	

Not Voting: 5		
Bridges	McCarran	Symington
Lennon	Murray	

On the key votes, however, Flanders voted first to substitute the George resolution for the Knowland-Ferguson text, then reversed himself and voted against the measure on the final ballot. He was troubled by the president's adamant opposition to the resolution, and he found alarming Senator Ferguson's warning just before the final vote that approval of the George amendment would increase the use of executive agreements instead of treaties. Denounced by the Chicago *Tribune* as the "Vermont Republican internationalist," Flanders worried too about the strong bias against the United Nations that was so prevalent in the letters he had received from proponents of the Bricker amendment. The senator believed that the UN, despite its problems, was essential to world peace and deserved America's continued support. He also thought that in many ways the Bricker amendment had already served its purpose. Senators would surely scrutinize treaties more carefully in the future, and members of the executive branch had certainly been made aware of the Senate's concern about its prerogatives in foreign affairs. Consequently, when he realized just how important his vote would be, Flanders chose to support the president by voting against the George resolution, secure in the belief that most of the measure's objectives had already been achieved.[42]

Administration officials had been confident that Flanders would support the president's position in the end, but they had not been nearly so sanguine about J. Glenn Beall of Maryland. Beall generally supported the president's programs (86 percent of the time during the 83d Congress—74 percent on foreign policy issues), but the administration was uncertain how he would vote this time. Gerald Morgan, one of the president's aides, had spoken to Beall to reiterate the administration's opposition to the Bricker and George amendments, and administration officials had thought he might be leaning their way until he had voted for Bricker's more stringent proposal the previous day. Having supported that measure, it seemed likely that he would vote for the George amendment as well. Much to everyone's surprise, however, Beall voted against the George resolution—the only senator who had voted for Bricker's amendment to do so. In a press release a few days later, Beall explained that he had opposed the George resolution because it would have impaired President Eisenhower's ability to conduct the nation's foreign affairs and resulted in presidents using executive agreements to avoid the problem of having treaties approved by a two-thirds majority in the Senate. As an aide to Senator Bricker pointed out, however, both of Beall's arguments applied to Bricker's text as well, yet Beall had supported that measure the day before. Why

---

[42]See 100 *CR* 1106–7, 2358, and 2374–75; Chicago *Tribune*, February 27, 1954, pp. 1, 4; and Flanders, *Senator from Vermont*, pp. 211–12.

then had Beall voted against the George amendment? The most plausible explanation is that pressure and lobbying from administration officials persuaded him to support the president.[43]

The importance of the Eisenhower administration's efforts against the George resolution cannot be overstated. It was the opposition of the president and his advisers to the measure and their opposition alone that led a number of Republican senators to vote against the bill. John Sherman Cooper, for example, almost always supported President Eisenhower on foreign affairs issues, and he did so again on the George amendment. Cooper had said in a Senate speech on January 29 that he expected to support Senator George's proposal unless administration officials pointed out problems with it which he had not seen. Subsequently, Cooper had reported on February 17 that members of the executive branch had advised him that the George resolution might impinge on the president's powers as commander in chief and his authority to conduct foreign relations. The senator had then suggested that the whole matter be referred back to the judiciary committee for further study. In the end, Cooper voted against the George amendment because of the administration's concern that the measure would create problems for the president in foreign affairs. Similarly, Leverett Saltonstall explained years later that he had "hated to do it," but he had voted against the George resolution in order to "support Eisenhower."[44]

Although it is true that not all Eisenhower Republicans (defined now as those senators who supported President Eisenhower at least 75 percent of the time on foreign policy issues) voted against the George resolution, the majority of them did in fact vote against the measure because of the administration's objections. Even though four senators who usually supported the president in foreign affairs (Cordon, Griswold, Kuchel, and Payne) deserted him early on in the fight over the Bricker amendment, and four more (Carlson, Hendrickson, Knowland, and Millikin) abandoned him on the final vote on the George resolution, the thirteen other Eisenhower Republicans remained loyal to the president throughout the

[43]See 100 *CR* 2262, 2374; statement by Senator J. Glenn Beall, "Senator J. Glenn Beall Comments on Senate Action on S.J. Res. 1," n.d.; and Charles Webb to Leila Edwards, March 12, 1954; both in JBP, Box 100, OHS; and list of senators and aides assigned to contact them, n.d., DDEP, OF 116-H-4 (a "yea" on the list meant a vote for the administration's position—against the amendment). On Beall's support for the president's policies, see *Congressional Quarterly Almanac, 1954,* p. 62; and Reichard, *Reaffirmation of Republicanism,* pp. 272–73.

[44]See 100 *CR* 1029, 1904–5, and 2374–75; and Leverett Saltonstall Oral History Transcript, p. 150, CUOHC. Cooper supported the president 87% of the time on foreign policy issues during the 83d Congress, Saltonstall 83%. See Reichard, *Reaffirmation,* pp. 272–73. On the importance of the administration's "all-out opposition," see also Richard Russell to Mrs. J. M. Haynes, February 22, 1954, Russell Papers, Series IX, Box 20, "Bricker Amendment."

controversy. Senators Aiken, Bush, Duff, Ferguson, Flanders, Ives, Purtell, Saltonstall, Smith (N.J.), Thye, and Wiley had all cosponsored the Bricker amendment at one time or another; yet they all voted against the George resolution after the president announced his opposition, as did Senators Cooper and Upton. H. Alexander Smith illuminated their reasons for voting as they did when he recorded in his diary not that he and the others had voted against the George resolution, but that they had "stood by the President and Dulles."[45]

It is interesting to note that the Eisenhower Republicans who stood by the president were more likely to be from the Northeast and tended to be more internationally minded than those who opposed him. Nine of the eleven Eisenhower Republicans from the Northeast supported the president by voting against the George resolution, but only three of the five Eisenhower Republicans from the Midwest and none of the four from the West did so (see Table 6). This reflects ideology as much as geography, since senators such as Aiken, Duff, Flanders, Ives, Saltonstall, and Smith (N.J.) were all more strongly committed to the idea of the United States playing an active role in world affairs than were legislators such as Carlson, Cordon, Knowland, and Millikin. Of those Republicans who upheld the president's position, only Ferguson could be described as nationalistically inclined.[46]

As important as the president and the Eisenhower Republicans were in the fight against the Bricker amendment, one must not lose sight of the key role liberal Democrats played in the measure's defeat. Despite all of Eisenhower's efforts, more than two-thirds of the Republicans who voted—32 out of 46—voted in favor of the George resolution; it was the liberal Democrats who supplied a majority of the votes that kept the amendment from passing. Thomas Hennings, Hubert Humphrey, Estes

---

[45]H. Alexander Smith Diary, February 27, 1954; and editorial, "They Listened to Reason," Pittsburgh *Post-Gazette,* March 2, 1954, clipping in Hennings Papers, Folder 4787. See also Reichard, *Reaffirmation,* pp. 272–73. Wiley had been a cosponsor of the Bricker amendment in 1952; Aiken, Bush, Duff, Ferguson, Flanders, Ives, Purtell, Saltonstall, Smith (N.J.), and Thye were all among the cosponsors of the amendment in 1953. See S.J. Res. 130, 82d Cong., 2d sess., February 7, 1952; and S.J. Res. 1, 83d Cong., 1st sess., January 7, 1953. Cooper had never cosponsored the Bricker amendment, and Upton had just recently been appointed to the Senate to replace the late Charles Tobey.

[46]Gary Reichard determined that, relative to other Republican senators, Duff, Ives, Saltonstall, and Smith (N.J.) could all be classified as strong internationalists; Aiken, Flanders, Thye, and Wiley as moderate internationalists; and Ferguson as a moderate nationalist. Carlson, Knowland, and Millikin were uncommitted, and Cordon and Hendrickson could not be scaled on this continuum because their voting records were too erratic. The other Eisenhower Republicans were new senators in the 83d Congress and Reichard did not include them in his ratings in this category. See Reichard, *Reaffirmation of Republicanism,* pp. 28–32, 66–67, and 250. See also editorial, "A Victory to Give Pause," St. Louis *Post-Dispatch,* February 27, 1954, p. 4-A.

TABLE 6.
Eisenhower Republicans and the George amendment

	For	Against
Northeast:	Hendrickson (N.J.) Payne (Me.)	Aiken (Vt.) Bush (Conn.) Duff (Pa.) Flanders (Vt.) Ives (N.Y.) Purtell (Conn.) Saltonstall (Mass.) Smith (N.J.) Upton (N.H.)
Midwest:	Carlson (Kan.) Griswold (Neb.)	Ferguson (Mich.) Thye (Minn.) Wiley (Wisc.)
West:	Cordon (Ore.) Knowland (Cal.) Kuchel (Cal.) Millikin (Colo.)	
Other:		Cooper (Ky.)

Kefauver, Herbert Lehman, and other liberal Democrats led the opposition throughout the debate. As Hennings explained in a letter to Eisenhower, the liberal Democrats opposed Bricker's resolution and all the so-called harmless substitutes. They regarded the various measures as an attack against "the historic separation of powers" and an attempt "to paralyze the traditional powers of the Presidency in our foreign relations." In the end, sixteen liberal Democrats and Independent Wayne Morse joined forces with fourteen Republicans to support the president and send the George amendment down to defeat (see Table 7).[47]

Another aspect of the vote on the George resolution that requires further comment is the sharp split between liberals and conservatives that emerges when one uses Americans for Democratic Action's liberal ratings of individual senators to analyze the vote (see Table 8). Interestingly, the 18 most reactionary Republicans and the 24 most conservative Democrats

[47]See Hennings to President Eisenhower, February 5, 1954, in 100 *CR* 1407. On the key role played by liberal Democrats, see also *New York Times*, February 27, 1954, pp. 1, 8, and editorial, "Sequel to Bricker," ibid., March 2, 1954, p. 24; Fletcher Knebel column, "Bricker May Return to Fight Another Day," Minneapolis *Star Journal*, February 28, 1954, copy attached to letter from Charles Webb to Mrs. J. A. Houle, March 15, 1954, JBP, Box 100, OHS; and *New Republic*, March 8, 1954, pp. 3–4.

TABLE 7.
Democrats who voted against the George resolution
(with their liberal ratings from Americans for Democratic Action) *

Douglas	100.%	Kefauver	100.%
Fulbright	76.9%	Kennedy	84.6%
Green	91.7%	Kilgore	90.9%
Hayden	92.3%	Lehman	100.%
Hennings	100.%	Magnuson	76.9%
Hill	84.6%	Monroney	76.9%
Humphrey	100.%	Neely	83.3%
Jackson	84.6%	Pastore	100.%

*Ratings are from ADA, press release for October 1, 1954, "ADA Papers."

all voted for the George amendment, while the vast majority of both parties' most liberal senators—"all the New Dealers" as the Chicago *Tribune* described them—voted against it. The Senate's 10 most liberal members—9 Democrats and Independent Wayne Morse—all voted against the proposal, as did 3 of the 4 most liberal Republicans: Senators Cooper (61.5%), Aiken (53.9%), and Thye (41.7%). The only liberal Republican who voted in favor of the amendment was Senator Langer (63.6%), a rabid isolationist. Of the 20 Democrats with liberal ratings of 75 percent or higher, only Thomas Burke (Ohio), Guy Gillette (Iowa), Mike Mansfield, and John Sparkman voted for the measure. Mansfield's reasons for voting as he did have already been discussed. Burke, Gillette, and Sparkman were all up for reelection in 1954, and that more than anything else led them to vote for the George resolution. Burke, who had just been appointed to the Senate to succeed the late Robert Taft, faced an especially difficult race in Ohio, where John Bricker and his amendment enjoyed considerable public support. Gillette and Sparkman both showed their true feelings about the proposal when they voted to send it back to committee, but they feared the political repercussions of opposing the measure directly. Sparkman's mail at one point ran 20 : 1 in favor of the Bricker amendment; hence, he tried to keep all his options open until the very last minute. When asked how he intended to vote, Sparkman replied that "if the final version of the amendment which comes before us protects the rights of our citizens without unduly hindering the Executive Department in its dealings with other nations, I shall be glad to support it." After such a statement, he could easily vote either way. Only after State Department officials informed him his vote would not be needed to defeat the George amendment did Sparkman vote in favor of the proposal.[48]

[48]See editorial, "Defeated by One Vote," Chicago *Tribune*, February 28, 1954, p. 20; and ADA, press release, October 1, 1954, "ADA Papers." On Langer's isolationist views, see

TABLE 8.
*Americans for Democratic Action liberal ratings of senators**

The most conservative Republicans

Bricker	0.%	Capehart	14.2%
Malone	0.%	Barrett	15.4%
Welker	0.%	Case	15.4%
Butler (Md.)	7.7%	Goldwater	15.4%
Dworshak	7.7%	Martin	15.4%
Schoeppel	7.7%	Mundt	15.4%
Williams	7.7%	Watkins	15.4%
Jenner	8.3%	McCarthy	16.7%
Butler (Neb.)	(12.5%)	Potter	16.7%

The most conservative Democrats

Byrd	0.%	Frear	38.5%
Holland	15.4%	Russell	38.5%
Robertson	15.4%	George	41.7%
McClellan	18.2%	Maybank	(43.%)
Stennis	23.1%	Hunt	(46.%)
Daniel	25.%	Clements	53.9%
Ellender	27.3%	Johnston	53.9%
Johnson (Colo.)	30.8%	Long	53.9%
Smathers	30.8%	Kerr	54.5%
Hoey	(33.%)	Anderson	69.2%
Johnson (Tex.)	33.3%	Gore	69.2%
Eastland	37.5%	Chavez	72.7%

The most liberal senators

Douglas	100.%	Morse	100.%
Hennings	100.%	Pastore	100.%
Humphrey	100.%	Hayden	92.3%
Kefauver	100.%	Green	91.7%
Lehman	100.%	Kilgore	90.9%

*Whenever possible, 1954 ADA liberal ratings are shown, but in some cases it was necessary to use 1953 ratings (indicated by parenthesis) for senators who died during 1954 and whose voting records for that year were not rated. See ADA, press releases, October 1, 1954, and September 24, 1953, both in "ADA Papers."

Doenecke, *Not to the Swift,* passim. On Sparkman, see 100 *CR* 2267; summary of telephone call, Sparkman to Secretary of State Dulles, January 9, 1954, in "Telephone Conversations, Dulles"; Sparkman to Professor Chafee, January 30, 1954, Chafee Papers, Box 12; Sparkman to Loren Berry, February 2, 1954, copy in JBP, Box 100, OHS; and letter from Ben H. Brown, Jr., to author, March 21, 1977.

Since the controversy over the Bricker and George amendments was a dispute over treaties and executive agreements, both of which are instruments of foreign policy, it seems surprising at first that senators divided along liberal and conservative lines—a split usually associated with domestic issues. The liberal-conservative dichotomy of the 1930s, for example, had been based on differences over domestic issues such as the expanding role of the federal government, and had not carried over into foreign affairs. The isolationists of that era had included among their ranks both liberals such as Maury Maverick (D-Tex.) and Gerald Nye (R-N.D.), and conservatives such as Hamilton Fish (R-N.Y.), Bennett Champ Clark (D-Mo.), and Robert Taft. Similarly, the internationalists had included both liberals like Alben Barkley (D-Ky.) and Claude Pepper (D-Fla.), and conservatives like Carter Glass (D-Va.) and Walter George.[49] The division between liberals and conservatives on the Bricker amendment makes sense, however, when one recalls that it had been primarily domestic concerns that had led Frank Holman and the leaders of the American Bar Association and Senator Bricker to propose their amendments in the first place. Holman and Bricker sought to limit the use and effects of international agreements to ensure that such compacts as the United Nations Charter and the draft covenant on human rights would not change social and economic conditions within the United States or allow international agencies to intervene in the nation's internal affairs. They also wanted to prevent the federal government from implementing such agreements by enacting legislation on economic and social matters previously regulated by the states. Hence, one would expect conservatives, who generally opposed federal action in such areas, to support such an amendment, and liberals, who favored national control over such matters, to vote against it. These expectations are borne out in the final vote on the George resolution.

One should not read too much significance into the fact that the George resolution fell just one vote short of the number required for approval, for there are some indications that the measure's opponents had a few votes in reserve that could have been called upon if necessary. Presidential counsel Bernard Shanley noted in his diary that Frank Barrett of Wyoming had promised to support the administration if his vote were needed, and a State Department aide confided years later that John Sparkman and others who wanted to vote for the amendment for political reasons were told that they could do so since there were already enough votes to block the

---

[49]See Patterson, *Congressional Conservatism and the New Deal*, pp. viii, 337, 348–49, and passim; Jonas, *Isolationism in America, 1935–1941*, esp. chapters 2 and 3 where he discusses both liberal and conservative isolationists; *New York Times*, January 19, 1941, p. 6-E; and Kimball, *The Most Unsordid Act: Lend-Lease, 1939–1941*, pp. 164, 207–9, and passim.

proposal. That of course had been based on the assumption that Harley Kilgore would be present to cast his vote against the resolution. One of Lyndon Johnson's biographers also reports that Johnson later claimed to have "engineered this cliff-hanging vote . . . in order to make the Administration sweat." There is no hard evidence supporting Johnson's boast, but it is possible that he would have prevailed upon Sparkman or others, or perhaps even changed his own vote, if necessary, to defeat the amendment.[50]

It should also be stressed that it was Senator George's rather innocuous substitute, not the Bricker amendment, that came close to being adopted. Bricker had realized that the resolution approved by the judiciary committee, including the "which" clause and giving Congress the authority to regulate executive agreements, had no chance of passing, and he had abandoned that measure in late January 1954, and submitted a less stringent proposal. But the Senate had rejected Bricker's modified resolution by a vote of 50–42, making it the only bill that failed to win the support of at least a majority of the legislators. Clearly, by February 1954, there was little enthusiasm among senators, especially in the face of Eisenhower's opposition, for imposing serious restrictions on the treaty-making power.[51]

As for the George amendment itself, it had become more of a symbolic issue than anything else by the time of the final vote. The first section of the proposal merely stipulated that international compacts conflicting with the Constitution would be null and void, and the second provision would simply have required congressional legislation to bring executive agreements into force as internal law within the United States. Treaties would not have been affected by the measure as long as they did not contravene the Constitution, nor would presidential agreements dealing only with foreign affairs. But as Paul Douglas, Ralph Flanders, and others had recognized, the controversy had come to be seen as a struggle between isolationists and internationalists, between those who believed the United States had to play an active role in world affairs, and those who sought to limit the impact of America's involvement in the United Nations and events overseas. Douglas and Flanders both decided in the end to vote against the George resolution because they feared that its adoption would be perceived as a victory for the isolationists.[52]

[50]See Shanley Diary, February 26, 1954; letter from Ben H. Brown, Jr., to author, March 21, 1977; and Steinberg, *Sam Johnson's Boy*, p. 359.

[51]See 100 *CR* 2262; Roscoe Drummond column, "What Happened on the Bricker Amendment," New York *Herald Tribune*, March 3, 1954, p. 3; and Lyman Tondel, Jr., letter to the editor, *New York Times*, January 12, 1955, p. 26.

[52]See Douglas, *In the Fullness of Time*, p. 478; Flanders's remarks in 100 *CR* 1106–7; Chicago *Tribune*, February 27, 1954, pp. 1, 4; and editorial, "Defeated by One Vote," Chicago

The Senate's rejection of the Bricker and George amendments represented a major victory for President Eisenhower over the "Old Guard" conservatives and isolationists. At first, Eisenhower had downplayed his opposition to S.J. Res. 1, talking of compromise and basing his objections on the secretary of state's analysis of the measure. The president and his advisers feared, however, that the enactment of anything but the most watered-down amendment would be interpreted as a triumph for Bricker and his cohorts, the Henry Dworshaks, William Jenners, George Malones, and Herman Welkers. When Eisenhower finally realized that more vigorous leadership was needed, he began speaking out frequently and forcefully against proposals that might weaken or be perceived as weakening the preeminent roles of the president and the federal government in foreign affairs. Eventually, he persuaded a majority of his supporters in the Senate to vote against such measures, and, with the help of liberal Democrats, they were able to defeat the Bricker and George amendments and preserve the Constitution intact.[53]

Tribune, February 28, 1954, p. 20. On isolationists and the Bricker amendment, see also Doenecke, *Not to the Swift,* pp. 235–38.

[53]See Hagerty Diary, January 14, 17, 19, 20, 22, and 31, 1954, DDEL; summaries of telephone calls, Dulles to the president, and Eisenhower to Brownell, both on January 9, 1954, and Eisenhower to Brownell, January 22, 1954; all in DDEP, Diary Series; and William S. White, "Bricker Fight Highlights Basic G.O.P. Split," *New York Times,* January 31, 1954, IV, 3. Dworshak, Jenner, Malone, and Welker were four of the more reactionary, isolationist Republicans in the Senate. Their liberal ratings according to ADA were 7.7%, 8.3%, 0%, and 0%, respectively, in 1954, and Reichard rated them all as very strong nationalists who supported Eisenhower's foreign policies only 30%, 25%, 10%, and 18% of the time during the 83d Congress. See ADA, press release for October 1, 1954, "ADA Papers"; and Reichard, *Reaffirmation of Republicanism,* pp. 57, 72–73, 86–87, 250, and 272–73.

CHAPTER ELEVEN

"The Fight Has Only Just Begun"

The Senate's rejection of the George resolution did not end the fight over the Bricker amendment. Despite being shunted off the front pages of the nation's newspapers by the growing controversy between the army and Senator McCarthy, the Bricker amendment remained a live issue as Senator Bricker and his supporters continued to press for the adoption of a constitutional amendment to limit the use and effects of treaties and executive agreements. Although Eisenhower complained in mid-1955 that he was "sick unto death of the term 'Bricker Amendment,'" the senator and his amendment remained a difficult problem which the president and his advisers had to contend with through most of the 1950s.[1]

I

President Eisenhower hoped that the defeat of the George resolution had laid the Bricker amendment to rest. Rather than dwelling on Knowland's desertion on the key vote or other disappointments, the president preferred to look ahead, emphasizing at his next meeting with the legislative leaders that he wanted to put the controversy behind them and get on with the job of selling their overall program to the public. When asked at a news conference if he was satisfied with the outcome in the Senate on the Bricker amendment, Eisenhower replied that he was pleased to be free now to concentrate on implementing his plans "for building a stronger and better America."[2]

[1] Dwight Eisenhower to Edgar Eisenhower, July 12, 1955, DDEP, Diary Series.

[2] See James Hagerty Diary, February 27 and March 1, 1954, in Ferrell, ed., *Hagerty Diary*, pp. 21, 23; Bernard Shanley Diary, March 1, 1954; legislative leadership meeting, March 1, 1954, supplementary notes, DDEP, Diary Series; president's news conference, March 3, 1954, in *Public Papers: Eisenhower, 1954*, p. 296; and *New York Times*, March 4, 1954, p. 12.

Eisenhower's relief proved to be short-lived, however. In a pamphlet released on March 2, 1954, Frank Holman promised that "the fight for an adequate constitutional amendment has only just begun." Holman asserted that the Senate would have adopted a meaningful amendment had it not been for "the unconstitutional interference of the President in a purely legislative process." Moreover, he charged, the measure would have passed regardless had not such "left-wing and world government senators as Kefauver, Humphrey, Lehman, and Fulbright" been joined by "such Republicans as Senators Wiley, Ferguson, Knowland, Saltonstall, Upton, and Flanders, who chose to placate the State Department and follow the Dulles-Acheson school of internationalism." Holman believed the battle could still be won though, and he urged all those who supported the Bricker amendment to continue the fight to see it enacted.[3]

A few days later, John Bricker echoed Holman's declaration that the conflict was far from over. In a speech before a regional conference of the American Bar Association, Bricker argued that his amendment was needed to counter the "revolutionary doctrines propounded in the United Nations" and protect America's internal affairs "from the consuming ambition of the United Nations and its specialized agencies to regulate those matters by treaty." The senator conceded that the defenders of "unhandicapped executive power" had won the first round because of the "furious lobbying of White House and State Department aides in the corridors of the Capitol, in the Senate cloakrooms, and by telephone," but he vowed to continue the fight until those who believed in "a philosophy of constitutional restraint" were victorious.[4]

The next round began on March 2 when Senator Alton Lennon (D-N.C.), who had been absent at the time of the vote on the George amendment, moved that the Senate reconsider its rejection of the measure. Bricker quickly endorsed Lennon's motion. He noted that thirteen senators who had supported some sort of limitation on international agreements had voted against the George resolution, and he doubted that those legislators would want "to be held responsible for depriving the House of Representatives of the opportunity to write a satisfactory constitutional amendment." Bricker expressed confidence that enough senators would now support the measure to give the House the chance to improve it.[5]

---

[3]Frank Holman, "The Fight for an Adequate Constitutional Amendment Has Only Just Begun," March 2, 1954, copy in JBP.

[4]"The Fight for a Treaty-Control Amendment—Round One," address by Senator Bricker at regional conference of the ABA, Atlanta, March 4, 1954, copy in JBP, Box 110, OHS; and *New York Times*, March 5, 1954, p. 6.

[5]100 *CR* 2460; statement issued by Senator Bricker, March 2, 1954, JBP; and *New York Times*, March 3, 1954, pp. 1, 7.

In the weeks that followed, however, neither Bricker nor Lennon pressed for another vote on the George resolution. They knew that of the five senators who had missed the final vote on the measure, Lennon, Pat McCarran (D-Nev.), and Styles Bridges (R-N.H.) were all conservatives who favored the amendment, while liberal Democrat James Murray (Mont.) opposed it. The three additional votes for the resolution and Murray's against it would make the count 63–32, leaving the amendment still one vote short of the two-thirds majority required for approval, with Stuart Symington (D-Mo.) yet to announce his position. The *New York Times* reported on March 3 that the amendment's supporters believed Symington would cast the decisive vote in favor of the resolution. That was just wishful thinking by the proponents, however. Senator Bricker explained years later that he could never get a firm commitment from Symington. Given Symington's liberal voting record (90.9 percent liberal rating from the ADA in 1954), his vote against the section of the Knowland-Ferguson amendment that would have invalidated international agreements conflicting with the Constitution, and the strong opposition to the measure from his fellow Missourians Harry Truman, Senator Hennings, and the editors of both the St. Louis *Globe-Democrat* and the *Post-Dispatch,* it seems highly unlikely that Symington would have voted for the George amendment. If Symington voted against the resolution, the only way it could be approved would be if a senator who had opposed it changed his mind and voted for the amendment now. Rumors were circulating that such was the case with various legislators, but Senator Bricker advised his supporters that he had received no such indications from any senator, and thus he had no reason to expect that the outcome would be any more favorable the second time around. If anything, Bricker worried that administration officials might persuade some of the resolution's previous supporters to vote the other way on a second roll call, and he feared the amendment would lose its momentum if it were defeated by more than one vote this time.[6]

Bricker had an additional reason for not pushing for a new vote. He had never been especially enthusiastic about the George resolution, which one

[6]See *New York Times,* March 3, 1954, pp. 1, 7; interview with Senator Bricker, June 26, 1975; ADA, press release for October 1, 1954, "ADA Papers," microfilm ed.; 100 *CR* 1740; editorial, "A Deal with Bricker?" St. Louis *Post-Dispatch,* January 6, 1954, p. 2-D; editorial, "No Compromise," St. Louis *Globe-Democrat,* January 13, 1954, copy in Harley Kilgore Papers, Box 25, FDRL; and Charles Webb to Mrs. Robert Murray, March 18, 1954; W. A. Schultz to Webb, May 12, 1954; Webb to Schultz, May 14, 1954; Senator Bricker to Loren Stark, May 24, 1954; Webb to Edward Rumely, June 1, 1954; and Bricker to Robert Vogeler, June 3, 1954; all in JBP, Box 101, OHS. Murray received an 84.6% liberal rating from ADA for 1954, while Bridges, Lennon, and McCarran had ratings of 22.2%, 16.7%, and 25% respectively.

of his followers had condemned as a "mutation which may quite possibly pass the Senate and be pawned off on your supporters as 'The Bricker Amendment.'" The senator recognized that there were problems with the proposal, particularly that it would allow executive agreements implemented by simple majority votes in both the House and the Senate to override state laws and constitutions. Consequently, rather than fighting for a flawed amendment, Bricker and members of the ABA's Committee on Peace and Law concentrated their efforts on drafting a new and stronger bill.[7]

Once again, however, the senator and his more ardent backers became embroiled in a dispute over the "which" clause. Bricker knew from previous experience that the Senate would never approve any resolution including such a provision; hence, he proposed dropping it. But Clarence Manion reported that "'States Rights' as a defense against the Communist conquest of the United States from the inside is capturing popular imagination," and although he would accede to eliminating the specific language of the "which" clause, Manion was adamantly opposed to any text "which surrenders the States Rights principle" of that article. Similarly, Frank Holman warned that if the amendment did not contain something along the lines of the "which" clause, then "much of our nationwide support which is based upon adequate protection of states' rights will be lost."[8]

As he had in the past, Bricker bowed to the wishes of his more extreme followers, and on August 5, 1954, he introduced a new amendment retaining the substance of the "which" clause. Section 1 of S.J. Res. 181 specified that "a provision of a treaty or other international agreement which conflicts with this Constitution, or which is not made in pursuance thereof, shall not be the supreme law of the land nor be of any force or effect." The second article, which was the key one, then stipulated that "a treaty or other international agreement shall become effective as internal law in the United States only through legislation valid in the absence of international agreement." Bricker had changed the wording slightly, but the provision was basically the same as the original "which" clause. Subsequent legislation would be required to implement international agreements, Congress would be limited to enacting only those laws already

[7]See W. Henry McFarland, Jr., executive chairman, American Flag Committee, to Senator Bricker, February 23, 1954; Edward Rumely to Bricker, February 15, 1954; Charles Webb to Eberhard Deutsch, March 3 and 4, 1954; Deutsch to Webb, March 6, 1954; Webb to Mrs. Robert Murray, March 12, 1954; Webb to Al Schweppe, April 5 and 21, 1954; and Frank Holman to Webb, June 18, 1954; all in JBP, Boxes 100, 101, and 102, OHS.

[8]See Bricker to Clarence Manion, June 30 and July 14, 1954; Manion to Bricker, July 9, 1954; Frank Holman to Bricker, July 15, 1954; and Bricker to Holman, July 16, 1954; all in JBP, Boxes 102 and 109, OHS.

authorized under its enumerated powers, and state action would be needed to bring into force agreements that dealt with matters normally reserved to the states by the Tenth Amendment.[9]

Bricker and Holman both stressed the importance of adopting this new amendment. The senator warned his colleagues that "the threat of treaty law has not abated," that "the treaty-making ambitions of the United Nations and its agencies" still reflected "a zeal to regulate the political, economic, and social rights and duties of people everywhere." His amendment was essential, Bricker emphasized, to protect the nation and the American people from those advocates of world government "who seek to set aside the American Declaration of Independence and nullify many of our constitutional protections." Holman, in another pamphlet, assailed the Eisenhower administration for failing to halt "the trend toward executive supremacy" that had begun under Roosevelt and been continued by Truman. He argued that the questions involved in this controversy were really quite simple, no matter how much "the politicians in Washington and the Eastern seaboard internationalists in New York attempt to confuse them." The only point in dispute, Holman declared, was "whether we and our children and our children's children are to have a government of men or a government of adequate constitutional safeguards." In his view, this was "the greatest issue which faces America today, greater than taxes or inflation or even Communist infiltration."[10]

II

In the spring of 1954, President Eisenhower seriously considered the possibility of a new, administration-backed version of the Bricker amendment. Senator Ferguson and a few other legislators who had stood by the president in the fight against the Bricker and George resolutions reported that they were in political trouble back home, and they suggested that their chances of winning reelection would improve significantly if they could vote for some sort of amendment that would reassure the American people that international agreements could not supersede the Constitution, while not crippling the powers of the chief executive. But Secretary

[9]S.J. Res. 181, 83d Cong., 2d sess., August 5, 1954; and 100 *CR* 13456–57. See Appendix L for the complete text of this measure. See also Alfred Schweppe to members of the Committee on Peace and Law, July 30, 1954, copy in JBP, Box 109, OHS.

[10]100 *CR* 13456–60, esp. 13457 and 13459; and Frank Holman, "Renewal of the Fight for an Adequate Constitutional Amendment on Treaties and Executive Agreements (The New Bricker Amendment)," August 6, 1954, copy in Irving Ives Papers, Box 48, Cornell University Library.

of State Dulles pointed out problems with all the various texts that were proposed, and along with the attorney general and the vice-president, he questioned the advisability of reopening the conflict so late in the congressional session when it might jeopardize the administration's legislative program. Consequently, the president decided to drop the idea.[11]

The Bricker amendment controversy actually had little impact on the 1954 congressional elections. Herbert Parmet has argued that Ferguson lost his bid for reelection in Michigan primarily because of his votes against the Bricker and George amendments, but the triumph of the entire Democratic state ticket in Michigan for the first time since 1936 shows that there were other, more important reasons for Ferguson's defeat, including the efforts of organized labor on behalf of the Democrats and the anger of people aroused by Secretary of Defense Wilson's comparison of unemployed workers to "kennel-fed dogs." Moreover, although three incumbent senators who had opposed the Bricker and George resolutions were defeated in 1954—Ferguson, John Sherman Cooper (R-Ky.), and Robert Upton (R-N.H.)—so, too, were three senators who had voted for the George amendment—Thomas Burke (D-Ohio), Guy Cordon (R-Ore.), and Guy Gillette (D-Iowa). And in Illinois, Democrat Paul Douglas won reelection easily despite a concerted effort to punish him for his vote against the George substitute.[12]

On January 6, 1955, John Bricker reintroduced as S.J. Res. 1, 84th Congress, the proposal he had submitted the previous August. Bricker knew that Senator George and his followers and most of the Eisenhower Re-

[11]See memorandum by the president to the secretary of state, May 26, 1954; paper prepared by the administrative assistant to the president, n.d.; memorandum by the secretary of state to the president, May 28, 1954; memorandum by the attorney general to the president, May 28, 1954; and memorandum by the president to the secretary of state, May 29, 1954; all in *Foreign Relations, 1952–54,* I, 1852–55.

[12]See Parmet, *Eisenhower and the American Crusades,* p. 312; E. W. Kieffer to President Eisenhower, November 5, 1954, and Karl Leibrand to Senator Ferguson, November 8, 1954; copies of both in JBP, Box 109, OHS; Lou Guylay to Leonard Hall, November 4, 1954, Leonard Hall Papers, Box 101, DDEL; "Analysis of 1954 Election," n.d., esp. pp. 6–10, 21, copy in Howard Pyle Records, Box 46, DDEL; and *New York Times,* November 4, 1954, pp. 1, 25, and November 7, 1954, IV, 5. For Secretary Wilson's remarks and the reaction, see *New York Times,* October 12, 1954, p. 13; October 13, 1954, pp. 1, 14; October 14, 1954, pp. 1, 24, 25; October 15, 1954, p. 10; October 24, 1954, p. 50; November 4, 1954, p. 23; and November 7, 1954, IV, 1, 5. On Senator Douglas's race in Illinois, see also Drew Pearson, "Coattail Ride Calls for Loyalty," Washington *Post,* June 20, 1954, p. 5-B; clipping from Chicago *Sun-Times,* August 22, 1954, DDEP, OF 138-A-4; Mrs. Magruder to John Bricker, April 18, 1954; Illinois Vigilant Women for the Bricker Amendment to fellow American, n.d.; and Bricker to Robert McCarthy, October 11, 1954; all in JBP, Boxes 101, 114, and 109, OHS; "A Digest from Reports of City Leaders Concerning the Last Campaign," November 23, 1954, copy in Leonard Hall Papers, Box 101; and Eisenhower, *Mandate for Change,* p. 433. After Ferguson's defeat in 1954, Eisenhower appointed him U.S. ambassador to the Philippines in 1955, and then to a judgeship on the U.S. Court of Military Appeals in 1956.

publicans would not endorse such a stringent amendment, so rather than highlight the measure's loss of support, he chose not to seek cosponsors this time. He had considered dropping the "which" clause and trying to achieve the same objectives through different language, but Charles Webb, his legislative assistant, had persuaded him not to change the text again. The only possible advantage to be gained by eliminating the "which" clause, Webb advised, was that it might induce Senator George to support the resolution, but he doubted whether George would join them in any event. Since the states' righters would resent the "which" clause's omission, Webb recommended that Bricker stay with his previous proposal.[13]

Webb's skepticism concerning Senator George proved to be well founded. In a private letter to Arthur Krock of the *New York Times,* George revealed that he had no intention of sponsoring another proposal similar to the amendment he had drafted in 1954. In fact, he confided, he had not yet decided if he would even support such a measure. He expected to be quite busy as the new chairman of the foreign relations committee, and he questioned the wisdom of introducing such a divisive issue into the new Congress. In mid-January, George confirmed publicly that he would not play an active role in 1955 in any debate over Bricker's new amendment.[14]

George's decision to stay out of the Bricker amendment controversy in 1955 reflected the close relationship that had developed between the senator and the president and the secretary of state. George had first gotten involved in the matter the previous year when Eisenhower and Dulles had sought his help in working out a bipartisan compromise, and he continued his efforts to help the administration in foreign affairs in 1955 and 1956. As chairman of the foreign relations committee, he did not want to create problems for the president by pushing for the Bricker amendment or similar restrictions on treaties or executive agreements.[15]

[13]See S.J. Res. 1, 84th Cong., 1st sess., January 6, 1955; 101 *CR* 109–12 (1955); and Webb to Bricker, December 21, 1954, and Webb to Frank Holman, December 27, 1954, both in JBP, Box 110, OHS. This is the same text as in Appendix L.

[14]Walter George to Arthur Krock, January 6, 1955, Krock Papers, Correspondence, Box 18, Princeton University Library; and *CQ Weekly Report,* 13 (week ending January 28, 1955), 99.

[15]See summaries of telephone calls, Eisenhower to Dulles, January 20, 1954, and Dulles to Phleger, January 7, 1955, both in "Telephone Conversations, Dulles," microfilm ed.; memorandum by the secretary of state to the president, January 20, 1954, and the legal adviser to the secretary of state, February 2, 1954, both in *Foreign Relations, 1952–54,* I, 1834–35, 1846–47; Dwight Eisenhower, memoranda for the record, January 17, 1955; January 24, 1956; and March 23, 1956; all in Ferrell, ed., *The Eisenhower Diaries,* pp. 292, 313, and 322–23; and Eisenhower to Senator George, January 27, 1955, DDEP, Diary Series. On the close relationship between George and the administration, see also Thruston Morton Oral History Transcript, p. 21, and Mike Mansfield Oral History Transcript, p. 2, both in Dulles Oral

Eisenhower met with his advisers in early January 1955 to review the new Bricker amendment. Dulles and Press Secretary James Hagerty both argued against giving in to its proponents. Hagerty in particular asserted that the resolution served as "a rallying ground for the Old Guard," and he warned that its adoption would be seen as an important victory for the isolationists and reactionaries in the party. Eisenhower agreed, and he promised to stand firm against the amendment; he would not endorse any proposal unless it merely reiterated that international agreements had to conform to the Constitution.[16]

When the Bricker amendment came up at the president's news conferences in the spring of 1955, Eisenhower stressed that his position was the same as it had always been. On March 23, 1955, when he was asked if he had changed his mind about the Bricker amendment, he simply said "no." When asked a month later if he was considering a substitute or compromise proposal, the president declared that he had not altered his position "one iota." In order to reassure the American people that international agreements could not violate the Constitution, he would accept an amendment stating that treaties and executive agreements in conflict with the Constitution would be null and void. He emphasized, however, that he would never accede to any arrangement that would weaken the national government's authority in foreign affairs and take the country back to the days before the Constitution.[17]

Administration officials were confident they could defeat the Bricker amendment if it reached the Senate floor during the 84th Congress. They noted that twelve senators who had either voted for or announced their support for the George resolution were no longer in Congress—Senators Burke, Butler (Neb.), Cordon, Gillette, Griswold, Hendrickson, Hoey, Hunt, Johnson (Colo.), Lennon, McCarran, and Maybank—but only three senators who had opposed the measure were missing in the new session—Cooper, Ferguson, and Upton. Since there were twenty-nine senators returning who had either voted against or declared their opposition to the resolution (thirty if one included Symington), only three or four votes would be needed from the new senators to ensure the amend-

---

History Project, Princeton University Library; and White, "Senator George—Monumental, Determined." When George decided in 1956 not to seek reelection rather than face a difficult primary contest against Herman Talmadge, Eisenhower immediately asked the senator to serve as a special ambassador to NATO. See Eisenhower to George, May 9, 1956, copy in Hagerty Papers, Box 61, DDEL; and *New York Times,* May 10, 1956, p. 1.

[16]See James Hagerty Diary, January 5 and 12, 1955, in Ferrell, ed., *Hagerty Diary,* pp. 157, 159; and minutes of cabinet meeting of January 7, 1955, DDEL.

[17]See president's news conferences, in *New York Times,* March 24, 1955, p. 18, and April 28, 1955, pp. 1, 8, and 12. See also *Public Papers: Eisenhower, 1955,* pp. 360–61 and 427–28.

ment's defeat. The president's aides believed that at least four of the new senators—Barkley (D-Ky.), McNamara (D-Mich.), Neuberger (D-Ore.), and Scott (D-N.C.)—would definitely vote against the amendment, while three others—Allott (R-Colo.), Case (R-N.J.), and O'Mahoney (D-Wyo.)—might also oppose it. Hence, they predicted the Bricker amendment would again fall short if it came to a vote in the Senate.[18]

III

Many of the administration's actions during these years also helped to undermine support for the Bricker amendment. Recognizing that concern over possible effects within the United States of the Genocide Convention and the draft covenant on human rights had led some people to favor the amendment, Secretary of State Dulles had announced during the hearings on S.J. Res. 1 in 1953 that the president would not ask the Senate to approve any of the United Nations human rights agreements. The administration had followed through on that promise; Eisenhower had not sought American ratification of the Genocide Convention, and the United States had withdrawn from the efforts to draft a binding covenant on human rights. As columnist Doris Fleeson had noted, Dulles and the Eisenhower administration had sacrificed the human rights agreements "to appease Republican nationalists led by Senator Bricker" and ward off the threat of the Bricker amendment.[19]

Shortly after the defeat of the Bricker and George amendments, administration officials sought to undercut support for such measures in the future by accepting in principle a bill proposed by Senator Ferguson requiring that executive agreements be transmitted to the Senate within thirty days of their execution. Ferguson hoped that his bill would have "a pacifying effect" and "relieve the pressure" for enactment of the Bricker amendment. Assistant Secretary of State Thruston Morton advised members of the foreign relations committee that the State Department would not object to the measure if the time period could be lengthened and some arrangement worked out to maintain the confidentiality of certain classified agreements. The committee amended the bill accordingly and reported it to the floor unanimously, but Congress adjourned before the full

[18]See "Legislative Outlook on Key Issues, 84th Congress," March 1955, copy in Howard Pyle Records, Box 30, DDEL. See also "Bricker Still Pitching for His Amendment," *CQ Weekly Report*, 13 (week ending July 1, 1955), 767–69.
[19]See Doris Fleeson, "Dulles Lifts Soviets off 'Rights' Hook," New York *Post*, April 8, 1953, copy in Mary Pillsbury Lord Papers, Box 2, DDEL; and *Hearings, 1953*, pp. 824–25. See also editorial, "Bricker Left in Midair," Washington *Post*, April 8, 1953, p. 16; and Eleanor Roosevelt, "My Day," St. Louis *Post-Dispatch*, April 9, 1953, p. 1-C.

Senate could act on the measure. The Senate did approve a similar bill, however, in 1956.[20]

In the spring of 1954, President Eisenhower had to decide whether to intervene militarily to help the French in their struggle against communist-led rebels in Vietnam. Some of the president's advisers recommended direct American intervention to relieve the pressure on the French garrison trapped at Dienbienphu, but Eisenhower refused to commit American forces to action in Indochina without congressional sanction. He believed Congress had a legitimate role to play in making such decisions, and the long debate over the Bricker amendment had just demonstrated how strongly the legislators resented having been ignored by Roosevelt and Truman in such matters. Eisenhower also remembered what had happened to Truman after he had sent American forces into Korea without congressional approval, and he was determined not to make the same mistake. If he took the nation into war, he wanted to be sure that the whole country was behind him and Congress was on record in support of his actions. Thus, when he was asked at a press conference if the United States might become involved in World War III in Indochina, Eisenhower promised that there would be "no involvement of America in war unless it is a result of the constitutional process that is placed upon Congress to declare it." Similarly, in a telephone conversation with Dulles, the president insisted that it would be "completely unconstitutional and indefensible" to use American forces to assist the French without congressional approval.[21]

In accordance with Eisenhower's wishes, Dulles and Admiral Arthur Radford, chairman of the joint chiefs of staff, met with the congressional leaders of both parties on Saturday, April 3, 1954, to discuss whether

---

[20]See S. 3067, 83d Cong., 2d sess., March 3, 1954; Homer Ferguson's comments at a meeting of the Senate Committee on Foreign Relations, May 5, 1954, in U.S., Congress, Senate, Committee on Foreign Relations, *Executive Sessions of the Senate Foreign Relations Committee* (Historical Series); Vol. 6: *1954*, 83d Cong., 2d sess. (made public in 1977), pp. 248–49; U.S., Congress, Senate, Committee on Foreign Relations, *Requiring International Agreements Other than Treaties to be Transmitted to the Senate within 60 Days After Execution Thereof*, S. Rept. 2340, 83d Cong., 2d sess., August 7, 1954; S. 147, 84th Cong., 1st sess., January 6, 1955; and 102 *CR* 12321–23 (1956). A similar measure sponsored by Senator Clifford Case (R-N.J.) was approved by Congress and signed into law by President Nixon in 1972. See S. 596, 92d Cong., 1st sess., February 4, 1971; 118 *CR* 4088–94, 28085–87, and 29307 (1972); and P.L. 92–403.

[21]President's news conference, March 10, 1954, in *Public Papers: Eisenhower, 1954*, p. 306; and memorandum of telephone call, Dulles to the president, April 5, 1954, in *Foreign Relations, 1952–54*, XIII, *Indochina*, 1241–42. See also the comments by Undersecretary of State Smith to the Senate Committee on Foreign Relations, February 16, 1954, in U.S., Congress, Senate, Committee on Foreign Relations, *Executive Sessions, 1954*, p. 127; and Herring, *America's Longest War*, pp. 28–36.

Congress would pass a joint resolution authorizing the president to employ air and naval forces as he saw fit in Southeast Asia. Dulles and Radford both emphasized that the administration had no plans to commit ground troops, but the legislators were skeptical, fearing that "once the flag was committed the use of land forces would inevitably follow." The congressmen also sought assurances that America's allies would be involved—that this would not turn into another Korea "with the United States furnishing 90% of the manpower." If the secretary of state could get definite commitments from the British and others that they would participate, then the leaders thought a resolution could be enacted authorizing the president to employ American forces. When the British refused to go along with the proposed intervention, however, and the French refused to make any moves toward granting real independence to the Vietnamese, the president, who had always had some misgivings about the plan, dropped the idea of direct American military involvement in Indochina.[22]

In the Formosa crisis of 1955, Eisenhower again sought congressional approval before taking steps that might lead to war. For a number of months the Chinese Communists on the mainland had been shelling the offshore islands of Quemoy and Matsu in what administration officials saw as a possible prelude to an attack against Chiang Kai-shek and the Chinese Nationalists on Formosa. The president believed that he probably had the legal authority to use American forces to protect Formosa, but, as he told the congressional leaders, he thought it would be "foolish to try to strain to the limit my constitutional powers" when a congressional resolution would make it clear to the Communists that the nation was united in its determination to defend Formosa. Accordingly, on January 24, 1955, Eisenhower asked Congress to pass a joint resolution authorizing the president to employ the armed forces as he deemed necessary to protect Formosa and the Pescadores against armed attack. As Dulles explained to members of the Senate Armed Forces and Foreign Relations committees, congressional approval of the resolution would show widespread support for the president's policy and increase its chances for success. Since there was "some doubt and uncertainty" over the respective powers of the

[22]See Dulles, memorandum of conversation with the president, April 2, 1954, and draft of joint resolution, April 2, 1954; memorandum for the file of the secretary of state, April 5, 1954, *re:* conference with congressional leaders concerning crisis in Southeast Asia, April 3, 1954; and memorandum of telephone conversation between the president and the secretary of state, April 3, 1954; all in *Foreign Relations, 1952–54,* XIII, 1211–12, 1224–25, and 1230. See also *New York Times,* April 4, 1954, p. 13; memorandum of discussion at the 192d meeting of the National Security Council, April 6, 1954, in *Foreign Relations, 1952–54,* XIII, 1250–65, esp. 1254; Hagerty Diary, April 26 and June 28, 1954, in Ferrell, ed., *Hagerty Diary,* pp. 48–49, and 79–80; Roberts, "The Day We Didn't Go to War"; Herring, *America's Longest War,* pp. 28–38; and Ambrose, *Eisenhower:* Vol. II: *The President,* pp. 173–85.

executive and the legislature in such matters, the secretary recommended that Congress and the president "work together to clarify and remove any such possible doubts from the arena."[23]

Although there was some criticism of the president's decision to seek congressional approval for actions that many believed he already had the authority to take, most people praised him for consulting with Congress in such a situation. Columnist Richard Rovere was part of a small minority when he complained that Eisenhower was acting as if the Bricker amendment "were so sound in principle that its provisions should be honored even without its being enacted into law." Much more typical were Walter George, John Bricker, and Mike Mansfield, who commended the president for working with Congress in this time of crisis. Bricker in particular asserted that the joint resolution authorizing the president to commit American troops would "demolish . . . the fallacious theory that the President, as Commander in Chief, has exclusive power to send Armed Forces of the United States anywhere in the world." Most legislators agreed with Bricker that Eisenhower had done the right thing in coming to Congress, and in just a few days the House and the Senate passed the Formosa Resolution by overwhelming margins.[24]

Bricker's comments about the Formosa Resolution illustrate his dilemma in trying to win support for a constitutional amendment to limit the internal effects of treaties and executive agreements. In view of Eisenhower's abandonment of the UN human rights agreements and his willingness to work with Congress in foreign affairs, there seemed to be little need for such a measure. Bricker and a few of the more moderate leaders of the ABA realized, therefore, that the only way an amendment would be adopted would be if it had the president's endorsement. At the same time, however, they knew that a less stringent measure that might be acceptable to the president would surely be denounced by Frank Holman, Clarence Manion, and others among the amendment's more extreme proponents. Unfortunately for Bricker, administration officials recognized that his position had

[23]Hagerty Diary, January 25, 1955, in Ferrell, ed., *Hagerty Diary,* pp. 173–74; and U.S., Congress, Senate, Committee on Foreign Relations, *Executive Sessions, 1955,* pp. 87 and 127. See also S.J. Res. 28, 84th Cong., 1st sess., January 24, 1955; U.S., Congress, Senate, Committee on Foreign Relations and Committee on Armed Services, *Authorizing the President to Employ the Armed Forces of the United States for Protecting the Security of Formosa, the Pescadores, and Related Positions and Territories of that Area,* S. Rept. 13, 84th Cong., 1st sess., January 26, 1955, esp. p. 9; summaries of telephone calls, Minority Leader Joseph Martin and Speaker Sam Rayburn to the president, January 20, 1955; Senator Knowland to the president, January 21, 1955; and Secretary Dulles to the president, January 25, 1955; all in DDEP, Diary Series; and Ambrose, *Eisenhower: The President,* pp. 212–14, and 231–45.

[24]Rovere, *Affairs of State,* pp. 250–51; and 101 *CR* 819–21 (George), 953–54 (Bricker), and 974–75 (Mansfield). The House of Representatives approved the joint resolution 410–3, and the Senate did likewise, 85–3. See 101 *CR* 680–81 and 994 for the votes.

deteriorated, and although they continued to meet with him in the interests of party unity, they saw no reason to make any concessions. Consequently, despite numerous conferences and much correspondence during 1955, Bricker and representatives of the ABA failed to reach an agreement with members of the administration on an amendment they would all support.[25]

IV

Events in 1956 and 1957 further demonstrated Bricker's predicament. When it became apparent that the talks between the amendment's proponents and administration officials had made no progress, the measure's supporters on the Senate Judiciary Committee took matters into their own hands. Led by Everett Dirksen (R-Ill.), they drafted a new proposal that was simpler and less legalistic than Bricker's amendment, but equally effective, or potentially so, in limiting the use and effects of international agreements. On March 5, 1956, the full committee approved the new text, recommending that the Senate adopt the following amendment:

Section 1. A provision of a treaty or other international agreement which conflicts with *any provision of* this Constitution shall not be of any force or effect. [Emphasis added.]
Section 2. On the question of advising and consenting to the ratification of a treaty the vote shall be determined by yeas and nays, and the names of the persons voting for or against shall be entered on the Journal of the Senate.[26]

[25]See John Bricker to Kenneth Colegrove, February 1, 1955, JBP, Box 115, OHS; Orie Phillips to Bernard Shanley, March 11, 1955; and Phillips to Attorney General Brownell, March 28, 1955; both in DDEP, OF 116-H-4; President Eisenhower, memorandum for the secretary of state, March 25, 1955; and Orie Phillips, "Memorandum for the Attorney General with Respect to Proposed Revised Draft of Resolution No. 1 Relating to the Treaty-Making Power," March 28, 1955; both in DDEP, Diary Series; draft prepared by Judge Phillips, Lloyd Wright, and Senator Bricker, and submitted to Bernard Shanley by Phillips and Wright on May 20, 1955; and Phillips to Wright, May 31, 1955; both in DDEP, OF 116-H-4; Gerald Morgan to Brownell, May 24 and June 1, 1955, and enclosures; Lloyd Wright to Morgan, June 6 and 8, 1955; Brownell to Wright, June 20, 1955; and Wright to Brownell, June 30, 1955; all in Gerald Morgan Records, A67-57, Box 3, DDEL; and Brownell to the president, July 30, 1955, and attached memorandum for the files, July 29, 1955, DDEP, administrative files, Box 8, "Brownell." See also Manion to Charles Webb, January 11, 1955; Mrs. Murray to Holman, January 12, 1955; Holman to Webb, April 12, 1955; Edward Rumely to Webb, May 11, 1955; and Mrs. Murray to Senator Bricker, May 24, 1955; all in JBP, Boxes 115 and 116, OHS.
[26]See Charles Webb to Alfred Schweppe, February 6, 1956, JBP; Phleger to Dulles, February 15, 1956, and Phleger to the secretary, March 19, 1956, both in Phleger Collection, Vol. 11; and U.S., Congress, Senate, Committee on the Judiciary, *Constitutional Amendment Relative to Treaties and Executive Agreements,* S. Rept. 1716, 84th Cong., 2d sess., March 27, 1956.

John Bricker immediately endorsed the revised resolution. In a letter to Winifred Barker, one of the leaders of the Vigilant Women for the Bricker Amendment, the senator asserted that the measure would prevent world government, prohibit American acceptance of the human rights covenants or the "socialistic" treaties of the International Labor Organization, bar the president from going to war without the consent of Congress or making domestic law by executive agreement, and keep the federal government from using a congressionally approved executive agreement to encroach on the reserved powers of the states. As he emphasized in a press release on March 5, Bricker believed that the new proposal embodied all the basic objectives of his original amendment. Anyone who opposed this measure, he declared, "must now answer this question: 'What provision of the Constitution do you want to violate by treaty or by executive agreement?'"[27]

Administration officials opposed Dirksen's resolution just as vehemently as they had opposed the original Bricker amendment. The president's advisers worried particularly that the insertion of the phrase "any provision of" in section one was more than just a stylistic change. They feared that the attempt to invalidate international agreements conflicting with "any provision of this Constitution" represented an attempt to resuscitate the "which" clause and overturn the Supreme Court's decision in the migratory bird case. If this proposal were adopted, they warned, it might be construed as applying the Tenth Amendment's restrictions to both treaties and statutes enacted to implement international agreements, putting some areas beyond the scope of the treaty-making power. Accordingly, at a meeting at the White House with Bricker, Dirksen, and the Republican Senate leaders, Eisenhower rejected this latest version of the Bricker amendment.[28]

---

[27]Bricker to Mrs. Lewis Barker, March 9, 1956, JBP, Box 122, OHS; and press release from the office of Senator Bricker, March 5, 1956, enclosed with Bricker to Senator Smith (N.J.), March 8, 1956, H. Alexander Smith Papers, Box 123.

[28]See the president's appointments, March 29, 1956; and Gerald Morgan, memorandum for Ann Whitman, March 30, 1956; both in DDEP, Diary Series. See also memorandum, "The Dirksen Substitute for the Bricker Amendment," n.d.; and Phleger to Dulles, February 15, 1956; both in Phleger Collection, Vol. 11; and summaries of telephone calls, Eisenhower to Brownell, March 13 and April 4, 1956, DDEP, Diary Series. Although it appears from a letter the president wrote to his brother Edgar in January 1956 that he had at one point agreed to accept an amendment containing the phrase "any provision of this Constitution," an examination of the president's correspondence on this matter in 1955 and 1956 indicates that he misspoke in the letter to his brother. None of the various texts proposed by Judge Phillips, Lloyd Wright, and Senator Bricker and tentatively agreed to by the president in 1955 included the phrase "any provision of this Constitution." In fact, Frank Holman denounced the 1955 text because it did not contain this phrase. See President Eisenhower to Edgar Eisenhower, January 18 and 30, 1956, both in DDEP, Diary Series; copy of draft prepared by Judge

The president's advisers were not the only ones who objected to the
Dirksen amendment; a number of Bricker's long-time supporters condemned the measure too. A Wyoming woman vowed to fight to the bitter
end against this "emasculated, truncated skeleton," and Clarence Manion
denounced it, incredibly enough, as an administration-backed compromise. Winifred Barker and Ruth Murray, the national coordinators of the
Vigilant Women for the Bricker Amendment, complained in their newsletter that the proposal would neither prohibit treaties "substituting supremacy of the United Nations for the sovereignty of the American people," nor protect United States citizens against "misinterpretations of the
Constitution by a partisan judiciary." In their opinion, the resolution
failed to reverse the "unsavory record of disastrous consequences to America that have come to us by reason of abandonment of the policies of
Washington and Jefferson which put our national interests as our *first*
concern." They did not think the Dirksen amendment would accomplish
any of their objectives, and they charged that Bricker's support for the
measure must have been based on "partisan and personal political concerns, rather than concern for our country."[29]

Bricker tried, to no avail, to reassure his supporters that he had not
"sold out" to the administration. He emphasized that the new proposal
"accomplishes about 85 percent" of what he had set out to achieve. As
proof of the measure's stringency, he pointed out that the president and
his advisers had rejected the amendment. Bricker predicted it would "soon
be obvious to all that left-wingers and One-Worlders fear the new text just
as much as any previous text."[30]

At this point, Bricker found himself trapped in the middle. Administration officials opposed the Dirksen amendment because they considered it
too restrictive, but a number of the senator's more vocal supporters were
already complaining that he had given away too much in his efforts to
reach a compromise with the executive branch. Bricker knew that no

Phillips, Lloyd Wright, and Senator Bricker, and submitted to Bernard Shanley, May 20,
1955; and Phillips to Wright, May 31, 1955; both in DDEP, OF 116-H-4; Gerald Morgan to
Herbert Brownell, May 24 and June 1, 1955, and attachments, Morgan Records, A67–57, Box
3; Brownell, memorandum for the files, July 29, 1955; President Eisenhower to Edgar
Eisenhower, August 1, 1955; and president to the attorney general, August 1, 1955; all in
DDEP, Administrative Files, Box 8, "Brownell"; and Frank Holman to Senator Bricker,
October 21, 1955, and Holman to Edgar Eisenhower, January 10, 1956, both in JBP.

[29]See Louise Pond to Bricker, April 10, 1956; and Vigilant Women for the Bricker Amendment Newsletter, April 1956; both in JBP, Box 122, OHS. For Manion's criticism of the new
text, see Frank Holman to Mrs. Barker, March 15, 1956, copy in JBP.

[30]See Bricker to Mrs. Lewis Barker, March 9, 1956; Bricker to Mrs. Barker and Mrs.
Murray, April 26, 1956; Charles Webb to Sally Snyder, March 20, 1956; and Webb to Mrs.
Barker, March 30, 1956; all in JBP, Box 122, OHS.

amendment would be adopted without the president's endorsement, and he realized that he would have to make even more concessions to win the administration's approval. Further concessions, however, would alienate his original supporters even more. Seeing no other possible solution to his dilemma, Bricker finally offered to shelve the whole matter until after the November elections if administration officials would promise to sit down with him at that time to try to draft a mutually acceptable resolution.[31]

The president and his advisers were more than willing to sidetrack the issue until after the elections. They were confident they could defeat the Dirksen amendment or any such measure, but they preferred not to engage in an all-out conflict with the party's right wing that might cost Eisenhower some votes in his campaign for reelection. Thus, they accepted Bricker's suggestion, and Sherman Adams pledged that administration officials would work with the senator before the convening of the new Congress to try to draft an amendment consistent with the following principles:

> 1. No treaty or executive agreement shall be valid if it conflicts with the Constitution.
> 2. Treaties and executive agreements are intended to be used in the conduct of our foreign relations, and not as a subterfuge to enact domestic law.
> 3. No amendment should change our traditional treaty-making power or hamper the President in his Constitutional authority to conduct foreign affairs.[32]

As promised, administration officials met with Bricker in December 1956, to discuss the senator's amendment. Bricker had revised the measure again in the intervening months in an effort to win back his supporters, and he now proposed a resolution very similar to the text he had introduced in February 1954. After studying the new amendment, however,

---

[31]See Bricker to Lloyd Wright, May 18, 1956, JBP; and Lloyd Wright to Sherman Adams, May 20, 1956; Adams to Wright, May 29, 1956; and Bricker to President Eisenhower, June 4, 1956; all in DDEP, OF 116-H-4.

[32]See Sherman Adams to Lloyd Wright, May 29, 1956; John Bricker to President Eisenhower, June 4, 1956; and Adams to Bricker, June 12, 1956; all in DDEP, OF 116-H-4; and President Eisenhower to Bricker, September 25, 1956, DDEP, Diary Series. On the administration's confidence that it could defeat the Dirksen substitute, see "Prospective Senate Vote on Dirksen's Substitute if Vote Taken During Second Session of 84th Congress," n.d., copy in Phleger Collection, Vol. 11. On the possibility of some Republicans deserting the president over this issue in the 1956 election, see President Eisenhower to Edgar Eisenhower, January 18, 1956, DDEP, Diary Series; Mrs. Murray to Senator Bricker, May 24, 1955; Bricker to Jacques Bramhall, Jr., July 2, 1956; Bricker to George Eusterman, July 9, 1956; and Mrs. Murray to Charles Webb, September 26, 1956; all in JBP, Boxes 116 and 123, OHS.

Justice Department officials concluded that it was "totally wanting in virtue" and would cripple both the treaty-making power and the president's authority in foreign affairs. Accordingly, the president and his advisers rejected Bricker's proposal, and negotiations between the two sides reached an impasse.[33]

While trying to work out an agreement with representatives of the administration, Bricker again encountered criticism from many of his previous allies. Edward Rumely of the Committee for Constitutional Government, Frank Holman and Eberhard Deutsch of the ABA, and the editors of the Chicago *Tribune* all complained that Bricker's new resolution represented a giant step backward. Deutsch believed the senator had gone too far and compromised essential principles, and Rumely and the editors of the *Tribune* charged that the new text failed to plug the loopholes in the Constitution and offered little or no protection to the American people. Holman asserted that the main reason the campaign for the Bricker amendment had bogged down so badly was that the last two proposals had been " 'watered down' under White House pressure." He recognized the difficulty of winning approval for any measure not endorsed by administration officials, but he refused to work actively for what he considered to be a meaningless amendment "drawn to placate the President." However long it took, Holman vowed, "the fight must go on until 'rightly won.' "[34]

Bricker believed, however, that he had no choice but to continue his negotiations with the attorney general and the president if he wanted to see an amendment enacted. He thought he was "making some headway" in his talks with Brownell, and he still hoped that a reasonable compromise could be worked out which the president would support. But once again the senator was being "over-bullish"; the president and his advisers continued to meet with Bricker, but they had no intention of endorsing any

[33]See Bricker to Eisenhower, December 10, 1956; Jack Martin, memorandum for the record on Senator Bricker's appointment with the president, December 27, 1956; and summary of telephone call between the president and the attorney general, December 27, 1956; all in DDEP, Diary Series; Acting Assistant Attorney General Nathan Siegel, memorandum for the attorney general re: analysis of 1957 Bricker amendment proposal, January 22, 1957, copy given to this author by Herbert Brownell; Brownell to the president, February 6, 1957, DDEP, Diary Series; Eisenhower to Bricker, February 7, 1957, and enclosed "Memorandum Re: 1957 Bricker Amendment," n.d.; and Bricker to Eisenhower, February 13, 1957; all in JBP; and Jack Martin, memorandum for the record on Senator Bricker's appointment with the president, May 22, 1957, DDEP, Diary Series. See Appendix M for the text of Bricker's latest proposal.
[34]See Frank Holman to Bricker, January 31, April 1, and May 16, 1957; Eberhard Deutsch to Bricker, February 18, 1957; and Edward Rumely to Bricker, May 4, 1957; all in JBP, Box 129, OHS; editorial, "Mr. Bricker Locks up an Empty Stable," Chicago *Tribune*, January 16, 1957, p. 16; and editorial, "You Can't Compromise," Chicago *Tribune*, February 7, 1957, p. 16.

amendment of the sort envisioned by Bricker. Finally, in February 1958, Bricker decided to defer further action until a new Congress convened in 1959.[35]

Although the president's opposition remained the key factor working against the Bricker amendment, Eisenhower's decision to consult with Congress concerning problems in the Middle East in 1957 also undermined support for Bricker's proposal. In the aftermath of the Suez crisis of 1956, administration officials feared that Russian influence was growing in the Middle East, especially under Nasser in Egypt, and the president sought to stabilize the situation by serving notice that the United States would not sit by idly while the Soviets gained a foothold in the region. Rather than relying on his inherent powers as president or his authority as commander in chief, however, Eisenhower chose to work with Congress, and on January 5, 1957, he asked the legislature to approve a joint resolution authorizing him to extend up to $200 million in aid to nations in the Middle East resisting Communist aggression, and allowing him to use the armed forces "as he deems necessary" to assist such nations.[36]

When Senator Fulbright and others raised questions concerning the Eisenhower Doctrine (as the proposal came to be known) and the respective powers of the executive and the legislature over use of the armed forces, the Senate Armed Services and Foreign Relations committees modified the resolution to minimize any controversy. Instead of authorizing the president to employ American forces as he saw fit, the senators changed the bill to proclaim that "if the President determines the necessity thereof, the United States is prepared to use armed forces" to help any nation in the Middle East requesting assistance against Communist aggression. The revised resolution made clear the importance that the American government—both president and Congress—attached to the Middle East, and it showed the readiness of the United States to intervene there militarily if necessary. It did so, however, by avoiding the question of

[35] See Bricker to Lloyd Wright, May 1, 1957; Bricker to Frank Holman, April 4 and May 23, 1957; and Charles Webb to Al Schweppe, February 3, 1958; all in JBP, Boxes 129 and 131, OHS; Bricker to President Eisenhower, February 13, 1957, JBP; and Eisenhower to Bricker February 18, 1957; Eisenhower to Brownell, February 21, 1957; and Jack Martin, memorandum for the record on Senator Bricker's appointment with the president, May 22, 1957; all in DDEP, Diary Series.

[36] See Eisenhower to Dulles, December 12, 1956; and summaries of telephone calls, Eisenhower to Dulles, December 8 and 28, 1956; all in DDEP, Diary Series; White House press release, January 1, 1957, DDEP, OF 99Q; U.S., Congress, House, *Middle East Situation: Address of the President of the United States delivered before a Joint Session of Congress, January 5, 1957*, H. Document 46, 85th Cong., 1st sess., 1957; H. J. Res. 117, 85th Cong., 1st sess., January 5, 1957; and president's news conference, January 23, 1957, in *Public Papers: Eisenhower, 1957*, pp. 86–87. On the crisis in the Middle East, see also Finer, *Dulles over Suez;* and Ambrose, *Eisenhower: The President,* pp. 314–18, 328–34, 338–40, 350–54, 356–73, and 381–88.

whether the president could take such action under his own authority or needed the consent of Congress.[37]

Nonetheless, most legislators praised the president for working with Congress in this situation rather than acting unilaterally. Arthur Watkins (R-Utah) contrasted Eisenhower's cooperation with Congress to Truman's decision to bypass the legislature during the Korean crisis, and emphasized that this president, unlike his predecessor, understood the Constitution and the limits it imposed on his authority. John Bricker asserted that if the United States again ended up in a war, this time there would at least be "unity at home and no suggestion that the war is 'unconstitutional.'" Similarly, Mike Mansfield hailed the final bill as a fine example of "responsible cooperation in foreign policy," and Senator Jacob Javits (R-N.Y.) commended the president for giving Congress the opportunity to influence foreign policy in a constructive way. With these sentiments predominating, Congress approved the Eisenhower Doctrine for the Middle East.[38]

V

While President Eisenhower was disarming proponents of the Bricker amendment by consulting with Congress on foreign policy matters, the courts dealt the resolution's supporters a further setback with a series of decisions holding that treaties and executive agreements could not abridge rights protected by the United States Constitution. Previous rulings on this question, particularly in *Missouri v. Holland* and *United States v. Pink,* had been ambiguous enough to lend some credibility to the warnings by Holman, Bricker, Walter George, and others that international agreements could violate the Constitution. But now, in the mid-1950s, new litigation provided the judiciary with the chance to clarify the relationship between the Constitution and treaties and executive agreements.[39]

[37]See U.S., Congress, Senate, Committee on Foreign Relations and Committee on Armed Services, *To Promote Peace and Stability in the Middle East,* S. Rept. 70, 85th Cong., 1st sess., February 14, 1957, esp. pp. 8–9; and Senator Lyndon Johnson's explanation of the changes the committees had made in the resolution, 103 *CR* 2230–31 (1957). Senators Fulbright, Morse, O'Mahoney, Humphrey, and Sparkman all raised questions concerning whether the president, as commander in chief, already had the authority to use the armed forces to protect American interests in the Middle East. See 103 *CR* 1855–69.

[38]See 103 *CR* 3023–26 (Watkins), 3129 (Mansfield), and 2594–98 (Javits); and John Bricker, "Memorandum on the Eisenhower Middle East Doctrine," March 5, 1957, JBP, Box 128, OHS. See also the remarks by Senators Green, Smith (N.J.), Wiley, Barrett, and Johnson, 103 *CR* 2232, 2240, 2990, 3128, and 3129.

[39]See Chapters 1 and 10, above, on *Missouri v. Holland,* 252 U.S. 416 (1920), and *United States v. Pink,* 315 U.S. 204 (1942).

The Senate had discussed the case of *United States v. Guy W. Capps, Inc.* at great length during the debate over the Bricker and George amendments in 1954, but when the Supreme Court decided the case the following year, it ignored the question of the validity of the executive agreement involved in the dispute. The justices ruled that the government had not proved that Capps had sold the potatoes for purposes other than seed, and they dismissed the suit without commenting on the constitutionality of the compact Truman had made with Canadian officials. Arthur Krock of the *New York Times* and a few other observers expressed concern that the court's finding that Capps had not violated his contract with a Canadian firm implied that the executive agreement under which the contract had been made was legal, but that conclusion was unwarranted. The justices had neither upheld nor invalidated the executive agreement; they had merely followed their customary practice of avoiding constitutional issues if they could base their decision on other grounds.[40]

While the *Capps* case was still in litigation, the federal Court of Claims ruled in *Seery v. United States* that an executive agreement could not deprive an American citizen of her constitutional rights. Opera singer Maria Jeritza Seery, a naturalized American citizen, had asked the United States Army to pay her for damages to a luxurious home she owned in Austria that had been taken over and used as an American officers' club between 1945 and 1947. Army officials had refused, citing an executive agreement with Austria that had assigned a specific sum of money to that nation to be used to satisfy any claims resulting from the American occupation. When the Austrians offered Madame Jeritza $600, she sued the United States government, asserting that it had no authority to enter into an agreement negating her right under the Fifth Amendment to "just compensation" for the taking of her property for public use. The Court of Claims rejected the government's motion to dismiss the suit, ruling that the president could not, through an executive agreement, "destroy the Constitutional right of a citizen." Although the judges chose not to speculate as to the validity of a treaty dealing with such matters, they declared that "there can be no doubt

---

[40]See *United States v. Guy W. Capps, Inc.,* 348 U.S. 296 (1955); Arthur Krock, "Supreme Court Unloaded the Gun," *New York Times,* February 17, 1955, p. 26; William Fitzpatrick, "Supreme Court's Silence on Spuds Gives New Ammunition to Treaty-Curb Backers," *Wall Street Journal,* February 15, 1955; and Justice Harold Burton, draft opinion, n.d., Burton Papers, Box 274, Library of Congress. For the view that the court's silence on the constitutionality of the executive agreement should not be interpreted either way, see Zechariah Chafee, Jr., to John Chafee, February 21, 1955, Zechariah Chafee Papers, Box 12. On the court's preference for avoiding constitutional issues if it could, see *Spector Motor Co. v. McLaughlin,* 323 U.S. 105 (1944), which Burton cited in a footnote to his draft opinion, but omitted from the final version at the request of Justice Black. See Black to Burton, January 28, 1955, esp. p. 14; and Black to Burton, January 31, 1955; both in Burton Papers, Box 274.

that an executive agreement, not being a transaction which is even men-
tioned in the Constitution, cannot impair Constitutional rights." Eventually, Madame Jeritza was awarded $11,000 in damages, and the Supreme
Court refused to grant certiorari when the government tried to appeal the
decision.[41]

In *Rice v. Sioux City Memorial Park,* the courts went a long way toward
reasssuring people that the human rights provisions in the United Nations
Charter were not self-executing and thus could not be enforced by the
judiciary unless implemented by subsequent legislation. Evelyn Rice had
sued when the Sioux City Memorial Park Cemetery had refused to bury
her husband, a Winnebago Indian, because its bylaws stipulated that only
Caucasians could be buried within its grounds. She had charged that the
cemetery's discriminatory policy violated, among other things, the equal
protection clause of the Fourteenth Amendment and various articles of the
United Nations Charter. The Iowa Supreme Court rejected Mrs. Rice's
arguments, ruling in part that further legislative action was required before the general statements in the UN Charter became law within the
United States. When Mrs. Rice appealed to the United States Supreme
Court, the justices, in a series of split decisions, upheld the state court's
ruling against her. Moreover, Justice Frankfurter emphasized in the majority opinion that the disagreement among the justices should not be taken
to mean that they were divided over the applicability and status of the UN
Charter. Even the justices who found for Mrs. Rice did so not on the basis
of the UN Charter, but on the grounds that the cemetery's actions were
contrary to the Fourteenth Amendment. None of the justices held that the
charter was part of the supreme law of the land or relevant to the case at
hand.[42]

In 1957, the Supreme Court finally ruled directly on the relationship
between international agreements and constitutional rights. An American
woman named Clarice Covert had killed her husband, an American ser-

[41]See *Seery v. United States,* 127 F. Supp. 601 (1955). See also memorandum, "Maria Jeritza
Seery v. United States," n.d., Hennings Papers, Folder 4774A, University of Missouri
Library; B. F. Crane, memorandum for Mr. Maw, February 16, 1955, copy in Corwin Papers,
"Bricker Amendment," Princeton University Library; and Arthur Krock, "Still Another
Court Test of Executive Agreements," *New York Times,* March 8, 1955, p. 26. For the award in
Madame Jeritza's favor and the Supreme Court's refusal to hear the government's appeal, see
161 F. Supp. 395 (1958); and 359 U.S. 943 (1959).
[42]See *Rice v. Sioux City Memorial Park,* 348 U.S. 880, and 349 U.S. 70 (1955), esp. pp. 73
and 80. See also Fred Arner, Library of Congress, "Summary of the Judicial Decisions
Arising out of the Refusal of a Private Cemetery in Iowa to Bury Sgt. John Rice, American
Indian," March 24, 1955, copy in Hennings Papers, Folder 4774A; Charles Webb to Sally
Jones, December 3, 1954, JBP, Box 110, OHS; and George Sokolsky, "Political Effects of UN
Charter on U.S.," June 27, 1955; Jesse Marshall to the editor, Sioux City *Journal-Tribune,*
June 30, 1955; and Bricker to Sokolsky, June 26, 1955; all in JBP.

viceman, while they were residing at an American air base in England. Even though she was a civilian, Mrs. Covert had been tried by a court-martial and convicted of murder. She later challenged the legitimacy of such a procedure, arguing that she had been deprived of her right to indictment and trial by jury as guaranteed in Article III and the Fifth and Sixth Amendments of the Constitution. The government claimed that an executive agreement between the United States and Great Britain gave American military officials exclusive jurisdiction over offenses committed in England by American soldiers or their dependents. Attorneys for the government also pointed out that the Uniform Code of Military Justice, which had been enacted into law in 1950, authorized military trials for those accompanying the armed forces if so provided in an agreement with the host nation, and they contended that the statute should be sustained as legislation "necessary and proper" to carrying out the nation's obligations under the agreement with Great Britain.[43]

When Mrs. Covert's case first reached the Supreme Court in 1956, a majority of the justices upheld her conviction. They ruled that the constitutional right to a jury trial did not extend to Americans overseas even if they were tried by an agency of the United States government. The justices decided that Congress could set up different mechanisms to handle such cases as long as the methods established were reasonable and consonant with due process, and they determined that court-martial trials met those requirements, even when applied to civilian dependents. Hence, the court refused to overturn the verdict against Mrs. Covert.[44]

A few months later, however, after rehearing arguments on the case, the Supreme Court reversed itself and ruled 6–2 that Mrs. Covert's trial by military authorities had violated her constitutional rights. Justice Black, writing for himself and Justices Warren, Douglas, and Brennan, held that "no agreement with a foreign nation can confer power on the Congress, or on any other branch of Government, which is free from the restraints of the Constitution." The prohibitions in the Constitution, the justices stressed, applied to all branches of the federal government, and could not be nullified or circumvented by treaties and executive agreements or laws enacted to implement such compacts. In this particular case, the court ruled that those sections of the Uniform Code of Military Justice that

---

[43]See *Reid v. Covert*, 354 U.S. 1 (1957), for the details of the case. The killing occurred before the NATO Status of Forces Agreement had gone into effect, so it was a similar agreement entered into between the United States and Great Britain in 1942 that was cited by the government attorneys. The situation would have been virtually the same if the Status of Forces Agreement had applied.

[44]See *Reid v. Covert*, 351 U.S. 487 (1956). See also the opinions in *Kinsella v. Kreuger*, 351 U.S. 470, a companion case.

authorized court-martials for civilian dependents were unconstitutional, even if they had been adopted pursuant to the agreement with Great Britain. Neither a treaty nor an executive agreement could deprive Mrs. Covert of her constitutional right as a civilian to a jury trial.[45]

Some of Black's colleagues objected to his discussion of the constitutionality of international agreements and statutes enacted thereunder. Justices Frankfurter and Harlan, who found in favor of Mrs. Covert, and Justices Clark and Burton, who found against her, all believed that the key question in the case was whether the court-martial of a civilian could be sustained under Congress's power to regulate the armed forces, a power not dependent on any treaty or executive agreement, and they saw no need to deal with treaty issues. Frankfurter tried to persuade Black to remove the section on treaties and executive agreements from his opinion to avoid "needlessly fanning the flames of the Bricker amendment controversy," but Black kept the offending passage in the opinion, hoping perhaps that his comments about the treaty power might finally quiet the agitation to enact the Bricker amendment.[46]

As Senator Thomas Hennings and the editors of the Washington *Post* noted, the court's decision in *Reid v. Covert* undermined the case for the Bricker amendment by showing that there was no need to amend the Constitution to protect the American people against treaties and executive agreements. Although the justices disagreed over various aspects of the case, none of them had held that the agreement with Great Britain authorized proceedings that would otherwise have been unconstitutional. But instead of being reassured by the decision, John Bricker denounced it as "judicial irresponsibility" and warned that "it would be manifestly foolish to rely on the politically motivated dicta of a minority of four justices as adequate protection against the loss of fundamental human rights." He charged that the justices had "manufactured a completely phony issue" in order to make "a gratuitous proclamation" which they hoped would convince people that the Bricker amendment was unnecessary. Bricker was confident, however, that the nation's lawyers would never "swallow this kind of legal gymnastics," and he promised to continue the fight for a

[45] See *Reid v. Covert*, 354 U.S. 1, esp. pp. 16–19; and Washington *Post*, June 11, 1957, pp. 1, 8. See also "Criminal Jurisdiction over American Armed Forces Abroad"; Currie, "Court-Martial Jurisdiction of Civilian Dependents"; Warren, "The Bill of Rights and the Military," pp. 103–4; and Wiener, *Civilians under Military Justice*, pp. 237–40, 305–14. Justices Frankfurter and Harlan wrote separate concurring opinions to make up the six-judge majority in favor of Mrs. Covert. See 354 U.S. 41–78.

[46] See Felix Frankfurter, memorandum for the conference re: Nos. 701 and 713, O.T. 1955, June 5, 1957, Hugo Black Papers, Box 326, Library of Congress; and the concurring and dissenting opinions in *Reid v. Covert*, 354 U.S. 41–90, esp. pp. 66 and 79–80.

constitutional amendment that would truly safeguard the liberties and freedoms of the American people.[47]

VI

Despite his pledge to keep fighting, Senator Bricker decided early in 1958 not to push ahead with his amendment at that particular time. Bricker feared that he had just one more chance to win approval for his resolution, and he believed the administration's continued opposition to the measure would block the amendment in the current Congress. He hoped that after the elections the next Congress might be more favorably disposed toward the measure.[48]

Before he could reintroduce his amendment, however, Bricker first had to win reelection to the Senate in 1958. A proven vote-getter who had triumphed by large margins in the past, Bricker expected to win easily in his race against Democrat Stephen Young, a former congressman-at-large who had been out of public office for the last eight years. Much to Bricker's dismay, however, the Ohio Chamber of Commerce sought to place on the ballot that year a referendum on adding a right-to-work provision to the state constitution. A right-to-work provision would prohibit contracts that required workers to join a union to retain their jobs, and unions bitterly opposed efforts to adopt such measures. Bricker and other Republican leaders in Ohio worried that the referendum would attract to the polls hundreds of thousands of pro-Democratic union workers, and they urged the businessmen to postpone it to 1959 so as not to jeopardize the chances of Republican candidates. But the leaders of the Chamber of Commerce wanted to capitalize on reports of widespread corruption in the unions, and they refused to put the matter off until the following year.[49]

Bricker tried to minimize the effects of the right-to-work issue on his own candidacy. Reluctant to take a forthright stand on the matter, the senator finally announced that, personally, he would vote for the provision, but he emphasized that this was an individual decision that each citizen had to make for himself, and he declined to campaign actively on

[47]On Hennings, see St. Louis *Post-Dispatch,* June 25, 1957, p. 4-A. On Bricker, see ibid., and Chicago *Tribune,* June 26, 1957, II, 7. See also editorial "Trial of Civilians Abroad," *Washington Post,* June 12, 1957, p. A-14; and editorial, "Down Bricker's Alley," ibid., June 13, 1957, p. A-18.

[48]See Charles Webb to Al Schweppe, February 3, 1958, JBP, Box 131, OHS.

[49]See *New York Times,* August 24, 1958, p. 54, and October 29, 1958, p. 1; and interview with Senator Bricker, June 26, 1975. See also Miller and Ware, "Organized Labor in the Political Process: A Case Study of the Right-to-Work Campaign in Ohio."

that issue. Nonetheless, the referendum's presence on the ballot transformed what probably would have been an easy victory for Bricker into a closely contested race.[50]

Republicans took a drubbing all across the nation in the 1958 elections, and nowhere was this more true than in Ohio. As Bricker and the Republican leaders in the state had feared, election day was a complete disaster for them. With record numbers of ballots being cast, Ohioans rejected the right-to-work amendment by almost one million votes, the Democrats won control of both houses of the state legislature for the first time in nine years and with their largest majorities since the 1930s, and Republican Governor C. William O'Neill lost his bid for reelection by 460,000 votes. As for John Bricker, he ran well ahead of the rest of the Republican ticket, but he still came in 165,000 votes behind Stephen Young. He could not overcome the effects of the right-to-work referendum on the ballot.[51]

Bricker's defeat in 1958 marked the end of his public career and ended the fight for the Bricker amendment as well. Between 1951 and 1958, Bricker had introduced a number of proposals to limit the effects of treaties and executive agreements, but the only time the full Senate had considered the measure had been in 1954, when his own amendment had been soundly defeated, and the George substitute had fallen just one vote short of approval. From then on, Bricker had been caught in an untenable position. He knew that the administration's opposition could block any measure he submitted, but he also learned that any changes in the resolution to try to satisfy the president would cost him the support of the amendment's original proponents. Consequently, Bricker had spent much of his time from 1954 to 1958 drafting new proposals and revising them again and again in a futile effort to write an amendment that would somehow be acceptable to both sides. With Bricker's defeat in 1958, however, the controversy was finally over, and Congress would not concern itself again with the president's powers in foreign affairs until the war in Vietnam led J. William Fulbright, Jacob Javits, and others to reopen these issues in the late 1960s and early 1970s.

[50]See *New York Times*, August 24, 1958, p. 54, and October 29, 1958, p. 1.

[51]See ibid., November 5, 1958, pp. 1, 24, and November 6, 1958, pp. 1, 15, 19; Miller and Ware, "Right-to-Work Campaign in Ohio"; and interview with Senator Bricker, June 26, 1975. Nationally, the Republicans lost 13 Senate seats, 47 House seats, and 5 governorships in 1958.

Conclusion

For some thirty years now, journalists, historians, political scientists, and others have been discussing and evaluating the Eisenhower presidency and the role that Dwight Eisenhower played within his own administration. Most of the first accounts were highly critical of Eisenhower's leadership, or, more precisely, his lack thereof. They portrayed him as an indifferent, uninterested, and uninformed chief executive who was more concerned about his next round of golf than he was about the nation's affairs, and who delegated most of his authority to his advisers and members of his cabinet, most notably chief of staff Sherman Adams and Secretary of State John Foster Dulles. The memoirs that appeared in the early 1960s did little to change the prevailing view among scholars that Eisenhower had been a weak and ineffective president whose limited conception of the presidency and reluctance to deal directly with difficult problems had undermined his own policies and objectives.[1]

A new picture of Eisenhower began to emerge in the literature of the late 1960s and early 1970s, as Eisenhower and the 1950s looked better and better when judged against Lyndon Johnson and Richard Nixon, the war in Vietnam, and the turbulence of the 1960s. Newly opened materials in the Eisenhower Library and other archives have since substantiated this revisionist portrait of Eisenhower as a knowledgeable, astute, and involved president who exerted a "hidden-hand leadership" to determine and implement his policies and programs.[2]

[1]See DeSantis, "Eisenhower Revisionism"; Reichard, "Eisenhower as President: The Changing View"; Schlesinger, "The Eisenhower Presidency: A Reassessment"; and McAuliffe, Commentary: "Eisenhower, the President."

[2]See for example Kempton, "The Underestimation of Dwight D. Eisenhower"; Parmet, *Eisenhower and the American Crusades;* and Greenstein, *The Hidden-Hand Presidency: Eisenhower as Leader.* See also the articles cited in the previous note.

Conclusion

Eisenhower's actions during the Bricker amendment controversy provide evidence to support this revisionist view. Arthur Krock of the *New York Times* and others even noted at the time that the Bricker amendment conflict transformed Eisenhower into a more active and involved president.[3] Although he relied heavily on others for advice concerning such a technical legal and constitutional issue, Eisenhower devoted considerable time and effort to the Bricker amendment, meeting countless times with Bricker, the congressional leaders, and his own advisers in attempts to resolve the problem. The president's handling of the Bricker amendment makes it clear, moreover, that he did not simply affirm Dulles's policies and suggestions; rather, Eisenhower often challenged the secretary of state's ideas and always retained for himself the ultimate authority. In his advice and comments preceding Dulles's testimony before the Senate Judiciary Committee, the president showed that he understood the political and institutional aspects of the dispute better than the secretary of state. Before making up his mind on the amendment, Eisenhower also consulted with Attorney General Brownell, John W. Davis, and others whose opinions he respected, instead of relying solely on Dulles's recommendation. And even though Dulles cabled from Berlin that the George amendment was acceptable if necessary for political reasons, Eisenhower decided to oppose the measure.

This study of the Bricker amendment shows some of the advantages and disadvantages of Eisenhower's "hidden-hand leadership." William Bragg Ewald, Jr., who worked on Eisenhower's staff in the 1950s and later assisted on his memoirs, has written that Eisenhower drew "an uncrossable line with speed and effect" on the Bricker amendment,[4] but the president was anything but clear and direct in his opposition to the measure during most of 1953. Eisenhower's maneuverings against the amendment were all behind the scenes—at cabinet meetings or in comments on drafts of statements by administration officials. Publicly, the president based his opposition to S.J. Res. 1 on Dulles's analysis of the amendment, making it appear that it was the secretary of state who was responsible for the administration's opposition. As a result, it was Dulles who had to endure the wrath of the amendment's proponents, while Eisenhower was able to maintain cordial relations with them. Eisenhower's apparent reluctance to take a firm stand against the amendment almost backfired. Bricker, Holman, and others continued to believe that the president did not really understand the issue, and that, in time, he could be won over to their point of view.

[3]See Arthur Krock, "Eisenhower's Changing Concept of his Job," *New York Times,* January 17, 1954, IV, 3; and editorial, "The 'Different' Eisenhower," St. Louis *Post-Dispatch,* February 7, 1954, p. 2-C.

[4]Ewald, *Eisenhower the President: Crucial Days, 1951–1960,* p. 142.

Accordingly, they persisted in their campaign to see an amendment enacted, and the conflict dragged on for years. When the president finally came out strongly against the measure in January 1954, it was almost too late. Many legislators were already committed by then, and administration officials had little luck in changing their minds. Consequently, the amendment came closer to passing than it would have if Eisenhower had opposed it more vigorously and directly from the start. Dulles and Brownell were both certain that if the president had taken a strong stand against the amendment from the beginning, its support would have collapsed immediately.[5]

The fight over the Bricker amendment had important consequences. Even though the amendment was defeated, the conflict made Eisenhower and his advisers more aware of Congress's resentment over past encroachments by previous presidents on legislative prerogatives. Thus, when faced with crises in Indochina in 1954, the Far East in 1955, and the Middle East in 1957, Eisenhower worked closely with Congress rather than acting unilaterally under his powers as commander in chief. In the latter two instances, he specifically asked Congress to authorize the use of American troops if he deemed it necessary. It would become apparent in the 1960s, after the Gulf of Tonkin Resolution and American escalation in Vietnam, that this method of joint action by the president and Congress had its imperfections too, but in the 1950s it was widely regarded as a marked improvement over President Truman's sending American troops to Korea without congressional approval. In other instances, however, Eisenhower chose not to consult with Congress. He bypassed Congress completely by resorting to the Central Intelligence Agency and covert operations to overthrow legitimate but leftist governments in both Iran and Guatemala. These were important exceptions to his general practice of working with Congress in foreign affairs, exceptions which he felt were necessary to ensure plausible deniability of any U.S. role.[6]

The Bricker amendment controversy also led the courts to rule clearly that international agreements could not abridge rights guaranteed by the United States Constitution. In *Seery v. United States* in 1955 and *Reid v. Covert* in 1957, the courts firmly established the Constitution's supremacy

---

[5]See memorandum of telephone conversation between the secretary of state and the attorney general, June 4, 1953, in *Foreign Relations, 1952–54,* I, 1812–13.

[6]See Roosevelt, *Countercoup: The Struggle for the Control of Iran;* Ambrose, *Ike's Spies: Eisenhower and the Espionage Establishment;* Cook, *The Declassified Eisenhower: A Divided Legacy,* pp. 184–88, and 217–92; Immerman, *The CIA in Guatemala: The Foreign Policy of Intervention;* and Schlesinger and Kinzer, *Bitter Fruit: The Untold Story of the American Coup in Guatemala.*

over treaties and executive agreements.

Another effect of the Bricker amendment conflict, regrettably, was that it delayed American ratification of the Genocide Convention for thirty-five years. Dulles tried to appease Bricker and his followers by announcing during the hearings on S.J. Res. 1 that the Eisenhower administration would not ask for approval of the Genocide Convention or other agreements on human rights, and Holman and Bricker later took solace from the fact that they had, in Holman's words, "exposed and stopped the attempt by Mrs. Roosevelt and her do-gooders to superimpose upon our own Bill of Rights so-called 'human rights' covenants." Eisenhower's successors, fearful of reopening old wounds, did not actively seek ratification of the convention until Richard Nixon did so in 1970. At that point, Alfred Schweppe, Eberhard Deutsch, and Orie Phillips of the ABA's Committee on Peace and Law helped lead the fight against the agreement, resuscitating many of the same arguments they had used in the 1940s and '50s. John Bricker even wrote to many of his former colleagues in the Senate to urge them to vote against the agreement. Presidents Jimmy Carter and Ronald Reagan later recommended that the Senate give its consent to the Genocide Convention, but not until 1986 did the United States finally ratify the agreement.[7]

It is important that we understand the Bricker amendment controversy because the conflict involved issues that are still relevant today. The Bricker amendment concerned the relationship between the United States and the United Nations, between the states and the federal government, and between Congress and the president. When the Senate rejected the Bricker amendment and all the various substitute proposals in February 1954, it resolved these issues, but only for a time. They would come up again in the future when the struggle over civil rights came to the fore, when the Senate considered the Genocide Convention again, and when legislators sought to rein in "the imperial presidency."

[7]See *Hearings, 1953,* p. 825; Holman to Bricker, October 13, 1958, JBP; Arthur Goldberg to President Lyndon Johnson, May 4, 1966, Johnson Papers, White House Central Files, HU, LBJL; *New York Times,* February 20, 1970, pp. 1, 14; Phillips and Deutsch, "Pitfalls of the Genocide Convention"; John Bricker to George Aiken, December 10, 1970, Aiken Papers, Crate 38, Box 3; U.S., Congress, Senate, Committee on Foreign Relations, *Genocide Convention, Hearing,* before a Subcommittee of the Committee on Foreign Relations, 92d Cong., 1st sess., 1971, pp. 12–104 (statements and testimony by Deutsch and Schweppe); and *New York Times,* May 25, 1977, p. 8; August 3, 1977, p. 5; September 6, 1984, pp. 1, 9; October 17, 1985, p. A-4; and February 20, 1986, pp. 1, 4.

APPENDIXES

Texts of Proposed Amendments

APPENDIX A

S.J. Res. 102—Introduced by Senator Bricker

on September 14, 1951

Section 1. The second paragraph of Article VI of the Constitution of the United States is hereby repealed.

Section 2. This Constitution, and all treaties and laws of the United States made, or which shall be made, in pursuance thereof, shall be the supreme law of the land; and the judges in every State shall be bound thereby, anything in the constitution or laws of any State to the contrary notwithstanding.

No treaty shall be made abridging any of the rights and freedoms recognized in this Constitution.

Section 3. No treaty or executive agreements shall be made respecting the rights and freedoms of citizens of the United States recognized in this Constitution, the character and form of government prescribed by the Constitution and laws of the United States, matters which involve no substantial mutuality of interest as between the United States and other sovereign states, or any other matters essentially within the domestic jurisdiction of the United States.

Section 4. Executive agreements shall not be made in lieu of treaties.

Executive agreements, other than those expressly authorized by the Congress, shall, if not sooner terminated, expire automatically six months after the end of the term of office for which the President making the agreement shall have been elected, but the Congress may, at the request of any President, extend for the duration of the term of such President the life of any such agreement made or extended during the next preceding presidential term.

The President shall publish all executive agreements except that those which in his judgment require secrecy shall be submitted to appropriate committees of the Congress in lieu of publication.

APPENDIX B

Text of Constitutional Amendment Recommended by the American Bar Association's House of Delegates, February 1952

A provision of a treaty which conflicts with any provision of this Constitution shall not be of any force or effect. A treaty shall become effective as internal law in the United States only through legislation by Congress which it could enact under its delegated powers in the absence of such treaty.

APPENDIX C

S.J. Res. 130—Introduced by Senator Bricker on February 7, 1952

Section 1. No treaty or executive agreement shall be made respecting the rights of citizens of the United States protected by this Constitution, or abridging or prohibiting the free exercise thereof.

Section 2. No treaty or executive agreement shall vest in any international organization or in any foreign power any of the legislative, executive, or judicial powers vested by this Constitution in the Congress, the President, and in the courts of the United States, respectively.

Section 3. No treaty or executive agreement shall alter or abridge the laws of the United States or the constitution or laws of the several States unless, and then only to the extent that, Congress shall so provide by act or joint resolution.

Section 4. Executive agreements shall not be made in lieu of treaties. Executive agreements shall, if not sooner terminated, expire automatically 1 year after the end of the term of office for which the President making the agreement shall have been elected, but the Congress may, at the request of any President, extend for the duration of the term of such President the life of any such agreement made or extended during the next preceding presidential term.

The President shall publish all executive agreements except that those which in his judgment require secrecy shall be submitted to appropriate committees of the Congress in lieu of publication.

APPENDIX D

S.J. Res. 1—As Introduced by Senator Bricker on January 7, 1953

Section 1. A provision of a treaty which denies or abridges any right enumerated in this Constitution shall not be of any force or effect.

Section 2. No treaty shall authorize or permit any foreign power or any international organization to supervise, control, or adjudicate rights of citizens of the United States within the United States enumerated in this Constituion or any other matter essentially within the domestic jurisdiction of the United States.

Section 3. A treaty shall become effective as internal law in the United States only through the enactment of appropriate legislation by the Congress.

Section 4. All executive or other agreements between the President and any international organization, foreign power, or official thereof shall be made only in the manner and to the extent to be prescribed by law. Such agreements shall be subject to the limitations imposed on treaties, or the making of treaties, by this article.

APPENDIX E

S.J. Res. 43—Introduced by Senator Watkins on February 16, 1953, at the Request of Frank Holman and the American Bar Association

Section 1. A provision of a treaty which conflicts with any provision of this Constitution shall not be of any force or effect. A treaty shall become effective as internal law in the United States only through legislation which would be valid in the absence of treaty.

Section 2. Executive agreements shall be subject to regulation by the Congress and to the limitations imposed on treaties by this article.

APPENDIX F

S.J. Res. 1—As Reported by the Senate Judiciary Committee on June 15, 1953

Section 1. A provision of a treaty which conflicts with this Constitution shall not be of any force or effect.

Section 2. A treaty shall become effective as internal law in the United States only through legislation which would be valid in the absence of treaty.

Section 3. Congress shall have power to regulate all executive and other agreements with any foreign power or international organization. All such agreements shall be subject to the limitations imposed on treaties by this article.

APPENDIX G

Knowland Substitute (Eisenhower Administration's Proposal), July 1953

Section 1. A provision of a treaty or other international agreement which conflicts with the Constitution shall not be of any force or effect. The judicial power of the United States shall extend to all cases, in law or equity, in which it is claimed that the conflict described in this amendment is present.

Section 2. When the Senate consents to the ratification of a treaty the vote shall be determined by yeas and nays, and the names of the persons voting for and against shall be entered on the Journal of the Senate.

Section 3. When the Senate so provides in its consent to ratification, a treaty shall become effective as internal law in the United States only through the enactment of appropriate legislation by the Congress.

APPENDIX H

Tentative Brownell-Bricker-Ferguson Compromise, January 1954

Section 1. A provision of a treaty or other international agreement which conflicts with this Constitution shall not be of any force or effect.

Section 2. The power to make treaties shall extend to the international relations of the United States but shall not be employed to regulate matters which are not necessary and proper for the conduct of our foreign affairs and which are normally and appropriately within the local jurisdiction of the States. A treaty or other international agreement shall become effective as internal law in the United States only through acts of Congress provided however that treaty provisions relating to the rights and obligations of aliens in the United States shall take effect as provided in such treaties.

APPENDIX I

George Substitute, January 1954

Section 1. A provision of a treaty or other international agreement which conflicts with this Constitution shall not be of any force or effect.

Section 2. An international agreement other than a treaty shall become effective as internal law in the United States only by an act of the Congress.

APPENDIX J

Knowland-Ferguson Proposal, February 1954

Section 1. A provision of a treaty or other international agreement which conflicts with this Constitution shall not be of any force or effect.

Section 2. Clause 2 of Article VI of the Constitution of the United States is hereby amended by adding at the end thereof the following: "Notwithstanding the foregoing provisions of this clause, no treaty made after the establishment of this Constitution shall be the supreme law of the land unless made in pursuance of this Constitution."

Section 3. On the question of advising and consenting to the ratification of a treaty the vote shall be determined by yeas and nays, and the names of the persons voting for and against shall be entered on the Journal of the Senate.

APPENDIX K

Bricker Proposal, February 1954

Section 1. Clause 2 of Article VI of the Constitution of the United States is hereby amended by adding at the end thereof the following: "Notwithstanding the foregoing provisions of this clause, no treaty made after the establishment of this Constitution shall be the supreme law of the land unless made in pursuance of this Constitution."

Section 2. A provision of a treaty or other international agreement which conflicts with this Constitution shall not be of any force or effect.

Section 3. A treaty or other international agreement shall become effective as internal law in the United States only through legislation by the Congress unless in advising and consenting to a treaty the Senate, by a vote of two-thirds of the Senators present and voting, shall provide that such treaty may become effective as internal law without legislation by the Congress.

Section 4. On the question of advising and consenting to the ratification of a treaty the vote shall be determined by yeas and nays, and the names of the persons voting for and against shall be entered on the Journal of the Senate.

APPENDIX L

S.J. Res. 181—Introduced by Senator Bricker on August 5, 1954

Section 1. A provision of a treaty or other international agreement which conflicts with this Constitution, or which is not made in pursuance thereof, shall not be the supreme law of the land nor be of any force or effect.

Section 2. A treaty or other international agreement shall become effective as internal law in the United States only through legislation valid in the absence of international agreement.

Section 3. On the question of advising and consenting to the ratification of a treaty, the vote shall be determined by yeas and nays, and the names of the persons voting for and against shall be entered on the Journal of the Senate.

APPENDIX M

Constitutional Amendment Proposed by Senator Bricker
to the Administration, December 1956

Section 1. A provision of a treaty or other international agreement not made in pursuance of this Constitution shall have no force or effect. This section shall not apply to treaties made prior to the effective date of this Constitution.

Section 2. A treaty or other international agreement shall have legislative effect within the United States as a law thereof only through legislation, except to the extent that the Senate shall provide affirmatively, in its resolution advising and consenting to a treaty, that the treaty shall have legislative effect.

Section 3. An international agreement other than a treaty shall have legislative effect within the United States as a law thereof only through legislation valid in the absence of such an international agreement.

Section 4. On the question of advising and consenting to a treaty, the vote shall be determined by yeas and nays, and the names of the Senators voting for and against shall be entered on the Journal of the Senate.

Bibliography

MANUSCRIPT COLLECTIONS

Dean Acheson Papers. Harry S. Truman Library.
George Aiken Papers. University of Vermont Library.
Joseph Alsop Papers. Library of Congress.
Stewart Alsop Papers. Library of Congress.
Americans for Democratic Action Papers. Microfilm edition. Sanford, N.C.: Microfilming Corporation of America, 1978.
Warren Austin Papers. University of Vermont Library.
Dana Backus and Theodore Pearson Collection of Reports and Documents on the Bricker Amendment. Association of the Bar of the City of New York Library.
Adolf Berle Papers. Franklin D. Roosevelt Library.
Hugo Black Papers. Library of Congress.
John Bricker Papers. Ohio Historical Society.
Harold Burton Papers. Library of Congress.
Harry Byrd Papers. University of Virginia Library.
Francis Case Papers. Excerpts on microfilm, Truman Library.
Emanuel Celler Papers. Library of Congress.
Zechariah Chafee, Jr., Papers. Harvard Law School Library.
Will Clayton Papers. Truman Library.
Clark Clifford Papers and Files. Truman Library.
Sterling Cole Papers. Cornell University Library.
Tom Connally Papers. Library of Congress.
Edward Corwin Papers. Princeton University Library.
Virginius Dabney Papers. University of Virginia Library.
John W. Davis Papers. Yale University Library.
Democratic National Committee Clipping Files. Truman Library.
John Foster Dulles Papers. Princeton University Library.
Minutes of Telephone Conversations of John Foster Dulles and of Christian Herter, 1953–1961. Microfilm edition. Washington, D.C.: University Publications of America, 1980.

Dwight D. Eisenhower Papers. Dwight D. Eisenhower Library.
George Elsey Papers and Files. Truman Library.
Harold Enarson Papers. Truman Library.
Ralph Flanders Papers. Syracuse University Library.
Felix Frankfurter Papers. Library of Congress.
Frank Gannett Papers. Cornell University Library.
James Hagerty Diaries and Papers. Eisenhower Library.
Leonard Hall Papers. Eisenhower Library.
Bryce Harlow Records. Eisenhower Library.
Robert Hendrickson Papers. Syracuse University Library.
Thomas Hennings, Jr., Papers. University of Missouri Library.
Manley Hudson Papers. Harvard Law School Library.
Irving Ives Papers. Cornell University Library.
Philip Jessup Papers. Library of Congress.
Lyndon Baines Johnson Papers. Lyndon Baines Johnson Library.
Philip Kaiser Papers. Truman Library.
James Kem Papers. University of Missouri Library.
Eugene Keough Papers. Syracuse University Library.
Harley Kilgore Papers. Roosevelt Library and West Virginia University Library.
Arthur Krock Papers. Princeton University Library.
Herbert Lehman Papers. Columbia University.
Fulton Lewis, Jr., Papers. Syracuse University Library.
Mary Pillsbury Lord Papers. Eisenhower Library.
Carl McCardle Papers. Eisenhower Library.
Harry McPherson Files. Johnson Library.
Vito Marcantonio Papers. New York Public Library.
Jack Martin Records. Eisenhower Library.
Sherman Minton Papers. Truman Library.
Gerald Morgan Records. Eisenhower Library.
Charles Murphy Papers and Files. Truman Library.
Philleo Nash Papers and Files. Truman Library.
Richard Nixon Papers. Federal Archives and Records Center, Los Angeles.
Dorothy Norman Papers. Columbia University Library.
Larry O'Brien Papers and Files. Johnson Library.
Leo Pasvolsky Papers. Library of Congress.
Herman Phelger Collection of Materials Relating to the Bricker Amendment and
    the Treaty-Making Power of the United States. Princeton University Library.
President's Committee on Civil Rights Papers. Truman Library.
Howard Pyle Records. Eisenhower Library.
Sam Rayburn Papers. Sam Rayburn Library, Bonham, Texas.
William P. Rogers Papers. Eisenhower Library.
Eleanor Roosevelt Papers. Roosevelt Library.
Franklin D. Roosevelt Papers. Roosevelt Library.
Richard Russell Papers. Richard Russell Memorial Library, University of Georgia.
Bernard Shanley Diary. Seton Hall University Library and Eisenhower Library.
H. Alexander Smith Diaries and Papers. Princeton University Library.

Howard Smith Papers. University of Virginia Library.
Stephen Spingarn Papers and Files. Truman Library.
Harold M. Stephens Papers. Library of Congress.
Harlan Fiske Stone Papers. Library of Congress.
David Stowe Papers and Files. Truman Library.
Arthur E. Sutherland, Jr., Papers. Harvard Law School Library.
John Taber Papers. Cornell University Library.
Robert A. Taft Papers. Library of Congress.
Theodore Tannenwald Papers. Truman Library.
Jack Tate Papers. Truman Library.
Elbert Thomas Papers. Roosevelt Library.
Dorothy Thompson Papers. Syracuse University Library.
Harry S. Truman Papers. Truman Library.
Louis Waldman Papers. New York Public Library.
William Allen White Papers. Library of Congress.
Sidney Yates Papers. Truman Library.

ORAL HISTORY COLLECTIONS

Columbia University Oral History Collection
  Sherman Adams Oral History Transcript.
  John Bricker Oral History Transcript.
  Herbert Brownell Oral History Transcript.
  Ralph Flanders Oral History Transcript.
  Leverett Saltonstall Oral History Transcript.
  Alexander Wiley Oral History Transcript.
John Foster Dulles Oral History Project—Princeton University Library
  Steward Alsop Oral History Transcript.
  Robert Bowie Oral History Transcript.
  John Sherman Cooper Oral History Transcript.
  Dwight D. Eisenhower Oral History Transcript.
  Homer Ferguson Oral History Transcript.
  Ernest Gross Oral History Transcript.
  Charles Halleck Oral History Transcript.
  Bourke Hickenlooper Oral History Transcript.
  Mary Pillsbury Lord Oral History Transcript.
  Mike Mansfield Oral History Transcript.
  Gerald Morgan Oral History Transcript.
  Thruston Morton Oral History Transcript.
  Herman Phleger Oral History Transcript.
  James Richards Oral History Transcript.
  Bernard Shanley Oral History Transcript.
  John Sparkman Oral History Transcript.

Dwight D. Eisenhower Library
  Clarence Manion Oral History Transcript.
Lyndon Baines Johnson Library
  George Reedy Oral History Transcript.
  William S. White Oral History Transcript.
Harry S. Truman Library
  George Elsey Oral History Transcript.
United States Senate Historical Office
  Pat Holt Oral History Transcript.

PERSONAL INTERVIEWS AND CORRESPONDENCE

Dana Backus. Interview with author. May 19, 1976. New York City.
John Bricker. Interviews with author. June 26, June 30, and July 10, 1975. Columbus, Ohio.
Ben H. Brown, Jr. Letter to author. March 21, 1977.
Herbert Brownell. Interview with author. June 23, 1975. New York City.
Robert Carr. Letter to author. September 17, 1976.
Lucius Clay. Letter to author. December 21, 1976.
Robert Eichholz. Interview with author. December 29, 1976. Washington, D.C.
J. William Fulbright. Interview with author. November 11, 1976. Washington, D.C.
Carlyle Maw. Interview with author. January 26, 1977. New York City.
Endicott Peabody. Interview with author. November 10, 1976. Washington, D.C.
Theodore Pearson. Letter to author. September 12, 1979.
Bernard Shanley. Interview with author. November 8, 1976. Newark, N.J.
Gerald Siegel. Interview with author. December 23, 1980. Washington, D.C.
Bethuel Webster. Interview with author. May 18, 1976. New York City.
Nancy Wechsler. Interview with author. June 30, 1976. New York City.

GOVERNMENT DOCUMENTS

Documents in this section have been arranged in chronological order.

  U.S. Congress. *Congressional Record.*
  U.S. Department of State. *Department of State Bulletin.*
  U.S. Department of State. *Foreign Relations of the United States.*
  U.S. Congress. Senate. *The Internal and External Powers of the National Government,* by George Sutherland. S. Doc. 417, 61st Cong., 2d sess., 1910.
  Public Papers of the Presidents: Harry S. Truman, 1945–1953. Washington, D.C.: United States Government Printing Office, 1961–1966.

Bibliography

U.S. Congress. Senate. *The Charter of the United Nations*. S. Doc. 70, 79th Cong., 1st sess., July 2, 1945.

U.S. Congress. Senate. Committee on Foreign Relations. *The Charter of the United Nations*. *Hearings* before the Committee on Foreign Relations, Senate, 79th Cong., 1st sess., 1945.

U.S. Congress. Senate. Committee on Foreign Relations. *The Charter of the United Nations*. S. Exec. Rept. 8, 79th Cong., 1st sess., July 16, 1945.

U.S. Congress. Senate. Committee on Foreign Relations. *Executive Sessions of the Senate Foreign Relations Committee* (Historical Series). 80th Cong.–86th Cong., 1947–1960 (made public in 1976–1982).

President's Committee on Civil Rights. *To Secure These Rights: The Report of the President's Committee on Civil Rights*. Washington, D.C.: United States Government Printing Office, 1947.

U.S. Congress. Senate. Committee on Labor and Public Welfare. *Prohibiting Discrimination in Employment because of Race, Religion, Color, National Origin, or Ancestry*. S. Rept. 951, 80th Cong., 2d sess., March 2, 1948.

U.S. Congress. Senate. Committee on Foreign Relations. *North Atlantic Treaty*. *Hearings* before the Committee on Foreign Relations, Senate, 81st Cong., 1st sess., 1949.

U.S. Congress. Senate. *International Convention on the Prevention and Punishment of the Crime of Genocide: Message from the President of the United States*. Executive O, Senate, 81st Cong., 1st sess., June 16, 1949.

U.S. Congress. House. Committee on Education and Labor. *The Federal Fair Employment Practice Act*. H. Rept. 1165, 81st Cong., 1st sess., August 2, 1949.

U.S. Congress. Senate. Committee on Foreign Relations. *The Genocide Convention*. *Hearings* before a Subcommittee of the Committee on Foreign Relations, Senate, 81st Cong., 2d sess., 1950.

U.S. Congress. House. Committee on Foreign Affairs. *Background Information on Korea*. H. Rept. 2495, 81st Cong., 2d sess., July 11, 1950.

U.S. Department of State. *Our Foreign Policy*. Department of State Publication 3972, General Foreign Policy Series 26. Washington, D.C.: United States Government Printing Office, 1950.

U.S. Congress. Senate. Committee on Foreign Relations and Committee on Armed Services. *Assignment of Ground Forces of the United States to Duty in the European Area*. *Hearings* before the Committee on Foreign Relations and the Committee on Armed Services, Senate, 82d Cong., 1st sess., 1951.

U.S. Congress. Senate. Committee on Foreign Relations and Committee on Armed Services. *Assignment of Ground Forces of the United States to Duty in the European Area*. S. Rept. 175, 82d Cong., 1st sess., March 14, 1951.

U.S. Congress. Senate. Committee on the Judiciary. *Treaties and Executive Agreements*. *Hearings* before a Subcommittee of the Committee on the Judiciary, Senate, 82d Cong., 2d sess., 1952.

Public Papers of the Presidents: Dwight D. Eisenhower, 1953–1961. Washington, D.C.: United States Government Printing Office, 1958–1961.

U.S. Congress. Senate. Committee on the Judiciary. *Treaties and Executive*

Agreements. Hearings before a Subcommittee of the Committee on the Judiciary, Senate, 83d Cong., 1st sess., 1953.

U.S. Congress. Senate. Committee on Foreign Relations. *Agreements Relating to the Status of the North Atlantic Treaty Organization, Armed Forces, and Military Headquarters. Hearings* before the Committee on Foreign Relations, Senate, 83d Cong., 1st sess., 1953.

U.S. Congress. Senate. Committee on the Judiciary. *Constitutional Amendment Relative to Treaties and Executive Agreements.* S. Rept. 412, 83d Cong., 1st sess., June 15, 1953.

U.S. Congress. Senate. Committee on Foreign Relations. *Requiring International Agreements Other Than Treaties to be Transmitted to the Senate within 60 Days After Execution Thereof.* S. Rept. 2340, 83d Cong., 2d sess., August 7, 1954.

U.S. Congress. Senate. *The Southeast Asia Collective Defense Treaty and the Protocol Thereto.* Executive K, Senate, 83d Cong., 2d sess., November 10, 1954.

U.S. Congress. House. Committee on Foreign Affairs. *Authorizing the President to Employ the Armed Forces of the United States for Protecting the Security of Formosa, the Pescadores, and Related Positions and Territories of that Area.* H. Rept. 4, 84th Cong., 1st sess., January 24, 1955.

U.S. Congress. Senate. Committee on Foreign Relations and Committee on Armed Services. *Authorizing the President to Employ the Armed Forces of the United States for Protecting the Security of Formosa, the Pescadores, and Related Positions and Territories of that Area.* S. Rept. 13, 84th Cong., 1st sess., January 26, 1955.

U.S. Congress. Senate. Committee on the Judiciary. *Treaties and Executive Agreements. Hearings* before a Subcommittee of the Committee on the Judiciary, Senate, 84th Cong., 1st sess., 1955.

U.S. Congress. Senate. Committee on the Judiciary. *Constitutional Amendment Relative to Treaties and Executive Agreements.* S. Rept. 1716, 84th Cong., 2d sess., March 27, 1956.

U.S. Congress. House. *Middle East Situation. Address of the President of the United States Delivered before a Joint Session of Congress, January 5, 1957.* H. Doc. 46, 85th Cong., 2d sess., January 5, 1957.

U.S. Congress. House. Committee on Foreign Affairs. *Authorizing the President to Undertake Economic and Military Cooperation with Nations in the General Area of the Middle East.* H. Rept. 2, 85th Cong., 1st sess., January 25, 1957.

U.S. Congress. Senate. Committee on Foreign Relations and Committee on Armed Services. *To Promote Peace and Stability in the Middle East.* S. Rept. 70, 85th Cong., 1st sess., February 14, 1957.

U.S. Congress. Senate. *Message from the President of the United States.* Executive B, Senate, 91st Cong., 2d sess., February 19, 1970.

U.S. Congress. Senate. Committee on Foreign Relations. *Genocide Convention. Hearings* before a Subcommittee of the Committee on Foreign Relations, Senate, 91st Cong., 2d sess., 1970.

U.S. Congress. Senate. Committee on Foreign Relations. *Genocide Convention. Hearing* before a Subcommittee of the Committee on Foreign Relations, Senate, 92d Cong., 1st sess., 1971.

U.S. Congress. Senate. Committee on Foreign Relations. *War Powers Legislation. Hearings* before the Committee on Foreign Relations, Senate, 92d Cong., 1st sess., 1971.

U.S. Congress. Senate. Committee on Foreign Relations. *Transmittal of Executive Agreements to Congress. Hearings* before the Committee on Foreign Relations, Senate, 92d Cong., 1st sess., 1971.

U.S. Congress. Senate. Committee on Foreign Relations. *Transmittal of Executive Agreements to Congress.* S. Rept. 92–591, 92d Cong., 2d sess., January 19, 1972.

U.S. Congress. Senate. Committee on Foreign Relations. *International Convention on the Prevention and Punishment of the Crime of Genocide.* S. Exec. Rept. 94–23, 94th Cong., 2d sess., April 29, 1976.

U.S. Congress. Senate. Committee on Foreign Relations. *Genocide Convention. Hearing* before the Committee on Foreign Relations, Senate, 95th Cong., 1st sess., 1977.

U.S. Congress. Senate. Committee on Foreign Relations. *The Genocide Convention. Hearings* before the Committee on Foreign Relations, Senate, 98th Cong., 2d sess., 1984.

U.S. Congress. Senate. Committee on Foreign Relations. *International Convention on the Prevention and Punishment of the Crime of Genocide.* S. Exec. Rept. 98–50, 98th Cong., 2d sess., 1984.

U.S. Congress. Senate. Committee on Foreign Relations. *Crime of Genocide. Hearing* before the Committee on Foreign Relations, Senate, 99th Cong., 1st sess., 1985.

U.S. Congress. Senate. Committee on Foreign Relations. *Genocide Convention.* S. Exec. Rept. 99–2, 99th Cong., 1st sess., 1985.

BAR ASSOCIATION DOCUMENTS

Documents in this section have been arranged in chronological order.

American Bar Association. *Reports of the American Bar Association.*

American Bar Association. Section of International and Comparative Law. *Proceedings.*

Association of the Bar of the City of New York. *Record of the Association of the Bar of the City of New York.*

Association of the Bar of the City of New York. *Reports.*

New York State Bar Association. *Proceedings.*

American Bar Association. "Report and Recommendations to the House of Delegates by the Committee for Peace and Law Through United Nations, With the Action Voted by the House of Delegates upon the Recommendations." September 7, 1948.

American Bar Association. "Documents for Study in the 1949 Series of Regional Group Conferences." February 1949.

American Bar Association. "Report of the Special Committee on Peace and Law Through United Nations." September 1, 1949.

American Bar Association. "Report and Recommendations to the Section of International and Comparative Law by the Committee on United Nations." September 5, 1949.

American Bar Association. "Report and Recommendations of the Section of International and Comparative Law." September 8, 1949.

American Bar Association. "Report of the Committee for Peace and Law Through United Nations." September 1, 1950.

American Bar Association. "Summary of Action Taken by the House of Delegates." September 1950.

American Bar Association. "Report of the Committee on Peace and Law." February 1, 1952.

Association of the Bar of the City of New York. Committee on Federal Legislation and Committee on International Law. "Report on 'Joint Resolution Proposing an Amendment to the Constitution of the United States Relative to the Making of Treaties and Executive Agreements' (S. J. Res. 130)." April 28, 1952.

American Bar Association. Section of International and Comparative Law. Committee on Constitutional Aspects of International Agreements. "Report on S. J. Res. 1 and the Knowland Substitute Amendment." August 24, 1953.

Association of the Bar of the City of New York. Committee on Federal Legislation and Committee on International Law. "The Risks of the 1956 Bricker Amendment." May 21, 1956.

DISSERTATIONS AND THESES

Berquist, Goodwin F., Jr. "A Comparative Study of Non-Congressional Arguments Against the League of Nations and the United Nations." M.A. thesis, Pennsylvania State University, 1954.

Bradford, Nancy Dixon. "The 1952 Steel Seizure Case." M.A. thesis, University of Southern California, 1967.

Bullard, Anthony. "Harry S. Truman and the Separation of Powers in Foreign Affairs." Ph.D. diss., Columbia University, 1972.

Engelland, Charles. "The Bricker Amendment." Ph.D. diss., State University of Iowa, 1954.

Juhnke, William. "Creating a New Charter of Freedom: The Organization and Operation of the President's Committee on Civil Rights, 1946–1948." Ph.D. diss., University of Kansas, 1974.

Koo, Youngnok. "Dissenters from American Involvement in World Affairs: A Political Analysis of the Movement for the Bricker Amendment." Ph.D. diss., University of Michigan, 1966.

Truitt, Wesley. "The Troops to Europe Decision: The Process, Politics, and Diplomacy of a Strategic Commitment." Ph.D. diss., Columbia University, 1968.

Bibliography

BOOKS

Abell, Tyler, ed. *Drew Pearson Diaries, 1949–1959*. New York: Holt, Rinehart and Winston, 1974.

Acheson, Dean. *Morning and Noon*. Boston: Houghton Mifflin, 1965.

———. *Present at the Creation: My Years in the State Department*. New York: W. W. Norton, 1969.

Adams, Sherman. *Firsthand Report: The Story of the Eisenhower Administration*. New York: Harper & Brothers, 1961.

Adler, Selig. *The Isolationist Impulse: Its Twentieth Century Reaction*. New York: Free Press, 1966.

Albertson, Dean, ed. *Eisenhower as President*. New York: Hill and Wang, 1963.

Alexander, Charles. *Holding the Line: The Eisenhower Era, 1952–1961*. Bloomington: Indiana University Press, 1975.

Alsop, Joseph, and Alsop, Stewart. *The Reporter's Trade*. New York: Reynal, 1958.

Ambrose, Stephen. *Ike's Spies: Eisenhower and the Espionage Establishment*. Garden City, N.Y.: Doubleday, 1981.

———. *Eisenhower*. 2 vols. New York: Simon and Schuster, 1983–84.

Asher, Robert; Kotschnig, Walter; Brown, William Adams, Jr.; Green, James Frederick; and Sady, Emil J. *The United Nations and Promotion of the General Welfare*. Washington, D.C.: Brookings Institution, 1957.

Auerbach, Jerold. *Unequal Justice: Lawyers and Social Change in Modern America*. New York: Oxford University Press, 1976.

Beal, John Robinson. *John Foster Dulles*. New York: Harper & Brothers, 1957.

Bell, Daniel, ed. *The Radical Right*. Garden City, N.Y.: Doubleday, 1963.

Berding, Andrew. *Dulles on Diplomacy*. Princeton, N.J.: D. Van Nostrand, 1965.

Berman, William. *The Politics of Civil Rights in the Truman Administration*. Columbus: Ohio State University Press, 1970.

Bernstein, Barton, ed. *Politics and Policies of the Truman Administration*. New York: New Viewpoints, 1974.

Berry, Mary Frances. *Stability, Security, and Continuity: Mr. Justice Burton and Decision-Making in the Supreme Court, 1945–1958*. Westport, Conn.: Greenwood Press, 1978.

Binkley, Wilfred. *The Man in the White House*. Baltimore: Johns Hopkins Press, 1978.

Bishop, Donald. *The Roosevelt-Litvinov Agreements: The American View*. Syracuse, N.Y.: Syracuse University Press, 1965.

Block, Herbert. *Herblock's Here and Now*. New York: Simon and Schuster, 1955.

Browder, Robert. *The Origins of Soviet-American Diplomacy*. Princeton: Princeton University Press, 1953.

Brown, Seyom. *The Faces of Power: Constancy and Change in United States Foreign Policy from Truman to Johnson*. New York: Columbia University Press, 1968.

Burns, James MacGregor. *Roosevelt: The Lion and the Fox*. New York: Harcourt, Brace & World, 1956.

237

————. *The Deadlock of Democracy: Four-Party Politics in America*. Englewood Cliffs, N.J.: Prentice-Hall, 1963.

————. *Roosevelt: The Soldier of Freedom, 1940–1945*. New York: Harcourt Brace Jovanovich, 1970.

Byrd, Elbert M., Jr. *Treaties and Executive Agreements in the United States: Their Separate Roles and Limitations*. The Hague: Martinus Nijhoff, 1960.

Campbell, Angus; Converse, Philip; Miller, Warren; and Stokes, Donald. *The American Voter*. Abridged ed. New York: John Wiley, 1964.

Campbell, Thomas, and Herring, George, eds. *The Diaries of Edward R. Stettinius, Jr., 1943–1946*. New York: New Viewpoints, 1975.

Caridi, Ronald. *The Korean War and American Politics: The Republican Party as a Case Study*. Philadelphia: University of Pennsylvania Press, 1968.

Carr, Robert. *Federal Protection of Civil Rights: Quest for a Sword*. Ithaca, N.Y.: Cornell University Press, 1947.

Carroll,. Holbert. *The House of Representatives and Foreign Affairs*. Pittsburgh: University of Pittsburgh Press, 1958.

Chafee, Zechariah, Jr. *Free Speech in the United States*. Cambridge: Harvard University Press, 1942.

Cheever, Daniel, and Haviland, H. Field, Jr. *American Foreign Policy and Separation of Powers*. Cambridge: Harvard University Press, 1952.

Childs, Marquis. *Eisenhower: Captive Hero—A Critical Study of the General and the President*. New York: Harcourt, Brace, 1958.

Clemens, Diane Shaver. *Yalta*. New York: Oxford University Press, 1970.

Cochran, Bert. *Harry Truman and the Crisis Presidency*. New York: Funk & Wagnalls, 1973.

Cohen, Benjamin V. *The United Nations: Constitutional Developments, Growth, and Possibilities*. Cambridge: Harvard University Press, 1961.

Cohen, Bernard C. *The Press and Foreign Policy*. Princeton: Princeton University Press, 1963.

————. *The Public's Impact on Foreign Policy*. Boston: Little, Brown, 1973.

Connally, Tom. *My Name is Tom Connally*. New York: Thomas Crowell, 1954.

Cook, Blanche Wiesen. *The Declassified Eisenhower: A Divided Legacy*. Garden City, N.Y.: Doubleday, 1981.

Cornwell, Elmer, Jr. *Presidential Leadership of Public Opinion*. Bloomington: Indiana University Press, 1965.

Corwin, Edward. *National Supremacy: Treaty Power vs. State Power*. New York: H. Holt, 1913.

————. *The Constitution and What It Means Today*. Princeton: Princeton University Press, 1947.

————. *The President: Office and Powers, 1787–1948*. New York: New York University Press, 1948.

————. *The Constitution and What It Means Today*. 1974 ed. Revised by Harold Chase and Craig Ducat. Princeton: Princeton University Press, 1974.

Cotton, Norris. *In the Senate: Amidst the Conflict and the Turmoil*. New York: Dodd, Mead, 1978.

Cowles, Willard. *Treaties and Constitutional Law: Property Interferences and Due Process of Law*. Washington, D.C.: American Council on Public Affairs, 1941.

Crabb, Cecil V. *Bipartisan Foreign Policy: Myth or Reality?* Evanston, Ill.: Row, Peterson, 1957.

Crandall, Samuel. *Treaties: Their Making and Enforcement*. 2d ed. Washington, D.C.: J. Byrne, 1916.

Crosby, Donald, S. J. *God, Church, and Flag: Senator Joseph R. McCarthy and the Catholic Church, 1950–1957*. Chapel Hill: University of North Carolina Press, 1978.

Dahl, Robert. *Congress and Foreign Policy*. New York: Harcourt, Brace, 1950.

Dalleck, Robert. *Franklin D. Roosevelt and American Foreign Policy*. New York: Oxford University Press, 1979.

DeConde, Alexander. *A History of American Foreign Policy*. 2d ed. New York: Charles Scribner's Sons, 1971.

Divine, Robert. *Foreign Policy and U.S. Presidential Elections, 1952–1960*. New York: New Viewpoints, 1974.

———. *Eisenhower and the Cold War*. New York: Oxford University Press, 1981.

Doenecke, Justus. *Not to the Swift: The Old Isolationists in the Cold War Era*. Lewisburg, Pa.: Bucknell University Press, 1979.

Donovan, Robert. *Eisenhower: The Inside Story*. New York: Harper & Brothers, 1956.

Dorough, C. Dwight. *Mr. Sam*. New York: Random House, 1962.

Douglas, Paul H. *In the Fullness of Time: The Memoirs of Paul H. Douglas*. New York: Harcourt Brace Jovanovich, 1972.

Drury, Allen. *Three Kids in a Cart: A Visit to Ike, and Other Diversions*. Garden City, N.Y.: Doubleday, 1965.

Dulles, John Foster. *War or Peace*. New York: Macmillan, 1950.

Dunne, Gerald. *Hugo Black and the Judicial Revolution*. New York: Simon and Schuster, 1977.

Eagleton, Thomas. *War and Presidential Power: A Chronicle of Congressional Surrender*. New York: Liveright, 1974.

Eichelberger, Clark. *Organizing for Peace: A Personal History of the Founding of the United Nations*. New York: Harper & Row, 1977.

Eisenhower, Dwight D. *The White House Years*. Vol. 1: *Mandate for Change, 1953–1956*. Garden City, N.Y.: Doubleday, 1963.

———. *The White House Years*. Vol. 2: *Waging Peace, 1956–1961*. Garden City, N.Y.: Doubleday, 1965.

———. *At Ease: Stories I Tell to Friends*. Garden City, N.Y.: Doubleday, 1967.

Evans, Rowland, and Novak, Robert. *Lyndon B. Johnson: The Exercise of Power*. New York: New American Library, 1966.

Ewald, William Bragg, Jr. *Eisenhower the President: Crucial Days, 1951–1960*. Englewood Cliffs, N.J.: Prentice-Hall, 1981.

Farnsworth, David. *The Senate Committee on Foreign Relations*. Urbana: University of Illinois Press, 1961.

Ferrell, Robert, ed. *The Eisenhower Diaries*. New York: W. W. Norton, 1981.

———, ed. *The Diary of James C. Hagerty: Eisenhower in Mid-Course, 1954–1955.* Bloomington: Indiana University Press, 1983.

Finer, Herman. *The Presidency: Crisis and Regeneration.* Chicago: University of Chicago Press, 1960.

———. *Dulles Over Suez.* Chicago: Quadrangle Books, 1964.

Fisher, Louis. *President and Congress: Power and Policy.* New York: Free Press, 1972.

Flanders, Ralph. *Senator from Vermont.* Boston: Little, Brown, 1961.

Fleming, Denna. *The Treaty Veto of the American Senate.* New York: G. P. Putnam's Sons, 1930.

Free, Lloyd, and Cantril, Hadley. *The Political Beliefs of Americans.* New Brunswick, N.J.: Rutgers University Press, 1967.

Fried, Richard. *Men against McCarthy.* New York: Columbia University Press, 1976.

Gallagher, Hugh. *Advise and Obstruct: The Role of the United States Senate in Foreign Policy Decisions.* New York: Delacorte, 1969.

Galloway, John. *The Gulf of Tonkin Resolution.* Rutherford, N.J.: Fairleigh Dickinson University Press, 1970.

Gallup, George. *The Gallup Poll: Public Opinion, 1935–1971.* New York: Random House, 1972.

Gerson, Louis. *John Foster Dulles.* Vol. 17 of *The American Secretaries of State and Their Diplomacy.* Edited by Robert Ferrell and Samuel Flagg Bemis. New York: Cooper Square, 1967.

Gilbert, Amy. *Executive Agreements and Treaties, 1946–1973: Framework of the Foreign Policy of the Period.* Endicott, N.Y.: Thomas-Newell, 1973.

Goldman, Eric. *The Crucial Decade—and After: America, 1945–1960.* New York: Vintage Books, 1960.

Goldsmith, William. *The Growth of Presidential Power: A Documented History.* 3 vols. New York: Chelsea House, 1974.

Goodrich, Leland; Hambro, Edvard; and Simons, Anne Patricia. *Charter of the United Nations: Commentary and Documents.* 3rd and rev. ed. New York: Columbia University Press, 1969.

Goold-Adams, Richard. *The Time of Power: A Reappraisal of John Foster Dulles.* New York: Appleton-Century-Crofts, 1962.

Gorman, Joseph. *Kefauver: A Political Biography.* New York: Oxford University Press, 1971.

Graebner, Norman. *The New Isolationism: A Study in Politics and Foreign Policy Since 1950.* New York: Ronald Press, 1956.

Grassmuck, George. *Sectional Biases in Congress on Foreign Policy.* Baltimore: Johns Hopkins Press, 1951.

Greenstein, Fred. *The Hidden-Hand Presidency: Eisenhower as Leader.* New York: Basic Books, 1982.

Griffith, Robert. *The Politics of Fear: Joseph R. McCarthy and the Senate.* Lexington: University of Kentucky Press, 1970.

Guhin, Michael. *John Foster Dulles: A Statesman and His Times.* New York: Columbia University Press, 1972.

Gunther, John. *Inside U.S.A.* Rev. ed. New York: Harper & Brothers, 1951.

Halberstam, David. *The Best and the Brightest.* Greenwich, Conn.: Fawcett, 1973.

Hamby, Alonzo. *Beyond the New Deal: Harry S. Truman and American Liberalism.* New York: Columbia University Press, 1973.

Harbaugh, William. *Lawyer's Lawyer: The Life of John W. Davis.* New York: Oxford University Press, 1973.

Hardin, Charles. *Presidential Power and Accountability: Toward a New Constitution.* Chicago: University of Chicago Press, 1974.

Hartmann, Susan. *Truman and the 80th Congress.* Columbia: University of Missouri Press, 1971.

Haynes, Richard. *The Awesome Power: Harry S. Truman as Commander in Chief.* Baton Rouge: Louisiana State University Press, 1973.

Henkin, Louis. *Foreign Affairs and the Constitution.* New York: W. W. Norton, 1972.

Herring, George. *America's Longest War: The United States and Vietnam, 1950–1975.* New York: John Wiley, 1979.

Hofstadter, Richard. *The Paranoid Style in American Politics and Other Essays.* New York: Vintage Books, 1967.

Holman, Frank. *The Life and Career of a Western Lawyer, 1886–1961.* Baltimore: Port City Press, 1963.

Holt, W. Stull. *Treaties Defeated by the Senate.* Baltimore: Johns Hopkins Press, 1933.

Hoopes, Townsend. *The Devil and John Foster Dulles.* Boston: Atlantic/Little, Brown, 1973.

Hughes, Emmet John. *The Ordeal of Power: A Political Memoir of the Eisenhower Years.* New York: Atheneum, 1963.

———. *The Living Presidency.* Baltimore: Penguin Books, 1974.

Immerman, Richard. *The CIA in Guatemala: The Foreign Policy of Intervention.* Austin: University of Texas Press, 1982.

Jackson, Robert H. *The Struggle for Judicial Supremacy: A Study of a Crisis in American Power Politics.* New York: Alfred A. Knopf, 1941.

James, Dorothy Buckton. *The Contemporary Presidency.* New York: Western Publishing Company, 1969.

Javits, Jacob, with Kellerman, Don. *Who Makes War: The President Versus Congress.* New York: William Morrow, 1973.

Jessup, Philip. *A Modern Law of Nations.* New York: Macmillan, 1948.

Jewell, Malcolm. *Senatorial Politics and Foreign Policy.* Lexington: University of Kentucky Press, 1962.

Johnson, Walter, ed. *The Papers of Adlai Stevenson.* Vol. 4: *Let's Talk Sense to the American People.* Boston: Little, Brown, 1974.

Jonas, Manfred. *Isolationism in America, 1935–1941.* Ithaca, N.Y.: Cornell University Press, 1966.

Jones, Joseph. *The Fifteen Weeks.* New York: Viking Press, 1955.

Kemper, Donald. *Decade of Fear: Senator Hennings and Civil Liberties.* Columbia: University of Missouri Press, 1965.

Key, V. O., Jr., with Cummings, Milton. *The Responsible Electorate: Rationality in Presidential Voting, 1936–1960.* New York: Vintage Books, 1968.

Kimball, Warren. *The Most Unsordid Act: Lend-Lease, 1939–1941.* Baltimore: Johns Hopkins Press, 1969.

Kluger, Richard. *Simple Justice: The History of Brown v. Board of Education and Black America's Struggle for Equality.* New York: Alfred A. Knopf, 1976.

Koenig, Louis. *The Chief Executive.* Rev. ed. New York: Harcourt Brace & World, 1968.

Ladd, Everett, Jr., and Hadley, Charles. *Transformations of the American Party System: Political Coalitions from the New Deal to the 1970s.* New York: W. W. Norton, 1975.

LaFeber, Walter. *America, Russia, and the Cold War, 1945–1984.* 5th ed. New York: Alfred A. Knopf, 1984.

Larson, Arthur. *Eisenhower: The President Nobody Knew.* New York: Charles Scribner's Sons, 1968.

Lash, Joseph. *Eleanor: The Years Alone.* New York: New American Library, 1973.

Leigh, Michael. *Mobilizing Consent: Public Opinion and American Foreign Policy, 1937–1947.* Westport, Conn.: Greenwood Press, 1976.

Leopold, Richard. *The Growth of American Foreign Policy.* New York: Alfred A. Knopf, 1962.

Leuchtenburg, William E. *Franklin D. Roosevelt and the New Deal, 1932–1940.* New York: Harper & Row, 1963.

Levering, Ralph. *The Public and American Foreign Policy, 1918–1978.* New York: William Morrow, 1978.

Lora, Ronald. *Conservative Minds in America.* Chicago: Rand McNally, 1971.

Lubell, Samuel. *The Future of American Politics.* 2d ed., rev. Garden City, N.Y.: Doubleday Anchor Books, 1956.

———. *Revolt of the Moderates.* New York: Harper & Brothers, 1956.

Lyon, Peter. *Eisenhower: Portrait of a Hero.* Boston: Little, Brown, 1974.

McClure, Wallace. *International Executive Agreements: Democratic Procedure Under the Constitution of the United States.* New York: Columbia University Press, 1941.

McLellan, David. *Dean Acheson: The State Department Years.* New York: Dodd, Mead, 1976.

MacNeil, Neil. *Dirksen: Portrait of a Public Man.* New York: World, 1970.

Manchester, William. *The Glory and the Dream: A Narrative History of America, 1932–1972.* Boston: Little, Brown, 1974.

Manion, Clarence. *The Conservative American.* New York: Devin-Adair, 1964.

Marcus, Maeva. *Truman and the Steel Seizure Case: The Limits of Presidential Power.* New York: Columbia University Press, 1977.

Marks, Frederick W. III. *Independence on Trial: Foreign Affairs and the Making of the Constitution.* Baton Rouge: Louisiana State University Press, 1973.

Martin, Joseph. *My First Fifty Years In Politics.* New York: McGraw-Hill, 1960.

Matthews, Donald R. *U.S. Senators and Their World.* Chapel Hill: University of North Carolina Press, 1960.

Miller, Merle. *Plain Speaking: An Oral Biography of Harry S. Truman*. Berkeley, Calif.: Berkeley Publishing Corporation, 1974.

Murphy, Paul. *The Constitution in Crisis Times, 1918–1969*. New York: Harper & Row, 1972.

Neustadt, Richard. *Presidential Power: The Politics of Leadership*. New York: John Wiley, 1960.

Paige, Glenn. *The Korean Decision*. New York: Free Press, 1968.

Parmet, Herbert. *Eisenhower and the American Crusades*. New York: Macmillan, 1972.

Patterson, James T. *Congressional Conservatism and the New Deal*. Lexington: University of Kentucky Press, 1967.

———. *Mr. Republican: A Biography of Robert A. Taft*. Boston: Houghton Mifflin, 1972.

Pauly, Karl. *Bricker of Ohio: The Man and His Record*. New York: G. P. Putnam's Sons, 1944.

Phillips, Cabell. *The Truman Presidency: The History of a Triumphant Succession*. New York: Macmillan, 1966.

Pious, Richard. *The American Presidency*. New York: Basic Books, 1979.

Porter, Kirk, and Johnson, Donald, comps. *National Party Platforms, 1840–1968*. Urbana: University of Illinois Press, 1970.

The President's Powers: Should the Power of the Presidency Be Significantly Curtailed? College Debate Series. Washington, D.C.: American Enterprise Institute for Public Policy Research, 1974.

Pruessen, Ronald. *John Foster Dulles: The Road to Power*. New York: Free Press, 1982.

Pusey, Merlo. *Eisenhower the President*. New York: Macmillan, 1956.

Radosh, Ronald. *Prophets on the Right: Profiles of Conservative Critics of American Globalism*. New York: Simon and Schuster, 1975.

Reedy, George. *The Twilight of the Presidency*. New York: World, 1970.

Reichard, Gary. *The Reaffirmation of Republicanism: Eisenhower and the Eighty-Third Congress*. Knoxville: University of Tennessee Press, 1975.

Reinhard, David. *The Republican Right since 1945*. Lexington: University of Kentucky Press, 1983.

Richardson, Elmo. *The Presidency of Dwight D. Eisenhower*. Lawrence: Regents Press of Kansas, 1979.

Rieselbach, Leroy. *The Roots of Isolationism: Congressional Voting and Presidential Leadership in Foreign Policy*. Indianapolis: Bobbs-Merrill, 1966.

Robinson, Edgar; DeConde, Alexander; O'Connor, Raymond; and Travis, Martin, Jr. *Powers of the President in Foreign Affairs, 1945–1955*. San Francisco: Commonwealth Club of California, 1966.

Rogin, Michael Paul. *The Intellectuals and McCarthy: The Radical Specter*. Cambridge, Mass.: M.I.T. Press, 1967.

Roosevelt, Kermit. *Countercoup: The Struggle for the Control of Iran*. New York: McGraw-Hill, 1979.

Roper, Elmo. *You and Your Leaders: Their Actions and Your Reactions, 1936–1956*. New York: William Morrow, 1957.

Roseboom, Eugene. *A History of Presidential Elections*. New York: Macmillan, 1957.

Rossiter, Clinton. *The American Presidency*. Rev. ed. New York: Harcourt, Brace and World, 1960.

———. *Conservatism in America: The Thankless Persuasion*. 2nd ed., rev. New York: Vintage Books, 1962.

Rovere, Richard. *Affairs of State: The Eisenhower Years*. New York: Farrar, Straus and Cudahy, 1956.

———. *Senator Joe McCarthy*. Cleveland: World, 1960.

Russell, Ruth, and Muther, Jeannette. *A History of the United Nations Charter: The Role of the United States, 1940–1945*. Washington, D.C.: Brookings Institution, 1958.

Schlesinger, Arthur, Jr. *The Age of Roosevelt*. 3 vols. Boston: Houghton Mifflin, 1956–1960.

———, ed. *History of United States Political Parties*. 4 vols. New York: Chelsea House, 1973.

———. *The Imperial Presidency*. Boston: Houghton Mifflin, 1973.

———, and Israel, Fred, eds. *History of American Presidential Elections, 1789–1968*. 4 vols. New York: Chelsea House, 1971.

Schlesinger, Stephen, and Kinzer, Stephen. *Bitter Fruit: The Untold Story of the American Coup in Guatemala*. Garden City, N.Y.: Doubleday, 1982.

Scott, William, and Withey, Stephen. *The United States and The United Nations: The Public View, 1945–1955*. Prepared for the Carnegie Endowment for International Peace, under the auspices of the Survey Research Center, University of Michigan. New York: Manhattan, 1958.

Smith, Donald. *Zechariah Chafee, Jr.: Defender of Liberty and Law*. Cambridge: Harvard University Press, 1986.

Smith, John Cabot. *Alger Hiss: The True Story*. New York: Penguin Books, 1977.

Snell, John, ed. *The Meaning of Yalta*. Baton Rouge: Louisiana State University Press, 1956.

Sofaer, Abraham. *War, Foreign Affairs and Constitutional Power*. Cambridge, Mass.: Ballinger, 1976.

Steinberg, Alfred. *The Man from Missouri: The Life and Times of Harry S. Truman*. New York: G. P. Putnam's Sons, 1962.

———. *Sam Johnson's Boy: A Close-Up of the President from Texas*. New York: Macmillan, 1968.

Stennis, John, and Fulbright, J. William. *The Role of Congress in Foreign Policy*. Washington, D.C.: American Enterprise Institute for Public Policy Research, 1971.

Stone, I. F. *The Haunted Fifties*. New York: Random House, 1963.

Sutherland, George. *Constitutional Power and World Affairs*. New York: Columbia University Press, 1919.

Taft, Robert A. *A Foreign Policy for Americans*. Garden City, N.Y.: Doubleday, 1951.

Bibliography

Theoharis, Athan. *The Yalta Myths: An Issue in U.S. Politics, 1945–1955.* Columbia: University of Missouri Press, 1970.

Truman, Harry S. *Memoirs.* 2 vols. Garden City, N.Y.: Doubleday, 1955, 1956.

Truman, Margaret. *Harry Truman.* New York: William Morrow, 1973.

Tugwell, Rexford, and Cronin, Thomas. *The Presidency Reappraised.* New York: Praeger, 1974.

Vandenberg, Arthur, Jr., ed. *The Private Papers of Senator Vandenberg.* Boston: Houghton Mifflin, 1952.

Vose, Clement. *Caucasians Only: The Supreme Court, the NAACP, and the Restrictive Covenant Cases.* Berkeley: University of California Press, 1959.

Waldman, Louis. *Labor Lawyer.* New York: E. P. Dutton, 1944.

Weinstein, Allen. *Perjury: The Hiss-Chambers Case.* New York: Alfred A. Knopf, 1978.

Westerfield, H. Bradford. *Foreign Policy and Party Politics: Pearl Harbor to Korea.* New Haven: Yale University Press, 1955.

Westin, Alan. *The Anatomy of a Constitutional Law Case: Youngstown Sheet and Tube Co. v. Sawyer—The Steel Seizure Decision.* New York: Macmillan, 1958.

White, William Allen. *The Autobiography of William Allen White.* New York: Macmillan, 1946.

White, William S. *Citadel: The Story of the U.S. Senate.* New York: Harper & Brothers, 1957.

Wiener, Frederick Bernays. *Civilians under Military Justice.* Chicago: University of Chicago Press, 1967.

Wilcox, Francis. *Congress, the Executive, and Foreign Policy.* New York: Harper & Row, for the Council on Foreign Relations, 1971.

Williamson, Samuel D. *Imprint of a Publisher: The Story of Frank Gannett and His Independent Newspapers.* New York: Robert M. McBride, 1948.

Wills, Gary. *Nixon Agonistes: The Crisis of the Self-Made Man.* Boston: Houghton Mifflin, 1970.

Wright, Quincy. *The Control of American Foreign Relations.* New York: Macmillan, 1922.

Young, Roland. *Congressional Politics in the Second World War.* New York: Columbia University Press, 1956.

ARTICLES

Anderson, Chandler. "The Extent and Limitation of the Treaty-Making Power under the Constitution." *American Journal of International Law,* 1 (1907), 636–70.

Aumann, Francis. "Ohio Government in the Twentieth Century: From White to Bricker (1931–1940)." *Ohio in the Twentieth Century, 1900–1938.* ed. Harlow Lindley. Columbus: Ohio State Archaeological and Historical Society, 1942.

Belair, Felix, Jr. "Advice and Comment." *Saturday Review,* July 8, 1961, p. 34.

Bendiner, Robert. "Retrogression in Ohio." *Nation,* November 2, 1946, pp. 493–94.

Bielitsky, Frank. "The Danger in the Treaty-Making Power—A Mirage." *Temple Law Quarterly,* 25 (1952), 463–71.

Black, Forrest. "*Missouri v. Holland*—A Judicial Milepost on the Road to Absolutism." *Illinois Law Review,* 25 (1931), 911–28.

Borchard, Edwin. "Confiscations: Extraterritorial and Domestic." *American Journal of International Law,* 31 (1937), 675–78.

———. "Extraterritorial Confiscations." *American Journal of International Law,* 36 (1942), 275–82.

Boyd, Julian. "The Expanding Treaty Power." *North Carolina Law Review,* 6 (1928), 428–56.

Brandon, Henry. "Witness in the White House." *Saturday Review,* March 16, 1963, pp. 85–86.

Bricker, John. "UN Blueprint for Tyranny." *Freeman,* January 28, 1952, pp. 265–68.

———. "Safeguarding the Treaty Power." *Federal Bar Journal,* 13 (December 1952), 77–84.

———. "Constitutional Insurance for a Safe Treaty-Making Policy." *Dickinson Law Review,* 60 (January 1956), 103–20.

———, and Webb, Charles. "Treaty Law vs. Domestic Constitutional Law." *Notre Dame Lawyer,* 24, (August 1954), 529–50.

Burdick, Charles. "The Treaty Making Power and the Control of International Relations." *Cornell Law Quarterly,* 7 (1921), 34–41.

Burnham, Walter Dean. "Eisenhower as Man, Eisenhower as Mystique." *Commonweal,* December 27, 1963, pp. 408–9.

Carroll, Wallace. "Light on Yesterday's Headliners." *New York Times Book Review,* June 25, 1961, pp. 1, 28.

Cater, Douglas. "'Mr. Conservative'—Eugene Millikin of Colorado." *Reporter,* March 17, 1953, pp. 26–31.

———. "Congress and the President." *Reporter,* May 12, 1953, pp. 15–16.

Catudal, Honoré Marcel. "Executive Agreements: A Supplement to the Treaty-Making Procedure." *George Washington Law Review,* 10 (1942), 653–69.

Chafee, Zechariah, Jr. "Federal and State Powers under the UN Covenant on Human Rights." *Wisconsin Law Review,* May 1951, pp. 389–473.

———. "Amending the Constitution to Cripple Treaties." *Louisiana Law Review,* 12 (May 1952), 345–82.

Chamberlain, Joseph. "Migratory Bird Treaty Decision and Its Relation to Labor Treaties." *American Labor Legislation Review,* 10 (1920), 133–35.

Commager, Henry Steele. "Presidential Power: The Issue Analyzed." *New York Times Magazine,* January 14, 1951, pp. 11, 23–24.

———. "The Perilous Folly of Senator Bricker." *Reporter,* October 13, 1953, pp. 12–17.

———. "A Reluctance to Reflect." *Washington Post Book Week,* November 10, 1963, pp. 1, 18.

"Constitutional Basis for Federal Anti-Lynching Legislation." *Lawyers Guild Review,* 6 (November–December 1946), 643–47.

Cornwell, Elmer, Jr. "The Truman Presidency." *The Truman Period as a Research*

Field. Ed. Richard Kirkendall. Columbia: University of Missouri Press, 1967, pp. 213–43.

Corwin, Edward. "Who Has the Power to Make War?" *New York Times Magazine,* July 31, 1949, pp. 11, 14–15.

———. "The Steel Seizure Case: A Judicial Brick without Straw." *Columbia Law Review,* 53 (January 1953), 53–66.

"Criminal Jurisdiction Over American Armed Forces Abroad." *Harvard Law Review,* 70 (1957), 1043–67.

Currie, Donald. "Court-Martial Jurisdiction of Civilian Dependents." *Washington and Lee Law Review,* 15 (1958), 79–88.

Dean, Arthur. "The Bricker Amendment and Authority over Foreign Affairs." *Foreign Affairs,* 32 (October 1953), 1–19.

De Santis, Vincent. "Eisenhower Revisionism." *Review of Politics,* 38 (April 1976), 190–207.

Deutsch, Eberhard. "The Treaty-Making Clause: A Decision for the People of America." *American Bar Association Journal,* 37 (1951), 659–62, 712–14.

———. "Proposed Changes in United States Treaty-Making Power." *Louisiana Bar Journal,* 1 (July 1953), 3–11.

———. "Eminent Domain under a Treaty: A Hypothetical Supreme Court Opinion." *American Bar Association Journal,* 43 (1957), 699–702.

Devaney, John. "Why the Guild?" *National Lawyers Guild Newsletter,* 1 (June 1937), 1, 4.

Divine, Robert. "The Case of the Smuggled Bombers." *Quarrels That Have Shaped the Constitution.* Ed. John Garraty. New York: Harper & Row, 1964, pp. 210–221.

Dulles, John Foster. "International Law and Individuals: A Comment on Enforcing Peace." *American Bar Association Journal,* 35 (1949), 912–13.

Fairman, Charles. Editorial Comment: "Finis to Fujii." *American Journal of International Law,* 46 (1952), 682–90.

Fensterwald, Bernard, Jr. "Trojan Horse or Don Quixote's Windmill?" *Federal Bar Journal,* 13 (December 1952), 85–98.

Ferguson, Edwin. "The California Alien Land Law and the Fourteenth Amendment." *California Law Review,* 35 (March 1947), 61–90.

Finch, George. "The Treaty-Clause Amendment: The Case for the Association." *American Bar Association Journal,* 38 (1952), 467–70, 527–30.

———. "The Need to Restrain the Treaty-Making Power of the United States Within Constitutional Limits." *American Journal of International Law,* 48 (1954), 57–82.

Forrester, Ray. "Mr. Justice Burton and the Supreme Court." *Tulane Law Review,* 20 (1945), 1–21.

Graebner, Norman. "Eisenhower's Popular Leadership." *Current History,* 39 (October 1960), 230–36, 244.

Green, Andrew Wilson. "A Comment on the Bricker Amendment." *Dickinson Law Review,* 40 (January 1956), 121–22.

Greenstein, Fred. "Eisenhower as an Activist President: A Look at New Evidence." *Political Science Quarterly,* 94 (Winter 1979–80), 575–99.

Griffith, Robert. "Dwight D. Eisenhower and the Corporate Commonwealth." *American Historical Review,* 87 (February 1982), 87–122.

Handlin, Oscar. "The Eisenhower Administration: A Self-Portrait." *Atlantic Monthly,* November 1963, pp. 67–72.

———. "Reader's Choice." *Atlantic Monthly,* October 1965, pp. 166–68.

Hendrick, James. "Progress Report on Human Rights." *Department of State Bulletin,* 19 (August 8, 1948), 159–72.

Henkin, Louis. "The Treaty Makers and the Law Makers: The Law of the Land and Foreign Relations." *University of Pennsylvania Law Review,* 107 (May 1959), 903–36.

Hilsman, Roger. "Congressional-Executive Relations and the Foreign Policy Consensus." *American Political Science Review,* 52 (September 1958), 725–44.

Hoffman, Paul. "How Eisenhower Saved the Republican Party." *Collier's,* October 26, 1956, pp. 44–47.

Holman, Frank. "An 'International Bill of Rights': Proposals Have Dangerous Implications for U.S." *American Bar Association Journal,* 34 (1948), 984–86, 1078–81.

———. "Must America Succumb to Statism?" *American Bar Association Journal,* 35 (1949), 801–05, 877–79.

———. "Treaty Law-Making: A Blank Check for Writing a New Constitution." *American Bar Association Journal,* 36 (1950), 707–10, 787–90.

———. "Let's Stop Giving America Away." *Women Lawyers Journal,* 39 (Spring 1953), 7–8, 28–29, 32–35.

———. "The Greatest Threat to American Freedom." *Wyoming Law Journal,* 8 (Fall 1953), 24–38.

———. "Need for a Constitutional Amendment on Treaties and Executive Agreements." *Washington University Law Quarterly,* December 1955, pp. 340–54.

Holt, Pat. "And Besides, It's Constitutional." *New Republic,* February 10, 1947, pp. 30–33.

Hudson, Manley. Editorial Comment: "Charter Provisions on Human Rights in American Law." *American Journal of International Law,* 44 (1950), 543–48.

Hyman, Sidney. "The Failure of the Eisenhower Presidency." *Progressive,* May 1960, pp. 10–13.

———. "The General's Lieutenant-in-Command." *New Republic,* July 24, 1961, pp. 20–22.

Immerman, Richard. "Eisenhower and Dulles: Who Made the Decisions?" *Political Psychology,* 1 (Autumn 1979), 21–38.

Jackson, Jay Lloyd. "The Tenth Amendment Versus the Treaty-Making Power Under the Constitution." *Virginia Law Review,* 14 (1928), 331–57, 441–68.

Jackson, Robert H. "The Lawyer: Leader or Mouthpiece?" *Journal of the American Judicature Society,* 18 (October 1934), 70–75.

Jacobs, Paul. "That Man, Those Years." *Nation,* November 15, 1965, p. 368.

Jessup, Philip. "The Litvinov Assignment and the Belmont Case." *American Journal of International Law,* 31 (1937), 481–84.

———. "The Litvinov Assignment and the Pink Case." *American Journal of International Law,* 36 (1942), 282–88.

Bibliography

Jones, Harry. "The President, Congress, and Foreign Relations." *California Law Review,* 29 (1941), 565–85.

Kauper, Paul. "The Steel Seizure Case: Congress, the President, and the Supreme Court." *Michigan Law Review,* 51 (December 1952), 141–82.

Kelley, Wayne. "Senator Russell Vows to Speak His Mind." *Atlanta Journal and Constitution Magazine,* February 4, 1968, pp. 9, 22.

Kempton, Murray. "The Underestimation of Dwight D. Eisenhower." *Esquire,* September 1967, pp. 108–9, 156.

Kepley, David. "The Senate and the Great Debate of 1951." *Prologue,* 14 (Winter 1982), 213–26.

King, Archibald. "Jurisdiction Over Friendly Foreign Armed Forces." *American Journal of International Law,* 36 (1942), 539–67.

———. "Further Developments Concerning Jurisdiction Over Friendly Foreign Armed Forces." *American Journal of International Law,* 40 (1946), 257–79.

Korey, William. "America's Shame: The Unratified Genocide Treaty." *Midstream,* 27 (March 1981), 7–13.

Korns, William. "Target: The President." *New Republic,* April 27, 1963, pp. 25–26.

Kraft, Joseph. "Inside the Void." *Commentary,* 32 (September 1961), 264–66.

Lawrence, David. "Let San Francisco Review Yalta." *United States News,* February 23, 1945, pp. 28–29.

Leuchtenburg, William E. "The Constitutional Revolution of 1937." *The Great Depression: Essays and Memoirs from Canada and the United States.* Ed. Victor Hoar. Vancouver: Copp Clark, 1969, pp. 31–83.

———. "Franklin D. Roosevelt's Supreme Court 'Packing' Plan." *Essays on the New Deal.* Ed. Harold Hollingsworth. Austin: University of Texas Press, 1969, pp. 69–115.

Levitan, D. M. "The Foreign Relations Power: An Analysis of Mr. Justice Sutherland's Theory." *Yale Law Journal,* 55 (1946), 467–97.

Lofgren, Charles. "*Missouri v. Holland* in Historical Perspective." *Supreme Court Review,* 1975, pp. 77–121.

McAuliffe, Mary. Commentary: "Eisenhower, the President." *Journal of American History,* 68 (December 1981), 625–32.

MacChesney, Brunson. "The Fallacies in the Case for the Bricker Amendment." *Notre Dame Lawyer,* 29 (August 1954), 551–82.

McDougal, Myres, and Lans, Asher. "Treaties and Congressional-Executive or Presidential Agreements: Interchangeable Instruments of National Policy." *Yale Law Journal,* 54 (1945), 181–351, 534–615.

McGovney, Dudley. "The Anti-Japanese Land Laws of California and Ten Other States." *California Law Review,* 35 (March 1947), 7–60.

McGowan, Lewis, Jr. "The Pink Case, the Recognition of Russia, and the Litvinov Assignment." *Georgetown Law Journal,* 30 (1942), 663–73.

McHargue, Daniel. "One of Nine—Mr. Justice Burton's Appointment to the Supreme Court." *Western Reserve Law Review,* 4 (1953), 128–31.

Magnusson, Jon. "Our Membership in the United Nations and the Federal Treaty Power under the Constitution." *Virginia Law Review,* 34 (February 1948), 137–64.

Maurer, David. "Relief Problems and Politics in Ohio." *The New Deal*. Vol. 2: *The State and Local Levels*. Ed. John Braeman, Robert Bremner, and David Brody. Columbus: Ohio State University Press, 1975, pp. 77–99.

Mayer, George. "The Republican Party, 1932–1952." *History of United States Political Parties*. Vol. 3: *1910–1945: From Square Deal to Fair Deal*. Ed. Arthur Schlesinger, Jr. New York: Chelsea House, 1973, pp. 2259–2292.

Miller, Glen, and Ware, Stephen. "Organized Labor in the Political Process: A Case Study of the Right-to-Work Campaign in Ohio." *Labor History*, 4 (Winter 1963), 51–67.

Morgenthau, Hans. "John Foster Dulles." *An Uncertain Tradition: American Secretaries of State in the Twentieth Century*. Ed. Norman Graebner. New York: McGraw-Hill, 1961, pp. 289–308.

Ober, Frank. "The Treaty-Making and Amending Powers: Do They Protect Our Fundamental Rights?" *American Bar Association Journal*, 36 (1950), 715–19, 793–96.

Oliver, Covey. "Executive Agreements and Emanations from the Fifth Amendment." *American Journal of International Law*, 49 (1955), 362–66.

Orfield, Lester. "Jurisdiction of Foreign Courts Over Crimes Committed Abroad by American Military Personnel." *South Carolina Law Quarterly*, 8 (1956), 346–54.

"Our Best and Worst Senators." *Pageant*, October, 1949, pp. 9–16.

Parker, John J. "The American Constitution and the Treaty Making Power." *Washington University Law Quarterly*, April 1954, pp. 115–31.

Pepper, Claude. "Observations on the Policy of the Bricker Amendment." *University of Florida Law Review*, 7 (Spring 1954), 58–67.

Perlman, Philip. "On Amending the Treaty Power." *Columbia Law Review*, 52 (November 1952), 825–67.

Phillips, Orie. "The Genocide Convention: Its Effect on Our Legal System." *American Bar Association Journal*, 35 (1949), 623–25.

―――. "The Treaty-Making Power—A Real and Present Danger." *Montana Law Review*, 15 (Spring 1954), 1–14.

―――, and Deutsch, Eberhard. "Pitfalls of the Genocide Convention." *American Bar Association Journal*, 56 (1970), 641–46.

Plesur, Milton. "The Republican Comeback of 1938." *Review of Politics*, 24 (October 1962), 525–62.

Quarles, James. "The Federal Government: As to Foreign Affairs, Are Its Powers Inherent as Distinguished From Delegated?" *Georgetown Law Journal*, 32 (1944), 375–83.

Re, Edward. "The NATO Status of Forces Agreement and International Law." *Northwestern University Law Review*, 50 (1955), 349–94.

Reichard, Gary. "Eisenhower and the Bricker Amendment." *Prologue*, 6 (Summer 1974), 88–99.

―――. "Eisenhower as President: The Changing View." *South Atlantic Quarterly*, 77 (Summer 1978), 265–81.

Rhodes, Richard. "Ike: An Artist in Iron." *Harper's Magazine*, July 1970, pp. 70–77.

Bibliography

Richberg, Donald. "The Bricker Amendment and the Treaty Power." *Virginia Law Review*, 39 (October 1953), 753–64.

Riesenfeld, Stefan. "The Power of Congress and the President in International Relations: Three Recent Supreme Court Decisions." *California Law Review*, 25 (1937), 643–75.

Rix, Carl. "Human Rights and International Law: Effect of the Covenant under Our Constitution." *American Bar Association Journal*, 35 (1949), 551–54, 618–21.

Roberts, Chalmers. "The Day We Didn't Go to War." *Reporter*, September 14, 1954, pp. 31–35.

———. "Strong Man from the South." *Saturday Evening Post*, June 25, 1955, pp. 30, 109–12.

Rovere, Richard. "The Unassailable Vandenberg." *Harper's Magazine*, May 1948, pp. 394–403.

———. "Eisenhower Revisited: A Political Genius? A Brilliant Man?" *New York Times Magazine*, February 7, 1971, pp. 14–15, 54, 58–59, 62.

Sayre, Paul. "*Shelley v. Kraemer* and United Nations Law." *Iowa Law Review*, 34 (November 1948), 1–11.

Schlesinger, Arthur, Jr. "Congress and the Making of Foreign Policy." *The Presidency Reappraised*. Ed. Rexford Tugwell and Thomas Cronin. New York: Praeger, 1974, pp. 83–116.

———. "The Eisenhower Presidency: A Reassessment." *Look*, May 14, 1979, pp. 40–48.

———. "The Ike Age Revisited." *Reviews in American History*, 11 (March 1983), 1–11.

Schubert, Glendon. "Politics and the Constitution: The Bricker Amendment during 1953." *Journal of Politics*, 16 (May 1954), 257–98.

Schwartz, Murray. "International Law and the NATO Status of Forces Agreement." *Columbia Law Review*, 53 (1953), 1091–1113.

Seasongood, Murray. "John W. Bricker: Personally Honest." *Public Men in and out of Office*. Ed. J. T. Salter. Chapel Hill: University of North Carolina Press, 1946, pp. 395–414.

Shannon, William. "Eisenhower as President: A Critical Appraisal of the Record." *Commentary*, 26 (November 1958), 390–98.

Simsarian, James. "United Nations Action on Human Rights in 1948." *Department of State Bulletin*, 20 (January 2, 1949), 18–23.

———. "Proposed Human Rights Covenant." *Department of State Bulletin*, 22 (June 12, 1950), 945–49.

———. "Economic, Social, and Cultural Provisions in the Human Rights Covenant." *Department of State Bulletin*, 24 (June 25, 1951), 1003–8.

Sohn, Louis. "A Short History of United Nations Documents on Human Rights." *The United Nations and Human Rights: Eighteenth Report of the Commission to Study the Organization of Peace*. Dobbs Ferry, N.Y.: Oceana Publications, 1968.

Sutherland, Arthur E., Jr. "Restricting the Treaty Power." *Harvard Law Review*, 65 (June 1952), 1305–38.

———. "The Bricker Amendment, Executive Agreements, and Imported Potatoes." *Harvard Law Review,* 67 (December 1953), 281–92.

———. "The Flag, the Constitution, and International Agreements." *Harvard Law Review,* 68 (June 1955), 1374–81.

Tananbaum, Duane. "The Bricker Amendment Controversy: Its Origins, and Eisenhower's Role." *Diplomatic History,* 9 (Winter 1985), 73–93.

Thompson, L. L. "State Sovereignty and the Treaty-Making Power." *California Law Review,* 11 (1923), 242–58.

"The United Nations Charter and the Constitution." *American Bar Association Journal,* 36 (1950), 652–53.

Warren, Earl. "The Bill of Rights and the Military." *The Great Rights.* Ed. Edmond Cahn. New York: Macmillan, 1963, pp. 87–113.

Weinfeld, Abraham. "Are Labor Conditions a Proper Subject of International Conventions and May the United States Government Become a Party to Such Conventions though They Regulate Matters Ordinarily Reserved to the States?" *California Law Review,* 24 (1936), 275–87.

White, William S. "Senator George—Monumental, Determined." *New York Times Magazine,* March 13, 1955, pp. 12, 42, 44, 47.

Wright, Quincy. "National Courts and Human Rights—The Fujii Case." *American Journal of International Law,* 45 (1951), 62–82.

Index

Acheson, Dean, 24, 28–29, 67, 70, 114, 180

Adams, Sherman, 67, 76, 116, 206, 216

Aiken, George: and Bricker amendment, 70, 141, 154, 168, 184; Eisenhower Republican, 141, 158, 184–85; and George amendment, 176, 181, 184–86; internationalist, 184; liberal Republican, 186

Allott, Gordon, 199

America, 117, 129

American Association for the United Nations, 56, 60, 126

American Bar Association: background and history of, 8; Committee on Peace and Law Through United Nations, 7, 11, 13–14, 32–34, 39–41, 54, 81, 91, 194, 219; and constitutional amendment, 15, 33–34, 38–41, 45–46, 126–27, 188, 202–3; and covenant on human rights, 11, 32–33; criticism of, 8, 45–47; and Genocide Convention, 12–15, 219; Section of International and Comparative Law, 13, 34, 38, 45–47, 55, 59–60, 126; and Universal Declaration of Human Rights, 7. *See also* Holman, Frank; Schweppe, Alfred

American Civil Liberties Union, 86, 126

American Federation of Labor, 86, 126

American Flag Committee, 55

American Jewish Congress, 55, 60, 86, 126

American Legion, 38, 119

American Medical Association, 118–19

Americans for Democratic Action, 56, 126; liberal ratings of senators, 159, 162n6, 170–71n23, 173n29, 175n33, 177n35, 185–87, 190n53, 193

Anderson, Clinton: and Bricker amendment, 168; and George amendment, 158, 176, 181; liberal rating of, 187

Associated Press, 128

Association of Physicians and Surgeons, 131

Association of the Bar of the City of New York, 58–59, 86, 90. *See also* Backus, Dana; Maw, Carlyle; Pearson, Theodore

Backus, Dana: and Committee for Defense of the Constitution by Preserving the Treaty Power, 121–24; Frank Holman on, 90; and 1952 hearings on Bricker amendment, 59; and 1953 hearings on Bricker amendment, 86, 90. *See also* Association of the Bar of the City of New York

Baggett, Sam, 127

Bar Association of St. Louis, 126

Barker, Winifred, 204, 205. *See also* Vigilant Women for the Bricker Amendment

Barkley, Alben, 188, 199

Barrett, Frank: and Bricker amendment, 158, 168; and Eisenhower administration, 174, 188; and George amendment, 174, 176, 181, 188; liberal rating of, 187

Beall, J. Glenn: and Bricker amendment, 95, 168, 182; and Eisenhower administration, 182; and George amendment, 175, 176, 179, 181, 182–83

Bennett, Charles, 34

Bennett, Wallace: and Bricker amendment, 158, 168; and George amendment, 176, 181

Benson, Ezra Taft, 102

Bernstein, Bernard, 86

Black, Hugo: *Capps* case, 210n40; *Oyama v. California*, 5; *Reid v. Covert*, 212–13; steel seizure case, 50

B'nai B'rith, 86

Fosdick, Harry Emerson, 128

Foundation for the Study of Treaty Law, 113–15

Fowler, Cody, 37–38

Frankfurter, Felix: on Bricker amendment, 128; *Reid v. Covert,* 213; *Rice v. Sioux City Memorial Park,* 211; steel seizure case, 50–51; on United Nations Charter, 211

Frear, Allen: and Bricker amendment, 43n31, 69n9, 158, 168; and George amendment, 176, 181; liberal rating of, 187; and Status of Forces Agreement, 106n30

Fujii case. *See Sei Fujii v. State of California*

Fulbright, J. William: and Bricker amendment, 167–68; and Eisenhower Doctrine, 208; and George amendment, 176, 181, 186; Frank Holman on, 192; liberal rating of, 159, 186; and motion to refer amendments back to committee, 169n19; opposed to all amendments, 159; and presidential power, 208, 215

Gallup Polls: on Bricker amendment, 128–29, 131–32; on United Nations, 2n2, 16n1

Gannett, Frank, 117

Garrett, Garet, 6

Genocide Convention: American Bar Association opposes, 12–15, 219; John Bricker opposes, 25, 219; drafting of, 12; Dulles on, 61–62, 74, 199, 219; and Eisenhower administration, 74, 199, 219; Frank Holman opposes, 13–15; U.S. approval of, 219

George, Walter: background of, 144–45; and Bricker amendment (1954), 154, 157–58; and Bricker amendment (1955), 196–97; and *Capps* case, 172; conservatism of, 144, 187, 188; and Eisenhower administration, 144, 146–47, 164–65, 197–98; and executive agreements, 146, 154, 160, 169–72; and Formosa Resolution, 202; and George amendment, 146–47, 149, 154, 158, 160, 164–65, 169–72, 175, 176, 179, 181; and Knowland-Ferguson amendment, 161; liberal rating of, 187; and motion to refer amendments back to committee, 167, 169; and *Pink* case, 169–71

George amendment, 146–50, 154–55, 164–66, 167, 169–90, 192–94, 225

Gerard, Sumner, 118

Gillette, Guy: absence from 84th Congress, 198; and Bricker amendment, 43n31, 69n9, 168; and George amendment, 158, 176, 181, 186; liberalism of, 186; and mo-

tion to refer amendments back to committee, 169n31, 186; and 1954 election, 186, 196

Glass, Carter, 188

Goldwater, Barry: and Bricker amendment, 158, 168; and George amendment, 176, 181; liberal rating of, 187

Gore, Albert: and Bricker amendment, 168; and George amendment, 158, 176, 181; liberal rating of, 187

Green, Theodore Francis: and Bricker amendment, 168; and George amendment, 176, 181, 186; liberal rating of, 159, 186–87; opposed to all amendments, 159

Greenstein, Fred, 78

Griswold, Dwight: absence from 84th Congress, 198; and Bricker amendment, 158, 159, 168; Eisenhower Republican, 159, 183–85; and George amendment, 176, 181, 183–85

Griswold, Erwin, 124–25, 138

Guatemala, 218

Gulf of Tonkin Resolution, 218

Gunther, John, 24

Gurley, Fred, 115

Hagerty, James, 139, 198

Hall, Leonard, 114

Halleck, Charles, 116, 138

Harlan, John Marshall, 213

Hayden, Carl: and Bricker amendment, 168; and George amendment, 176, 181, 186; liberal rating of, 159, 186–87; and motion to refer amendments back to committee, 169n19; opposed to all amendments, 159

Hendrickson, Robert: absence from 84th Congress, 198; and Bricker amendment, 44, 53, 92, 143, 168; and covenant on human rights, 30; Eisenhower Republican, 143, 158, 183–85; and George amendment, 176, 179, 181, 183–85; and Status of Forces Agreement, 106

Hennings, Thomas: and Bricker amendment, 92–93, 168; and *Capps* case, 172; and Eisenhower, 165–66, 185; and George amendment, 165–66, 170–72, 174, 176, 181, 185–86, 193; and Knowland-Ferguson amendment, 163; liberal rating of, 159, 186–87; and motion to refer amendments back to committee, 169n19; opposed to all amendments, 159, 165–66, 185; and *Pink* case, 171; and *Reid v. Covert,* 213

Hickenlooper, Bourke: and Bricker amendment, 157–58, 168; and George amend-

Index

Library of Congress Cataloging-in-Publication Data

Tananbaum, Duane, 1949–
   The Bricker Amendment controversy : a test of Eisenhower's political leadership / Duane
Tananbaum.
     p.   cm.
   Bibliography: p.
   Includes index.
   ISBN 0-8014-2037-7 (alk. paper)
   1. Eisenhower, Dwight D. (Dwight David), 1890–1969. 2. International and municipal
law—United States. 3. Treaty-making power—United States. 4. United States—Foreign
relations—Executive agreements. 5. Executive power—United States. 6. Legislative
power—United States. 7. Bricker, John W. (John William), 1893–1986. I. Title.
E836.T36   1988   973.921—dc19   88-3614

DATE DUE